Sam Steele

# Sam Steele
## A Biography

ROD MACLEOD

◲ The University of Alberta Press

Published by

The University of Alberta Press
Ring House 2
Edmonton, Alberta, Canada T6G 2E1
www.uap.ualberta.ca

Copyright © 2018 Rod Macleod

LIBRARY AND ARCHIVES CANADA
CATALOGUING IN PUBLICATION

Macleod, R.C., 1940–, author
    Sam Steele : a biography / Rod Macleod.

Includes bibliographical references and index.
Issued in print and electronic formats.
ISBN 978-1-77212-379-1 (softcover).—
ISBN 978-1-77212-433-0 (EPUB).—
ISBN 978-1-77212-434-7 (Kindle).—
ISBN 978-1-77212-435-4 (PDF)

    1. Steele, Samuel B. (Samuel Benfield),
1848-1919. 2. North West Mounted Police
(Canada)—Biography. 3. Police—Canada,
Western—Biography. 4. Soldiers—Canada—
Biography. 5. Northwest, Canadian—History.
6. Canada—History—1867-1914. 7. Biographies.
I. Title.

FC3216.3.S77M33 2018      363.2092
C2018-905855-2
C2018-905856-0

First edition, first printing, 2018.
First printed and bound in Canada by Friesens,
Altona, Manitoba.
Copyediting and proofreading by Brian Mlazgar.
Maps by Wendy Johnson.
Indexing by Judy Dunlop.

All rights reserved. No part of this publication
may be reproduced, stored in a retrieval system,
or transmitted in any form or by any means
(electronic, mechanical, photocopying,
recording, or otherwise) without prior written
consent. Contact University of Alberta Press for
further details.

University of Alberta Press supports copyright.
Copyright fuels creativity, encourages diverse
voices, promotes free speech, and creates a vibrant
culture. Thank you for buying an authorized
edition of this book and for complying with the
copyright laws by not reproducing, scanning, or
distributing any part of it in any form without
permission. You are supporting writers and
allowing University of Alberta Press to continue
to publish books for every reader.

University of Alberta Press is committed to
protecting our natural environment. As part of
our efforts, this book is printed on Enviro Paper:
it contains 100% post-consumer recycled fibres
and is acid- and chlorine-free.

University of Alberta Press gratefully acknow-
ledges the support received for its publishing
program from the Government of Canada, the
Canada Council for the Arts, and the Government
of Alberta through the Alberta Media Fund.

This book has been published with the help of
a grant from the Canadian Federation for the
Humanities and Social Sciences, through the
Awards to Scholarly Publications Program, using
funds provided by the Social Sciences and
Humanities Research Council of Canada.

This book was funded in part by the Alberta
Historical Resources Foundation.

*For Elaine*

## Contents

Acknowledgements IX
Introduction XI

1 || Early Life: Orillia and the Red River Expedition, 1848–1873   1
2 || The North-West Mounted Police, 1873–1885   29
3 || Steele's Scouts in the Rebellion, 1885   71
4 || Frustrated Ambition, 1886–1888   91
5 || The Love of His Life: Marie Harwood, 1888–1890   113
6 || Fort Macleod and Family, 1890–1898   137
7 || The Klondike Gold Rush, 1898–1899   165
8 || Fighting for Queen and Country: Lord Strathcona's Horse, 1899–1901   193
9 || Imperial Interlude: The South African Constabulary, 1901–1907   229
10 || Preparing for War, 1907–1914   257
11 || An Old Soldier Fades Away: General Steele, 1914–1919   285
|| Epilogue   323

Notes   327
Bibliography   365
Index   375

# ‖ Acknowledgements

I AM DEEPLY GRATEFUL to the people who helped me in the writing of this book. My wife Elaine was my chief research assistant, spending countless hours transcribing documents, especially Marie's letters to her husband. Her insights from that work were invaluable in understanding the most important relationship in Steele's life. The University of Alberta Libraries provided me for two summers with an outstanding research assistant, Dan Watson, who cheerfully and competently performed every assigned task. He even willingly took on trying to untangle Steele's business investments, something that Steele himself clearly failed to understand.

Charlotte Gray, Vern Paetkau, and Laura Macleod read the whole manuscript and their comments and suggestions made this a much better book. Their willingness to take the time from busy lives went beyond friendship, or in the case of Laura, family ties. Peter German and Don Smith very kindly read parts of the book.

The staff at Bruce Peel Special Collections, University of Alberta, could not have been more helpful. At times getting through the mass of Steele material seemed like an endless task, but they always made working there a pleasure. When a renovation project closed the library for some months, they went out of their way to ensure uninterrupted access to the papers. Thanks to Robert Desmarais, Linda Quirk, Jeff Papineau, Carolyn Morgan, and Carol Unwin. Lynn McPherson, the archivist for the collection and the person who knows more about Steele than anyone else, was an indispensable resource. All images in this volume are courtesy of Bruce Peel Special Collections.

The book would never have been written if the University of Alberta had not taken the initiative to acquire and preserve the Sir Samuel Steele Collection. Cameron Treleaven of Aquila Books in Calgary alerted Ernie Ingles and Merrill Distad about the availability and importance of the papers and they, with the support of then Vice-President Academic Carl Amrhein, raised the necessary money (approximately $1.8 million) in an amazingly short time. Their foresight and initiative prevented the collection from a likely fate of being broken up or sold out of the country.

I have published a number of books with University of Alberta Press over the years. Peter Midgley, Cathie Crooks, Mary Lou Roy, and Alan Brownoff are always a great team to work with. Brian Mlazgar's meticulous and insightful copyediting was a great help. I have the privilege of being the last author signed by Linda Cameron before she retired as Director. Thanks to all.

## Introduction

IN NOVEMBER 1899, as the last weeks of the 19th century ran their course, Superintendent Sam Steele of the North-West Mounted Police (NWMP) paid a rare visit to the area around Orillia where he had grown up. He travelled to the farm a few miles west of the town where he was born fifty-one years previously, and to the churchyard where his parents were buried. He thoroughly enjoyed reconnecting with old family friends and staying with his half-brother, John Steele, at the nearby town of Coldwater. Sam Steele made strong and lasting friendships throughout his life and valued his family and childhood ties. On this visit he also relished the role of returning hero. Although his departure from the Yukon Territory a month before had been involuntary and under something of a political cloud, the circumstances were not widely known and his reputation as the man who had tamed the gold rush was undimmed. "Had to talk Yukon all day," he noted in his diary for November 16.[1]

Happy as he was to regale the citizens of Orillia with tales of the world-famous gold rush, Steele's own future was very much in doubt at this point in his life. He had served the NWMP with distinction for twenty-six years and had long hoped to cap his career with command of the Force, but in the fall of 1899 that prospect seemed increasingly remote. The commissioner of the NWMP, Lawrence William Herchmer, showed no sign of being ready to resign. Herchmer was a Conservative appointee and not popular with Sir Wilfrid Laurier's federal Liberal government, but even if the Liberals decided to replace him it was unlikely that they would appoint Steele, whose political connections were also Tory and whose father-in-law was a Conservative insider. There were a few Mounted Police officers with Liberal connections, and although none had Steele's combination of ability and experience, this was unlikely to count for much. In fact, as Steele was well aware, Superintendent A. Bowen Perry was being groomed for the job; to make matters worse, Perry was one of the few NWMP officers he actively disliked.

Steele could certainly have had his choice of the available commands in the NWMP but none were remotely as interesting or important as the Yukon. He had invested in mining ventures in southern British Columbia and in the Yukon, and devoting himself to those businesses seemed a likelier career prospect. Then, just as he was about to make his choice, events elsewhere presented him with a new opportunity. In October, fighting had begun in South Africa between Great Britain and the Boer republics of the Orange Free State and the Transvaal. While Steele was visiting Orillia the British seemed to be winning the first encounters but as he was returning to his family in Montreal in early December the situation changed drastically. In what became known as "Black Week," December 10–17, the British lost three major battles in succession[2] and quickly made it known to the Canadian government that they would welcome military assistance.

Canada's tiny permanent military could only provide the nucleus of an expeditionary force, which would have to be raised largely from current and former members of the militia—and men like Sam Steele who had gone into the Mounted Police because it offered a career of active service not available in the army of the time. Before the end of the year Commissioner Herchmer had been given command of a new unit, the 2nd Battalion, Canadian Mounted

Rifles (CMR) to be raised in western Canada. Steele was offered the position of second in command. He accepted reluctantly because he disliked Herchmer and had little respect for his abilities, but the combination of the call of duty and the prospect of action was irresistible. But another, longer-term possibility began to form in Steele's mind as well. A short, victorious campaign could result in Steele and Herchmer returning to Canada covered in glory. Herchmer, after a suitably short interval, could then retire, turning the NWMP over to Steele, whose reputation would now overshadow that of Perry and make him impossible to ignore.

Even better things were in store. Steele had just finished assembling the western contingents of the CMR and sending them to Ottawa when he was offered command of another new regiment financed by the enormously wealthy Canadian high commissioner in London, Lord Strathcona, who had made his fortune with the Hudson's Bay Company (HBC) and the Canadian Pacific Railway (CPR).[3] Steele would turn out to be a highly successful commanding officer of Lord Strathcona's Horse but the other parts of his vision did not work out as planned. Instead, Steele would spend seven years in South Africa as a senior officer in Lord Baden-Powell's South African Constabulary. When he eventually returned to Canada it was as a colonel in the militia. His promotion to major general at the beginning of the First World War marked the culmination of a remarkable career that had begun forty-four years earlier as a private in the Red River Expedition.

Steele's rise from backwoods Ontario farm boy to Major General Sir Samuel Benfield Steele was a narrative assiduously promoted by Steele himself in his 1914 autobiography *Forty Years in Canada*, and in later years by his son, Harwood Steele. Comparing the version of events in the autobiography to Steele's diaries and letters reveals no inventions or significant exaggerations, but it does reveal that many things were systematically omitted. Steele had rivals—enemies and people he intensely disliked—but this was not apparent in the memoir.[4] Similarly, his wife and family, to whom he was devoted, barely get a mention in the book. It would be easy, and totally misleading, to get the impression that family life was unimportant to him. On the contrary, from his marriage until the end of his life, every major decision he made about his career revolved around their interests.

In spite of the picture that emerges from his autobiography, which makes it easy to dismiss him as a stereotypical bombastic imperialist, Sam Steele always defined himself as a Canadian, even when he was living and working in South Africa or England. He was often bitterly resentful of the Canadian government for what he regarded as mistreatment, but that never changed his pride in his native country, or his determination to help shape its identity. When he was in South Africa at the end of the South African War, with no prospect of returning to the NWMP or Canada, and despite being paid roughly double his Mounted Police salary, his letters and diaries are full of longing for his native land. He thought of himself as a citizen of the British Empire, but was privately scornful of many of the British officers with whom he worked, constantly comparing them unfavourably with Canadians. He got along well with individual Americans but thought that too many of them as immigrants in western Canada were a threat. In 1908 he confided to his diary, "The Americans would be all right but they can never be loyal, and it is doubtful if their children would be."[5] He was indignant when a visitor from New Zealand compared the First Nations of western Canada unfavourably to the Maori, and even the Canadian forests were a matter of pride. In a letter to his wife from South Africa in 1901 he described the country where Lord Strathcona's Horse was fighting:

> *This is what the people call the bush veldt and the whole of them talked of it as if it was like our bush, but I can now understand an old Country man. It really is nothing more than a nice park like country, with lots of room to go through it. My youthful experiences taught*

me different and our great Canadian forests make one laugh at the thought of calling it bush.[6]

Sam Steele was an ambitious man and he rose high, but always, it seemed, with the ultimate prize just beyond his reach. He was the top Mountie in the Yukon and far enough away from Ottawa that he was subject to few controls, but that position lasted less than two years and did not lead to the commissioner's job. He was the commanding officer of Lord Strathcona's Horse—in many ways the most satisfying part of his career—but that was over in a year. He became a general in 1914 at a time when there were virtually no officers of that rank in the Canadian Army, but within a year or two there were many, all younger, many of them his former subordinates, with the active commands that he coveted.

The Steele Collection at the University of Alberta is a rich source, and it is clear from the various drafts of his autobiography in the collection that he started keeping a diary in 1870 when he was part of the Red River Expedition. Those diaries existed in 1909–1913 because he quotes from them in the unpublished drafts.[7] The earliest surviving diaries at the University of Alberta, however, date from 1885. What happened to the early diaries? The most likely possibility is that Steele's son Harwood, who was extremely protective of his father's reputation and who started on a biography, deleted entries in the early diaries that he thought discredited Sam. The diary for 1887 is also missing. This was one of the low points in Steele's career, when he considered leaving the NWMP; there are also hints that he was having a drinking problem at that time.

From January 1885 until his death in 1919, it is possible to reconstruct his life on almost a daily basis. Steele's diary has daily entries for most of those years and after meeting his future wife in 1889, he wrote lengthy letters to her several times a week, some as long as forty pages, whenever they were apart. However, there are almost no sources for his childhood, his family life, his education or his early adulthood—gaps which are exceedingly frustrating for a biographer attempting to understand Steele's formative years. In effect, Sam Steele emerges fully formed in his diaries and surviving letters at age thirty-seven, a senior officer in the NWMP, approaching middle age with an adventurous career already behind him. His opinions on world affairs, Canadian politics, literature, music, religion, and of course on his work as a policeman and soldier, are clearly evident in the diaries and letters, but exactly how those ideas were formed in his youth is likely to remain mysterious.

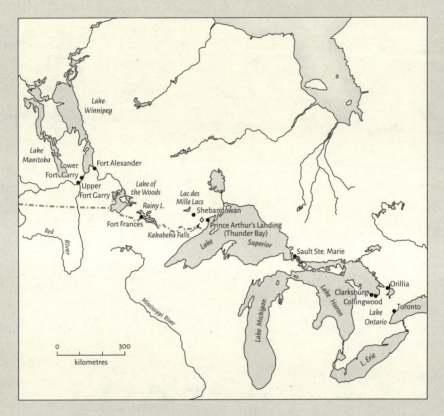

The Red River Expedition, 1870.

# 1 | Early Life
*Orillia and the Red River Expedition*
1848-1873

SAM STEELE WAS BORN JANUARY 5, 1848 on a farm west of the town of Orillia in Simcoe County, Canada West. It was still a fairly remote frontier settlement on the edge of the immense rocky wilderness of the Canadian Shield, but a place that was rapidly developing links to the economic and political centres of Canada by railways and the potent forces of economic growth they unleashed. By the time Sam was approaching adulthood, the dynamism of the Canada of his birth was powerful enough to make a great leap westward to the Pacific and later northward to the Arctic Ocean. His adult life corresponded with the first half century of the new transcontinental Canada and he did more to help create it than all but a handful of his contemporaries. By the time he died in 1919, he had missed very few of the epic adventures that shaped Canada during the previous fifty years, and had been a leading figure in several of them.

Sam Steele's childhood and early life are shrouded in obscurity. In his autobiography, *Forty Years in Canada*, he covers the first twenty-two years of his life in less than five pages. Even that brief account reveals almost nothing about his relationships with his parents and siblings or the childhood experiences that formed him. There is no mention in the autobiography, or his later diaries and letters, of the Chippewa people who inhabited the area where he grew up—perhaps because they had been moved onto one of Canada's first reserves a couple of years before the Steele family arrived. He tries to portray his upbringing as conventional for the time and place, the Upper Canadian frontier one generation removed from the first settlements. In many ways it probably was, but in at least one way it was quite unusual. His father was sixty-seven when Sam was born and his mother was nineteen.

Elmes Yelverton Steele, Sam's father, had an adventurous career in Nelson's navy during the Napoleonic Wars.[1] The middle son of the large family of a country doctor in Gloucestershire, Elmes Steele joined the navy as an officer cadet in 1798 at age seventeen. This was a relatively advanced age to start a naval career and suggests that Steele lacked the family or political connections to set him immediately on the path to becoming an officer. Energy, intelligence and being at the right place at the right time (that is, surviving actions in which those above you in rank were killed) led to promotion to Midshipman, Master's Mate, Lieutenant, and eventually Captain. Steele just missed the battle of Trafalgar but did take part in the battle of the Basque Roads. As an officer in HMS *Leopard* in 1807 he was present when that ship fired on the USS *Chesapeake*, one of the incidents leading to the War of 1812.

Fortunately for Steele, much of his service was on frigates, smaller warships which had a greater likelihood of capturing enemy ships and giving their crews a chance at prize money. In 1799, his frigate HMS *Triton* with three others captured a Spanish treasure fleet on its way from the Caribbean. This was one of the largest prizes of the war and the share, even for a recently appointed midshipman, was £750. That amount was many times his annual pay and would be roughly the equivalent of $200,000 in today's money. The prize money was a life-changing event for Steele. It transformed him overnight from a penniless junior officer to a man of some substance. It allowed him to marry Elizabeth Coucher, the sister of a fellow officer, in 1809. The income it provided supplemented his naval pension after the war when he moved his growing family to France. When the disturbances surrounding the 1830 revolution in that country made it uncomfortable for English residents, Elmes Steele moved his family back to England and then took advantage of an offer of free land grants in Upper Canada for former soldiers and sailors. By that time the family had six children and, although the oldest son was studying medicine and would remain behind, providing for the future of the rest in the colonies seemed a better prospect than anything England could offer.

Elmes Steele, accompanied by his second son John, age fourteen, sailed to Canada in 1832 and travelled upriver to the capital, York. They went first to Hamilton, intending to take up land in the Niagara Peninsula near London, but met someone who suggested that the area farther north would be better, so they returned to York and travelled up Yonge Street until they found land to their liking in Simcoe County a few kilometres west of Orillia. The prize money Elmes had won more than thirty years earlier was crucially important for the kind of life the Steele family would have in their new home. The 1,000-acre grant Steele received was enormous by English standards but as every immigrant to Canada quickly realized, land without capital to develop it was quite meaningless. A modest amount of cash meant the difference between the kind of daily struggle for existence recorded by Steele's contemporaries, Susanna Moodie and Catharine Parr Traill,[2] and a reasonably comfortable life within a short period of time. Elizabeth Steele and the four younger children came to Canada a year later, taking the longer, more expensive, but much more comfortable route through New York.

The land that the Steeles acquired was part of the Lake Simcoe–Lake Huron Purchase (Crown Treaty Number Sixteen) of 1815. It was one of the earliest post–War of 1812 treaties by which the government of Upper Canada solidified its control of the agricultural land south of the Canadian Shield. Unlike later treaties, this one provided for a one-time cash payment with no annuities or reserves. First Nations were under the direct control of the British government during this period and its policy was based on the hope that, once treaties were signed, the First Nations would quickly make the transition to an agricultural economy.[3] This did not happen and within a decade or so, starvation and disease prompted the government to move the surviving Chippewa from the area west of Lake Simcoe to a reserve at Coldwater Narrows.[4] Growing up in this area, Steele presumably came to understand the relationship between the settler population and the First Nations they had displaced as an inevitable transition to marginality, however benevolently intentioned.

Elmes Steele's capital enabled him to hire an old soldier named Butcher and his wife along with two other men.[5] Elmes, John and the other three men cut a road through the bush to the Steele property and began clearing the land and building a house. With this start, Elmes Steele had no difficulty establishing himself as a successful farmer and community leader. He donated land and paid for the construction of an Anglican church near his farm, became a magistrate in 1833 and colonel of the local militia unit. John soon moved to his own farm near Orillia and the other children married into the community.

When the 1837 Rebellions broke out, Elmes and John Steele turned out with the militia to defend the government. Upper Canada's ruling Family Compact had sought to attract retired British officers with the expectation that they would be solid supporters of the status quo. Many were, but Captain Steele's politics had been Whig in England and while he was more than willing to defend "Queen and Country," it soon became apparent that he was not prepared to accept the Compact's assertion that they were the sole embodiment of loyalty to the British Empire.[6] In the wake of the Rebellions, Lord Durham produced his famous report recommending a union of

Upper and Lower Canada to be governed under what the opponents of the Tory Family Compact called a system of "responsible government." In October 1839, Elmes Steele chaired a meeting at a tavern on Yonge Street of those who supported Durham's proposals. The Family Compact–appointed sheriff, William Jarvis, organized a mob to break up the meeting and one participant was killed.

The British government carried through with the union of the two Canadas but instructed the new governor, Lord Sydenham, that responsible government could not be reconciled with imperial control. Some political leaders, notably Robert Baldwin of Toronto, as York was now called, believed that if they could assemble a solid majority in the assembly, they could force the British authorities to accept the system. The first election for the new assembly of the Province of Canada was held in the spring of 1841. The constituency of Simcoe where the Steeles lived was usually solid Tory country, represented for almost all the period from 1830 to 1857 by a stalwart of the Family Compact, W.B. Robinson; the only election Robinson lost during these years was to Elmes Steele running as a Baldwin Reformer in 1841. Steele seems to have stepped in as a candidate at the last minute when a neighbour backed out, although his earlier involvement with the cause suggests that he acted out of conviction. After his 1839 experience he would not have been unaware of what he might be up against in the election, but a man who had stood on bullet-swept decks in major naval battles was unlikely to be intimidated. Elections in Canada until the introduction of the secret ballot in 1874 were not for the faint of heart. Voters had to show up at the polling places and announce their choice to the returning officers before everyone who happened to be present. Candidates who could get their supporters to the polls, and prevent their opponents from showing up, won the election.

The 1841 contest brought out the full range of electioneering techniques of the period and went down as one of the bloodiest of the century in Canada. There was only one polling place in the constituency, in the town of Simcoe, carefully chosen because it was the most solidly Tory location. Steele's supporters were mainly in the outlying parts of the county; his slogan was "The Backwoodsman's Friend." While there were no deaths in Simcoe during the election, there were plenty of broken heads as gangs— several hundred on each side and armed with cudgels—fought to control the polling place.[7] The poll was open for a week and Robinson's men held out for the first few days, but Steele's followers coming in from the outer townships drove them off and won the election.

After the violence of the election, Steele turned out to be an unremarkable member of the assembly, working for roads and other public works in his county and generally staying out of the complex political infighting that swirled around Robert Baldwin and his Canada East partner, Louis-Hippolyte Lafontaine, as they manoeuvred to attain responsible government. When the next election came along in 1844, Steele chose not to run. Money seems to have been the principal reason for his decision. Elections ran on liquor and large quantities were needed to keep up the morale of the troops during the contest. One source claims that Steele spent £700 on the 1841 election and, although that amount seems exaggerated, he let it be known that the earlier election had exhausted his finances.[8] There are also indications that his lukewarm support for Baldwin's hard line on responsible government had disappointed his supporters. Elmes Steele seems to have been a moderate by conviction and was prepared to stand up for his beliefs. Later in life, Sam Steele received a letter from his former militia commander and remembered, "My father and his nearly fought a duel, all was ready when their friends brought a party of police on the scene. The old Colonel O'Brien was very intolerant and my governor was the very reverse so they never could agree."[9]

Two years after he left political life, Steele's wife Elizabeth died. There is no indication in any of the records what the cause of death might have been but life on the frontier was certainly much more precarious for women than for men. Steele wasted no time marrying again, this time to a neighbour, Ann MacIan Macdonald, in 1847. Although Elmes Steele's grandchildren, Harwood and Flora, had an almost obsessive interest in family history, they showed no curiosity whatever about the nature of the relationship between their grandfather and his second wife. Whatever a nineteen-year-old girl saw in a sixty-seven-year-old man, the marriage turned out to be productive. The first child, Samuel Benfield Steele, was born less than a year after the marriage and Ann went on to have five more children before her early death in 1859.

Around the time that Sam was reaching school age the family left the farm and moved into Orillia. Elmes Steele was well into his seventies by that time and no doubt rented out the farm. Schooling for the growing family was one of the reasons for the move, although Elmes did some home instruction. Sam's relationship with Elmes was admiring but rather distant, more like that with a respected grandparent than a father. The ties to his mother seem to have been closer. Writing to his wife from South Africa in 1902 in a reminiscent mood he said, "I used to be my mother's (champion) and fight for her when saucy Irish children used to say things to us as we passed. It was rare of course but she used to be very much pleased to see me in my five or six years bristle up and make for them with stones and sticks."[10] In all the thousands of pages of his diaries and letters, this is the sole mention of his mother. Perhaps he felt abandoned when she died, leaving him with an elderly father and five younger siblings at age nine.

The death of Ann Steele created an immediate family crisis since Elmes Steele, now close to eighty, was in no position to care for six young children. In *Forty Years in Canada*, Steele wrote of his mother's death, "Our years were very happy before that, but there came afterwards much sorrow and a great deal of unhappiness, brightened, of course, at times by the kindly sympathy of our relatives."[11] What exactly this means is hard to decipher. It would appear that the children were parcelled out among the children of Elmes's first marriage and that some fared better than others. Sam was apparently the only one of the family who went to live with his half-brother John. That relationship quickly became one of the most important of Sam Steele's life. John was forty years his senior and was much more of a father than his biological parent had been. The breakup of the family left Sam Steele with a powerful urge to look out for his siblings whenever possible. He kept in close touch with them throughout his life, lending them money and finding them jobs. His sense of responsibility for them was one of the forces behind his drive to succeed. The drive to excel and make his way in the world appeared early in Sam's life and never left him. In one of his letters home from South Africa he recounted a telling incident from his youth:

> The McCullochs were a very respectable Hieland Scotch family settled next to John's old place. There were two daughters and a son, all quiet and kindly...(Their mother) used to think and say that I was a wild boy and a great flirt and even hinted though without reason that I went even farther than flirting, and that is one thing absolutely true that I never was guilty of anything of the sort. One of the girls tried to seduce me and I coyly objected to her soft embrace and so she told Mrs Mc and John's wife that I had tried to take her virtue(!) from her. I left John's at once. I was just visiting at the time and did not see them for many years when they reported of their accusations.[12]

One might suspect that the details of the incident were not quite as Sam presented them but clearly he was not about to let a romantic entanglement in his late teens tie him down to a farm in Simcoe County.

Farming was never in Sam Steele's future. He acquired a homestead in Alberta while serving in the Mounted Police and put money into cattle-raising ventures with friends, but these were strictly speculative investments. Later in life he entertained romantic notions of retiring as a gentleman farmer on the prairies, in the Niagara Peninsula, or near Orillia, but farming never really attracted him, and it attracted his wife even less. Once he left Orillia he lived the rest of his days in towns and cities. After finishing school he worked for an unidentified business in Orillia and then moved west to the town of Clarksburg where he found a better job as a clerk. But by that time he had already discovered that what he really wanted, and what he was good at, was being a soldier.

In the 1860s the American Civil War brought several serious diplomatic crises between Great Britain and the United States. The Canadian government reluctantly took some steps to reorganize its defence force, the aptly named "Sedentary Militia," which existed largely on paper. Although tensions with the United States relaxed with the end of the war, there were cross-border raids into British North America in 1866 by the Fenian Brotherhood, an Irish nationalist organization with many members in the northern states. The Fenians hoped that their incursions would inspire the British North American colonies to rise up and throw off the British yoke or, failing that, encourage the Irish to do so. The raids had the opposite effect in Canada, stimulating a nascent nationalism and providing an impetus for Confederation in 1867.[13]

Even though the only serious skirmish of the raids, the Battle of Ridgeway, was a clear defeat for the Canadian militia, exposing a woeful lack of training and equipment, the willingness of the militia to defend their country inspired young men like Sam Steele. There was not much money for modern arms and equipment but volunteer soldiers who were keen and willing to devote the time could take three-month courses of instruction run by British regulars that qualified them to become officers. Sam Steele, age sixteen in 1866, took one of these courses in Toronto and received a commission in the 35th Simcoe Battalion of Infantry.[14] When he moved to Clarksburg he organized an infantry company there for the 31st Battalion. He says in his memoirs that he was asked to take command but declined because he believed he was too young. He goes on:

*I left there after putting the company in good order and well organized, parting from them with much regret. I was still interested in the force, however, and made a close study of all military matters, at the same time looking well after the interests of my employers, until the disturbances of the Red River Metis under Louis Riel changed my life.*[15]

This sounds distinctly odd. If he loved the organization and the military life, why leave and resign his commission? Throughout his life, Sam Steele reacted strongly against people he considered incompetent, particularly if they were above him in the hierarchy. This was probably an early example of this attitude. Later in life he would not always have the luxury of leaving when he found superior officers wanting.

Canada's westward expansion got off to an uncertain start in the fall of 1869 when Louis Riel organized the population of the Red River Settlement to resist the transfer of the HBC's territories until they had been consulted. Without a military force at hand to impose its terms the Canadian government was forced to negotiate. The result was the *Manitoba Act*, which created a new province in the area immediately around Red River. An effort to disrupt the negotiations and overthrow Riel's provisional government by some of the recent arrivals from Canada in Red River led to the execution of one of their number, Thomas Scott. The death of Scott created a furor in Ontario that overshadowed the fact that he was the sole casualty in what could easily have been a much more deadly situation. The agreement that led to the *Manitoba Act* meant that the whole vast western territory from Lake Superior to the Rockies passed to Canada without military action. The Canadian North-West would not be conquered territory.

Nevertheless, the Canadian and British governments believed that a military demonstration was necessary to assert Canadian sovereignty and make it clear to American expansionists in the northern border states that they had every intention of defending the territory. Agreement was reached after lengthy negotiations

*The earliest photograph of Sam Steele in his late teens in militia uniform.*
[BPSC, 2008.1.2.1.6.1.1.1]

that a force would be sent to reinforce this message. The force consisted of 400 British regulars of the King's Royal Rifle Corps with a few Royal Engineers, Royal Artillery and medical personnel, and two battalions of Canadian militia of 350 men each, one from Ontario and one from Quebec, under the command of Colonel Garnet Wolseley, an exceptionally competent British officer serving in Canada at the time.[16] Volunteers from militia units in the two provinces were recruited for the two Canadian battalions. Sam Steele volunteered immediately, not through the 31st Battalion in Clarksburg where he was living and working, but through the 35th in his old hometown. When he was accepted as part of the Simcoe County Company (No. 4) Steele did something else that revealed what he had learned from the Clarksburg episode. Officers for the company had been chosen already but not the non-commissioned officers (NCOs). The commanding officer, Captain D.H. McMillan, paraded the men and asked all those who had earned officer's certificates to identify themselves. Steele decided not to reveal that he held these papers so that he could remain a private.

He was young. The Ontario Rifles was an elite unit made up of the pick of the province's militia battalions and commanded by men Steele knew and respected. He could learn more about leadership, he decided, watching from the ranks. It was a good decision, a sign of rapidly maturing judgement. Steele had a lot to learn and at this point in his life he set about learning it methodically—a pattern that would last until the end of his life. In any case for someone like Steele—strong, active, accustomed to frontier life—the Red River Expedition was not just a learning experience, but also offered a chance to serve his country in the national project of western expansion while simultaneously promising adventure and fun. Without any of the burdens of command he was free to compete with his fellow soldiers in the formal and informal tests of strength and endurance on the journey. He absorbed their point of view so thoroughly that when he did become an NCO, an officer and ultimately a general, he always understood their needs and how to motivate them.

The British and Canadian governments wrangled over details through the winter months but by May everything was settled and the soldiers made their way to Toronto to receive their uniforms and rifles and do a few days of drill before heading off into the wilderness.[17] They then travelled by rail to Collingwood, where they boarded ships to take them across lakes Huron and Superior to Thunder Bay. Just what the Ontario soldiers expected to do when they reached Manitoba varied considerably. Although anyone who had previous connections to Red River was ineligible for selection to the Canadian battalions, many of Sam Steele's fellow soldiers joined with the intention of following the Toronto *Globe*'s urgings to avenge the death of Thomas Scott. An officer of Steele's company noted in his diary a few days after leaving Thunder Bay:

> *July 7 12 o'clock Mr. Kennedy has returned bringing us the news that we must be in the Lake on Sunday. He also tells us that as fighting is expected our Battalion will accompany the 60th Rifles all the way through. This news satisfies all our men, as they are all afraid that our Company might be left at Fort Frances.*[18]

Others signed up with the intention of staying in the west as settlers once their enlistment expired, like the commanding officer of Steele's company, Captain McMillan, who stayed on, prospered, and several decades later became lieutenant governor of Manitoba. Those who wanted to stay at the end of their year of enlistment were offered land grants of 160 acres (roughly sixty-four hectares), exactly what the homestead system would adopt two years later. The smallest group of volunteers, which included among others the prime minister's son, Hugh John Macdonald, and James F. Macleod, later Sam's boss as commissioner of the NWMP, joined for the military experience. Sam Steele certainly fell into this category; he showed no hostility toward the Métis while stationed at Red River, only curiosity about their customs and way of life.

The American authorities at Sault Ste. Marie were not disposed to be helpful in permitting passage to the Expedition. Although the Oregon Treaty of 1846 had settled the western boundary, many Americans continued to believe that the land west of the Great Lakes should be part of their country.[19] In any case, no self-respecting country would permit a foreign military force to move through its territory. The Canadians were therefore forced to unload all military supplies before Steele's ship, the sidewheel steamer *Chicora*, was allowed to pass through the locks. Transshipping the many tons of supplies required to get 1,200 men to Manitoba took so much time and effort that it was mid-June before all troops and supplies were assembled at Thunder Bay. The route west from there to Red River was difficult but well known by 1870. Fur traders from Montreal who eventually coalesced into the North West Company started using the route a century before and it remained a highway of the western trade until the HBC absorbed the North West Company in 1821. The HBC immediately switched its heavier freight traffic to the northern route from York Factory on Hudson Bay through Lake Winnipeg to the North Saskatchewan River, because it allowed the use of more capacious York boats instead of canoes. The waterway from Thunder Bay now saw only local traffic along with the occasional messenger canoe unencumbered with cargo.

The Hudson Bay route was out of the question this late in the year, so a way had to be found to get boats, about 150 in all, over places where only canoes had travelled. A railway through the region to connect central Canada with its new western empire was already envisaged and work had started on improvements to the route that would support the eventual construction. An engineer named Simon J. Dawson was hired in 1869 to make it usable. Dawson immediately recognized that the biggest problems were at each end of the route: the first 100 kilometres or so west from Thunder Bay and the 160 kilometres between Lake of the Woods and Red River. He started work on roads at each end that would connect to the relatively easy water passage that ran some 400 kilometres from Lac des Mille Lacs to Lake of the Woods. Dawson was naturally consulted on the best way for the soldiers to get to their destination. He advised that he had speeded up work on the road from Thunder Bay so it would be ready on time for wagons to haul the boats from Lake Superior to Shebandowan Lake past the daunting obstacle of Kakabeka Falls. However, the western road would not be ready. The Expedition would have to take the old fur trade loop north through Rat Portage to the Winnipeg River and down its cataracts to Lake Winnipeg.

This was the best possible plan under the circumstances and Wolseley accepted it. Even so, it promised to be a gruelling journey and before the first troops could set out from Thunder Bay it got a lot harder. The weather had been hot and dry to this point and a forest fire swept through, destroying all the bridges and culverts completed on the road and burning up the timber set aside for others. Wolseley decided that he would have to abandon the road and take his boats up the shallow and rocky Kaministiquia River and portage around the falls. This might not have been possible but now the weather broke and heavy rain set in, causing the streams to rise. Still, the boats had to be tracked most of the way, a procedure Steele described vividly in his memoirs:

*When at this work the voyageurs were in the bow and stern of the boat, each with a pole to keep it out from the rocky shore or to steer clear of boulders. The remainder of the men took hold of the line, one of them leading it the best way over land or along the shore, while the rest passed the line over their shoulders. Often when the water was too deep near the shore they ascended the bank, the leader passing the rope in front of the trees while the others hauled on the line as was most convenient, running along and passing one another when necessary. As a rule wading was preferred to taking to the high banks. Frequently, owing to the swiftness and depth of the water, one would miss his footing and would have to hang on to the towline whilst the other men steadied themselves until he had regained his feet.*[20]

The constant rain now turned the portage trails into mud holes that needed to be corduroyed with logs to be made passable. Officers as well as men worked long hours with picks, shovels, and axes. Then the boats could be skidded over, followed by the stores and supplies. Each boat had a crew of ten to twelve soldiers and three civilian voyageurs, many of them Ojibway from around Fort William and Iroquois from Kahnawake, and carried a standard load of eight barrels of biscuit (45.4 kg each), six barrels of flour (45.4 kg each), eight barrels of pork (91 kg each), two sacks of beans (45.4 kg each), two cases of dried potatoes (22.6 kg each), a barrel of sugar (36 kg), a chest of tea (22.6 kg), an arms chest (91 kg), two ammunition boxes (29 kg each), a tent (34 kg), and miscellaneous supplies adding up to another 40 kg. For each boat, close to two tonnes of supplies had to be hauled on men's backs over the slippery and often steep portage trails, amidst clouds of mosquitoes and black flies. Steele's account of the trip in his autobiography is very much in the "band of brothers" tradition, but in fact some of the soldiers quickly decided they had had enough, as the Mulvey Diary recorded: "July 8 One of our men Pt Van Malder was very disorderly—he threw down his knapsack and positively refused to carry it farther. So I halted the Company and ordered him under arrest...This place is 25 miles from Thunder Bay."[21]

Steele, on the other hand, ignored the discomforts and thrived on the challenges and competitions among the stronger men to see who could carry the heaviest loads. He was one of the men who could manage a ninety-one kilogram pork barrel or arms chest and one or more additional items with relative ease. As Steele pointed out, they were all in good shape to start with and became stronger with the constant exertion. As well, as the food was consumed the loads grew lighter. Much of the middle part of the trip from Rainy Lake through Lake of the Woods allowed for sails to be hoisted, which gave a welcome rest from rowing. Steele complained that his boat, which the crew had derisively named *The Flying Dutchman*, was the slowest and clumsiest of the expedition. At Fort Frances they managed to exchange it for a lighter one.

The last part of the journey took the soldiers across Rat Portage and down the steep descent of the Winnipeg River to Lake Winnipeg. Like most of the others, after a month in boats, Steele considered himself an experienced voyageur and found running the rapids exhilarating. There was a large HBC post, Fort Alexander, a few kilometres from the mouth of the river where Wolseley had planned to concentrate all his troops before moving on to Red River. That would have been a prudent move if there was a realistic possibility that Riel and his followers were planning to forcibly oppose the expedition, but the word at Fort Alexander was that Riel did not intend to do so and furthermore, could not do so because most of the Métis capable of bearing arms were far off on the annual summer buffalo hunt. So instead of waiting for the Ontario and Quebec battalions to arrive, when Wolseley reached Fort Alexander on August 20 he and the regulars set off the following day for Red River. They reached Upper Fort Garry on August 24 with guns at the ready to find that Riel and the remaining members of his provisional government had left. Wolseley was very disappointed to be cheated of a fight. He said so in his farewell speech to the Canadian troops as recorded by Captain McMillan: "Altho the Banditti who have been oppressing this people fled at your approach without giving you an opportunity of proving how men capable of such labor could fight you have deserved as well of your country as if you had won a battle."[22]

Wolseley was far too much the professional to try to provoke a fight, however, or to allow his soldiers to do so. Keeping the rank and file under control was easy enough with the 60th Rifles and the other British regulars who were given a day off to spend in the saloons of the village of Winnipeg, a kilometre from Fort Garry, with strict orders not to involve themselves in local quarrels. Everyone realized that the tensions in the settlement between the recently arrived settlers from Ontario and the Métis, unresolved since the execution of Thomas Scott by Riel's provisional government the previous fall, were explosive. The voyageurs who had delivered the soldiers to Red River were not under military discipline and probably sided with the Métis. The two Canadian militia units certainly aligned with the opposing sides. They were under military discipline, but it would not take much to fracture those bonds. The newly appointed lieutenant governor, Adams G. Archibald, had been delayed en route and did not reach the settlement until

September 2. Ottawa had assumed that Riel's provisional government would stay in place until Archibald took over but when the Métis leader left, there was no civil authority to appoint justices of the peace, appoint constables, or authorize the military to arrest civilians. Wolseley asked Donald Smith (later Lord Strathcona), the ranking HBC official on the scene, to assume authority until the lieutenant governor arrived. Smith reluctantly agreed but clearly his orders would carry little weight with a population who saw their troubles as the result of being abandoned by the Company.

Steele's company and the rest of the Ontario Rifles were encamped in front of Fort Garry by August 29, waiting for the British troops to leave so that they could move in, a process which started the same day. Riel's enemies in the settlement clearly expected that the Ontario troops would join them in punishing the "rebels" for what they regarded as the murder of Thomas Scott; if the troops would not arrest them, at least they would look the other way while scores were settled. Wolseley understood the dangers. In his farewell address to the militia on handing over command to Colonel Jarvis of the Ontario Rifles, in addition to praising the men for their performance, he urged them to remain strictly neutral:

> *Some evil designing men have endeavored to make a Section of this people believe that they have much to dread at your hands. I beg of you to give the lie to such a foul aspersion upon your character as Canadian Soldiers by continuing to comport yourselves as you have hitherto done. I desire to warn you especially against mixing yourselves up in party affairs here, to be present at any political meeting or to join in any political procession is strictly against her Majesty's orders & regulations a fact which I am sure, you have only to know to be guided by.*[23]

Sam Steele thoroughly approved of this exhortation to order and discipline, although some of his fellow soldiers did not. Steele was peripherally involved in the ugliest incident that took place in the few days after the departure of the regulars. On September 13 he was part of a work party taking the boats out of the water for winter storage at the fort. As he recounted it,

> Suddenly two travel-stained horsemen, one on a black horse and one on a grey, rode up to us and asked if we had seen a man named Elzear Goulet who, one of them stated, had commanded the firing party which shot Thomas Scott. As we could give them no information they wheeled quickly and rode off at full speed towards Winnipeg. The same night it was reported in camp that they had found Goulet seated on a bench at the Davis House, a hotel in the village, and when they had accosted him he had taken flight towards the Red River, pursued by his accusers. When he arrived at the bank he turned and threatened to shoot, but they called to him "Fire Away!" Seeing that they would not be denied, he jumped into the river, and when he attempted to swim across, shots were fired and he sank. The horsemen had been followed by a crowd of people, amongst whom were two of our buglers, mere lads. No other soldiers were present, and neither of these took part in the chase, nor is it likely that any of our men would have taken part in the pursuit of the unfortunate man, even had they known that he was one of the murderers of Scott. We had amongst us about a dozen very wild spirits, but they were kept in control by the strict discipline maintained in the regiment, and, what is sometimes better, the fear of the displeasure of their comrades, who in ways soldiers have, could make their lives intolerable.[24]

Much of this account is based on hearsay and the last part of it sounds self-serving but it largely agrees with other eyewitness accounts and the best historian of the Red River Expedition, George Stanley, concludes, "it has a certain ring of truth about it."[25] Steele's personal sympathies were entirely with Riel's opponents but that counted for nothing against his inherent belief in the overriding importance of duly constituted authority. A few days after the Goulet episode, he got a chance to put those beliefs to the test when he was promoted to corporal and moved from No. 4 Company to No. 7. His new company housed a concentration of the bad boys of the regiment, the "wild spirits" referred to above. Most of these men were older than Steele and resented the promotion of a younger man from a different company. Now that the prospect of combat had vanished, there was a long winter of tedious routine ahead before they could take their discharge and land grants or return to Ontario. This gave them plenty of leisure time to entertain themselves by harassing a young and inexperienced corporal.

Steele showed early evidence of skill at handling difficult situations by ignoring provocations and refusing to lose his temper. When one situation turned violent, he met that challenge equally well. One of the Privates in No. 7 Company, John Kerr, indulged in some horseplay which angered one of the troublemakers, a man named Joe Case; Case stabbed him in the leg with a carving knife. Kerr responded by knocking Case unconscious with a poker. When Case's supporters rushed into the room to avenge their friend, Steele drove them off with a rifle butt before further damage could be done. Both men were patched up successfully and when the colonel got wind of the incident both refused to make a complaint. Steele wisely concluded that natural justice had been satisfied and was far better than the strict letter of military law.[26] This combination of tact backed with force established Steele's authority. Drill and parades three times a day with full thirty-two kilogram packs soaked up any residual resentments and life in the barracks settled into a peaceful routine for the winter.

Outside the fort, Manitoba's first election in the fall of 1870 revived tensions and led to some rioting. The police handled most of it but Sam's company was called out on one occasion and managed to disperse the crowd without bloodshed. As the bitter winter weather set in, he had plenty of time to think about the choice he would have to make when his enlistment expired in the spring. He knew farming was not for him, so the land grant held little interest. John Kerr and many of his friends were joining the police force being recruited for Manitoba but that did not appeal. Military life was what Steele sought. He could have signed on for another year with the reduced force the government decided to maintain to help keep order in the new province. In addition to this, the Canadian intelligence network in the United States was reporting that the Fenians might be planning an incursion from Minnesota. While this was not public knowledge, there had been hints of it, and the prospect of action might have tempted Steele to stay. In any case, the Fenians were reined in by the United States Army before the Canadian forces could meet them. Steele's assessment that soldiering in Manitoba would be a dead end proved correct. He decided to return to Ontario and see if anything more promising might develop there.

Wolseley and his British soldiers had gone straight from Red River to the United Kingdom, one of the last groups to leave Canada as part of the general British military withdrawal from North America. Steele and others assumed that some kind of professional Canadian army would have to replace them, if only to carry on the training of the militia. He intended to be first in line to sign up. Perhaps rumours to that effect had influenced his decision not to stay in Manitoba. The Canadian government was in no hurry to get on with creating an army, however. Money was short, in part because of the expenses of the Red River Expedition, and the government was desperately searching for the massive sums necessary to build a railway to the Pacific coast. Arriving back in Toronto in July, Steele found nothing happening and went home for a few months. In October, Ottawa finally announced that its plan was to create central schools for each of the three branches of the military (infantry, artillery, and cavalry), which would eventually develop into a small professional army, which would have as a primary role the training of the volunteer militia. Artillery came first because it was the most technically complex and difficult to improvise, and because it was essential for manning the fortifications at key places on Canada's frontier.

The School of Gunnery was to have two batteries, "A" at Kingston under the command of British officer Lieutenant-Colonel George Arthur French and "B" at Quebec. Steele did not make it to Kingston in time to be the first to sign up, but he was number twenty-two and his brother Richard was twenty-three. They were to undertake a one-year training course, after which some might sign on as regular soldiers in Canada's embryonic professional army. Almost all of the Steele brothers' fellow students and some of the instructors were familiar faces from the Red River Expedition. The instructors were experienced NCOs from the British Army, which was undergoing a series of fundamental structural changes known as the Cardwell Reforms after the secretary of state for war in Gladstone's government. Enlistment prior to the 1870s had been for life but was now fixed at twelve years. Many relatively young veterans, who had no prospects for civilian employment, jumped at the opportunity to serve in Canada.

Both instructors and students were a select group. Sam Steele thoroughly enjoyed absorbing the lessons of men who had served in the Indian Mutiny, the Crimean War, and other imperial conflicts all the way back to Waterloo. His experience was not unique. Colonel Thomas Bland Strange, who commanded "B" Battery at Quebec, looked back on it as one of the highlights of a career that took him around the world.[27] Sam did well and began his service as a regular soldier instructing militia gunners at Fort Henry in Kingston. He was then sent to Toronto to what at the time was called New Fort (now Stanley Barracks) in charge of a party with the task of organizing the guns and stores left behind the previous year by the departing British troops. When that was complete he did some militia instructing and filled in his spare time by taking courses at Toronto Commercial College. Early in 1873 he was transferred back to Kingston once again as an instructor.

By the summer of that year, it seems clear that peacetime soldiering was losing some of its appeal. Steele was also realizing that this was not the road to the kind of social standing he craved.

One of his sisters had married a successful merchant in Toronto but Steele did not get in touch with her during the year he spent in the city. In a revealing passage in a letter to his fiancé in 1889 he wrote:

> I knew that I was not thought to be doing the right thing although steady and well thought of...I had been passed in the street and not recognized by them and took my own road which I found suited me the best, and I had many friends on high who were not likely to be annoyed not being relations. Of course, I know they were not aware I was in Toronto or they would have made a great deal of me, for I kept away and they had no idea that I was in existence. I was a rolling stone they thought with a love of adventure and all that sort of thing.[28]

So when rumours began to circulate that the government was organizing a force to be known as the North-West Mounted Police, Steele at once began to explore the prospects of joining up. Steele's autobiography, the only source for this period of his life, skips lightly over the decision, as it does for many of the significant turning points in his life, but it cannot have been taken without considerable soul searching. He had been completely focused on a military career from his early teens. When his enlistment in the Ontario Rifles ran out he had unhesitatingly rejected the possibility of joining a Manitoba police force. Now he eagerly sought an opportunity in a similar force in the same part of Canada.

There are several possible motivations for this momentous change in the trajectory of Steele's life. One is certainly the maturing process. The early to mid-twenties are a time when many people reassess their youthful ambitions and adjust them to take account of experience and changing circumstances. Steele was highly intelligent and the two years since he had left Manitoba must have made a couple of things apparent to him. In the first place, the growth of the Canadian army was going to be painfully slow, with very limited prospects for promotion. Steele had no intention of remaining at non-commissioned rank for the rest of his life. At just this time, the government was planning to open the Royal Military College at Kingston for the education of officers, but Steele seems to have decided that he was too old to go back to school. The second consideration was that, even if he did become an officer, the prospects of action for the army in the foreseeable future seemed remote. The Treaty of Washington in 1871 had settled all major differences between the United States and Britain in North America, effectively eliminating the only possible enemy.

The Red River Expedition had given Steele an idea of the immensity of Canada's new empire in the west and it is likely that he was inspired by the challenges involved. One of the British soldiers Steele had encountered at Red River, Captain William F. Butler, had been hired by the Canadian government to tour the North-West Territories and report on conditions. He published a lively and enormously popular book detailing his journey, *The Great Lone Land*, in 1872, painting a vivid, if somewhat romanticized picture of the region.[29] Steele read it, and it clearly made a strong impression since he refers to it in *Forty Years in Canada*, and it may have stimulated his sense of the allure of novelty and adventure, never far below the surface throughout his life. Probably some combination of all these reasons lay behind his decision to head west again.

The North-West Mounted Police also had a more distinctively military character than the Manitoba Mounted Police. They were to be equipped as a light cavalry regiment of the period and placed under military discipline. Their equipment included several field guns. Obviously they were prepared to confront something beyond the average bank robber or even a criminal gang. The Canadian government had learned some hard lessons as a result of the Red River Resistance and this time it took the trouble to learn something about the new territory before launching its representatives into the wilderness. Information was collected from the HBC and missionaries residing in the area. In addition to Captain Butler's reconnaissance, the adjutant general of the Canadian militia, Colonel Patrick Robertson-Ross, travelled across the prairies to

British Columbia in 1872 and reported at length on his observations. All accounts agreed that the most likely trouble spot was just north of the 49th parallel in what is now southern Alberta, where American traders had established posts on Canadian territory and were selling large amounts of illicit liquor to the Blackfoot. This situation was a clear challenge to Canadian sovereignty and it would be the primary mission of the Mounted Police to arrive with sufficient force to deal with it. To underline the dangers of the situation, as the Mounted Police were being recruited in the summer of 1873, word arrived that twenty Assiniboine had been massacred in the Cypress Hills by a group of "wolfers" from Montana Territory.

Canadian governments, then as now, were close observers of what the United States was doing. What they saw was not encouraging. Washington repeatedly signed treaties with the Native peoples of the vast area west of the Mississippi and then stood by while those documents were ignored by incoming settlers, railroad builders, and gold miners. When some of the tribes responded with violence, the army was sent in to deal with them. The wars that resulted were brutal and sometimes came close to being genocidal.[30] Worse, perhaps, from the point of view of Ottawa, the American policy was both expensive and ineffective. The army was costing Washington close to a million dollars a year and there was no peace on the plains in the 1870s. The total Canadian budget at that time was around $19 million, so a radically different solution would have to be found. It arose from Prime Minister John A. Macdonald's recognition that the essence of the problem was exerting control over the settler population. If that could be achieved, treaties could be enforced and the cycle of retaliation avoided. Although the Mounted Police were to some degree modelled on the Royal Irish Constabulary and on British police forces in India, as adapted to the circumstances of the North-West Territories, they were quite unlike anything in the history of European colonialism.[31]

Steele learned that recruiting in his area was to be handled by a militia officer from Brockville, Major James Morrow Walsh, who had been appointed as one of the officers of the Mounted Police. He obtained a letter of introduction, met Walsh and discovered that Walsh knew some members of his family. Steele must have impressed Walsh since he agreed to appoint him as staff constable (the equivalent army rank was sergeant major, which Steele uses in his autobiography; the NWMP eventually changed the rank designation to troop sergeant major). The original NWMP consisted of 300 men divided into six "divisions" of fifty men each. Walsh was one of three commissioned officers in "A" Division and, as staff constable, Steele would be the senior NCO and fourth in command. The next step was to get permission to leave "A" Battery. As Steele related it in his autobiography, "So we went to Colonel French, who was in the city, and with a twinkle in his eye, as if he knew all about it, he gave four others and myself permission to leave the battery and join the police."[32] French did know all about it, of course, since he was about to become the first commissioner of the NWMP.

Steele went back to Kingston to wind up his affairs with "A" Battery and after a "jolly send-off" returned to Brockville where he was sworn in on October 1. It took no more than a few days to sign up the full contingent and then it was off to Toronto to join two other divisions and leave for the west before the lakes froze over. Sam Steele was now on the road to becoming one of the most celebrated Canadians of his generation.

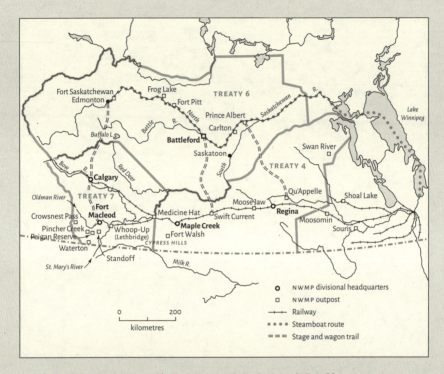

The March West and NWMP Divisional Headquarters before 1885.

## 2 ‖ The North-West Mounted Police
### 1873-1885

SAM STEELE AND ABOUT 150 OTHER MEMBERS of the first three divisions of the North-West Mounted Police left Toronto in October 1873 for Manitoba. This was very late in the year for travel to the west and the original plan had been for the police to spend the winter organizing and training in Toronto. The hastened departure was the result of news of an incident that quickly became known as the Cypress Hills Massacre.[1] In the anarchic society of the border area between Montana and the North-West Territories in the early 1870s, whites, Métis, and several First Nations mingled uneasily. Traders bought buffalo hides from anyone who had them, with whiskey as the principal currency. The most widely despised group in the border country were known as "wolfers," men who poisoned wolves because it was easier than shooting or trapping them and provided undamaged pelts. Coyotes, foxes, and other wildlife, along with the dogs of the First Nations, were collateral damage.

In the spring of 1873 several hundred people were gathered around trading posts in the Cypress Hills as the winter trading season wound down. About 300 were Assiniboine in bands led by

Chiefs Maniputosis and Inihan Kinyen. On the last day of May, a group of wolfers led by Thomas Hardwick and John Evans arrived. They had been on their way to Fort Benton, Montana, when forty of their horses were stolen. The horses had been taken by a Cree band, but the wolfers did not know this and headed back for the Cypress Hills in the hope of recovering them. Although the Assiniboine had few horses after a very hard winter, they were a convenient target. The wolfers began drinking heavily the following day, June 1, and when one of their number accused the Assiniboine of taking another horse, they set off to get it back. Although the wolfers were heavily outnumbered, they were armed with modern repeating rifles, while most of the Assiniboine had muzzleloaders or, in some cases, bows and arrows. The inevitable result was that more than twenty Assiniboine, including women and children, died in the attack and only one of the wolfers.[2]

Although the Canadian government had already passed legislation creating the NWMP when the Cypress Hills Massacre occurred, the incident gave urgency to their plans. The Mounted Police were central to the goal of peopling the prairies with agricultural settlers. That end was universally regarded as an inevitable extension of the dispossession of the Indigenous peoples of the Americas that had been going on for three and a half centuries. If the outcome, broadly speaking, was not in doubt, the means of achieving it and perhaps the ultimate place of the First Nations in the new order, were still open to some degree. In earlier centuries in the Americas the Indigenous peoples often faced extermination through disease or deliberate colonial policies of genocide.[3] If any survived, they were often subjected to some form of slavery. The newly independent United States in the early 19th century developed a legal regime that allowed the confiscation of Indian lands and the removal of entire nations west of the Mississippi over the aptly named "Trail of Tears."[4] When settlement moved onto the Great Plains, the process continued relentlessly. In the words of the classic American study of the period,

*Having destroyed one "Indian barrier," an aggressively westering America now faced another. In less than half a century this barrier too would be destroyed, and white civilization would reign unchallenged over the plains, mountains and deserts of the Trans-Mississippi west.*[5]

The instrument for carrying out the transformation was the United States Army; too weak to prevent treaty violations by settlers but, when Indians retaliated for their losses, strong enough to crush resistance by large-scale massacres at Sand Creek (1864) and Wounded Knee (1890) and many smaller ones.[6]

Canadians a century and a half ago were just as interested observers of the United States as they are now, and what they saw made Ottawa's western ambitions a daunting prospect. Inadequate as the American army was for the task of keeping order on the plains, it was vastly stronger than anything Canada could afford. Sir John A. Macdonald's creative solution was to send out police instead of soldiers. This was based on the insight that any serious conflicts with the First Nations were likely to arise from treaty violations by white ranchers or settlers. Perhaps a police force could prevent these from getting out of control. Police forces were quite a recent phenomenon in the 1870s. Sir Robert Peel's London Metropolitan Police were only a few decades old and had been copied by just a few large North American cities. The only police covering large rural areas were in Ireland (the Royal Irish Constabulary) and India, where circumstances were vastly different from those in North America. The idea of controlling the process of settlement from Ottawa was a remarkably ambitious notion, given the enormous distances involved and the primitive communications of the day, but there seemed no option. The new police force would have to make up most of its own methods of keeping the peace as it went along. Sam Steele would be one of the central figures in that process.

In the three years since Steele and many others of the first contingent of the NWMP had set out over the same route with the

Red River Expedition, the way had been improved to the point that it was almost routine. Prospective settlers were now using it and Steele noted that the police were starting to fulfill their mandate by helping them on the way. Wagons could now be used on many places where boats had been hauled painfully over portages and the long detour north via the Winnipeg River was no longer necessary. Still, it was November, and winter had set well in by the time they reached Manitoba. The last group of recruits had to cross the Red River on the ice and the final leg of the trip from Winnipeg to Lower Fort Garry was done in sleighs.

Before they left for their winter quarters at Fort Garry, the new mounted policemen were sworn in by the acting commissioner, Lt. Col. W. Osborne Smith. Steele was the third man to take the oath, a fact which has led to the frequent assertion that he was the third to enlist in the NWMP, but his regimental number was 40, which meant that thirty-nine others had joined before he did. All members, including commissioned officers, took the oath on November 3 in Winnipeg. It might seem odd that the government would recruit members of the Mounted Police and ship them to Manitoba before swearing them in, but the reason was quite a simple one. Nobody got paid until sworn in so the procedure saved the treasury two months' salary. Official penury also lay behind the curious rank structure of the NWMP in its early years. Every man below the commissioned level of sub-inspector was appointed as a constable ($1.00 a day) or sub-constable ($0.75 a day). Steele was one of three staff constables ($1.25 a day). In practice, it was quickly found necessary to create the traditional military ranks of corporal and sergeant with appropriate pay differentials and the government reluctantly acquiesced.[7]

Later in November, the men got their uniforms and the first permanent commissioner, George Arthur French, arrived to take over command and set about organizing his new police force. French immediately added his voice to those of the lieutenant governor and the North-West Council in urging that the second half of the 300 men authorized for the NWMP be recruited and organized over the winter in Ontario, ready to join the first group in the spring. Complicating the situation was the fact that the government of John A. Macdonald was forced to resign in October under the weight of the Pacific Scandal. The Liberal leader who took over as prime minister in November, Alexander Mackenzie, was even more devoted to economy in government than his predecessor and seriously proposed doing away with the NWMP altogether. The British government, still responsible for Canada's foreign relations, insisted that the police force was essential for maintaining Canadian sovereignty in the west.[8] French probably did not know how close he came to losing his new command before it got started and Sam Steele certainly had no idea of the high politics of the situation.

French was fortunate in having a lot of competent men with military experience in the new force. Any who proved less than satisfactory were quickly weeded out and replaced by soldiers from the small garrison at Red River. For the Manitoba contingent there was much to do. Buying and training horses was the most important task. The available mounts were half-wild prairie broncos that had never seen a saddle or bridle. Stables had been constructed at Lower Fort Garry to house the horses but all training had to take place outdoors through the bitter Manitoba cold. Steele had what was surely the toughest job in the Mounted Police that winter. He was in charge of breaking the horses, training them, and instructing the riders. This meant five training sessions a day, six days a week, except when the temperature dropped below −38°C. The temperature limit was for the benefit of the horses, not the men. In his autobiography Steele claimed, "Even when we had them 'gentled' so as to let the recruits mount, the men were repeatedly thrown with great violence to the frozen ground; but no one lost his nerve, they always 'had it with them.'"[9] The numbers tell a somewhat different story. By the spring, even with replacements from the local militia, there were only 120 men left from the original 150. New recruits had to be brought with the second contingent to replace them.

Doubling the size of the Mounted Police meant the appointment of new officers and promotion for some of those in Manitoba. Sub-inspector Walsh, for example, was made inspector and given command of "D" Division. Superintendent James F. Macleod became assistant commissioner. Steele hoped to be among those promoted. When a sub-inspector named Bredon resigned, Steele wrote to Commissioner French asking for the job but did not get it. French's correspondence to Ottawa reveals that while Steele was well thought of, he was considered too junior and there were four or five others ahead of him on the promotion list.[10] Steele's letter shows clearly that, unlike the case four years earlier, he was confident of his abilities now and would have welcomed advancement, but he probably did not have high hopes. He knew by this time that political connections were at least as important as educational qualifications or demonstrated ability. James F. Macleod, for example, had a degree from Queen's University and had articled in the law office of Alexander Campbell, John A. Macdonald's minister of Justice. Steele had no such educational and political advantages and he was, in any case, a decade younger. The realization that he would have to make up for his lack of education and influence spurred him on to greater efforts. He took little part in the dances and parties of the Red River community, although on one occasion he rode thirty kilometres to Winnipeg in −30°C weather to go to a ball. As he wrote in his memoirs, "I much preferred an evening either with the old settlers, who could tell me something about the country, or in attending their dances and weddings. I took notes of all the information I received, and was pretty well acquainted with the customs of the Indians, hunters and traders before I left Fort Garry."[11] He had always worked to prepare himself, but taking notes at dances and weddings showed a new level of seriousness.

Steele's personal information gathering was a reflection of the preparations the Mounted Police were making for moving in the summer from their temporary base in Manitoba to the foothills of the Rockies, 1,200 kilometres to the west. The original plan was for the second contingent to go west by rail to North Dakota, meet the Manitoba group just north of the border and then head west. The 49th parallel had recently been surveyed by a joint American-Canadian team, which had created camps with caches of food and animal fodder along the international boundary. The police were to travel along the boundary to take advantage of the supplies and avoid the difficulties of finding their way in an area that had no maps and few available guides.[12] When they reached what is now southern Alberta, they would establish a post to control the reported influx of American traders from Montana who were selling liquor to the Blackfoot people there. Then some of the members would return to the HBC post at Fort Ellice (near the modern city of Brandon) and establish a headquarters.

Just before they left, Commissioner French received a telegram from Ottawa informing him of trouble between the American authorities and Native people south of the border. He was ordered to change his route and go farther north to avoid possible involvement. Guides were quickly hired who claimed to know the country on the new route west, although this proved not to be the case. Steele knew nothing of all this and was fully occupied with problems of his own. Assistant Commissioner Macleod put him in charge of organizing the move from Fort Garry to Dufferin and setting up the camp where the second contingent was to join them. The second contingent brought its horses with it and rode north from the railhead at Fargo, arriving at the camp on June 19. Neither horses nor men among the new arrivals were prepared for an exceptionally violent prairie thunderstorm that struck the camp that night. The horses stampeded out of the camp and could not be stopped. Steele's western broncos quickly recovered and returned to the camp but some of the eastern mounts ran eighty kilometres south of the border.

Recovering the horses and allowing them to rest for a few days delayed the start west but by July 8 they were ready. The four-kilometre long column of 300 Mounted Police, about 200 carts and wagons, ninety-three cattle for slaughter, two field guns, mowing machines, portable forges and field kitchens left in the afternoon and, by design, made only about fifteen kilometres the first day. Known in the west as a "Hudson's Bay Start," the abbreviated first day of the march allowed deficiencies to be discovered and remedied while still close to home. After that, the routine was one of very early starts; the column was often on the way by 3 or 4 A.M. It did not take long for serious trouble to develop. Hot and dry weather set in, exacerbating the difficulties of finding sufficient water for the livestock in a dry country. Small sloughs were often the only available sources and their water quality, reduced to begin with by the heat and muddied by hundreds of horses and cattle, had disastrous effects on the digestive systems of animals and men. The Ontario horses, unused to prairie conditions, were particularly severely affected. To add to the expedition's woes, a large infestation of grasshoppers stripped most of the vegetation on the route.

Three weeks after leaving Dufferin, so many horses and cattle were sick that Commissioner French ordered a halt at the Souris River on July 25. Even after five days' rest with adequate water and pasture, many of the horses and cattle were not in condition to go on. French reluctantly decided to detach twenty men of "A" troop with the weakest animals and send them north to the HBC post at Fort Ellice, then via the well-travelled Carlton Trail to Edmonton. Inspector W.D. Jarvis and Sub-Inspector Sévère Gagnon were in command with Steele as the senior NCO. Steele was probably chosen for his skill with horses and general reliability so the assignment was in one sense a vote of confidence but he, unsurprisingly, did not see it that way, although he was pleased that his brother Richard was part of the group. Edmonton was a long way from the place where the primary mission of the NWMP would be carried out. To be shuffled off to what promised to be a backwater and denied the opportunity to take part in possible armed confrontations with the American whiskey traders was a bitter pill for someone with Steele's ambitions. The best chances for glory and promotion were with the main body of the Force and he was not there. His disappointment was still tangible forty years later when he wrote in his memoirs, "We were a disconsolate lot when we saw the force depart on their long trek."[13]

After a few more days of rest, the group headed slowly for Fort Ellice.[14] The leisurely pace and better feed and water brought improvement for the animals but it was August 18 before they were ready to leave Fort Ellice. Although the Carlton Trail was in constant use and Inspector Jarvis had travelled it the year before, getting to Edmonton with heavily loaded ox carts and wagons would not be easy. The fur trade traffic on the trail consisted mainly of individuals and small groups; heavy freight went by river. It took Steele's group two weeks longer to reach their destination than the main body to the south. The only bright spot was that they ate better than the others since game, especially geese and ducks, was much more plentiful along the northern route. If the weather stayed dry, travelling was relatively easy but a couple of weeks of rain in late August and early September turned the trails into quagmires. Then the only recourse was to chop trees to build corduroy roads over the worst stretches. Small streams could be forded but crossing the South and North Saskatchewan rivers by ferry took more than a week.

By the end of September the NWMP were getting close to the present Alberta–Saskatchewan border, more than two-thirds of the way to Edmonton. The country on the north bank of the Saskatchewan along this final stretch is wetter and more heavily wooded than the prairies south and east. This meant that the trail was much worse. Winter was also approaching but the weather was not so cold that it froze the ground, just enough to prevent it from drying out. It took a month of cold, exhausting struggle to bring the remnants of the wagons and livestock into the welcoming precincts of Fort Edmonton on November 2. One of the principal reasons any of them made it was the work and leadership of Sam Steele. His reward was a commendation in Inspector Jarvis's report on the trip in which he wrote, "Sergeant-Major Steele has been undeviating in his efforts to assist me, and he has also done the manual labour of at least two men."[15]

Fort Edmonton had been the HBC's western transportation hub for half a century by 1874. It received trade goods from Europe and rest of the world via its York boat brigades and the river steamers just coming into service. The pemmican collected from the buffalo hunters on the prairies to the south provided the essential food supply for the network of northern posts that stretched to the Arctic Ocean. The HBC's Columbia Brigade based at Edmonton provided courier service across the mountains to posts on the Pacific. In 1874 when the NWMP arrived, Edmonton was at the beginning of a period of rapid change. A few dozen settlers had started to build outside the walls of the fort. Most of them were there because government surveyors were busy planning the route of the proposed Canada Pacific Railway through the Yellowhead Pass to British Columbia. That project was in the process of self-destructing as a result the Pacific Scandal, which had brought the government of John A. Macdonald down late in 1873. As Steele's group was making its painful way from Fort Ellice, the Mackenzie government was struggling, without much success, to come up with an alternative strategy. Nevertheless, few people doubted that large-scale agricultural settlement on the prairies was inevitable.

The great land rush to the area was all in the future in the last months of 1874, so Inspector Jarvis and his men experienced the kind of fur trade hospitality that travellers had traditionally received at the fort. Warm, comfortable quarters and plenty of food helped the recovery from the gruelling journey. In a gesture of appreciation and as a way of introducing the police to the community, Steele set about organizing a Christmas dance for those in the fort and anyone for many kilometres around who cared to make the journey. The men voted a month's pay to cover the expenses, mostly for food, and took care of the cooking. The dancing and feasting stretched over two days and from the lively description in Steele's memoirs, it is clear that everyone had a very good time.

A week after the ball Inspector Jarvis got word that some whiskey traders were heading for the settlement at Buffalo Lake, 120 kilometres southeast of Edmonton. Bison had been hunted by the plains nations for millennia and for the last century the meat, made into pemmican, was a staple of the fur trade. The hunting at Buffalo Lake represented a new phenomenon—killing the animals just for their hides, which were now in great demand for industrial use in the United States. Repeating rifles along with steamboats and railways to haul away the hides allowed killing on an industrial scale that virtually eliminated the bison in a decade or two. Sam Steele, who was familiar with the traditional hunt from his days at Red River, was appalled by the scale of what he called "the most wanton destruction."[16] In the brief period that the commercial hunt lasted, between 1872 and 1877, Buffalo Lake was the largest community in the North-West Territories, with about 400 houses when Steele visited it in 1875.[17]

Jarvis and Steele, with ten men, rented dog sleds and ponies and set off in early January for Buffalo Lake in the midst of the coldest stretch of weather the area had experienced in thirty years. For two weeks on the trip the temperature went as low as −48°C and did not rise above −40°C. When the police got to Buffalo Lake they were welcomed by the hunters; new faces and word from the outside were a welcome diversion in the long winter. No trace of the reported whiskey traders came to light although they and their wares were undoubtedly present. The Mounted Police would soon develop the techniques and intelligence network for tracking illicit booze, but in January of 1875 they were neophytes and do not appear to have tried very hard to search out the whiskey traders. This trip was mainly about showing the flag and making their presence known, so they joined in the feasting and dancing for a few days then went back to Edmonton.

The rest of the winter at Edmonton was quiet and monotonous, relieved only by a couple of mail deliveries from the east. One of them brought Steele information that he seized upon as a possible way of getting out of a posting that seemed to offer no prospects for excitement or advancement. Some of his friends from "B" Battery were being sent to England for training at the Army's School of Gunnery at Shoeburyness. Surely the NWMP would benefit from similar cavalry training for some of its members at the cavalry school at Canterbury. Sam wrote to the commissioner suggesting that he would be the ideal person to do this and that he would even pay some of the expenses and would promise to re-enlist when his three-year term was up.[18] There was no reply, perhaps because Commissioner French was at that time struggling with his orders from Ottawa to establish a headquarters for the police at Swan River, a bleak location that had nothing to recommend it.

With the arrival of spring there was at least work to occupy the little Edmonton force. Orders had arrived to build a permanent post on the south bank of the North Saskatchewan River where it was expected most agricultural settlement would take place. The initial surveys for the Pacific railway ran the main line south of the river, not crossing to the north side until sixty kilometres west of Edmonton. For the small group of settlers outside the walls of the fort, this decision was a severe blow and they responded by meeting with Jarvis and demanding that the NWMP post be built at Edmonton. This was the wrong approach for someone who, according to Steele, "was of a fiery temperament, and would carry out his orders as he pleased."[19] Jarvis had apparently been thinking of building directly across the river in what would later become the town of Strathcona—and eventually part of Edmonton—but his annoyance with the tone of the demand led him to select a site forty kilometres downstream. This location was named Fort

Saskatchewan and as soon as the snow melted, the men started building the new post at that location.

In April the Mounted Police, with some help hired from the local settlers, began clearing the site and in May the timber provided by contractors arrived. The new post consisted of a three-metre high stockade with a bastion at one corner. Inside the walls there were quarters for officers and men, a guard room, and stables, all built of squared logs. Steele was in his element doing this kind of work. As he noted in his memoirs, he and the other Canadians in the group had grown up with an axe in their hands and were happy to show "ex-graduates and Irish land agent's sons," how to square timbers and cut shingles.[20] The work was well under way by July when the HBC steamer *Northcote* made her first trip of the season upriver, bearing, among other things, mail for the police. Some of it directly concerned Steele. While his suggestion for being sent to England was ignored, the letter, with its polite hint that he might be considering resigning when his term of enlistment ended, had attracted the right kind of attention. He was promoted, not to officer status as a sub-inspector, but to chief constable, the equivalent of regimental sergeant major and the senior NCO in the Force. Better still for his future ambitions, he was ordered to the NWMP headquarters at Swan River where his abilities would be noticed by those in charge.

When the *Northcote* headed back downriver, Sam Steele was the happiest passenger aboard. The boat could only go as far as Grand Rapids where the drop of twenty-five metres into Lake Winnipeg ended navigation. Another steamer from Winnipeg was supposed to be waiting but it was delayed. After a few restless days waiting Steele hitched a ride with two canoes on their way from Norway House to Fort Garry. When they arrived no boats were going upstream so Steele decided to walk to Winnipeg since, as he said in his memoirs, "the distance was but 22 miles."[21] Here he quickly found transportation to Swan River with a wagon train of public works men on their way to work on the police buildings there. Steele, like every other mounted policeman stationed there, intensely disliked the Swan River headquarters, with its drafty prefabricated buildings located on a site filled with very large, half-buried glacial boulders. Swan River was also the location of one of the mass hibernation sites for prairie garter snakes—not dangerous, but not exactly a selling point when they emerged by the thousands from their dens in the spring. The site of the NWMP headquarters had been changed from Fort Ellice because it was on the proposed main line of the Pacific railway, but since that project had collapsed, its future as the headquarters of the NWMP was very much in doubt.

Promotion and the move to headquarters was certainly an improvement for Steele, but most of the interesting developments for the Force were still happening somewhere else. Two important new posts, Fort Walsh and Fort Calgary, were established from Fort Macleod in the summer of 1875. Most public attention that year was focused on the sensational efforts to track down the perpetrators of the Cypress Hills Massacre and have them extradited from the United States for trial in Winnipeg. Steele says almost nothing about his duties at Swan River during the summer and fall of 1875 beyond a comment that the adjutant and commissioner were happy to see him and promised him lots of work.[22] The work consisted partly of helping to finish the buildings at Swan River and partly of administrative efforts to make sure that the growing network of western posts received enough food to keep the men alive over the winter.[23] That much was accomplished, although pay was often weeks or months late and there were no replacements for the increasingly worn-out uniforms. At Fort Walsh some constables were even forced to buy parts of United States Army uniforms from traders to replace their tattered police clothing, which almost led to a violent incident when some Sioux warriors driven north by American cavalry accused the police of being Americans in disguise.[24]

Steele got to Swan River in late July just as the commanding officer of the Canadian militia, Major General Edward Selby-Smyth, passed through on a tour of inspection. The Conservative opposition in Ottawa had recovered its self-confidence after the debacle of the Pacific Scandal and was loud in its complaints about the government's western policies. Selby-Smyth's trip was apparently designed to quiet the opposition's accusations that not enough was being done to secure the west, and that it would be better if the NWMP were absorbed into the militia. If so, the results were mixed. The report praised the work of the police and firmly rejected the notion of converting them into a purely military force, but it was also critical of the choice of headquarters and the lack of training in some areas. All members of the Force could ride, he admitted, "but there is a material difference between sitting on a horse without falling off...and horsemanship proper."[25] He also hinted strongly that there were not enough mounted policemen to cover the enormous extent of the North-West Territories.

Steele had arrived at Swan River too late to be included in the Mounted Police escort that accompanied the general on his trip across the prairies, which certainly disappointed him. Swan River had been made reasonably habitable by the time winter set in, however, and it had advantages not enjoyed by posts farther west. There was a regular weekly mail service from Winnipeg and, better still, the telegraph had reached Swan River and the operator provided a daily summary of news from the outside. Although Steele does not mention it in his memoirs, he must have been aware that by the beginning of 1876 relations between his commanding officer and Ottawa were deteriorating rapidly. Commissioner French's criticism of the choice of Swan River as headquarters did not go down well with the government. His requests for additional money to make up the deficiencies that operating in the west had revealed were ignored and French believed, quite correctly, that his political masters had only a dim conception of the difficulties imposed by the size of the area. In July he submitted his resignation and left for England.

This might have harmed Steele's prospects for promotion since French had singled him out and brought him to headquarters, but the new commissioner, James F. Macleod, had known Steele since the Red River Expedition and was fully aware of his abilities. Macleod had been the original assistant commissioner of the NWMP, and then left the Force when he was appointed stipendiary magistrate on January 1, 1876. He was hastily recalled when French resigned and accepted the job as commissioner. Plans were already underway for the negotiation of Treaty 6 at Fort Carlton that summer. The police were to provide an escort and logistical support for this very important event and Macleod quickly put Steele in charge of organizing it. This was the kind of job that he had been waiting for, one that suited his energy and talents and put him at the centre of events.

The new commissioner arrived at Swan River at 6 A.M. on August 6, 1876. He brought the good news that the government had agreed to abandon Swan River as headquarters and move it to Fort Macleod, which was the real centre of police activity. The bad news was that almost all the forty men at Swan River had to be packed and ready to move by 9:30 that same day to Fort Carlton to support the treaty negotiations.[26] Planning for the talks had been going on for over a year and an advance party had already left, so the order was not entirely a surprise, and Steele had the men on the road half an hour early. The plan was to travel to Fort Carlton to meet the treaty negotiating party and provide support for them until the treaty was signed. Then they would move on to Fort Macleod to set up the headquarters there. By drawing in constables from as far away as Fort Saskatchewan, it was possible to concentrate eighty-two men, including the police band, to provide the visual spectacle that the occasion seemed to demand.

Steele's group escorted the three treaty commissioners, Alexander Morris, lieutenant governor of Manitoba, Chief Factor William Christie of the HBC, and James McKay, a Métis member of the North-West Territorial Council who had helped negotiate

Treaties 1, 2, 3, and 5. McKay greatly impressed Steele, partly because of his fluency in several Indigenous languages and partly because of his great size; he apparently weighed close to 400 pounds. Treaty negotiations started at Fort Carlton on August 19. Treaty 6 encompassed a huge swath of territory that stretched from the present-day border of Manitoba and Saskatchewan west to the Rocky Mountains and included most of what is now central Alberta and Saskatchewan. Most of the signatories were Plains Cree and Woods Cree nations, with some Stoneys, eventually fifty bands in all. Many of these were powerful bands with long experience of dealing with the HBC. The negotiations were prolonged and complex and resulted in the addition of two new clauses, known as the "medicine chest" and "famine" clauses, that significantly extended the Canadian government's obligations. Chief Poundmaker's insistence on these additions delayed the signing for some days but on August 23 it took place.[27]

Treaty payments and the presentation of medals and uniforms for the chiefs lasted for more than a week, then the entourage moved on to Fort Pitt, an HBC post located almost exactly on the present Alberta–Saskatchewan border. Negotiations here began September 7 and concluded much more quickly. By the middle of September everything was wrapped up and the police could head for Fort Macleod. They were anxious to get there because winter was approaching and also because there was serious trouble immediately south of the border between the United States government and the Lakota led by Sitting Bull. At the end of June, part of George Armstrong Custer's 7th Cavalry had been defeated and wiped out at the Little Bighorn, provoking a massive response by the American government. Constable A.R. Macdonell, one of a party of NWMP recruits on its way west on the Missouri in July, noted in his diary: "Had great difficulty in securing a boat for Fort Benton the American Government pressing every boat to carry supplies & men up the Yellowstone line to fight Indians."[28]

When Sam Steele first set eyes on Fort Macleod, a place that would play a very significant part in his life, the police post was located on an island in the Oldman River. This had undoubtedly seemed like a defensible and prudent location when the NWMP arrived two years earlier, but high water in the spring made it untenable for extended periods of time; in 1884 the site would be abandoned in favour of a new location on top of the high south bank of the river. Traders and other civilians attracted by the large police presence were already sensibly building out of the river valley. Moving the headquarters to Fort Macleod meant more accommodation was needed, so Steele and the others set about the familiar routine of putting up log buildings and improving those already in place with such luxuries as wooden floors to replace the existing dirt ones. Some of the police even used their own money to buy bolts of fabric from the traders to cover the interior walls.

Fort Macleod quickly became the administrative hub for the North-West Territories with transfer of the headquarters there. Together with its most important outpost, Fort Walsh, 250 kilometres to the east, it had two-thirds of the strength of the Mounted Police, who were the only executive arm of the Canadian government. They ran the postal system, collected customs at the international boundary, and acted as Indian agents. Some of the mail came through Canadian territory by steamboat to Edmonton and was then carried south by contractors hired by the police. The alternate and increasingly important route was through the United States. Railways and river steamers brought mail and freight to Fort Benton, Montana, where it was loaded on ox trains by the I.G. Baker Company for the trip north. For mail, the northern route was just as quick; a letter to eastern Canada either way took two weeks. For freight of any kind, the United States route had a very big advantage, as supplies including food for men and horses came that way. The wagon trains loaded up with thousands of buffalo robes for the return journey. Fort Benton also offered services like banking, which were not available in Canada closer than Winnipeg.

Steele was very busy in the fall of 1876 with the normal administrative routine of headquarters and, as the horse expert of the police, he spent much of his time breaking and training broncos. Although he would not have admitted it at the time, his skill at the job and the letters he had written asking for equestrian training in England were in danger of blocking the career advancement he hungered for. Steele loved horses and enjoyed the recognition of his specialist talents but if he remained in that role, while he might eventually become a commissioned officer, he would never have a chance at becoming commissioner, which he already knew was his goal. He did not hesitate to re-enlist for another three-year term in September.[29]

Following the Battle of the Little Bighorn, Sitting Bull and some 3,000 of his Lakota crossed the border into what is now southern Saskatchewan and informed Superintendent Walsh that they intended to stay. Keeping the peace among various First Nations of the region was an absolute requirement for the Mounted Police. It was already a very challenging job with the rapidly diminishing herds of buffalo. With thousands of extra mouths to feed belonging to groups who had never been on good terms with the Blackfoot and Cree, whose traditional territories were mainly north of the international boundary, the situation promised to push the diplomatic skills of the NWMP to the limit. The international aspect of the situation meant that every move would be under intense scrutiny. Once the public demand for revenge for Custer died down, the United States government was in no hurry to have Sitting Bull return. The Canadian government, on the other hand, wanted the Lakota gone as quickly as possible to avoid upsetting the nations they hoped to persuade to sign treaties. Clearly, the 300 mounted policemen were not going to be able to force ten times their number of Lakota to do something they did not want to do.

Extraordinary pressure fell on the shoulders of Superintendent James Morrow Walsh and even on very junior individuals under his command. Constable A.R. Macdonell, who had joined the NWMP in July 1876, found himself barely six months later in charge of the new post at Wood Mountain, established to monitor the Lakota. Macdonell and two other policemen as green as he was had no additional resources to make their task easier. In February 1877, with his post surrounded by more than 100 lodges he noted in his diary: "I find it extremely difficult to get along without the aid of an interpreter. [Lakota] Scouts are arriving from across the line, impossible to understand them."[30] Macdonell spent the next year and a half mediating disputes among the Lakota and other First Nations groups in the area. American newspapers were fascinated by the Mounted Police success in managing the Lakota and dubbed Superintendent Walsh "Sitting Bull's boss."

Steele gives no hint that he resented the fact that Walsh revelled in the public attention the situation created, but other members of the Force certainly did. Commissioner Macleod reprimanded Walsh for giving too many interviews and Prime Minister John A. Macdonald believed that the superintendent was deliberately encouraging Sitting Bull to stay in Canada for reasons of self-promotion.[31] Walsh was forced to resign from the Mounted Police as soon as the Lakota returned to the United States and the government thought it was safe to get rid of him. What Steele learned from this episode and never forgot was that being in command at the centre of events was essential for advancement but required careful management. Self-deprecating modesty was the best possible public persona, whatever one's personal opinions might be.

While attention was focused on police activities around Fort Walsh, Steele and his colleagues at the headquarters were busy with what was, in the long run, a more important issue—the negotiation and signing of Treaty 7 covering the southwestern prairies. The Mounted Police were even more closely involved in this process than they had been with Treaty 6 the previous year. The nations of the Blackfoot Confederacy made it clear to the representatives of the Canadian government that the relationship of trust they had established with the police over the three years since their arrival was crucial to an agreement. Commissioner Macleod, who had a particularly good understanding with the highly respected Siksika chief Crowfoot, was therefore named as one of the two Canadian negotiators.[32] Although the bond of trust between the two ultimately held, Crowfoot was in no sense a paramount chief and many, particularly in the Kainai (Blood) nation were more skeptical. In the spring of 1876, when the war south of the border was heating up, Sitting Bull had offered an alliance to the Blackfoot with the aim of making war on both the United States Army and the Mounted Police, accompanied by a threat that, if they refused, the Lakota would come north and wipe out the Blackfoot after they had finished with the Americans. The Blackfoot rejected this proposal because it came from their traditional enemy, but some thought that fighting the government was not a bad idea. In any case, why were the police allowing enemies of the Blackfoot to stay in Canadian territory?

Steele's account of the treaty negotiations is one of the most disappointing passages in his autobiography. Living at Fort Macleod in the midst of Kainai territory, he and the other mounted policemen could not have been unaware of the tensions in the Blackfoot Confederacy. The negotiations were originally planned to take place at Fort Macleod but when Crowfoot refused, the venue was changed to Siksika territory at Blackfoot Crossing on the Bow River. This change in turn irritated the Piikani and Kainai who refused to attend for the first several days. It was only intense negotiation by Crowfoot and a few others that finally won the others over.[33] Steele's account ignores all the difficulties and echoes the bland official government report which gave a completely misleading picture of how dangerously close the treaty negotiations came to failure.

By the end of September 1877, the treaty had been signed and treaty payments made. On September 28, Commissioner Macleod, Inspector L.N.F. Crozier, Steele, and twenty-eight men left for Fort Walsh, where an American delegation was expected to talk with Sitting Bull about returning to the United States. Ottawa had put all the pressure at its disposal through the British government to persuade the reluctant Americans to make the effort and when that bogged down, a Canadian cabinet minister broke all precedents by going to Washington for direct talks with President Hayes and his cabinet.[34] Minister of the Interior David Mills succeeded in getting the Americans to agree to send a commission north to discuss a possible return with Sitting Bull. This display of direct diplomacy by Canada annoyed the British embassy in Washington but they had little choice but to go along. More delays followed as the American State and Interior Departments wrangled over who would foot the bill. Astonishingly, the two American representatives eventually appointed had to pay their own expenses and hope Congress would eventually reimburse them, although they did get some assistance from the army. The representatives, General Alfred Terry and retired General A.G. Lawrence were not permitted any discretion—they could only present the American terms, which amounted essentially to unconditional surrender. By the time they left for Canada, no one on either side of the border expected a successful outcome.

Steele's party arrived at Fort Walsh on October 1 to find that an already difficult situation had become worse. General Terry had been delayed at Fort Benton because the soldiers designated to escort him to Canada had been pulled away to join the fight against Chief Joseph and the Nez Perce, who were at the end of an epic running battle from their home territory in Oregon in an effort to join Sitting Bull. The few wounded and starving Nez Perce who escaped the final confrontation in the Bear Paw Mountains just south of the 49th parallel arrived at the Lakota camp just as Commissioner Macleod was making his way to Fort Walsh. Superintendent Walsh had gone to Pinto Horse Butte near Wood Mountain to check on the situation and found the Lakota very disturbed, as the Mounted Police clearly were, by the sight of women and children with gunshot wounds. Macleod and his men headed east to assist if necessary and met Walsh, Sitting Bull, and nineteen of the Lakota along the way. They returned to Fort Walsh to await the Americans.

General Terry arrived at the border on October 15 with three companies of the 2nd Cavalry; two remained there and one accompanied him to Fort Walsh, travelling in army ambulances. Steele was part of the Mounted Police escort and found his first encounter with the United States Army very interesting. He envied their equipment, especially their tents and camp stoves and was fascinated by the portable desks they carried with them to keep up with the endless paperwork that all armies generate.[35] Steele always enjoyed meeting new people and his professional interests were aroused because several of the Americans were veterans of the Civil War. The stories he heard marked the beginning of a lifelong interest in that conflict. Like all the others present, Steele had no expectation that the Lakota could be persuaded to return. General Terry presented the American take-it-or-leave-it position; Sitting Bull and the other chiefs spoke at length about why they had no intention of going back. It was all over in a day and everyone left knowing that nothing had been settled.

Steele and the headquarters group went back to Fort Macleod for the winter. That season turned out to be one of the mildest ever recorded on the prairies. There was almost no snow and the Mounted Police were able to play a game of cricket at Fort Macleod on New Year's Day, 1878. There were prairie fires in mid-winter, an exceptionally rare occurrence. The fires drove the buffalo away from southern Alberta, threatening to push the Blackfoot peoples east into conflict with the refugee Lakota over the diminishing herds. The police were kept busy trying to keep the situation under control. Steele complained that he never got to bed before midnight and often had to work all night.[36] By the spring of 1878 the situation had become so tense that headquarters was moved to Fort Walsh in May along with as many men as could be spared from other posts. The Force was also shorthanded because some officers and men had left to take up ranching while a good many others had deserted. Pay for constables had actually been reduced from 75¢ to 50¢ a day and those who were unhappy found it easy to slip across the border and make their way east through the United States.

Shortly after the headquarters moved to Fort Walsh, a group of new recruits arrived from the east by way of Montana. They were accompanied by a batch of unbroken replacement horses. As the senior NCO, Steele spent most of the summer training both men and animals. His work was rewarded at the end of August when he was promoted to sub-inspector. Several of the original officers retired that year, making room for Steele and others. The step up to commissioned rank was very important to Steele but in typical fashion he does not mention it in his memoirs. The biggest change it brought was that he would now spend less time with his training and administrative duties and be given more interesting and independent assignments.

As often happens on the prairies, the extremely mild winter of 1877–1878 was followed by a brutally cold one in 1878–1879. Early in 1879 the Mounted Police were instructed to conduct a census of the Métis population and Steele was assigned the area between Calgary and Fort Macleod. He set off with two constables and an interpreter. On their way back they were caught in a blizzard on the Belly River. They ran out of food and had to abandon their sleighs and baggage in hopes of making it to Fort Macleod. Luckily they found a welcoming ranch house with food and warmth where they stayed until the storm blew itself out.

Shortly after surviving the blizzard, Steele was sent off in charge of a party of sixteen—which included the legendary guide, Jerry Potts—to investigate a report that Cree Chief Wandering Spirit had attacked another band. The police found the Cree camped on the Red Deer River 150 kilometres north of Fort Walsh. They arrested several without difficulty and brought them back to Fort Walsh for trial. In June 1879 Steele was ordered to Montana to pick up a group of recruits. While waiting for their boat to arrive he socialized with the American soldiers, among other things playing whist with them—a game he enjoyed throughout his life until it was replaced

Steele on his promotion to inspector, 1879. [BPSC, 2008.1.2.1.6.1.22]

by bridge early in the 20th century. After Steele returned to Fort Walsh, the community was struck by a severe outbreak of typhoid fever. The disease mainly affected the population of the town surrounding the fort, where several died. There were no deaths in the fort but Steele came close to succumbing and, at one point, Surgeon George Kennedy asked him if he wanted to send any last messages to his family.[37]

It took weeks for Steele to recover but by November he was well enough to take part in the hunt for the murderer of the first mounted policeman killed on the job. Constable Marmaduke Graburn was posted at the horse camp a few kilometres up the valley from Fort Walsh during the day. On November 17 he failed to return and a search party discovered his body with a bullet wound in the back of the head. Suspicion fell on a group of Kainai who had been in the vicinity but, with a heavy snow covering the Cypress Hills, they could not be found.[38] The storm turned out to be the beginning of another severe winter. Buffalo had been in short supply and now they disappeared altogether. The Mounted Police spent most of their time distributing food to prevent widespread starvation among the First Nations. Fort Walsh was the hub for this activity with herds of cattle and other supplies coming up from Montana. The town around the fort was the largest settlement in the North-West Territories in 1880. An ex-member of the Mounted Police built a hall that saw service as theatre, dance hall, and church. Steele and Superintendent L.N.F. Crozier, who had taken over command of the post from James Walsh, used it to hold the first Masonic banquet in the North-West Territories.[39]

By the spring of 1880, two cold winters in succession and the disappearance of the buffalo had reduced the Lakota to starvation and many were going back across the border to the United States. The Canadian government decided it was safe to move Superintendent Walsh to Fort Qu'Appelle where he would be close enough to be recalled if Sitting Bull reacted negatively. With summer, more and more of the old chief's followers began to move to reservations in the United States. John A. Macdonald, back in power in Ottawa, was convinced that Walsh had been deliberately discouraging the Lakota from returning because he enjoyed the publicity he received. Walsh had made himself vulnerable by having a child with a Siksika woman while he had left his wife behind in Brockville.[40] In July 1880 Walsh was sent to Ontario on leave and when he returned was kept away from Sitting Bull. After a suitable passage of time to avoid the hint of scandal, he was forced to resign from the NWMP in 1883. Walsh's misfortune was Steele's opportunity. On July 21, Steele moved to Qu'Appelle and took over command of "B" Division and the post, which had thirty-nine police assigned to it.

The Qu'Appelle post was not as large and important as Fort Macleod and Fort Walsh in 1880 but it represented the future for the Mounted Police. Much of the work was still with the First Nations, such as distributing rations, making treaty payments and carrying out an extensive smallpox vaccination program during an epidemic in 1881. The few farmers in the Qu'Appelle Valley provided a welcome source of food for the men and animals of the police, but they also presented a new problem. Up to this point the only Europeans in North-West Territories had been HBC men, other traders, and a few missionaries. These people worked daily with the First Nations; their work and their lives would otherwise have been impossible. The settlers, on the other hand, did not need the Indigenous inhabitants of the prairies and there was great potential for conflict. When David Mills was in Washington to discuss Sitting Bull in 1877, he was asked by American Secretary of the Interior Carl Schurz, "How do you keep your whites in order?"[41] Law enforcement in the American west was entirely controlled by the settler population who ran roughshod over the agreements with the Native Americans whenever it suited their purposes. When conflicts inevitably arose, using the Army was the only option.[42] Qu'Appelle was the first test of whether or not the Mounted Police could provide a different way of doing things and Sam Steele was at the centre of the situation.

He rose to the occasion. Steele's memoirs recount a very telling episode that took place while he was in command at Qu'Appelle. It is worth quoting at length:

> On August 6 [1880] the division had as guests, with quarters in the guard-room, two English gentlemen, settlers from the vicinity of Rapid City, 200 miles east. They had been arrested by our Shoal Lake magistrate, who had refused bail. One was Captain B., a retired Indian Mutiny veteran, the other a much younger man, Mr. J. The circumstances of their arrest were ludicrous. A complaint had been made against them for a mere trifle and a warrant issued, but, instead of placing the warrant in the hands of our constable, the magistrate, who had been on bad terms with my predecessor, employed a young and very green settler to carry out the arrest. On arriving at the home of the accused he spent a pleasant forenoon, and lunched with them at their invitation, not saying a word about his errand until he was leaving, when he turned at the door and said, "Oh, by the way, I have a warrant for your arrest!" The Englishmen laughed and refused to believe it, but, as the "special" [constable] insisted, B. got his rifle and said, "J., you count one, two, three, and I shall put a bullet through his hat!" No sooner said than done, and the terrified special rode for dear life to the magistrate, who, after all, had to employ our constables. They, as a matter of course, met with no resistance. The poor fellows were taken from their homesteads to Qu'appelle, where they remained in the guard-room until they knew the names, characteristics and nickname of every officer, man and horse in the force. Judge Richardson tried them some months later, and taking into consideration the delay, released them the same day.[43]

The two settlers in this incident were at the very top of the social and political hierarchy in the Canadian west at that time, but Steele did not hesitate for a moment to apply the letter of the law. The message for everyone in the area could hardly have been clearer.

When Superintendent Walsh returned from his leave the following year, Steele reverted to second in command of the division. How the two men got along personally and professionally is unknown. Steele says almost nothing in his memoirs about Walsh but his distaste for Walsh's flamboyant and self-promoting personal style occasionally leaks through, as when Walsh greeted a group of visiting journalists by staging a mock attack on their train. Steele commented, with an almost audible sniff of disapproval, "Their visit gave Major Walsh an opportunity to welcome them to the west in the spirited manner peculiar to him."[44] The highlight of the summer of 1881 was the first visit of a Canadian governor general to the North-West Territories. The Marquess of Lorne started out from Qu'Appelle in mid-August and spent three weeks travelling throughout the region. Steele trained the police guard of honour that welcomed the governor general and organized the escort that accompanied him on the trip, although he did not accompany the party as it made its way northwest to Edmonton and south to Montana. He was much too busy with the work at Qu'Appelle.

The Conservative government of Sir John A. Macdonald, back in office since 1878, had now managed to revive the Pacific railway project and the new CPR, incorporated at the beginning of 1881, was aggressively pushing construction west from Winnipeg by the summer. The CPR immediately moved its main line far to the south; instead of following the old Carlton Trail to Edmonton and through the Yellowhead Pass into British Columbia, it now ran much closer to the United States border through what was to become Regina, Medicine Hat, through Calgary, and then into British Columbia. The change had momentous consequences for the Mounted Police and even greater ones for Sam Steele's career. By the end of the construction season the rails had reached what was to become the city of Brandon and surveyors were working as far west as the future city of Swift Current. The main line would now pass a few kilometres south of the police post at Fort Qu'Appelle and Steele and his men had to deal with a rush of land speculators hoping to snap up future town sites along the line. These individuals were mostly a nuisance until the winter set in, after which, as many were completely unprepared for winter travel on the open prairie, they often had to be rescued by the police.

In the fall of 1880 Commissioner James F. Macleod had left the NWMP to become a justice of the Supreme Court of the North-West Territories. His replacement, Acheson Gosford Irvine, lost no time in asking the government to increase the size of the Force from 300 to 500 men. Ottawa reluctantly agreed late in January 1882, perhaps spurred on by the rapid progress of CPR construction the previous summer. Snow and cold generally slowed all activities during the prairie winter so Steele applied for and received permission to take a leave to visit family and friends in Ontario early in February. It was nine years since he had left and he was ready for a break and undoubtedly pleased to be able to show off his hard-earned status as an inspector. He got as far as Winnipeg where he was ordered to stay and set up a recruiting office to find some of the 200 new men the Force required. After a few weeks a replacement was available to take over and he finally made it home where, he says, "all treated me as if I had been the prodigal son!"[45] Arriving back at Qu'Appelle as the CPR's spring construction season was starting, Steele was put in charge of all the detachments along the railway.

The experience of the previous year had shown that the huge workforce constructing the line had little or nothing on which to spend their pay during their few off hours except liquor and gambling. Both led to trouble that could slow the work and both the company and the government were determined not to let that happen. Liquor was officially prohibited in the North-West Territories, indeed one of the primary missions of the NWMP in its first years had been to keep it out of the hands of the First Nations. That had largely been successful but the numerous, highly concentrated gangs of navvies with money in their pockets were a much more tempting market for purveyors of illicit booze. The answer was to locate a police detachment at every construction site and move whenever they did. The officer in charge, Steele, like all commissioned NWMP officers, was also a justice of the peace and could try minor cases on the spot. Holding court in his tent, he often worked far into the brief northern summer night. At the end of July he got a short respite of sorts when the government abruptly decided to move the territorial capital from Battleford to a place on the railway west of Qu'Appelle, known as "Pile of Bones" for the massive stack of bison bones collected there for shipment south. The new capital was renamed Regina and the NWMP headquarters was ordered to move there from Fort Walsh. Steele was given the job of choosing the location of the headquarters and laying out the sites for the prefabricated buildings that would house it. Steele wanted the site where the Saskatchewan Legislature now stands but it was the prime location in the area and Steele was overruled by the lieutenant governor. The police were obliged to settle for a less desirable spot a couple of kilometres west. Both sites were on a small creek to which Steele claims to have given the name "Wascana" (Sioux for Pile of Bones).[46]

As soon as the railway reached Regina a town began to spring up around the government buildings. By the spring of 1883 it even had a newspaper, the *Regina Leader*, edited by the talented Irish-born journalist Nicholas Flood Davin. Since police headquarters was some distance away from the emerging town centre, Steele found it necessary to station some men there, the first of many municipal NWMP detachments. The prefabricated headquarters buildings, shipped in from Ontario, were a step up from the dirt floors at Fort Macleod and the sod roofs at Qu'Appelle, but they still left much to be desired. Steele noted that in the depth of winter at Regina, ink bottles had to be kept on the office stove to prevent them from freezing.[47] Nevertheless, he enjoyed the much greater variety of social life that the little territorial capital offered. In March 1883 he was once again sent to Winnipeg to recruit new constables for the police. Here he was an interested observer of the frothy mix of railwaymen, land speculators, English remittance men, and con artists who populated the town. As always he enjoyed meeting interesting individuals such as Major A.B. Rogers, who had found the crucial pass through the Rockies the previous year, and the CPR's chief engineer, the former Confederate general Thomas L. Rosser.

At the beginning of the construction season the CPR labourers at Maple Creek threatened to go on strike and Steele was rushed from Winnipeg to sort out the situation. Although trade unions had been legal in Canada for about ten years, in the 1880s only small groups of skilled workers in major cities were effectively organized. The CPR construction workers certainly had no kind of organization and, isolated on the line of construction, completely dependent on the company for food, shelter, and transportation, were quite powerless. If they tried to quit, they could be charged with the offence of "deserting employment" or with vagrancy. Their frustrations erupted from time to time in what would later be called wildcat strikes. The Mounted Police had no choice but to enforce the laws, although some of them privately objected to the high-handed actions of the CPR and tried to mediate.[48] There is no indication that Steele was one of these. At this time and throughout his career he had no sympathy for workers who threatened the public peace, however legitimate their grievances might be. The incipient Maple Creek strike was quickly put down.

Construction went very rapidly in the summer of 1883, crossing the South Saskatchewan River at Medicine Hat and heading for the mountains. While he was at Medicine Hat, Steele received another interesting assignment. Far to the east a boundary dispute between the provinces of Ontario and Manitoba had been simmering since 1870. Both provinces claimed a large slice of territory that included Lake of the Woods and the town of Kenora. Ottawa had ruled in Manitoba's favour in 1881 but Ontario refused to accept the decision and appealed the case to the Judicial Committee of the Privy Council in London. In 1883 both provinces were trying to assert their claims by appointing magistrates in Kenora and violence threatened. Steele was instructed to go there with sufficient men to assert the authority of the federal government and calm the situation. He picked out a group of the most imposing constables he could find and hurried to Winnipeg. Reports of their presence were enough to convince the disputants that it would be better to leave the issue to the courts. Steele's men spent a few days at Fort Garry and then headed back to the construction camps, while he stayed in Winnipeg to do some recruiting. It is clear that by the summer of 1883, Steele had emerged as one of the chief troubleshooters of the Mounted Police, a man who could act coolly and decisively in an emergency.

In November 1883 Steele was sent to Calgary to take command of the detachment there. This was a very significant step for him since Calgary had replaced Qu'Appelle as the third-largest concentration of Mounted Police after the headquarters at Regina and Fort Macleod in the heart of Blackfoot country. The command structure of the force at this time consisted of the commissioner, six superintendents and thirteen inspectors. The Calgary detachment in the fall of 1883 was under the command of Superintendent J.H. McIlree but he had been given leave to return east to deal with family matters. Steele's appointment to take over in his absence—with another officer, Inspector Thomas Dowling, under his command—was a clear indication that he was at or near the top of the list for promotion, should a vacancy arise among the ranks of superintendents.

Calgary was a tiny village when Steele arrived there, but growing fast because of the CPR construction. Although the railway crews left for the winter, Steele was confronted with his first murder case after Christmas. A cook at a restaurant in Calgary named Jesse Williams got into a dispute with a store owner over his account. There was an intense argument in the store and when it closed that night Williams broke in and cut the owner's throat with a straight razor, making off with the day's receipts. When the man did not show up as expected to light the fire at the Presbyterian church, his friends found his body and reported the death as a suicide. Steele, after the police surgeon dismissed that possibility, organized search parties who found Williams outside the town before midnight. Blood on his hands and clothing, and the discovery of his discarded razor beside the trail of his footprints in the snow leading away from the scene of the murder, were enough to convince a jury of his guilt when he was brought to trial, although he was defended by the town's most prominent lawyer (and later senator), James Lougheed. Some of Calgary's outraged citizenry thought it might be a good idea to string Williams up immediately but Steele confronted the mob and had no difficulty convincing them that lynching would not be tolerated.[49]

Relations with First Nations across the prairies were deteriorating in the latter half of 1883 and into 1884. The arrogance of the CPR, building its mainline through the middle of the Siksika Reserve without any form of consultation, was one cause. The other was the fact that the Department of Indian Affairs and its agents had begun taking over management from the police. One of their first initiatives was to try to introduce a system which would require all First Nations travelling off their reserves to have a permit or pass issued by the Indian agent. The Mounted Police leadership thought that this policy was foolish and probably illegal. Commissioner Irvine took the extraordinary step of denouncing it in his published annual report for 1884.[50] Indian Affairs backed off but not before much damage had been done to relations and, most unfortunately, it would again try to institute the system after the 1885 Rebellion.[51] Steele first encountered the unhappy mood among the First Nations in January, when Sergeant William Fury and a constable met with obstruction on the Siksika Reserve while trying to make an arrest on a charge of horse stealing. Steele responded by going with twenty-five men to the reserve and bringing the leaders of the resistance to Calgary, where they were released with a reprimand by Judge James F. Macleod.

Steele, in his memoirs, tells of another encounter with the Siksika in early June which was potentially more serious. The Indian agent on the reserve reported that a Métis emissary from Louis Riel named Bear's Head was there spreading disaffection. Steele sent a sergeant and constable to arrest him on the all-purpose charge of vagrancy, which they managed without difficulty, but on the way back to Calgary by train, Bear's Head managed to slip out of his handcuffs, grab the sergeant's rifle, jump off the train, and escape in the direction of the reserve. When the sergeant arrived in Calgary and reported the escape, Commissioner Irvine and Superintendent W.M. Herchmer were there to officiate at the change of command of the district to Herchmer so that Steele could move west to supervise CPR construction. The changeover was put on hold while Steele was ordered to deal with the situation on the reserve. He took two constables and an interpreter and headed for Chief Crowfoot's camp, arriving at dawn in the midst of pouring rain, which he welcomed, "as we did a blizzard in winter when on the same sort of errand, for under the circumstances the Indians would not be stirring or wandering about the precincts of the camp as they would in fine weather."[52]

Leaving the two constables outside, Steele and the interpreter went into Crowfoot's lodge where they found the chief, the leading men of the Siksika, and the fugitive, seated, Steele says, in the place of honour. Steele demanded the surrender of Bear's Head but Crowfoot at first refused. There was an angry confrontation after which Steele grabbed the man by the collar and dragged him out of the lodge. The two constables put the prisoner on their buckboard, this time with handcuffs that were the right size. A large crowd had gathered by this time and Steele delivered a stern lecture about the importance of cooperation with the police. He gave Crowfoot a railway ticket so that he could travel to Calgary to observe the trial and then took the prisoner away. According to Steele's account, Bear's Head appeared before the commissioner the following day and was acquitted.

The *Calgary Herald* reported the incident shortly after it occurred, so it seems to have happened much as Steele's memoirs relate, but with a few interesting differences.[53] Steele's speech to the Siksika was more of a negotiation than he admitted later. Crowfoot's biographer, Hugh Dempsey, states that Steele and his prisoner were only allowed to leave *after* the chief was promised his rail ticket to Calgary to observe the trial.[54] Bear's Head's acquittal clearly bothered Steele. He had risked his life and that of his men for nothing. Worse still, the encounter exacerbated relations with the Siksika at a time when Louis Riel was back in Canada actively seeking support for a move against the government. The acquittal, according to Dempsey, had convinced Crowfoot that he was right to shelter the Métis fugitive and the police were wrong. The situation was saved by the quick action of the lieutenant governor of the North-West Territories, Edgar Dewdney, who immediately arranged a train trip to Regina and Winnipeg for Crowfoot and three other Blackfoot chiefs. It is probable that the sight of large buildings and 15,000 people at Winnipeg was what convinced the Blackfoot to stay out of the Rebellion, not Steele's homily.

In his memoirs, Steele wrote that it was Commissioner Irvine who tried and acquitted Bear's Head and hinted that Superintendent Herchmer was at fault for not handing over Steele's report on the arrest. In fact it was Herchmer who tried the case and undoubtedly dismissed it because it failed to meet even the very flexible evidentiary standards for vagrancy.[55] The man who gave the orders that set the whole event in motion, Commissioner Irvine, became a convenient scapegoat for the government and was fired in the wake of the Rebellion. He moved to a new job as warden of Stony Mountain Penitentiary near Winnipeg. He and Steele remained friends and visited each other often while Steele was writing *Forty Years in Canada*. Shifting the responsibility for the unfavourable outcome to Superintendent Herchmer, whom Steele resented for later getting a job that he thought was rightfully his, suited both men.

Whether or not the incident took place exactly as Steele remembered it three decades later, at the time he had no leisure to ponder what had happened. The railway had moved into the mountains by the time work ceased for the winter in late 1883, ending up at a station called Laggan (later Lake Louise) near the British Columbia border. Unlike the North-West Territories, British Columbia had no laws prohibiting liquor sales, nor did the Mounted Police have jurisdiction there, so Steele had much planning to do for the following year. Ottawa solved the jurisdiction problem easily by appointing Steele as a commissioner of police for British Columbia, which gave him essentially the same powers as a NWMP superintendent in the North-West Territories. The critical problem of keeping too much booze from reaching the navvies was dealt with by proclaiming a law called the *Public Works Peace Preservation Act*. This legislation outlawed liquor in a strip ten miles on each side of the CPR right of way, but after two seasons of experience Steele had a healthy respect for the ingenuity of both buyers and sellers. He asked for the width of the strip to be doubled to twenty miles on each side and got his way.

Railway construction in the mountains was much slower than it had been across the prairies, although by the summer of 1884 it had moved through the Kicking Horse Pass and into the valley of the Columbia River. Steele moved his headquarters from Laggan to Golden as soon as he arrived from Calgary, in the process almost losing his life when a skittish horse was startled and nearly threw itself off the narrow cut above the canyon. Later in the summer, headquarters moved to a place called Beaver River near the entrance to Rogers Pass. Here the CPR built a police headquarters complete with cells for thirty prisoners, a courtroom, stables, and accommodation for Steele and his men. The formidable challenges of construction through Rogers Pass that made it possible to create this semi-permanent headquarters certainly had advantages from Steele's point of view. The Beaver River location was far more comfortable than living in tents on the prairie. The downside of not moving every week was that it gave the liquor sellers, prostitutes, and gamblers time to catch up with the camp and establish themselves.

Steele's daily routine was a round of dealing with assault and drunk-and-disorderly cases from the illicit alcohol that made its way into the camps, and trying to keep prostitution and gambling more or less under control. Serious crime was relatively rare. The only homicide while Steele was supervising construction grew out of a political dispute. There were many Americans working on the railway and 1884 was a presidential election year. At one of the camps near Kicking Horse, a conductor who supported the Democratic candidate, Grover Cleveland, got into an argument with a Black barber who naturally sided with the Republicans, the party of Lincoln. The fight heated up to the point that the barber attacked the conductor with a straight razor. A friend of the conductor saved his life by pulling out a pistol and shooting the barber dead. Steele concluded that this was a case of self-defence and let the man go.

In British Columbia construction slowed during the winter but did not cease completely as it had on the prairies. This meant less work for the police and in late January Steele was able to get a full night's sleep for the first time in weeks.[56] For some of his men, a little leisure tempted them to partake of the recreational activities they were trying to keep from the navvies. On January 31 he recorded in his diary, "Fined Const Duburn (?) ten dollars and 2 mos. C.B. for being absent from watch station until 1245, using insolent language to Sergts Fury & King found in a house of ill fame when not there on duty."[57] Steele himself found more harmless amusements. There were several people in the camp who enjoyed his favourite card game, whist, and they played regularly during the long winter nights. Most were senior railway employees who also had appointments as justices of the peace and helped Steele try cases. The exception was a young Scottish immigrant named George Hope

Steele and his detachment at Farwell (now Revelstoke), BC, during the construction of the CPR, 1884. The man on the far left is Sergeant Fury. [BPSC, 2008.1.2.1.6.2.1]

Johnston, who had managed to obtain from the very compliant British Columbia government both a licence to sell liquor outside the railway belt and an appointment as justice of the peace.

Johnston had several different careers later in life, including some years as a journalist with the *Calgary Herald*, and became a lifelong friend of Steele's and a fellow investor in mining ventures in British Columbia. Their relationship got off to a somewhat rocky start in January 1885 when Johnston reported that 110 gallons of liquor he had stored, allegedly for sale outside the railway exclusion zone, had been stolen.[58] The liquor was quickly recovered by the Mounted Police, but when Johnston applied to have it returned and shipped out of the zone, Steele refused.[59] He took every possible opportunity to destroy confiscated alcohol because, as Johnston's experience showed, the lack of secure storage meant it inevitably found its way onto the market. Although this meant a major monetary loss for Johnston, he does not seem to have resented it. Within a few weeks he and Steele were socializing and trying cases together.[60]

As the weather began to improve and construction activity picked up, labour issues came to a boil on the railway. Steele began to get complaints from the labourers that they were not being paid. Most of the actual construction work was done by CPR subcontractors, with different gangs of men clearing the right of way, grading, building bridges, and hauling supplies. The CPR took no responsibility for the actions of its subcontractors and allowed the situation to get out of hand. Steele's account of the incident that followed in his memoirs is not short of drama. In the book he says that he was worried about the situation building with the unpaid workers for about a month before it erupted in violence at the end of March. Things were complicated by the fact that he became seriously ill just as events were coming to a head, probably with a bout of the typhoid fever that was endemic in the construction camps. On April 1, about 1,200 men went on strike, refusing to go back until they were paid. At this point a telegram arrived bringing word that rebellion had broken out on the prairies and ordering Steele and his men to Calgary. He wired back saying that the situation was too serious and that he could not leave until it was resolved. He met with the strike leaders, urged them to go back to work, and arranged a meeting with the CPR construction manager, James Ross, who promised to do what he could about the wages.

About 500 men went back to work but the rest refused and did their best to prevent work from resuming. The situation was tense and not a little confused, as evidenced by the fact that a confrontation was precipitated by the arrest, not of a striker, but of a contractor named Behan, who seems to have been in sympathy with the men.[61] A constable who tried to arrest Behan for drunkenness was roughed up by a crowd of strikers who made off with the contractor. Sergeant William Fury and two constables tracked him down in one of the saloons, but a mob of about 200 prevented them from making the arrest. Fury then went to Steele's sickbed and asked for instructions. Steele told Fury to make the arrest with pistol drawn and to shoot anyone who tried to interfere. He dragged himself out of bed and found George Hope Johnston and a copy of the Riot Act in preparation for the reaction to the arrest.

It was not long in coming. As he and Johnston were getting ready, they heard a shot and went out of the police headquarters to find Fury and his men retreating across the bridge that separated the police buildings from the camp, bringing the prisoner and pursued by an angry mob led by "a woman in scarlet [who] followed them with wild shrieks and curses."[62] Steele grabbed a rifle and used it to hold off the crowd while Johnston read the Riot Act, which orders any group of twelve or more assembled to disperse immediately. If they refuse, the police are permitted to use force to disperse them.[63] The bridge was a huge advantage for Steele and the police, since it was the only access to the police headquarters and prevented the crowd from surrounding them. One man had been wounded by Sergeant Fury while trying to prevent the arrest and no one in the mob doubted Steele's willingness to use his Winchester. They backed off and dispersed. Steele immediately got the CPR to organize a special train to take the prisoner east so his friends would not be tempted to attempt a rescue. A few more arrests of prominent members of the mob the following day cooled things further. Several days later the cause of the trouble evaporated when all the arrears of wages were finally paid. Steele and his men left for Calgary on April 7 to take part in the suppression of the Rebellion.[64]

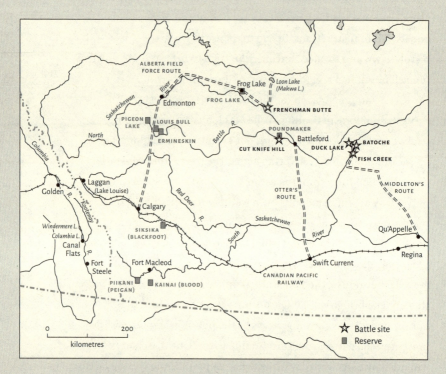

Steele's Scouts, 1885.

# 3 ‖ Steele's Scouts in the Rebellion
## 1885

AS STEELE'S TRAIN PULLED INTO CALGARY on April 11, he had only the sketchiest notion about why he had suddenly been pulled away from the mountains. He knew that serious trouble had broken out among the Métis settlements along the South Saskatchewan River and that shots had been fired at a place called Duck Lake. He quickly discovered that the situation on the prairies was deteriorating rapidly. Riel and his followers had set up a provisional government at Batoche on the South Saskatchewan River near Prince Albert and had ordered all government representatives out. Warriors from Big Bear's band had murdered nine people, including two priests, at Frog Lake. They had then driven the small Mounted Police detachment out of Fort Pitt and taken a number of settlers prisoner. Other Cree bands in the Edmonton area were reportedly planning to join the fighting. These reports were almost entirely unfounded, but alarm spread quickly among the white population.[1]

Steele's assignment on the CPR had kept him isolated from the growing crisis centred in the area between Prince Albert and St. Laurent on the South Saskatchewan. Although all the Cree nations in the area had reluctantly signed Treaty 6, they were deeply unhappy about the failure of Indian Affairs to appoint competent farm instructors to help them with their transition to agriculture or to make up for that deficiency by distributing food to prevent starvation.[2] The settlers who had taken up land around Prince Albert had suffered crop failures in the early 1880s and were bitterly disappointed by the abrupt decision to change the route of the CPR to the south. The Métis community there had been trying to get their traditional river lots recognized by the government survey. Other Métis settlements, such as St. Albert near Edmonton, had their river lots officially recorded by the surveyors but those in the Batoche–St. Laurent area were missed in the original survey and Ottawa ignored requests to spend the money necessary to do it over.[3]

With every section of the population unhappy and resentful about being ignored by Ottawa, the situation was ripe for serious trouble. The first step in that direction came in June 1884 when a meeting of the Métis voted to ask Louis Riel to return from the United States to lead negotiations with Ottawa. Since his success in uniting the population at Red River and bringing the province of Manitoba into existence in 1870, Riel had lived a difficult life. Driven out of Canada by threats of prosecution for the killing of Thomas Scott, Riel had suffered a mental breakdown and spent several years in asylums. By 1884 he had married and become an American citizen, and was teaching at a Jesuit mission school in Montana. When the delegation from the South Branch (as the Métis settlement on the Saskatchewan was known) reached him, he cautiously agreed to come north and help.

When Riel arrived in July his goals appear to have been modest; to forward negotiations for the Métis and pursue some claims of his own against the government for the land grant he was entitled to as a Red River Métis and services performed while he headed the provisional government in 1869–1870. It quickly became apparent that Riel had lost none of his charisma and the enthusiasm of his welcome, not just from the Métis but from the citizens of Prince

Albert and the discontented Cree, fundamentally altered his position. Unfortunately for all concerned, Prime Minister Sir John A. Macdonald chose to dismiss the Cree as impotent, the Prince Albert settlers as Liberal malcontents, and Riel as a self-seeking extortionist. By the fall of 1884 it was apparent that Ottawa was not about to listen to any protests. Early support from all groups in the community convinced Riel that he could repeat what he had achieved in Manitoba; perhaps he could do much more. Riel had studied for the priesthood and had always been deeply pious. Now his religious ideas took an increasingly bizarre turn.

He began to talk of himself as a prophet, Louis "David" Riel, sent to reform the Catholic Church by making Archbishop Ignace Bourget of Montreal the new Pope and moving the seat of the Church from Rome to a new republic carved out of the Canadian prairies for the Métis and First Nations as well as settlers from Ireland, Poland, and other Catholic parts of Europe.[4] Although this messianic vision began to alarm some of those who had originally welcomed Riel, especially the priests working in the community, most of the Prince Albert settlers, and even a few of the South Branch Métis, enough were willing to follow wherever Riel chose to lead to make it a highly explosive situation. The Mounted Police, the Oblate fathers, Lieutenant Governor Edgar Dewdney, and Judge Charles Rouleau all recommended that Ottawa move immediately to resurvey the river lots along the South Saskatchewan and increase the distribution of food rations to the Cree. Some of the western advisors even suggested that settling Riel's personal claims for a sum of about $35,000 would convince him to go back to the United States.

The only dissent from this advice in the west came from the Indian Affairs Department officials who continued to maintain that there would be no trouble and that giving the Cree food without demanding work in return would destroy their moral fibre. If the First Nations failed to adapt quickly to an agricultural way of life, they would suffer the fate of the buffalo herds that had been the foundation of their traditional economy; unfortunate, perhaps, but inevitable. The government's point man on this social Darwinist policy was Hayter Reed, Indian agent at Battleford from 1881 to 1883 and assistant Indian commissioner for the North-West Territories, 1883 to 1888.[5] Reed not only cut rations to his charges at every opportunity with an enthusiasm that took no account of the disastrous consequences for their health, but also made it clear that he despised First Nations people and considered them inferior. The fact that so few of the Cree ultimately took an active part in the Rebellion is quite astonishing.[6]

The survey and ration demands were embodied in a petition sent to Ottawa in mid-December. The government rejected the petition at the end of January 1885, promising only to investigate the claims of the Métis about the survey. Prime Minister Macdonald tried to hedge his bets by ordering the Mounted Police to begin recruiting enough men to double the size of the Force from 500 to 1,000. Both measures were too little and too late. By March, Riel had decided to ignore the opposition of the Roman Catholic Church, his lukewarm support among the First Nations, and the fact that, apart from his secretary, William Henry Jackson, it had collapsed altogether among the settlers.[7] At a public meeting at St. Laurent on March 8, Riel announced his intention to form a provisional government. A governing council was appointed March 19 and as a first step ordered Superintendent L.N.F. Crozier to surrender the police post at Fort Carlton and leave the North-West Territories. The provisional government began seizing arms and food supplies from stores in the area. On March 26, Crozier sent a small force of police and civilian volunteers from Prince Albert and Fort Carlton to secure the store at Duck Lake, about ten kilometres west of Batoche. Shooting started when they met a Métis force led by Gabriel Dumont. The Rebellion had begun.

Steele's location at the start of the fighting might have seemed disadvantageous for his career advancement. Once again, as in 1874 and 1877, he was far from the centre of the action. This time it turned out to be a stroke of luck. By 1885 the NWMP were widely dispersed in small detachments across the prairies. Headquarters at Regina was the only place where a sizeable group of police could be quickly detached from other duties to respond to the emergency. Commissioner Irvine assembled a force of ninety and headed north on March 18 to reinforce Superintendent Crozier at Fort Carlton. The most direct route took them via the river crossing at Batoche, which they found in the hands of the rebels. Irvine therefore detoured to another crossing downriver and reached Prince Albert late on March 24. He paused for a day to rest men and horses, then headed for Fort Carlton early on March 26. By the time he got there, Crozier had already retreated from the fight at Duck Lake with a dozen killed and about the same number wounded; a clear victory for the rebels who lost less than half that number. Irvine quickly decided, correctly, that Fort Carlton was indefensible and moved all his force back to Prince Albert. This was a sensible move, but one that kept the only sizeable concentration of Mounted Police out of action for the duration of the Rebellion since the military commander, General Middleton, ordered them to stay there.[8]

The only Mounted Police who took an active part in the fighting after Duck Lake were Steele's group from British Columbia and a small detachment from Fort Macleod under Inspector A. Bowen Perry, both of which were attached to General Thomas Bland Strange's Alberta Field Force. The Canadian government was as quick to react to the outbreak of the Rebellion as it had been slow to respond to the difficulties of the communities on the Saskatchewan, putting together a small army of militia units mostly from central Canada under the British officer commanding the Canadian militia, General Frederick Middleton. The CPR was able to move the troops and their equipment and supplies west over the nearly complete main line within a month. General Middleton initially organized his forces into two columns moving north from the railway at Qu'Appelle in the direction of the Métis headquarters at Batoche, and from Swift Current toward Battleford, which had been occupied by Big Bear's Cree. News that Big Bear's band had massacred nine people at Frog Lake on April 2 further panicked the population of Edmonton, Calgary and Fort Macleod, forcing Middleton to create a third force there.

The Alberta Field Force was even more improvised than the other columns. The commanding officer, General Strange, was a retired British artillery officer who, after an adventurous career fighting the Empire's wars around the globe, had retired to raise horses at a ranch near the Siksika Reserve east of Calgary. General Middleton quite correctly discounted the threat to Alberta but recognized the political necessity of doing something to appease the population. Strange was a notable eccentric who referred to himself as "Gunner Jingo," but he was also a regular soldier of long experience who would be just fine for that job.[9] His appointment had the additional advantage that Middleton could give him the militia units he regarded as badly trained and untrustworthy, the Mount Royal Rifles from Montreal and the 9th Voltigeurs from Quebec City as well as a hastily organized western unit, the Winnipeg Light Infantry.

Strange, for his part, was more than happy to have them. His French was good and he had spent the last years of his army career commanding the Canadian artillery at Quebec City and Kingston. The Quebec militia units, however, were all foot soldiers, and what Strange needed most of all to prevent his infantry from being ambushed while marching through bush country was a competent mounted force to scout ahead. Strange was delighted to find that Steele was available for the job. They had met while Steele was in the permanent force artillery at Kingston, and again while Steele was in charge of the NWMP detachment at Calgary during the construction of the railway and had to deal with Strange's frequent complaints about horse thefts by the Siksika. It says much about Steele's diplomatic skills that he managed to remain on reasonably good terms with both the general and his neighbours. Strange was also able to strengthen his force by adding a nine-pounder Mounted

Police field gun from Fort Macleod manned by twenty men under Inspector A.B. Perry.

Steele was assigned the militia rank of major when he arrived in Calgary and was given command of all the mounted troops in the Alberta Field Force, which included his own scouts and a unit commanded by Major George Hatton, known as the Alberta Mounted Rifles.[10] Steele quickly recruited sixty-five cowboys and ranchers to add to his twenty-five Mounted Police to form Steele's Scouts.[11] Scouting on horseback was a lot more fun and certainly more glamorous than plodding along with the infantry or dragging the field gun through the mud, but it was also serious business. Good scouting required military knowledge, constant vigilance, and discipline. Steele had no concerns that the two groups under his command would be incompatible, "The cowboy has no superior in the world, and in spite of his free life he takes to the order of military experience as if he were born to it."[12] Steele also had two competent officers with militia experience, Captain J.K. Oswald and Lieutenant J.A. Coryell, a surveyor who had attended the Royal Military College, to look after the details. The more experienced Oswald was made second in command and given No. 1 Troop. Lieutenant Coryell was assigned all the NWMP and the remainder of the cowboys for No. 2 Troop.[13] Calgary was overcrowded with soldiers and anxious settlers who had moved in from their isolated farms and ranches, so Steele's Scouts had to be accommodated in the bowling alley.

Eight days after he got to Calgary, Steele had his men horsed, armed with Winchester rifles and revolvers, and given a distinctive uniform of sorts in the form of "a scarlet sash around the left shoulder."[14] Lieutenant Coryell with a few of his scouts were detailed to accompany a small band of settlers from Red Deer who had fled to Calgary on the outbreak of the Rebellion, but were now anxious to get back to their homes. There had been some minor incidents of looting but no signs of hostility from any of the First Nations in the area. In fact the Indian agents in the area reported that Riel's emissaries urging them to join the fighting had been rebuffed, so it was deemed safe for the settlers to return.[15] General Strange decided to waste no time waiting for his whole force to assemble and on April 20 the first group, consisting of Steele's men and half of the 65th Regiment, headed north for Edmonton. The rest, including the Winnipeggers and the field gun, would follow when they were ready. There was a well-established trail between the two future Alberta cities in 1885. Two stagecoach lines leaving Edmonton on Mondays and Thursdays respectively offered travellers a five-day trip south to connect with the CPR trains to Winnipeg.[16] Nothing like the several hundred soldiers with 175 teams and wagons had ever passed this way, however, and by mid-April a spring thaw was starting which meant a slow, muddy journey.

After five days the column reached the Red Deer River and the little settlement located where it was possible at most times of the year to ford the stream without too much difficulty. The spring runoff had raised the river level, however, and when the soldiers tried to cross, several of the wagons were swept downriver by the current. Orders to make the crossing early in the morning before the melting brought the water up solved that problem. The next day word arrived from the Reverend John McDougall that Edmonton was not under threat so Strange sent back orders to have boats built there to move men and supplies down the North Saskatchewan to the Mounted Police post at Fort Pitt, which he planned to use as a base to track down Big Bear.

The deliberate march allowed Steele to further assess his hastily recruited command but only one man had to be let go as "unsuitable" by the time they got to Red Deer.[17] The Scouts stayed on the alert, but much of their time was spent escorting the bridging parties from the 65th that went ahead of the main force making necessary repairs. The trail north from Red Deer took the Field Force through the territories of Bobtail's and Ermineskin's large Cree bands. The Oblate fathers Lacombe and Scollen were there with the chiefs to greet the soldiers, although Strange, typically, refused to shake hands with them as he considered them untrustworthy.[18] Edmonton was reached without any further hitches on May 1.[19]

Steele's men pitched their tents on the race track and enjoyed a few days' rest while General Strange waited for his other units to catch up and organized his troops for the move downriver. The Scouts were kept under strict discipline; no more than 10 per cent of them were allowed passes at a time and all had to be back in camp by midnight.[20] There was, in truth, not much in the way of temptation to be found in Edmonton in 1885. The Jasper House Hotel, advertised as "[t]he only brick building in Edmonton," was the best bet, while, on the other hand, there were enough churches to allow General Strange to order compulsory church parades for his whole force. The *Edmonton Bulletin*, whose editor, Frank Oliver, was no admirer of the Mounted Police, approved of Steele's men: "The police, 50 in number, do not look as jaunty as those we have been used to seeing, but do look a great deal more like business."[21]

At 6:30 on the morning of May 6, the Scouts broke camp and moved off along the north bank of the Saskatchewan. Most of the heavy supplies, especially food for men and horses, was now being transported on the boats General Strange had ordered built, but many wagons were still necessary to carry tents, bedding, and personal effects. As on the Calgary to Edmonton portion of the march, Steele's job for the first days of travel east of Edmonton was to check for signs of Cree activity and make sure the trails were passable for the larger group following. Those five days travelling brought them to the former HBC post at Fort Victoria, which Steele had passed through eleven years earlier on the March West. Fort Victoria was now a little settlement with some river lot farms clustered around the Methodist mission. This was only about forty kilometres from the Saddle Lake Reserve, which had been raided by Little Hunter's and Blue Quill's men on April 3. Another day's ride would bring them to Frog Lake and the scene of the killings. It was time to tighten up the security of the expedition.

Four troopers from the Scouts were designated as night herders, with extra pay for the job. The rest were instructed, "As the alarm may be given at any time, no man will take his clothes off at night but be ready to stand to his arms at a moment's notice."[22] Fires were strictly monitored at night and those thinking about leaving the camp after dark without permission were warned that they were liable to be arrested or even shot by sentries. The infantry caught up to the Scouts at Fort Victoria on May 16 and Steele's men moved out early the following morning with additional orders about avoiding unnecessary noise on the march. They paused for several days at Saddle Lake Reserve, sending out small parties north and east to see if they could find Cree who might be disposed to attack the column.

There were no signs of anyone, friendly or unfriendly, so on May 21 Captain Oswald was ordered to take a larger group of fifteen Scouts with several Métis guides and carefully check out the route to Fort Pitt, including the site of the killings at Frog Lake. His group left Saddle Lake at 6:30 on the morning of May 22 and got to within about twenty kilometres of Frog Lake before camping for the night at Moose Hill Creek. Oswald and half a dozen men, including Canon George McKay of Prince Albert, who had accompanied the force from Calgary, arrived at Frog Lake late in the afternoon of May 23. They were the first people on the scene since the massacre and quickly discovered one body in the cellar of the burned-out mission house. It had been three weeks since the killings and it was only possible to identify the body as one of the priests by his clothing.

The following day Oswald noted:

*Roused at 4 AM. Canon McKay, myself, Troopers Phillips, Robertson, Jardine, the Rowlands & Whitford unearthed 3 more bodies from Mission cellar & buried them in cemetery, Canon McKay reading the burial service. They were two priests & two others, all unrecognizable— a sad sight & terrible work to have to accomplish for humanity's sake.*[23]

As soon as this was done, the party moved on to Fort Pitt, finding it burned and abandoned. Two days later General Strange arrived with the main part of the force. Steele was ordered to find Big Bear and his captives while the infantry secured Fort Pitt and established contact with General Middleton's forces, which by this time had defeated the Métis at Batoche. All the other rebels had surrendered and Big Bear's people were the sole holdouts.

Steele now had several other small mounted units—the Alberta Mounted Rifles, Boulton's Scouts and the Surveyors Intelligence Corps—under his command and tracking the Cree was not difficult. Several hundred people moving though the partially wooded parkland left an unmistakable trail. The Cree had not gone far in any case. Although most Canadians at the time believed Big Bear to be the unchallenged leader of the Cree at Frog Lake, there were in fact deep divisions among them. Strictly speaking, Big Bear's people were the Plains Cree, who had lived by hunting buffalo on the prairie much as did their traditional foes, the Blackfoot. The Woods Cree, who occupied the adjoining reserve at Frog Lake, had been more reluctant participants in the events there and at Fort Pitt, although they felt compelled to go along. Leadership of the Plains Cree had largely passed to the war chief Wandering Spirit, who wanted to move south and east to join Poundmaker's people and continue the fight. With the news of the decisive defeat of the Métis at Batoche and the surrender of Riel, this appeared to be the only way of avoiding surrender, but the Woods Cree were not at all sure they wanted to continue with what increasingly appeared to be a hopeless pursuit. It was decided to hold a Thirst Dance to resolve the differences.

The place where they camped to hold the dance was a hilltop near a location known as Frenchman Butte, about twenty kilometres northeast of Fort Pitt. On May 26, some of Steele's men found a letter dropped by one of the women prisoners, confirming the direction the Cree had taken. Steele and ninety of his men set off in pursuit and as they were about to halt, around midnight, they ran into a Cree war party. A confused firefight erupted in which one of the warriors was killed before the rest faded into the darkness. At first light Steele's force moved on, discovering the remains of a large camp with 187 tipi rings. Shortly after that their advance party encountered the Cree once again. Shots were exchanged and both sides retreated. Moving forward cautiously once again Steele found that the Cree encampment was on the far side of a steep valley with a small marshy stream along the bottom. Wandering Spirit's men had dug rifle pits among the poplars that fringed the top of the hill. Steele sensibly decided that the position was too strong for his small force to attack and waited for General Strange to come up.

The infantry arrived later in the day, bringing the field gun with them. The Cree positions were within reach of the nine-pounder, which began to fire shrapnel rounds 1,500 metres across the valley. The fire scattered the Cree and allowed Steele to move his men down into the valley by late afternoon. In the morning the gun opened up again and Strange ordered Steele to try to find a way to his left that would permit the force to outflank the Cree position. The prospects were not promising; the horses sank up to their bellies in the swampy creek bottom and the farther left Steele pushed, the thicker the bush became. By the time Steele reported, it appeared to most of the soldiers that the Cree had abandoned the position, but General Strange decided he would wait for more of his soldiers to arrive before moving on. It seems clear that Steele thought Strange was being far too cautious, but as usual in his autobiography, when he thought a mistake had been made by a superior officer, he preferred silence to criticism.[24]

When Strange decided that he was ready to move on four days later, Steele's Scouts encountered no resistance and found the hilltop position abandoned.[25] The ground was littered with food, tools, and furs looted from Frog Lake and Fort Pitt, and even a note from one of the prisoners which strongly suggested that the Cree had been driven off by the fire from the field gun. In fact, the encounter at Frenchman Butte had split the fragile Cree alliance.

Some of the Woods Cree decided to surrender and took a few of the prisoners with them. Steele's men caught up with the party on June 1 and brought them back to the main camp.

Some of Steele's men had been attached to the infantry, his force was down to sixty-two men, and they were running short of ammunition and food, but General Strange ordered them to push on in pursuit of the Cree. General Middleton had just made his way up the river and Strange assured Steele that the commander in chief would send his mounted troops in support. Steele and his men followed Big Bear's trail in a northeasterly direction for two days, occasionally exchanging distant shots with the Cree scouts. Early on the morning of June 3 they came in sight of a large lake, called Loon Lake at the time, now Makwa Lake. The trail down to the water went through dense bush to a small open prairie on the water's edge, where Steele could see a Cree lodge. A fordable narrows (now called Steele Narrows) separated two parts of the lake and some of the Cree were observed moving across to the heavily wooded opposite shore.

Steele claims that he was about to call on the Cree to surrender when they opened fire on his men, and there is no reason to doubt him.[26] He had asked the redoubtable Canon McKay, who possessed both a fluency in Cree and a booming voice, to do the job, but the shots triggered an immediate attack by Steele's Scouts. The ensuing firefight killed the Woods Cree chief Cut Arm and wounded several others. Three of Steele's men were seriously wounded, including Sergeant William Fury, who was lucky to survive with a bullet in the chest.[27] The remaining Cree retreated to the other side of the lake, leaving Steele with the unappetizing prospect of crossing the water under fire from a hidden enemy. He wisely declined what would have been a useless sacrifice and ordered a ceasefire. Canon McKay called across to the Cree to surrender but they continued firing with, according to Steele, disturbing accuracy. A quick assessment showed that the Scouts were down to fifteen rounds of ammunition per man. There was no sign of the promised reinforcement so Steele pulled his men back about five kilometres and sent the wounded back to Fort Pitt. This action ended the last military conflict fought on Canadian soil.

The sentries around the camp fired a few more shots during the night at what they thought were Cree warriors. In fact, it was two of the captives, William McLean and James Simpson, who had convinced their captors to give up and who were trying to reach Steele to negotiate a surrender. This incident was unfortunate in a number of ways. Rescuing the captives would have capped a highly successful campaign for Steele and made him an instant celebrity. As it turned out the rebuff further fragmented the Cree and prolonged the ordeal of the captives as well as of the soldiers. The Woods Cree with the captives headed north toward the Beaver River and Lac des Iles. Most of the Plains Cree went in the opposite direction, hoping to join up with Riel. When they discovered that he had already surrendered, some fled to the United States. All the Plains Cree avoided the cordon of soldiers that General Middleton had created. Big Bear and one of his sons made their way to the Mounted Police detachment at Fort Carlton and surrendered on July 2, as one of the searchers who had missed him farther north commented, to the only four men in the North-West Territories who were not looking for him.[28]

The disintegration of the Cree was not apparent to the military command in the aftermath of the Loon Lake fight. General Middleton believed that there were still around 500 warriors in one body, a huge overestimate since there had never been that many at any time, so he organized four columns to move north from the North Saskatchewan to bottle up the enemy and force a surrender. Strange was sent in the direction of Cold Lake, Lt. Col. William Otter's force moved north from Battleford, and a party of Mounted Police under Commissioner Irvine from Prince Albert formed the easternmost column. Steele, with all the mounted units, stayed with Middleton in the centre and went back to the scene of the Loon Lake fight. There was no sign of any of the Cree except for the bodies of those killed in the exchange and that of one woman who apparently committed suicide when her husband was killed. All the mounted men were anxious to push on but when General Middleton discovered that he could not get his Gatling gun across the narrows, they were ordered to stop, much to Steele's disgust: "The staff, however, would not listen to any representations made by members of the Mounted Police, nor to the evidence of their own senses, but leaned on those with no experience to guide them, with the usual results."[29]

The whole of Middleton's force, now joined by Otter's Battleford contingent, gathered at Fort Pitt to await developments. A few days later, General Strange reported finding a large cache of flour at Beaver River. Middleton decided that this must be where the Cree were going and took his column there. The Woods Cree and the prisoners were, in fact, in the area but not where the soldiers were searching. The hunt was mainly in the direction of Cold Lake and the Cree were near Lac des Iles. There was more waiting for the troops who were increasingly bored and restless. Middleton had to issue strict orders against men going out of camp with their rifles to hunt since they were in danger of shooting each other.[30] Finally, on June 19, the prisoners persuaded the Cree to let them go and they made their way back to Loon Lake where some of Steele's men found them and brought them in. The surrender of Big Bear two weeks later brought the Rebellion to an official end.

|| The eastern troops headed for Battleford to be loaded onto river steamers for the trip home. Some of the soldiers were sent south to the railway to travel east to Winnipeg. Steele's Scouts and the Alberta Mounted Rifles were ordered back to Calgary on June 29 to be disbanded.[31] They retraced their route back upriver to Edmonton, arriving on July 6.[32] After a short rest to decide on the disposition of sick and lame horses that were to be left there, they crossed the river and moved south two days later. After an uneventful trip they reached Calgary on July 18 to a hero's welcome.

The mayor and council along with a large crowd of citizens met them as they rode in. There was a civic banquet and Steele was presented with a diamond ring.

Steele's celebrity resounded well beyond Calgary. The most detailed source of information about the Rebellion for Canadians at the time was a publication called *The Canadian Pictorial and Illustrated War News*, which sprang into existence on April 4, 1885 and appeared weekly until August. The *War News* was decidedly unambiguous in its take on events; its editors wanted heroes to give the public and if that required embellishment, their writers and artists were equal to the task. Steele met the requirements nicely; Ontario born and raised, handsome, man of action and already associated with two of the central institutions of Canada's western empire, the NWMP and the CPR. The July 11 issue of the *War News* featured the Loon Lake skirmish on the front page. An illustration, clearly drawn by an artist who got no closer to the action than the western outskirts of Toronto, showed Steele's men (in Mounted Police uniforms and white helmets) firing at the Cree from behind trees. The breathless caption read, "Gallant Attack on Big Bear's Band by a Handful of Mounted Police Under Inspector Steele and Squadron Sergt. Major Fury."[33]

Celebrity could be fleeting, but the summer of 1885 brought a more lasting reward. A telegram was waiting at Calgary informing Steele of his promotion to superintendent. This was not just a big step in rank, it almost doubled his salary, from $800 a year to $1,400. The Rebellion had not been kind to most of the officers of the Mounted Police. The relationship between the Mounted Police and the militia in the 19th century was close—almost all the inspectors and superintendents of the police came from the militia before the First World War—but that did not mean it was always a warm one. Many militia officers resented the publicity the Mounted Police seemed to generate so effortlessly and the Rebellion offered a rare opportunity to put the NWMP in its place. Much of their criticism focused on the fact that Commissioner Irvine, with the largest concentration of police, had stayed in Prince Albert until the fighting was over. That he had been ordered to do so by General Middleton could not save Irvine, who lost his job as a result.

If Irvine was unfairly targeted, another Mounted Police officer attracted criticism that was well deserved. Inspector Francis Jeffrey Dickens, son of author Charles Dickens, was deaf, alcoholic, and generally incompetent. Lord Dufferin, governor general of Canada from 1872 to 1878, was a family friend and had obtained the appointment for Francis after he had finished drinking up his share of his father's estate. Dickens's personnel file is filled with reports that describe him as "totally unfit to be a Mounted Police officer," but his political connections and his father's fame kept him from being fired.[34] He was put in charge of Fort Pitt in 1883, one of the smallest and most isolated police outposts where, it was hoped, he might stay out of trouble. Unfortunately, the outbreak of the Rebellion put him next door to Big Bear. His leadership inspired so little confidence that the two dozen or so settlers who came to Fort Pitt for protection after the Frog Lake Massacre chose to surrender to the Cree, rather than try to defend the fort. When they left, Dickens and his men abandoned Fort Pitt and retreated downriver by boat.

Steele and Inspector Perry, who was promoted the same day, were untainted by the real and perceived failures of some of their colleagues. Their promotions indicated clearly that they were considered the rising stars of the Mounted Police who would be in line for command of two of the new divisions being created with the doubling in size of the Force. Steele was therefore feeling very good about himself when he took ten days off for a holiday to visit friends in Winnipeg. While there he was alerted to the presence of a suspect in a dramatic murder that had taken place near Golden, British Columbia, the previous fall. A man named Baird, carrying $5,000 in cash for his company, was shot down from ambush. Evidence strongly implicated a drifter who went by the name of "Bull Dog Kelly" but he had disappeared before he could be arrested. Steele quickly notified the Winnipeg police but Kelly managed to get across the border to Minnesota before they caught him.

CPR *construction at the summit of Rogers Pass, BC, 1885.* [BPSC, 2008.1.2.1.6.5.8]

Back overseeing the completion of the CPR construction in September, Steele spent a good deal of time gathering evidence to support an extradition case.[35] To his disgust the British Columbia government decided it was too expensive to pursue the case, but he took some satisfaction from the fact that "Kelly," whose real name was McNaughton, died violently the following year. Steele had another reason to be unhappy with the government of British Columbia that fall. Now that the railway was nearing completion, the provincial authorities had started challenging the federal government authority on the line by selling liquor licences to all comers and arresting the special constables appointed to replace the Mounted Police while they were off suppressing the Rebellion. Steele arranged for North-West Territories Justice James F. Macleod, assisted by Superintendent Arthur Griesbach, to come in and sort things out. The British Columbia government quickly backed down and federal authority was restored.

A few weeks later the last rails were in place to join the eastern and western sections of the line and finish the great project. Plans for marking the completion called for a ceremonial driving of the last spike at a place near Eagle Pass known since that time as Craigellachie. A special train brought the CPR brass from the east, and picked up Steele on November 7. Sir Donald Smith (later Lord Strathcona) did the honours in front of a small crowd memorialized in one of the most famous Canadian photographs of the 19th century. The scene is an interesting mixture of several of the wealthiest and most powerful Canadians of the day side by side with the navvies who worked for around a dollar a day, some of whom undoubtedly spent time in Steele's jail cells. Sam Steele is in the front row, fittingly, because his contribution to the project was of the first importance.

Donald Smith, William Cornelius Van Horne, and the other CPR officials recognized Steele's work by including him in the triumphal tour that followed the Craigellachie ceremony. The first train trip through the mountains to the Pacific was a luxurious affair in the private cars of the railway moguls. The speed of the journey, which reached a hair-raising fifty-seven miles per hour (ninety kilometres per hour) in places, deeply impressed Steele.[36] Vancouver did not yet exist when the train reached tidewater; the company was just then in the process of making the harbour surveys that would bring the city into being. The company steamer *Olympia* was diverted from its survey duties and Steele and the magnates got aboard for the British Columbia capital, Victoria, where they were enthusiastically received by the government. Steele liked the city and enjoyed a few days of being a tourist, but he was more than happy to get back on a train going east. His future would be worked out on the prairies and he was anxious to get on with it. His description of coming out of the mountains in his autobiography captures his mood perfectly:

> When our train emerged from the Bow River Pass, and we again saw before us the magnificent expanse of prairie, with the beautiful sparkling Bow meandering to the eastward, pleasure beamed on every countenance, and was given vent to in cheers of delight, one stalwart engineer shouting at the top of his voice, "Hurrah! Civilization at last!"[37]

# 4 ‖ Frustrated Ambition
1886-1888

MOST PEOPLE, even the most motivated and successful, go through a stage at some point in their lives when they lose confidence in the vision that propels them. For some, it is a transitory experience from which they bounce back to pursue their goals with renewed energy. At the other end of the scale, it can destroy an individual completely. For Sam Steele, this stage of his life lasted about a year and a half, from the beginning of 1886 until the summer of 1887. The disillusion and perhaps depression that set in did not damage him irreparably but it did come close to derailing his career in the Mounted Police.

Steele and Perry were both rewarded for their successful performances during the Rebellion by being given commands in the heart of the affected areas; Perry got "F" Division at Prince Albert and Steele was assigned "D" Division at Battleford. In addition, Steele had "K" Division, headed by his friend Superintendent A.R. Macdonell, under his command. If Steele or Perry expected that this would put them in the centre of the action, they were soon to be disappointed. In 1886 and for years after the two places were the quietest locations in the North-West Territories. The settlers around Battleford were a little nervous, but as the months went by without any indication that the local Métis communities and Cree nations were interested in a repetition of the previous year's hostilities, those fears abated. In addition to the hundred or so men in each of "D" and "K" Divisions, a small Royal Canadian Artillery detachment, "A" Battery, remained in the town until March 1886. The government also acted to remove potential causes of discontent. In January Steele reported that the Cree on two reserves near Battleford were complaining about their farm instructors. They were immediately replaced by former Mounted Police NCOs.[1] Lumber to construct new police barracks had to be hauled from Prince Albert and Steele was instructed to give the contracts to Métis on the basis of need, whether or not they had taken part in the Rebellion.[2]

For the first month Steele was in Battleford the weather also played a part. January of 1886 was brutally cold with temperatures dropping below −45°C several times. The cold limited what Steele's new command could do in the way of training so he was able to relax a little. He often played whist with Macdonell, the medical officer, Dr. J.W. Rolph, some of the artillery officers, and a couple of the local clergymen. Perhaps it was his social contact with the men of the cloth that prompted a more regular church attendance in this period than at any other time in his life. In the eight months he spent at Battleford he often attended two services on a Sunday and he enforced mandatory church parade for the men. With his higher salary, he felt able to indulge himself in expensive cigars. Between January and July 1886, he spent the rather astonishing sum of $55.75 on them, the equivalent of about $1,400 in 2018 dollars.[3]

The other recreational activity that appears in Steele's diary for the first time in 1886 is drinking. This is interesting, because Steele unquestionably drank heavily at certain times in his life. In 1927 an American writer named T. Morris Longstreth published a book entitled *The Silent Force: Scenes from the Life of the Mounted Police of Canada*.[4] Longstreth never met Steele but he interviewed many older NWMP veterans who had served with him. Their recollections led him to include the following passage in the book: "Steele's ability to drink was the height of regimental envy; a quart bottle was the measure of his nightcap; yet, however inapposite an ideal such a figure might present on the Sabbath-school platform, to the men in the ranks the sight was more instructive, more inspiring, than even texts from Moses or Isaiah." When Harwood Steele read the passage he immediately threatened a lawsuit and lined up an impressive collection of distinguished former mounted policemen who were prepared to swear that his father was not a drinker, although some of the statements were quite carefully phrased.[5] Longstreth quickly agreed to remove the sentence from the second printing of the book.[6]

Steele's diary for March 23, 1886, contains an interesting comment: "Spent evening at Olivers at whist party some good whiskey there but did not touch it as I have decided not to while here. I have been at several parties and liquor has been at all but none have been able to persuade me to drink any."[7] Clearly Steele was familiar enough with whiskey to distinguish good from bad and the words, "I have decided not to [touch it] *while here*," imply that he had indulged earlier and regretted it. A few weeks later after another social engagement he wrote, "Spent evening at H____ and had a glass of ale did not indulge. I am temperate as usual and feel that indulgence in intoxicants is all rot."[8] Ale, apparently, didn't count as an intoxicant. The temperance pledge lasted through the summer but in early September, as Steele was leaving Battleford for Fort Macleod, his friend Superintendent A.R. Macdonell and a former mounted policeman named Nash came to see him off. Steele recorded in his diary, "Mac came out with me as far as camp and stayed all night. Harry Nash came over also and brought some of the joyful with him."[9]

Indications are that Steele found Battleford an uncomfortable place that he was happy to leave behind. One of the things that Steele found challenging was the fact that a large percentage of his men were new recruits brought in as part of the doubling in size of the Force the previous year. NWMP headquarters at Regina was not yet set up to train a recruit intake of anything approaching this size, so the responsibility for all instruction fell on the divisional commanders. Many of the recruits had signed on during the Rebellion with hopes of action and adventure. There was very little of that to be had in Battleford in 1886; instead what they experienced was overcrowded quarters and, once the cold weather broke in February, more than four hours of drill daily.[10] Similar conditions in Edmonton that year produced a minor mutiny when some police refused to turn out for duty when ordered to do so.[11]

Steele reacted quickly to signs of unrest in his command. When one of his constables got into a scuffle at a dance with some local Métis, Steele immediately investigated and fined the man.[12] In mid-February he received an anonymous letter from a constable claiming to represent "D" and "K" troops. The letter, "requested the removal of Insp Allan and Wilson who they say will drive the said troops to desperation."[13] Steele investigated for two weeks, satisfied himself that he knew who had written the letter, but did not approach the man directly. Instead he paraded the division and told them that anonymous letters were not the way to address their grievances.[14] If the unhappy constables thought they might get some sympathy from the public, they were disappointed. The Battleford newspaper commented, "The Mounted Police are putting in their spring 'setting up' drill. Some of them think it is a good deal like work."[15] A highly successful sports day on May 24 helped restore morale.

Sam Steele never had much trouble managing his constables and NCOs; his officers were sometimes another matter. This was the case in a mysterious episode that happened at Battleford in the spring of 1886. In the late stages of the Rebellion, the army had shipped a large quantity of oats to the town. Several tons left over when the troops departed became the responsibility of the police. Oats were the essential fuel for draft horses to move anything that could not be carried by the railways and were in universal demand.

At the end of February, the government decided to auction most of the stock at Battleford since oats were perishable and a constant temptation for theft.[16] Some of the oats were set aside for the Métis freighters hauling lumber from Prince Albert, because they were destitute and unable to purchase feed.

This sensible plan was badly mismanaged by the police officer who handled it, Inspector John Beresford Allan. The job was simple enough; when the price of the oats was determined by the auction on March 2, the value of the quantity of oats set aside for the Métis was established as $450 (about the equivalent of $14,000 today). The police would then send a cheque for the amount to the Militia Department. Inspector Allan did that, but in a remarkably casual way. He did nothing until June and then, instead of mailing the cheque, gave it to his brother W.A. Allan, an Anglican clergyman in Battleford, who was stopping in Ottawa on his way to England and asked him to drop it off to with Lt. Col. Whitehead, the Chief Supply Officer. The Rev. Mr. Allan, however, forgot the errand and the cheque did not reach the Militia Department until he returned to Canada in October.[17]

Inspector Allan's sloppiness might have passed unnoticed if Steele had not been transferred to Fort Macleod in the summer of 1886. Before he left on September 1, Steele had to make sure that all the detachment accounts were accurate and up to date. The missing payment for the oats led him to investigate the situation and to the conclusion that Inspector Allan, at the very least, had some explaining to do. He also seems to have concluded that another officer, Inspector W.D. Antrobus, had sold off some oats and pocketed the money. He reported these suspicions to headquarters.[18] The reaction did not come until he had moved to Fort Macleod, and when it did, came as a severe shock. Steele met with the commissioner in mid-October and was ordered to withdraw his allegations. The formal document to Steele's superior at Fort Macleod, Superintendent Percy Neale, a month later, was brusque and insulting:

> *On receipt hereof you will send for Supt. Steele to the Orderly Room, hand him the enclosed file of papers, direct him to read them attentively, and call upon him to report, (which is to be rendered without loss of time) as to whether upon final consideration he will elect to maintain or withdraw his imputations against his brother officers.*[19]

It is clear from the correspondence that Inspector Allan was guilty of nothing more than carelessness. The interesting thing is that the file contains nothing at all about the other officer named, Inspector Antrobus. The implication of the wording of the order quoted above is that Steele was reluctant to give a pass to both men. This, of course, raises questions about Antrobus. This officer, it turns out, had a decidedly up and down career in the Mounted Police. He joined as a constable in 1874 and seems to have been very competent, rising steadily through the ranks over the next ten years. Unfortunately, Antrobus suffered from a severe alcohol problem; he was a binge drinker who managed to stay sober for considerable periods between bouts of hitting the bottle. One of these episodes took place in the summer of 1884 when Antrobus was stationed at Swift Current. He went on a tear that ended when he locked himself in a bathroom in the railway hotel and refused to come out. A police doctor was rushed down from Regina and, with the help of a sergeant and corporal, broke down the door and got him out.

Antrobus managed to get away from the men trying to help him and almost fell under the wheels of a passing train in his effort to escape. He was restrained and sent to Regina where he smashed furniture and ripped up his bedding. In his report the police surgeon commented, "in a large experience extending over thirty-five years, I have never seen one so violent."[20] For most members of the Mounted Police, an episode like this would have brought about immediate dismissal, but in this case word came down from Ottawa that because there was some doubt as to the cause of "the attack of mania," Antrobus was to be returned to duty with a warning that he was on trial.[21] The inspector clearly had powerful political connections.

The next incident on record occurred seven years later in the spring of 1891. Antrobus, now a superintendent, was in charge of "C" Division at Battleford, when reports reached the commissioner that he was drinking on the job. The assistant commissioner went to check out the situation and quickly reported by telegram: "Shall I suspend Antrobus and place Howe in command. A shortage in cash used for private purposes, never replaced, admits it."[22] Fuller's investigation found that Antrobus had been stealing money by falsifying the accounts for the detachment's supply of oats. Antrobus's political friends made a last-ditch effort to save his job. The member of Parliament (MP) for Compton, Quebec, R.H. Pope, sent the following extraordinary note to Sir John A. Macdonald:

> One Antribus [sic] engaged in the Mounted Police has been suspended for being drunk. I think it is second offence. No doubt it is a very serious offence for any man to get drunk, this is a point upon which we will both agree, but for a man to lose his position because he did get drunk only makes it a greater calamity for the unfortunate who gives way to one of the weaknesses of Mother Civilization. I want this man reinstated and kept there for two years drunk or sober. At the expiration of that time he will be entitled to pension. Then they can sack the bugger as soon as they like.[23]

Unfortunately for Antrobus, Macdonald was in his final weeks of life and unable to protect him any longer.

It seems certain that something similar to the episode that ended Antrobus's career took place five years earlier in Battleford. The situation for Steele was complicated by the fact that the new commissioner who took over in April 1886, L.W. Herchmer, was an outside appointment (one of only two in the long history of the Mounted Police) and an unknown quantity.[24] In an organization as small as the Mounted Police before 1885, Steele could not have been unaware of the Swift Current incident. When questions arose about the behaviour of Inspector Antrobus, Steele could reasonably have expected that, at the very least, an investigation would result. Instead, Antrobus was promoted to superintendent and transferred to Calgary in the early summer of 1886. It seems likely that this decision was made before Steele's charges and that Antrobus's political backers got him out of the jam. This was one of the first important decisions that Commissioner Herchmer made in his new job and he clearly could not allow Steele's allegations to blow it up in his face. This is the only version of events that accounts for the ultimatum to Steele to drop the charges, along with the extensive evidence about Allan in the file and the complete absence of Steele's letter or any other documents concerning Antrobus.

As this situation was fermenting, an additional complication was added by Steele's decision to apply for the position of assistant commissioner. The position became open when Superintendent L.N.F. Crozier resigned over his resentment at not getting the top job when Herchmer was appointed. Steele quickly assembled some political backing of his own. The Conservative MP for Ottawa County, Alonzo Wright, sent a letter of support with the backing of the members from Barrie and Simcoe, Steele's home territory, and "many other Military M.P.s."[25] In addition to being a power in the ruling party, Wright was known as "The King of Gatineau." Wright was also related by marriage to the very influential NWMP Comptroller, Fred White. Steele got additional support from another prominent Tory MP, D'Alton McCarthy.[26] It was not enough. The commissioner chose instead to appoint his brother, W.M. Herchmer, and his handling of Steele in the fall of 1886 appears to have been designed to put him firmly in his place.

Steele got the message. It was at this point that he seriously considered leaving the Mounted Police. He met with Commissioner Herchmer about the Allan/Antrobus matter on October 15 and noted in his diary the following day, "Commissioner went away today at 9.30 Saw him and got his promise for leave at 16 November for four months."²⁷ The 1886 diary encloses two notes from Steele's friend George Hatton introducing him to J.G. Burrows in Montreal and J.E. Robertson in Toronto, describing Steele as his best friend in the country and asking them to take care of him.²⁸ At some time in the next month, Steele cancelled his plans to look for other employment; he did not take up the promised leave and the notes from Hatton were never used. Why Steele made this decision is not clear. His diary for 1886 ends on October 18 and that for 1887 has disappeared, but a comment in a letter to his future wife in 1889 provides a clue:

> *I do not think that he [Commissioner Herchmer] is passionately fond of me but he certainly shews that he has a great deal of confidence in me and if he does not think a good deal of me his actions belie him. I had a fearful falling out with him in 86 but it was settled by Sir John and since that time he has shown that he bears no malice and has openly given me a very high character to many friends of his and mine.*²⁹

One possible reason for Steele's change of heart might be that he discovered that Herchmer's treatment of him was not personal; the commissioner was habitually rude and insulting to all his subordinates, even his brother. Steele, throughout his life, strove to be the uncomplaining good soldier. Commissioner L.W. Herchmer was efficient and hard working but, as two of the RCMP official historians, William Beahen and Stan Horrall, point out in *Red Coats on the Prairies*, he was also, "overbearing, vindictive and ill-tempered."³⁰ Steele and Herchmer would have an often-contentious relationship over the next fifteen years.

The changing situation at Steele's new posting also probably influenced his decision. Unlike Battleford, which had no railway and was populated by many depressed and destitute survivors of the Rebellion, southern Alberta was experiencing strong economic growth. Completion of the CPR mainline created a boom in cattle ranching and Steele, with his larger salary, was interested in taking advantage of investment opportunities. Just south of Fort Macleod, the Galt family's North Western Coal and Navigation Company had started to exploit coal deposits along the Oldman River, creating the rapidly growing town of Lethbridge. By 1886, the new community needed its own police detachment and most of "D" Division under Steele was assigned to the job. Even so, this was a serious comedown from the previous year when he had been in overall command of two divisions at Battleford. It seems highly probable that in this period, as often happened when he was bored or unhappy, Steele drank heavily. Harwood Steele, as his reaction to the Longstreth book shows, was fiercely protective of his father's reputation. The missing diary for 1887 is part of a pattern that strongly suggests that Harwood weeded out any documents that contained direct evidence of his father's excessive use of alcohol.

Whatever happened in late 1886 and early 1887, things started to look up for Steele in the spring. The British Columbia government requested the assistance of the Mounted Police to deal with a situation involving the Kutenai First Nation in the southeastern part of the province and Steele and his "D" Division were given the job. As a separate British colony before joining Canada, British Columbia had negotiated only a few treaties with Indigenous nations on Vancouver Island and had assigned very small reserves. By the time British Columbia joined in 1871, Canada had a well-established policy of negotiating comprehensive treaties and establishing relatively generous reserves, allotting land according to population on the same scale as homesteads for European settlers. As part of becoming a Canadian province, British Columbia agreed to sign treaties covering the rest of its territory, presumably along the same lines as the other western treaties. It soon became apparent that the province had no intention of following through and, in fact, it was well over a century before it was finally forced by the courts to comprehensively address the process.

In order to allow settlement and mining operations in the late 19th century, the British Columbia government assigned reserves in many areas without any pretense at consultation and even without bothering with the elementary step of taking a census to determine the land needs of the First Nations. In most parts of the province's interior, the extreme isolation and lack of settlement pressure prevented conflict from becoming acute. This was not the case with the Kutenai in southeastern British Columbia. They had historic connections with the plains people on the prairies where they had once hunted buffalo and with others south of the United States border. They knew in detail the kind of land allotments provided in the United States and in Canada under Treaty 7. The ones they had received were nothing like as large and some traditional locations were arbitrarily taken from them and given to settlers. One particularly valuable and contentious piece of land known as Joseph's Prairie, where the city of Cranbrook now stands, was allotted to the member of the British Columbia legislature for the area, Lt. Col. James Baker, even though it was the heart of traditional Kutenai territory and had in recent years been farmed by them. The Kutenai in the 1880s had strong leadership in the person of Chief Isadore.[31] They had also enjoyed good relations with the priests at St. Eugene's Mission for twenty years. Their protests over what they rightly considered unjust treatment were interpreted by the local whites as threatening, causing them to demand protection.

In late 1886, the Canadian government ordered Mounted Police Assistant Commissioner W.M. Herchmer to investigate. Some idea of the isolation and difficulties of travel to the area at the time can be gleaned from the fact that to get there, Herchmer had to travel by train to Vancouver, by boat to Victoria, then south on another boat to Seattle, east on the Northern Pacific Railroad to Sand Point, Idaho Territory, and then north on horseback into Canada. The last part of the trip was actually on snowshoes over Moyie Pass. Herchmer found much unrest among the Kutenai, and an unsolved murder of two miners dating back to 1884—hardly surprising given the almost complete absence of British Columbia law enforcement. The province provided one constable for an area roughly the size of Ireland. Herchmer suggested sending in a large force of Mounted Police, but Ottawa was still bickering with Victoria about who should pay. Matters came to a head in March 1887 when the British Columbia constable arrested a Kutenai man named Kapula for the murders. Isadore and a group of armed followers freed Kapula and ordered the constable and the government surveyor out of the area.

This incident could not be ignored. The commissioner of Indian Affairs for the North-West Territories, Edgar Dewdney, investigated and reported that, in his opinion, the Kutenai had been treated unjustly. He feared that if violence broke out, it might easily spread across the mountains and south into the United States, where the authorities were already sending troops to deal with that possibility. In May, Assistant Commissioner Herchmer was sent back in and managed to persuade Chief Isadore that he should surrender Kapula when the Mounted Police arrived in the area and were prepared to conduct a proper trial.[32] Steele had received orders to be ready to move his division to British Columbia in May, but it was the next month before he was instructed to leave.[33] On June 10, "D" Division got on the narrow-gauge railway, known as the Dunmore Line, which connected to the CPR just outside Medicine Hat. Even then there was a delay caused by a false report of an uprising by Métis and First Nations near Swift Current. Steele took his command there and sent out patrols that found nothing threatening.

After ten days at Swift Current, it was obvious that nothing was going to happen there and the commissioner telegraphed Steele to come to headquarters at Regina for a consultation. There is no record of what passed between the two men at that time but it seems likely that Herchmer was reassuring himself about his subordinate, who had reacted to discipline like a good soldier. Steele may have considered leaving the Force but he showed no signs of joining the group of discontented officers whom the commissioner believed were trying to undermine his authority.³⁴ Certainly the tone of Herchmer's communications changed at this point; he now started his letters, "My Dear Steele," a distinct contrast to the earlier cold formality. After a couple of days at Regina, Steele was back at Swift Current organizing the special train that would carry men, horses, and equipment to British Columbia.

There was an overnight stop in Calgary on June 27 to take on a few extra horses and to feed and water the rest, then the train moved west through the mountains to Golden. Here they met the assistant commissioner and Steele got the latest intelligence about what was happening with Chief Isadore and his people. The plan was to load "D" Division and all of its horses and equipment on a sternwheel steamer called the *Duchess*, which offered service up the river through Lower Columbia Lake (now Windermere) to the end of Columbia Lake at Canal Flats. From there a pack trail ran south for sixty kilometres to the scene of the conflict. The *Duchess* turned out to be a rather dubious vessel. She was built by a former CPR surveyor named F.P. Armstrong out of scrap lumber left over from the railway construction and employed some very tired boilers and machinery previously used on boats in the St. Lawrence.³⁵ The *Duchess* had made a couple of trips upriver in 1886 but the contract to move the Mounted Police and more than sixty tons of supplies was her first big engagement.

The move to the Kootenay Valley got off to a terrible start. Just before they were due to leave Golden, Steele's senior NCO, Sergeant Major Tom Lake, committed suicide while suffering from what Steele described as "a severe attack of neuralgia."³⁶ There may have been more to it than that since Lake had been borrowing money from people in the Force. Lake had joined the Police in 1874 and Steele was undoubtedly sad at losing an old comrade. He paid an outstanding account of $25 that Lake left with a merchant at Golden and then spent several years trying to recover it from the government.³⁷ After the bad omen of Lake's death things got worse.

Captain Armstrong could not resist the temptation to overload the boat on the first trip and she promptly capsized. No lives were lost but almost all the supplies that did not sink immediately floated off down the Columbia. After two weeks' delay, the Mounted Police finally got away.

Steele was able to find another boat named the *Clive*, although this one was even less prepossessing than the *Duchess*, having been constructed from an old railway construction barge and parts of a steam tractor. The *Clive* managed two trips up the lakes before she too foundered, but by that time the *Duchess* had been refloated and was back in action. Between them the two vessels managed to get enough freight upriver to sustain Steele's men through the winter. When Steele got to the Kootenays in the last week of July, the first order of business was to select a site for the post. Assistant Commissioner Herchmer had recommended a place near a tributary called Six Mile Creek but Steele and his medical officer, Dr. F. Hamilton Powell, rejected it because the creek ran out of a large swamp.[38] They found a better location on high ground at the confluence of Wild Horse Creek and the Kootenay River. The site had the additional advantage of being close to a ferry operated by a man named Robert Galbraith, who also had the contract to pack in supplies for the police from the head of navigation on the lakes.

In addition to Surgeon Powell, Steele had two recently appointed inspectors under his command. Inspector Zachary Taylor Wood was a graduate of the Royal Military College who had already proved to be a very competent officer at Fort Macleod. He would go on to a distinguished career in the Mounted Police and became one of Steele's trusted friends. Inspector Albert Huot joined "D" Division shortly after Wood and turned out to be equally capable. Steele was able to turn the business of constructing the post over to these two while he set about dealing with the issue that had brought the Mounted Police there. He immediately issued an invitation to Isadore to visit the police encampment. The Chief came on August

20 and a discussion between the two men resulted in Kapula being handed over a few days later to await trial.

In his annual report and in his memoirs, Steele presents the encounter and its outcome as a simple matter of ordering Isadore to turn over the fugitive and the chief obeying. In fact, it was a situation that required a significant degree of tact and negotiating skill. The Kutenai were well armed, quite unused to government authority, and had strong connections both south of the border and across the Rockies. Father Nicolas Coccola, the Oblate priest who arrived at St. Eugene's Mission in September 1887, was quite startled to find that the Kutenai habitually came to church with guns and knives in their belts.[39] The mission, a few kilometres up the St. Mary's River from where it joined the Kootenay at Galbraith's Ferry, was a very important factor in Steele's success in coming to a peaceful resolution of the tense situation in the valley. Itinerant Catholic missionaries had travelled through the area from time to time since the early 19th century. Their influence was consolidated with the opening of St. Eugene's by Father Leon Fouquet in 1874.

The Oblate Fathers in British Columbia by this time were following the system introduced by Bishop Paul Durieu, who had adapted it from the Jesuits he worked with in the American Pacific Northwest.[40] The strategy emphasized community building centred around strict enforcement of church attendance and morality. The priests organized the election of chiefs and sub-chiefs in charge of government in the village. There were "watchmen" who monitored religious practices for signs of backsliding into paganism, "policemen" who administered punishments on the orders of the chief, catechists and the "bell-ringer" who summoned people to church. Punishments for transgressions like polygamy, gambling, and drunkenness were harsh, usually flogging administered publicly during feast days. Steele witnessed one of these events and noted in his diary, "Annual flogging administered to whores, adulterers, drunkards and gamblers. A ____ and 30 others punished in that way. All seemed contented."[41]

The system invested the chiefs like Isadore with an unusual amount of authority and his cooperation was critical. Just as the Mounted Police arrived, the priest who had founded St. Eugene's was replaced by Father Coccola. Fortunately for Steele, the transition went smoothly for two reasons. In the first place Coccola was well trained; before he arrived he had learned enough of the Kutenai language to communicate and he had great strength of character. Secondly, he already knew and respected Steele. Coccola had arrived in British Columbia from France in 1880 and after some instruction at New Westminster, was assigned to Kamloops. His first years there were spent among the local First Nations but when construction began on the CPR in 1883 he was instructed to offer his services to the workers in the camps. Steele immediately welcomed him and provided all the assistance he could.[42] Working closely with clergy of all kinds was a consistent theme in Steele's career in the Mounted Police. He recognized instinctively that law enforcement worked best when it came from a sense of community values, and churches of all denominations were hugely important allies. Steele's own religious beliefs can best be described as lukewarm and conventional, but he easily formed alliances and friendships with men of the cloth.[43]

Both Steele and Father Coccola recognized that Isadore and his people had been treated unfairly by the British Columbia authorities. They also knew that, although some additional reserve land would be set aside, it would be much less than the Kutenai claimed (Isadore ended up with 680 acres, the MLA, Col. Baker, who had acquired the disputed area at Joseph's Prairie, had 32,000 acres).[44] In September the British Columbia officials, in their usual ham-fisted way, without consulting the Kutenai who were on their annual trip to Idaho to buy winter supplies, allotted the additional reserves and departed. They left Steele with instructions "to acquaint Isadore and his Indians with their decision."[45] This took the form of a letter outlining the boundaries and concluding with a pompous lecture about how lucky Isadore was to be forgiven for making trouble.⁴⁶ There was nothing Steele could do to change the reserve land allotted to the Kutenai; that possibility would not emerge until a Canadian Supreme Court decision in 2014. The least harmful alternative was therefore to persuade them to work with what they had been given.

Steele set about doing that as best he could. One thing that was in his power was the case of Kapula. Steele quickly organized a trial, examined the almost complete lack of evidence and set him free. That demonstration that the police were not completely on the side of the settlers helped set the stage. When Isadore returned from Idaho on November 7, the real negotiation began. The chief once again asked for Joseph's Prairie to be returned. Steele told him that was not possible but that he would be paid for agricultural improvements to the site. Isadore then requested that an irrigation ditch be dug to his reserve land and Steele agreed to have his men do it; the work was completed before the end of the year.⁴⁷ He also promised help to build a school at the mission. With Father Coccola's support, these few concessions were enough to win Isadore's compliance. Steele had essentially accomplished what he was sent to British Columbia to do by December 1887, but he recommended that he and his men remain until the following summer to make sure that all parties abided by their agreements.

While Steele was conducting the delicate negotiations to resolve the situation with Isadore, he had to cope with other urgent tasks. One of these was a severe outbreak of typhoid fever. The disease was not fully understood at the time, although there was a general awareness that contaminated water was the cause. Surgeon Powell had taken great care with the selection of the site of what became Fort Steele and was baffled when eleven men, himself included, came down with the disease in late August.⁴⁸ In fact, typhoid typically takes a month to fully develop and the first symptoms began to appear in a few of the men just after the division arrived, making it almost certain that it had been contracted at Golden or during the trip upriver. The office of the Indian agent was taken over as a hospital and the British Columbia Indian commissioner, Dr. Israel Powell, who happened to be visiting at the time, filled in for his Mounted Police namesake when Surgeon Powell fell ill until a replacement could be sent in from Calgary. Three men died and the other eight gradually recovered.

The healthy members of "D" Division began building the post so that they could move out of their tents before winter set in. This was a very sizeable construction project, including barracks for the constables, quarters for the officers and sergeants, an orderly room with jail cells, hospital, stables, storage buildings, and workshops—eight major buildings in all. There was plenty of suitable pine timber nearby but the trees had to be cut, trimmed, hauled to the site, peeled, and cut to size. The 1,400 or so logs were then assembled into buildings. Rough lumber for the floors was rafted from a sawmill upriver at Wawa. A local contractor provided large blocks of cedar to be hand cut into shakes for roofing. All of this was completed by the end of November. Steele was justifiably proud of the buildings and recommended that they be turned over to the British Columbia government when the NWMP left. One of the structures, the officers' quarters, was used as a provincial police office for many years and survives at Fort Steele Heritage Town to this day.

By the beginning of 1888, all of "D" Division's essential tasks had been accomplished and boredom began to set in. Steele at least knew that they would probably be pulled out in the summer, but his men had no such reassurance. They were stuck in a remote valley with very little to do and morale became a serious problem. In the depth of winter, Steele tried to keep his men busy repairing equipment and adding finishing touches such as sidewalks to the post. The officers gave lectures on the law and constables' duties. It was not entirely successful. Crime was almost non-existent in the Kootenay Valley that year but the cells at Fort Steele were occupied by mounted policemen who had committed various breaches of discipline. Steele kept them busy cutting firewood. Discontent even spread to the normally reliable NCOs. At the end of January, Steele found it necessary to reprimand a corporal for causing "petty annoyances" to the men.[49] In March two sergeants got into a fight in the mess; both were "reprimanded severely" and one was sent off to another division.[50]

By April the snow had gone and Steele was able to keep his men busier. The narrow valley with its two entrances north and south meant that the kind of extensive patrolling carried out on the prairies was neither possible nor necessary. That left training. The division was put through many long hours of drill, both mounted and on foot. Steele set up a firing range a few kilometres upriver at a place called Bummer's Flats so that the constables could compete in shooting competitions with their pistols and carbines. These activities certainly helped. A total of eight men had deserted in the fall of 1887. Desertion was a constant problem for the Mounted Police in the 19th century but these numbers were unusually high, as Steele noted in his annual report. Isolation and boredom, combined with the ease of reaching the United States, were the reasons. It was much more convenient to desert from Fort Steele than from any of the prairie posts. All that was necessary was a stolen boat and the river would take one rapidly downstream across the border without any serious possibility of pursuit.[51] By the spring of 1888, Steele's disciplinary measures were taking effect and there was only one more attempt to abscond, this one unsuccessful.[52]

Tedium was just as much a problem for Steele himself. He could socialize with his officers, and did so, especially after Inspector Wood's wife joined him. He often spent the evenings playing his favourite card game, whist, with the families of Robert Galbraith, the ferry operator, and the postmaster, Charles Clark. He read books, including a biography of Daniel Webster, and, of course, he wrote letters to friends and family.[53] Two or three months of these sedentary diversions along with hours at his desk working on his monthly reports, pay sheets, and official correspondence seem, not surprisingly, to have given him concerns about putting on weight.

He began taking long walks, four to six kilometres a day, usually in the afternoons. Sometimes he visited local ranchers and other people he knew, but mainly it was for the exercise. Riding had always been his favourite form of exercise, but in March he was thrown from his horse, dislocating his shoulder, and it took the better part of a month to recover.[54]

Although Steele had recommended keeping the division in British Columbia for a full year, by the end of April he was becoming increasingly impatient to leave. It had already been decided that the unit would travel back to Fort Macleod through the Crowsnest Pass, taking as much of their equipment as possible on pack horses. The rest would have to go by boat to Golden to be shipped by rail to Alberta, or if that was too expensive, sold off before they left. Steele started to work on planning this part of the move on April 26.[55] A month later there was still no word about when the division would move, but on May 28, Steele ordered a party to look at the Crowsnest trail and do any necessary brush cutting to clear it.[56] He hopefully began working on bringing his accounts up to date, but as May passed into June, no word arrived. Steele's frustration showed through in a rare complaint is his diary: "Terribly dull here. It is simply frightful. If I had no place to go in the evenings occasionally I do not know what I could do."[57] A week later he noted: "Did nothing but loaf. Fell asleep in the afternoon and dreamt of insubordination drunkenness etc."[58]

Finally on June 18, a letter arrived from the commissioner that the division would depart at the end of July. Steele had already arranged with the legendary frontiersman John George "Kootenay" Brown to set up caches of basic food supplies ("oats and biscuits") along the trail and he now instructed Brown to proceed.[59] He decided to organize a Dominion Day celebration with sports and speeches to mark the departure of the unit. The event was a great success with participation from the whole community, and "Indians carried off most of the prizes in everything."[60] At the end of the festivities Isadore and a large deputation came to see Steele. The chief, "expressed himself as being very much pleased with the way he and tribe had been treated and that he will never forget the police and will when I am far away remember me. Said that the behaviour of the men was splendid and honourable."[61]

After that, the rest of the month was mainly tedious waiting. The weather was oppressively hot, so much so that Steele indulged in a rare swim in Wild Horse Creek. The mosquitoes were so bad that the Kutenai set small fires all along the valley to create smudges to drive them away. Fortunately none of these developed into a large-scale blaze. In the middle of the month, Assistant Commissioner W.M. Herchmer arrived to inspect the division and help with the preparations for the move. On July 21 Steele, Herchmer, two constables, and "Kootenay" Brown set out to examine the trail to the Crowsnest Pass. As usual on these trips, they went only a few kilometres the first day, then camped and made a very early start the next day (4:20 A.M.) to avoid the heat.[62] In two days they reached the ranch and trading post of Michael Phillips at Tobacco Plains just north of the international boundary. From there the trail to Crowsnest ran up the valley of the Elk River toward the pass. Satisfied that the route was suitable for so many men and horses, they returned to Fort Steele, arriving back late on July 25.

On August 4 the equipment and supplies that could not be economically shipped out were auctioned off. Then it was several days of goodbyes to the Galbraiths, the Clarks and other friends, including Father Coccola. At last, on August 7 at 7:00 A.M., the cavalcade moved out. There was a delay a few kilometres down the trail where Steele had arranged to have the scene recorded for posterity: "Halted to have the whole train photographed. Mr. Bourne came to meet us at Upper Fish Lake and did it there."[63] This diary entry is interesting because it is the first recorded example of Steele's lifelong love of recording significant moments in his life with photographs. What his hot, sweaty, mosquito-harassed men thought of the delay is not recorded.

On the second day out the weather turned cooler, to the relief of men and animals. The trip was almost leisurely, leaving very early each morning and stopping usually by noon after covering twenty-five to thirty kilometres. There were few difficulties on the trip, although they found that squirrels had eaten sizeable quantities of the oats cached along the trail. On August 12 they made a sharp right turn where Michel Creek flows into the Elk River (where the town of Sparwood is now located) and followed the creek up to its headwaters near the continental divide. On August 13, they began moving through the pass and Steele, with the trip nearly complete, began to relax and enjoy the scenery:

*Reached the summit in four miles and then descended in the valley of the Creeks forming Old Man R. middle fork. Passed a fine little lake [probably Summit Lake] with good feed for horses and wood and water. Then moving along the edge of a high Mt met Lees Lake, a beautiful sheet of water surrounded by Mts. Passed the wonderful cave with the stream and saw the waterfall on the opposite side.*[64]

On August 14, the division arrived at the police post in the pass and found an inspector from Fort Macleod waiting with teams and wagons to take over the loads from the pack horses. From there it was an easy ride to Pincher Creek and, on the evening of August 16, the division reached Fort Macleod and camped along the river near the post. Steele congratulated his men for the year's work and for performing well on the trip. Then he was greeted by his friend, Superintendent Macdonell, who invited him to meet his new wife and eat with them. Steele was happy to do so. And Macdonell's wife was not the only surprise. He noted in his diary, "Took supper at Macdonells and met his wife and Mrs Gillis and Miss Harwood came home at 11.30."[65] Sam Steele's life was about to change.

# 5 || The Love of His Life
Marie Harwood
1888-1890

IN THE FALL OF 1888, when he returned to Fort Macleod from British Columbia, Sam Steele was forty years old. He clearly enjoyed the company of women, and although his life to this point had afforded very few opportunities to spend time with them, he seems to have had at least one serious relationship.[1] As a mounted policeman, the women with whom he came in contact were almost exclusively the wives of fellow officers or First Nations women, but for Steele the latter would have been out of the question in terms of marriage or an extra-marital affair. He had seen what that had done to the career of Superintendent James Morrow Walsh, and affairs of the heart would never be allowed to jeopardize his own ambitions. As a policeman Steele came into contact with quite a number of prostitutes but there is no evidence that he availed himself of their charms, although some of his constables certainly did. Steele might have started thinking about marriage as early as 1878 when he was promoted to inspector, but it seems much more likely that he was too busy until January 1882, when he took a short leave to go back to Ontario. The search for a suitable marriage partner was probably part of his agenda on the trip, but his leave had to be cut short when he was ordered to Ottawa to take a group of recruits west. With the CPR construction, the Rebellion and the sojourn in British Columbia, there were no other opportunities for the next six years.

Fort Macleod was not a much more likely place to find a wife in 1888 than the other places Steele had been serving. There are even some indications that he might have given up on the prospect of marriage by this time. In an early letter to his future wife, after professing his love, he wrote, "If anyone had told me that I was to be what I now am, I would never have believed them. I used to consider the thing absurd but I find *that it is real.*"[2] The woman who brought about this revelation was Marie Elizabeth de Lotbinière Harwood. Marie was twenty-nine years old, petite and dark-haired.[3] She had come to Fort Macleod from her home in Vaudreuil just outside Montreal to visit her aunt Minnie, who had recently married Steele's friend and colleague, Superintendent A.R. Macdonell. Minnie was nearly the same age as Marie and was much more like a cousin than an aunt; the two women remained close friends for life. Although Minnie apparently did not know it until much later, Macdonell had proposed to Marie earlier and had been turned down. The visit must, at the start, have been more than a little tense for Marie until she discovered whether or not her relationship with Minnie would survive.

Marie Harwood, known as "Maye" to family and friends, was the second child and oldest daughter of Robert William Harwood, seigneur of Vaudreuil and a former Conservative MP.[4] The Harwoods, while not wealthy, were certainly members of the Quebec elite.[5] The original Canadian Harwood, Robert Unwin Harwood, came to Canada in 1822 and married Marie Louise Josephte de Lotbinière, daughter of Eustache Gaspard de Lotbinière, a landowner and political figure. Their children intermarried with other prominent Quebec families, notably the Taschereaus, the Panets and the Bellefeuilles. Robert William Harwood married Mary Charlotte McGillis, and the family appear to have been completely at home in both languages. Marie's

Steele in 1890, shortly after he met Marie. [BPSC, 2008.1.2.1.6.1.7.2]

six surviving brothers (two died in infancy) all attended St. Laurent College for high school, then either McGill or Bishop's universities. Marie and her three sisters seem to have been educated at convent schools, then at home. The family was warm and close growing up.

The marriage proposal from Alex Macdonell was not the first that Marie Harwood had received. By 1888 she had acquired a reputation of being very choosy and she was fast approaching the end of what was considered a marriageable age for someone of that period and social class. The immediate impetus for the trip west seems to have been some mild family disapproval over her rejection of a proposal by William Drayner, who later married her sister Louise. It seems highly unlikely that she went to Fort Macleod as a tourist to experience the wild frontier. Did Minnie hint that there were eligible bachelors about and few single women? Perhaps it was a combination of these motives. In any case, there is very little doubt about what happened when she and Sam Steele met that day in August. The two were instantly physically attracted to each other and there were less romantic considerations. Sam certainly saw Marie as a woman of sophistication and social position. In her eyes, Sam was not just a hero of the frontier; he was a man with a secure position on his way up.

In a letter to Sam after they were engaged, Marie admitted that the shadow of spinsterhood was on her mind:

> *I saw an old friend of mine this afternoon whom I had not seen for over two years. She found me looking so well & if anything younger & asked for my secret happiness! I might have told her, only she made a most unhappy marriage some eight years ago. She was a pretty girl & clever too, but fear of not finding a husband if she waited too long, made her accept a man in no way worthy of her. I told her at the time but she would not listen. Now she says "Ah! Maye you were wise to wait!" She is older than I by at least three years & is faded & careworn looking when only in her prime. Of course I too begin to feel the weight of the many years passed over my head, as another has lately been added to the number.*[6]

But as the passage makes clear, she was determined to wait for the right man and there was no doubt from the start that Sam was the one.

At the dinners at the Macdonell home, followed usually by music or whist, Sam and Marie for a month put on an elaborate show of ignoring each other, fooling none of the observers present. Beyond the home socializing, Fort Macleod offered little in the way of entertainment. But perhaps Miss Harwood might like to go riding? She did not know how to ride. In that case, who better to teach her than the former chief riding instructor of the Mounted Police? Steele was very busy at work in early September preparing for his new job and for the arrival of the commissioner on a tour of inspection in the middle of the month. The social occasion of the season was the fall race meet September 20–23, attended by Commissioner Herchmer and his wife, along with all the officers from Fort Macleod and Lethbridge and the local ranching elite. The chance to observe each other in this larger setting led to an exchange of notes, in which Marie agreed to equitation lessons.[7] The first excursion saw the roles completely reversed. Sam was thrown from his horse and Marie rushed to his assistance. He was not badly injured but the incident broke the ice and allowed the mutual attraction to break through the stiff Victorian social conventions. As Steele put it in a letter after Marie had returned to Vaudreuil, "I do not think that the fall I got when we took our first ride has done me any harm. I would not have *missed that fall for a great deal* for I am sure it made us better acquainted did it not?"[8]

This episode took place in late September and after that the relationship blossomed quickly, although Marie refused to allow Sam to kiss her until after they were engaged.[9] Fortunately for the course of the romance, the weather that fall at Fort Macleod was benign, as early fall in Alberta can sometimes be. The two rode daily for as long as four hours at a time. On October 18, Sam proposed and although Marie did not say yes, he was sufficiently encouraged by her response to repeat the proposal the next day. This time she promised to give him an answer the following week and strongly hinted that it would be positive. Steele was elated and confided to his diary, "I most likely will remember the ride for some time to come."[10] He clearly recognized the delay for what it was; Marie did not want to appear too eager. The following week, October 25, she accepted the proposal. The Macdonells discreetly withdrew from their living room to allow this to happen. Sam quickly got in touch with his brother in Winnipeg to order an engagement ring.

There followed a month when they saw each other almost every day, riding as often as the weather permitted. For Sam at least these outings were blissful. A typical diary entry was, "Rode out in the afternoon with Miss Harwood and enjoyed it immensely."[11] Marie gamely went along and claimed to enjoy them as well but after the fall of 1888 there is no indication that she ever rode a horse again. For his part, Sam professed a deep enthusiasm for music that had not been apparent earlier in his life. There were some potential snags before the engagement could become public. Marie was a devout Catholic and Steele was a Protestant in a period when these differences were regarded with great seriousness. Steele was not concerned but Marie's father and the church might put up roadblocks. There are hints that Sam, and perhaps Marie as well, consulted the famous Oblate priest, Father Albert Lacombe, on the matter and that he gave them his blessing, with the usual provisos about raising the children as Catholics.

It is hard to overestimate what a barrier religion could be in 19th-century Canada. Catholic–Protestant hostility was at the root of almost all the serious political crises in the country for half a century after Confederation from schools in Manitoba to conscription during the First World War. Religious riots, like the ones in Montreal in 1853 provoked by virulently anti-Catholic diatribes of the Italian activist Alessandro Gavazzi, which brought soldiers into the streets and killed ten people, were not uncommon; one historian counted twenty-two in the city of Toronto between 1870 and 1889.[12] Although Sir John A. Macdonald managed to negotiate the religious divisions within his party, the two strongest candidates to succeed him were both victims of the religious prejudices of the day. D'Alton McCarthy left the Conservatives because he could not stomach the idea of state-supported Catholic schools in Ontario and Manitoba. The brilliant Nova Scotia lawyer and politician, Sir John Thompson, was considered ineligible to lead the party because, raised a Baptist, he had married a Catholic and converted. The Conservatives only turned to him in desperation after Macdonald's death when the party was in terminal decline. Nor were the Liberals immune: Sir Wilfrid Laurier lost his minister of the Interior and western lieutenant, Clifford Sifton, over the Catholic school question.

With these concerns weighing heavily on them, in early December Sam drove Marie to Lethbridge where they got on the narrow-gauge railway to the Dunmore junction. There, Marie took the train for Montreal and home to announce the engagement and, they hoped, start making preparations for the wedding. The separation immediately set off a passionate correspondence. The two exchanged lengthy letters filled with expressions of love and longing two or three times a week. The first order of business, however, was for Steele to seek the formal permission of Marie's father. His letter was dated December 3, 1888, the day before Marie left Fort Macleod, and was hand-delivered. It was suitably stiff and Victorian and is worth quoting in full:

*Dear Sir:*

*You will, no doubt, be much surprised at the receipt of this letter from one who is an utter stranger, and especially as it is to ask you for the hand of your daughter—Miss Harwood, in marriage. I have only known her for a few months, but love her dearly, and should you regard with favor this request, will do my utmost to prove a kind and faithful husband to her.*

*I am a Protestant, which may be to you a serious objection, but I understand what the rules of your Church are in such cases, and I am ready to promise all that is required.*

*I am a Superintendent in the Northwest Mounted Police, and a soldier by profession, of good standing in the corps, and have held important posts in the interests of the Govt.*

*I naturally feel much diffidence in saying even what I have just stated and must leave to others any remarks with reference to any merits I may or may not possess.*

*Hoping to receive your favorable consideration of this, to me, all important matter, and that you will kindly favor me with an early reply.*

*I am, Dear Sir*
*Yours Sincerely,*
S.B. STEELE

Sam did not have to wait long for the reply. Robert Harwood sent it by return mail:

*Dear Sir*

*In answer to your letter handed to me by my daughter Maye, I give my consent relying on her good judgment in choosing her companion for life. I may tell you that she has been an ever obedient, loving daughter to father and mother. Therefore she should be a faithful loving wife. She reached us safe and sound.*

*11th December/88*
*Vaudreuil*
*Yours Truly*
R. HARWOOD

Robert Harwood was evidently not at all hesitant to give his consent. He had other daughters to marry off and family dynamics dictated that relations would be much easier if the oldest was first. The tone of the letter, along with the fact that consent was not solicited until Marie had talked to her father face to face, showed that her happiness and well-being were important to him.

Now that the engagement was official (it was hardly a surprise to Marie's parents since rumours from Fort Macleod had reached Montreal social circles well before she got back), the business of preparing for the marriage could begin. The wedding was planned for some time after Christmas, 1889. Convention mandated a two-year delay; in a letter Sam referred to "the stereotyped *two years.*"[13] He wanted it much sooner but Marie was determined not to rush things.[14] The compromise was a year and they reminded each other in the letters that they were, after all, not teenagers. Sam's ideas about the proper relationships between men and women were unconventional for the time, as he recorded in an interesting conversation on the subject of marriage with some of his fellow officers:

> We were talking yesterday evening in the mess about many things and among the topics, the question came up as to what kind of woman each would prefer for a wife. I said I preferred one with a will of her own and not one who would blindly follow where I would lead, and who was so sensible that she could make allowances for her own faults and mine. Starnes and all the rest said you can never be happy with a girl with a will like that. You are strong will[ed] and proud and you could never agree. I replied that I was not so inclined that I was not ashamed to yield when wrong. I could not convince them that a man should not marry a doll or a simpering little goose.[15]

Marie evidently agreed with those sentiments and responded, "You have won all the *mature love* of a *mature woman* who has given you all her heart."[16]

She hoped that he might be able to visit Vaudreuil at some time during the year to see her and meet her family. That was out of the question because Sam was too busy with his work. Fort Macleod was the only NWMP command apart from the headquarters at Regina that had more than one division. On December 8 Steele had taken over the command, which included both "H" Division, commanded by his friend, Superintendent A.R. Macdonell, and "D" Division headed by Inspector Z.T. Wood, who had been with him at Fort Steele. He was happy with his subordinates but not with the state of the command when he took over, as he confided to Marie:

> This is a fearful post for work. I have scarcely a minute to myself. I do not think that my predecessor "killed" himself with it, but there was a great deal of fault finding about it, and I find that if one does his

duty, he will have his hands full, all of the officers are kept upon the steady run, and then they cannot do it all. I am afraid my pet that if there had been as much to do when you were here I would never have been able to make time at all unless we sat up late as when Mrs Mac thought you were up too late.[17]

The lieutenant governor of the North-West Territories was due to visit Fort Macleod soon and the governor general was expected later in the year. The burden of paperwork was not made any easier when Steele's clerk deserted at the end of January.[18] As the commanding officer at Fort Macleod, Steele was entitled to the house on the base that had been occupied by his predecessor, Superintendent Neale, who was retiring. He had at no time in his life had more than a single room for his personal space and he found the situation a little difficult to deal with. Much of his correspondence with Marie in the early months of 1889 concerned the novel problem of getting the place ready for the two of them. There was a piano for sale in the town, and after much consultation he bought it. On other items of furniture, he admitted that he was out of his depth:

> I think it would be better to wait for the furniture until you and I are together in Montreal. It is a good place and only one line of railway from there to Dunmore and therefore less delay. I will not get anything that you have not chosen dear unless if you particularly wish it. A man is a fool that would do such a thing.[19]

Among the things that kept Steele busy early in 1889 were his judicial duties. He noted in his annual report, "Superintendent Macdonell and Inspector Wood were the only other Justices of the Peace, besides myself, until the arrival of Inspector Begin, and they shared the work of that exceedingly disagreeable office."[20] Steele, like other NWMP officers, had been hearing cases as a justice of the peace for years, but had never before found the responsibility particularly onerous. The difference this year was the growing public resentment over the territorial liquor laws. When Canada established the government of the North-West Territories in 1870, it was made illegal to manufacture, import or sell liquor. The objective, of course, was to keep booze out of the hands of the First Nations, and both their leaders and the government agreed that prohibition was essential to achieving this end. Many among the small settler population resented the restriction and put sufficient pressure on the government that a system of permits was introduced allowing individuals designated by the lieutenant governor to import liquor for their own use.

With the defeat of the 1885 Rebellion and the completion of the CPR the situation began to change rapidly, especially in the growing towns of the North-West Territories. When a judge ruled that the holder of a permit need not keep the liquor in his home, the law became effectively unenforceable and for the first time in the history of the NWMP, numbers of otherwise law-abiding citizens resented their activities. As Steele stated bluntly in his annual report, "I may say that nearly all classes in this district are strongly opposed to the existing liquor laws, and there are but few who will not assist either in smuggling or screening the smugglers."[21] In private he complained to Marie:

> *The longer a man lives and the more he tries in a public position to do what is right and the more friends he makes, the more his enemies will increase in number and perhaps in power. One who lives the calm life of one who is not working for a Government can form no idea of the hatred that exists sometimes or generally in a position like that which I hold.*[22]

|| Another matter that occupied Steele's attention was a cross-border raid by some of the Kainai from the reserve near Fort Macleod. In April, several young men went south and stole a number of horses from a rancher near Big Sandy, Montana, and from the Gros Ventres. The latter pursued them and forced them to abandon most of the

horses but in the accompanying firefight, two Gros Ventres were killed. Steele was not overly concerned at first. He wrote to Marie, "I have been powwowing with Red Crow, North Axe and the Indians today. Some of the horse thieves gave themselves up today and the men caught two more so there are only two yet to catch."[23] The other two did not turn up and that led to a dangerous and embarrassing incident. In July, the Kainai held their annual Sun Dance and the sergeant in charge of the detachment at Stand Off spotted Calf Robe, one of the alleged participants in the raid. He and two constables tried to arrest Calf Robe who responded by pointing a gun at the police, who were quickly surrounded by a large, threatening crowd. The police sensibly withdrew.

The following day Steele sent Inspector Z.T. Wood with a larger party to the reserve, where they arrested five men and charged them with obstructing the police. This was a serious offence that could not be tried before a justice of the peace so the men were committed for trial at the next sitting of the Territorial Supreme Court in August. Steele and the Crown prosecutor believed that the police had acted correctly but what happened next caught them both by surprise. Chief Red Crow, supported by the Indian agent, asked for bail for the men and they were released. When the case came to trial they argued that it should be dismissed because the sergeant who made the original attempt to arrest Calf Robe had no warrant. To Steele's dismay, the judge agreed and threw the case out.[24] Whether or not Steele was distracted by thoughts of his forthcoming marriage, he did not handle this incident well. If he had communicated effectively with Red Crow and the agent, he would have realized that the chief was as anxious as he was to stop incursions of this kind. The Kainai and the Gros Ventres had reached their own agreement a couple of years earlier to stop cross-border raids and this was a direct violation.[25] The ham-handed arrest effort at a sacred ceremony like the Sun Dance only served to decrease the authority of the police.[26]

The hundreds of letters that passed between Sam and Marie in 1889 were very largely focused on the details of their relationship and plans for the forthcoming marriage. He occasionally commented on incidents arising from his work and local Fort Macleod gossip. It is therefore somewhat surprising to find frequent references to one of the more obscure political issues of the day—the Jesuit Estates controversy. In the spring of 1889, the Quebec legislature attempted to solve a problem that went back more than a century. In 1774, the Roman Catholic Church had dissolved the Society of Jesus and its extensive land holdings in Canada reverted to the government. When the order was restored by the Catholic Church in 1842, Jesuit representatives in Canada began to ask for compensation. The Quebec government was willing enough to provide the money but other religious orders and the church hierarchy in Quebec could not agree on how to divide it up. The government's solution in 1889 was to pass an act referring the question to the Vatican.

This seemed logical to most Quebeckers but the Orange Order and other Protestant extremists were outraged. The idea that the Pope would be asked to rule on a Canadian political issue was, they said, intolerable interference in Canada's affairs. Since most of the outraged opponents of the legislation were outside the province, they demanded that Ottawa use its constitutional power to disallow the law. Prime Minister John A. Macdonald realized that disallowance would set off a major political crisis with Quebec and quickly made common cause with Liberal leader Wilfrid Laurier to oppose the idea. Thirteen Ontario Tories ignored their leader and voted in favour of disallowance. They subsequently formed their own party, the Equal Rights Association, for the 1896 election but managed to win only a single seat.[27]

Sam Steele was concerned about this issue because the leader of the group was his hometown MP, D'Alton McCarthy. He worried that McCarthy's anti-Catholic diatribes might lead members of

Marie's family to think that he shared these views or even that he might be a member of the Orange Order.²⁸ And in fact, he had been, as he finally admitted in a letter in July:

> When I was about twenty years old, I was among a great many of them but was not bigoted in the least. None of my family had ever belonged. I had no place to go in the evenings and I was coaxed to join. I attended for about three months but have never been in any of their lodges since nor acknowledged them in any way. I have no sympathy with them, although large numbers of them simply belong to them to gain popularity. I knew I could gain lots of it by being an active member but I did not for I bitterly regretted the step which in a moment of youthful folly I had taken I do not even know enough of them now to enter a lodge without being with another member of the order...I hope you will forgive me for not telling you before and that it will not be necessary for you to say anything about it as it does not really matter. My relatives were quite as much horrified at my step as the most devout Catholics could have been, and my elder brother of whom I spoke made me feel ashamed of myself.²⁹

McCarthy was also Steele's most powerful political supporter whose influence would vanish if he left the Conservative Party. The year 1889 was in many ways a high point in the history of the NWMP; they had enough men to carry out their duties, and apart from annoyances like the liquor laws, the country seemed increasingly calm and prosperous. There was talk within the Force that a second assistant commissioner was needed to help administer the growing network of posts across the prairies. Steele intended to be first in line if this position materialized, although he did not expect anything to happen soon. Father Lacombe wrote a letter of support for him and his family members in Ontario were doing what they could.³⁰ For the time being at least, he was happy to receive assurances from both the commissioner and the comptroller of the Force, Fred White, that he would remain at Fort Macleod for several years.³¹

Mounted Police officers were reasonably well paid by the standards of the time but Steele and others were always on the lookout for legitimate sources of additional income. In the summer of 1889 he and his friend, Superintendent Macdonell, became interested in a potential oil discovery in what is now Waterton National Park. There were seepages there of very light crude oil, known at the time as "coal oil." This was known to be a valuable commodity ever since the first North American discoveries near Sarnia, Ontario, in the 1850s, although the underlying geology was barely understood. The law treated oil wells as mines, so the procedure for prospective producers was to stake surface claims and start digging or possibly drilling with the primitive equipment available at the time. At the end of July Steele reported to Marie:

> *Lex has come back and has got a claim each for us and some for them. It is genuine coal oil and plenty of it. The owners of claims meet on Friday to decide upon the best course to adopt about the sale of the property. There is none left all is in the hands of the people here except one claim."*[32]

Steele was doubtful about the potential, correctly as it turned out. A company was eventually formed and a well drilled in 1902 but it failed after a short time.

In October 1889, Steele hosted a visit by the governor general, Lord Stanley, on his tour of western Canada. The highlight of the event in southern Alberta was a ceremonial meeting with Chief Red Crow and others on the Blood Reserve. Although the vice-regal party was under Steele's supervision for only two days, the preparations involved were extensive. Treaty payments were made two days before the event to make sure the Kainai were in a good mood.[33] The governor general and his entourage arrived in Lethbridge by train but from there they travelled in carriages and slept in tents for a couple of days. There were only nine people in the party but they certainly did not travel light; Steele had to provide a mounted escort and fourteen four-horse teams for the party and their baggage. A dismounted honour guard was required for the ceremonies on the reserve. Men had to be brought in from outposts all over the district to take part. In the event, all went well, although Steele complained that he had almost lost his voice as a result of hours of shouting drill instructions to the men of the honour guard, while they were training for the occasion.

The governor general spent the day after the visit to the reserve at Fort Macleod inspecting the post. Steele could not resist bragging to Marie:

> *He took in every mortal thing and was highly pleased at the appearance of everything as well he might. He particularly admired the state of the horses and quarters for the men and hospital. He was very nice to the men as well. The party lunched with us and stayed some hours, his Ex having a chat with Father Lacombe and all of the rest. He created a good impression on all. He said to Dr. Grant that he was simply amazed at the efficiency of my district and that fine as the turn out at Regina was the state of affairs here far surpassed it.*[34]

After that the vice-regal tourists moved on to the enormous Cochrane Ranch, where they were treated to a wolf hunt and demonstrations of cowboy skills.

Once the governor general departed, Steele could turn to getting ready for the trip east for his marriage in the new year. He spent a good deal of time readying the house he and Marie would occupy. He admitted to her that he knew next to nothing about how to make this happen so he relied on others. It helped that the Macdonells lived in a nearly identical house so Marie could send instructions in her letters, which Sam passed on to the carpenters. Many of them included passages like this:

> *I was thinking yesterday, it would be a good idea, my pet, to have about a foot wide painted around the floors in our dining room &*

*parlor; brown would be nice. Then when we get our carpets if perchance we should decide on large rugs, the floor would be ready—a border left uncovered they say hinders the moths from causing too much havoc.*[35]

Wallpaper for the house absorbed much attention over a period of months. The nearest source of supply was Winnipeg and at first Superintendent Macdonell was deputed to buy it on a trip east. As it turned out, he was not able to find time to make the purchase. In the end the commissioner himself chose the wallpaper and brought it to Fort Macleod.[36]

The end of the year always brought a blanket of white for the Mounted Police—not snow but paperwork. Steele had his own annual report to prepare as well as supervising those of his officers. This year, in addition, there was an ominous situation emerging involving Commissioner. L.W. Herchmer and his brother, William, who had made the mistake a few years earlier of antagonizing Nicholas Flood Davin, owner of the *Regina Leader*, and MP for the area.[37] Davin had been collecting stories about mistreatment by the Herchmers from disgruntled mounted policemen since that time and now he started publishing these anonymous attacks in his newspaper. He found a willing ally in the owner of the *Fort Macleod Gazette*, C.E.D. Wood, a former NWMP constable and cousin of Inspector Z.T. Wood. Their public attacks seemed likely to bring about a public inquiry that would, at best, be very disruptive and might even end careers. Steele had reached a tenuous truce with the commissioner but he was a friend of both the Woods and was directly involved in two incidents central to the allegations of misconduct.

A constable named Thomas Craig at Fort Macleod had taken advantage of a plan that allowed part of his pay to be deducted monthly and put into a savings account. In 1887 he closed the account and withdrew the total of $538.57. Two years later it was discovered that clerks in Ottawa had mistakenly credited deductions from a different Constable Craig to the wrong account.

Thomas Craig was ordered to repay $377. He refused to do so and Steele, who had just taken over command, investigated the situation and discovered that Craig was illiterate and unable to understand the documents involved. He concluded that there had been an honest mistake. Commissioner Herchmer, however, ordered Craig arrested for fraud.[38] The most prominent lawyer in Fort Macleod, F.W. Haultain, stepped forward to defend Craig but Herchmer insisted on going ahead with the prosecution. The chief clerk in charge of NWMP administration, Laurence Fortescue, was brought all the way from Ottawa to testify at the trial on December 19, causing him, as Steele commented in a letter, "to leave his Xmas dinner behind him."[39] At the trial, when the Crown prosecutor discovered that Steele was willing to testify in Craig's favour and that Craig was willing to pay back the money in installments, the charges were abruptly dropped.[40]

The conclusion of the case meant that Steele would be able to get away by the end of the year, but its effects lingered on. He had been forced to come out in public opposition to the commissioner, who was fighting to retain his own job and was unlikely to be in a forgiving mood. The Craig case provided plenty of ammunition for Herchmer's attackers, but the second incident was much more politically damaging. At the end of the governor general's visit, Assistant Commissioner Billy Herchmer got into a card game with some of the officers at Fort Macleod, lost some money and his temper, and exchanged insults with two of them. Steele ordered Inspector D.H. Macpherson to apologize, which he reluctantly did, but the other case was different. As he explained to Marie:

> it was not pleasant to have such things but the Asst Com was to blame for he cannot touch whiskey without making an arrant fool of himself. He made a most insulting attack on Starnes calling the French Canadians the most opprobrious names. I told him it was his duty to apologize to Starnes which he did pretty quickly but he has made one

*enemy and his trip here has made him lose a great deal of the respect he ought to be possessed of.*[41]

Steele knew that if word of this incident became public, the pressure to fire the commissioner, or at least to hold an inquiry into his management of the Force, might become irresistible.

Steele fretted that the NWMP might take advantage of his presence in Quebec to have him do some recruiting, thereby infringing on his honeymoon.[42] Those fears did not materialize and at the end of the year Assistant Commissioner Billy Herchmer came to Fort Macleod to fill in while Steele was away. On January 2, 1890, Sam drove to Lethbridge in bitterly cold weather and got on the train to Montreal the following day. The cold followed him for the whole five days of the journey and turned it into a minor ordeal. The dining car broke down at Medicine Hat so there was no food until they reached Winnipeg. A replacement car was found there but it lasted only as far as Fort William before the sub-zero temperatures froze its water supply and put it out of action. Steele and the other passengers had to snatch what food was available at stops along the way.[43] The train finally reached Montreal late on January 8 in the middle of a snow storm. Steele found a hotel, feeling grumpy and apprehensive about finally meeting Marie's family.[44]

Things started to look better the next day. Robert Harwood came to the city from Vaudreuil, picked him up, and took him to the house of a relative, Richard Hubert, where all the family assembled. The warm welcome from the family eliminated all concerns and after lunch Steele and Harwood went off to see the bishop and receive his permission for the marriage. Nothing had been left to chance in this area. As Steele noted in a letter in October, "I will see Father Lacombe as you suggest and get over the difficulty of proving my bachelorhood. It has happened before that men had wives in the West, Indian wives whom they thought they were not married to or could desert with impunity."[45] Steele might have been referring here to Superintendent James Morrow Walsh, but the wording suggests that his was not an isolated case. The bishop had clearly been thoroughly briefed by Father Lacombe and other prominent western clergy who were on good terms with Steele, and the interview was over in half an hour.

The only minor concern was that Marie was recovering from a severe cold and looked unwell to Sam. That did not stop her from shopping. They spent all of January 11 in the stores, with a short break for lunch with Marie's brothers. Then it was off to Vaudreuil for the weekend to meet more members of the extended family, including Marie's uncle Henry Hammond, a former military man who thoroughly approved of Sam. Monday it was back to Montreal to make the final arrangements for the wedding. His best man, Inspector Albert Huot, had arrived from Quebec City where he was visiting family. Huot had served under Steele's command in British Columbia where they became close friends. Steele was sorry when Huot was transferred to Prince Albert after they returned to Fort Macleod, and when he checked into the hotel in Montreal, the two sat up talking until 4 A.M.[46] Inspector Cortlandt Starnes, who like Huot had gone west with the 65th Mount Royal Rifles during the Rebellion before joining the NWMP, also attended the wedding.[47]

The wedding was held at the Harwood family home in Vaudreuil. Steele's uncertainty about when he would be able to get away had presumably prevented arranging for a larger church wedding. The lack of an elaborate ceremony seems not to have bothered Marie unduly. It definitely suited Steele very well. The laconic diary entry for the day read: "Married today to Miss Maye Harwood of Vaudreuil. Huot best man Starnes and Capt Labelle 65th Batt. came, well received and stood the ordeal very well so my wife says. Left for New York at 610 and left Montreal at 730."[48] After an exhausting overnight trip involving two changes of train, the couple arrived in New York where they stayed at a hotel on 40th Street and Broadway, close to what is now Times Square, in the city's burgeoning theatre district.

*Sam and Marie's wedding photograph.* [BPSC, 2008.1.1.5.3.1.2]

They spent several days visiting the mandatory tourist sights: Grant's Tomb, Riverside Drive, the Brooklyn Bridge, and Central Park. The park impressed Steele, but not the fashionable New York ladies in their carriages. "Women all plain," he recorded in his diary, "which is a notable fact in New York. The women cannot compare with Canadians for beauty. More than three fourths are plain and many ugly."[49] He was equally dismissive of Brooklyn, "dingy and mean for its size."[50] Steele then looked up a man named Walter Johnston, inspector of explosives for the New York Fire Department, who may have been related to his friend from British Columbia, George Hope Johnston. Steele had certainly met him before and was greeted like a long-lost friend. Sam and Marie dined with the Johnstons and then went off to see the latest Gilbert and Sullivan opera, "The Gondoliers."[51]

They saw the Johnstons frequently over the next week and went to several more theatrical performances as well as visiting museums during the day. Johnston introduced Steele to his superior, Captain Cassels, who arranged a tour of several stations and a demonstration of how they turned out for a fire call. Cassels, in turn, introduced Steele to the superintendent of the New York Police (as the police chief was called at the time), John Russell. While Marie did some more touring on the elevated railway and went shopping with Mrs. Johnston, Steele toured police headquarters and two of the precinct stations.

After two weeks in New York the Steeles got on the train back to Montreal. They spent several days at a hotel there, receiving a stream of congratulatory visits from family and friends. Then it was back to Vaudreuil for a few days with the family before spending two days in Ottawa. Marie went along but this was largely a business trip for Steele. He was mostly interested in finding out what the government was prepared to do about the accusations against Commissioner Herchmer. The Steeles dined with both Laurence Fortescue and Comptroller Fred White so they certainly got a full briefing.[52] Sam also had an interview with Sir John A. Macdonald.

As Steele describes it in *Forty Years in Canada*, the prime minister did not ask him anything about the NWMP but about the necessity for a Calgary–Edmonton railway.[53] It seems highly probable that the government had not yet made a decision about Herchmer and that Steele was being sized up as a possible replacement, should it be necessary to make a change. Steele knew exactly where he stood and commented, "I know Sir John too well and Fred White trims the ship of state to suit him."[54]

The dimming of prospects for advancement did nothing to interfere with the couple's state of domestic bliss. The rest of February was spent at Vaudreuil or in Montreal in a pleasant round of visits with family and friends. Steele had at last found the warm and stable family relationship he had missed for most his childhood. On February 10 he wrote in his diary, "I have never been so happy in my life."[55] Much of the time in Montreal was spent shopping for items for their home in the west. Marie seems to have enjoyed this more than Sam. His irritation began to show in his diary and on February 21 he commented, "Out shopping again & have no patience left. Matrimony is certainly very trying to a man of my stamp."[56] In spite of the trials of shopping, Steele was in no hurry to get back to work. In early March he requested and was granted a month's extension on his leave.[57]

The Steeles spent some of the extra time visiting Sam's relatives in Toronto and he travelled north to Coldwater to visit others there, especially his half-brother John. In mid-May they reluctantly said their goodbyes to both families and headed west, arriving in Fort Macleod on May 14. They stayed with the Macdonells for a few days while the final touches were being put on their house and then they moved in to truly begin their life together. There were no unrealistic expectations on either side. The year of separation, with its intense correspondence in which they poured out their souls to each other, provided a solid foundation for a marriage that would survive separations half a continent and even half a world apart, and that ended only with Sam's death.

# 6 ‖ Fort Macleod and Family
1890–1898

THE NINE YEARS between 1889 and 1898 at Fort Macleod were the longest period Sam Steele lived in one place in his adult life. Personally, it was a time of contentment and fulfilment; his marriage was very happy, his three children were born, and he was surrounded by friends. Professionally, the years before he went to the Yukon were difficult and unsettled. He remained in charge of the largest and most important operational Mounted Police post (Regina was largely occupied with training), but his relations with Commissioner Herchmer went rapidly downhill. The death of Sir John A. Macdonald in 1891 was a blow to Steele's personal ambitions, and left the NWMP open to attacks from the Liberal opposition in Ottawa that threatened the very existence of the force. By the middle of the decade, Steele was actively working on an exit strategy that would allow him to support his growing family.

When the newlyweds arrived back in Fort Macleod in the spring of 1890, they were clearly enjoying married life. In spite of Sam's worries about his inadequacies as an interior decorator, the house proved to be satisfactory. It was a two-storey frame building facing onto the parade square and situated between the officers' mess and the house occupied by the Macdonells.[1] The post no longer boasted a stockade since its move from the original fort on an island in the river in 1884, just a symbolic fence and gate. The Steeles, although not wealthy, lived a very comfortable life. There was a "servant girl," Emily Palmer by name, to help Marie run the household and Sam employed a constable, James Macdonald, part-time as his groom and driver.[2] The house had a small garden in front with lots of prison labour to do the digging and weeding.[3] Above all, the Steeles had social standing, something that was perhaps more important to Marie than to her husband. As the commanding officer, Steele was automatically the most important individual on the post and, since the police were the largest employer in the town as well, he was at the centre of the local elite. Steele's political sense was well developed by this stage in his life and he was well aware that his position required careful management to avoid alienating people both inside and outside the Force.

Steele had a large carriage with a four-horse team at his disposal and, when the weather was good, Marie (and later the children) often accompanied him on his tours of inspection throughout the district. These excursions sometimes included other officers and their wives or friends from the town. They usually stayed with friends in the towns of the district or with ranchers, but in summers they frequently camped. The Steeles developed friendships with prominent local ranchers like John Herron, Frederick Godsal, and especially the family of Allen Bean Macdonald, who managed the 50,000-acre Glengarry Ranch in the Porcupine Hills west of Claresholm. They also frequently visited the Mormon settlement at Lee's Creek (later Cardston) where they stayed with the founder of the community, Charles Ora Card and his wife Zina. There was a surprising variety of summer activities available around Fort Macleod in the 1890s. Tennis and golf were popular, although the Steeles do not seem to have participated in either sport. For spectators, there were race meets, sports days, rodeos, polo games, and lacrosse and cricket matches against teams from Pincher Creek and Lethbridge.

Winter was a time for indoor entertainments. Whist parties were popular among the Mounted Police officers. There were dances several times a year, put on by local groups like the St. Andrew's and St. Patrick's societies, and by the police themselves. Marie organized concerts that involved the townspeople as well as the police, like the one in honour of Father Lacombe in January 1891. Sam had his private thoughts about these gatherings, which he undoubtedly kept to his diary:

> Went to concert got up by Maye in the Hall it was a success. Most respectable gathering. Father LaCombe thanked the audience for their attendance and expressed his gratitude. Maye delighted, came back in a good humour with herself and the rest of the performers. I had a dull time of it waiting for the dance to conclude. Do not think I will go to any more concerts unless I decide to go home immediately after and not wait for the dance.[4]

On December 7, 1891, Marie gave birth to a girl whom they named Mary Charlotte Flora Macdonald Steele, known throughout her life as Flora. In later years Sam Steele was intensely devoted to all his children, although there is little room for doubt that Flora was his favourite. It is somewhat surprising, then, that he does not record the birth in his diary and it was six weeks before she received even this perfunctory mention: "Weather very fine drove out in the afternoon with Maye and the youngster."[5] There is an unexplained medical bill for Marie in the summer of 1890, so it is possible that she had a miscarriage and that Sam resisted forming an emotional attachment to the baby until she showed signs of thriving.[6] Thrive she did, and was soon accompanying her parents on their trips around the district. In July 1892, Marie and Flora left for Vaudreuil to spend the summer with the family there. By that time, Sam could hardly bear to be parted from his daughter, "the great Flora," as he called her in a letter to Marie. After they had been gone two weeks he worried that she might not recognize him when they got back.[7]

The second child, Gertrude Alexandra Elizabeth Steele, born August 2, 1895, rated an immediate mention in Sam's diary, as did the youngest; Harwood Elmes Robert Steele, who arrived May 5, 1897.[8] One of the immediate consequences of the arrival of the children was that Emily Palmer's wages increased from $10 to $15 a month. The younger children joined the family excursions within a month or two of their births and Sam frequently (and proudly) noted, "drove out with my wife and family."[9] The children were generally healthy; the only serious illness any of them suffered came when Gertrude contracted measles at eighteen months and nearly died.[10] This was perhaps the only time in her life that Gertrude was the centre of family attention; the rest of the time she was a classic middle child, content to go her own way by flying under the radar. She was the only one of Steele's children to marry and did not share her siblings' almost obsessive interest in their father's life and career.

In the months before the birth of Flora, the crisis surrounding the commissioner of the NWMP was coming to a head. Regina MP and journalist Nicholas Flood Davin had first brought his charges against Herchmer to the floor of the House of Commons in March 1890, demanding a judicial inquiry.[11] Prime Minister Macdonald decided to defend Herchmer, temporarily sinking Steele's hopes that he might get the job, but Sir John was forced to agree to an internal investigation of the charges to be carried out by Comptroller Fred White. At the end of July, White spent several days at Fort Macleod. Word of Assistant Commissioner W.M. Herchmer's insult to French-Canadian officers during the governor general's tour had reached Ottawa and Steele was ordered to write a full report.[12] This was by far the most damaging of the charges against Commissioner Herchmer, even though it was his brother who was directly involved. Macdonald could deflect charges against Lawrence Herchmer of mistreating his subordinates, but Billy Herchmer's indiscretion threatened the Conservative Party's support in Quebec with an election coming early in 1891.

White continued to gather evidence through the fall of 1890 and into the spring of 1891 with all deliberate speed. His work kept the issue out of the public eye until the general election in March returned Macdonald and his government to power. A few months later, in June, the Old Chieftain died, leaving a tired party with no obvious successor to the leadership. The very competent justice minister, John Thompson, was ruled out because he had married a Catholic and later converted to Catholicism himself, which made him unacceptable to many Ontario Conservatives. The party eventually settled on Senator John J.C. Abbott to replace Macdonald. This seemed to be a very positive development for Steele, since Abbott was a neighbour and friend of the Harwoods.[13] Abbott was a competent and vigorous leader until he began to suffer serious health problems in the spring of 1892, but he did not have Macdonald's intimate knowledge of the Mounted Police. Nicholas Flood Davin moved quickly to take advantage of the situation. He renewed his attacks on Herchmer and demanded that White's report be released.

At first the new government continued Macdonald's policy of defending Herchmer, but in July the Liberals and the Montreal newspaper *L'Étendard* got wind of the assistant commissioner's anti-French-Canadian tirade. That led John Thompson, the minister responsible for the NWMP in the House of Commons, to release White's report and to appoint Justice E.L. Wetmore of the Supreme Court of the North-West Territories to hold a judicial inquiry into all the charges. Commissioner Herchmer already knew that Steele had confirmed the charges against his brother to White, and had written to the comptroller accusing Steele and Inspector Z.T. Wood of spreading lies.[14] Steele did not know of this correspondence, but he must have realized that the commissioner knew of his testimony when Inspector Wood was abruptly transferred from Fort Macleod in June.[15] None of the story of Billy Herchmer's indiscretion became public with the release of White's report, since it dealt exclusively with the charges against his brother, but it would certainly do so when witnesses were required to testify under oath before Judge Wetmore. Steele would be the star witness against the assistant commissioner since the incident had happened under his command.

Wetmore's deadline for submitting complaints was December 19, 1891, and by that time he had accumulated a total of 137 charges against the commissioner in addition to those against his brother. It seemed to Steele and most other people in the North-West Territories that the Herchmers were on their way out. That became much less of a sure thing on New Year's Day, 1892, when Billy Herchmer died suddenly in Calgary. Steele and his friends thought at first that it might be suicide, but an autopsy revealed that it was a heart attack.[16] With the politically explosive charges against his brother now vanished, the commissioner had a chance to weather the storm. This was a double blow for Steele because a new assistant commissioner had to be appointed at once. A year earlier Steele would almost certainly have gotten the job, but now that was out of the question and it went instead to Superintendent John Henry McIlree, a conscientious but unimaginative officer.

In the days leading up to the opening of the hearings at Regina on February 19, the newspapers were full of the charges against Herchmer but Steele was becoming worried about the outcome. Herchmer had very able legal counsel and it did not take long for the most serious charges—of pressuring policemen under his command to vote against Davin, and of misappropriating public funds—to fail for lack of evidence. On February 7 Steele noted in his diary, "Did not go to church. Cannot do so as long as I am in the frame of mind caused by the Force."[17] He had every reason to be concerned. Although the hearings moved to Fort Macleod on February 23 and continued until mid-March, the decision had long since been made in the court of public opinion. On February 17 the *Calgary Herald* published a devastating editorial entitled "The Squabble at Regina" that concluded:

> The most serious of the charges—those in which the public had a real
> interest—have been either explained away or abandoned, and the
> Judge Commissioner is now engaged in dealing with personal squabbles
> between individuals, at an enormous public expense. In the name of
> everything that is decent and proper how much longer is this outra-
> geous farce to continue?[18]

Admittedly the Herald was the most faithful Conservative paper in Canada and regarded Nicholas Flood Davin as a traitor to the party, but no one else came forward to challenge its assessment of the inquiry.

The report of the commission did not appear for a year after the hearings wound up, leaving all those at the centre in limbo. Steele might well have considered leaving the Force, but he now had a wife and child to support. Finding suitable employment at a time when the country was in the midst of a severe depression was a problem. The local economy in Fort Macleod was also affected by the extension of the Calgary and Edmonton Railway through to Lethbridge in 1892, which quickly made that town the regional centre because of its connections east to the CPR main line and south to the United States. Rumours began to circulate that the government would replace the commissioner and that the position had been offered to Colonel Macleod.[19] Steele still had hopes that he might get the job, but when Prime Minister Abbott was forced to take his sick leave at the end of the summer, they faded. They disappeared altogether in December when Abbott resigned as prime minister. The stress led to Steele's only serious illness before the one that ended his life. It is not clear what he was suffering from, but he was off duty for a month and a half from Christmas of 1892 to mid-February 1893. He was convalescent for another six weeks and at the end of March wrote in his diary that he had attended church for the first time since December and that "I am better now and it does not hurt me to go out."[20]

In March 1893 the report of the Wetmore inquiry was finally released. Its conclusion was that fourteen of the 137 charges had

Steele and fellow officers at Fort Macleod. Back row, left to right: Inspector T.A. Wroughton, Inspector Z.T. Wood, Inspector Alex Macdonell, Steele. Front row, left to right: Inspector Cortlandt Starnes, Inspector Percy Neale, Inspector Albert Huot, unknown. [BPSC, 2008.1.2.1.6.23]

been proven and twenty-three partially substantiated. The essence of the report, confirming what the newspapers had concluded a year earlier, was summed up in a couple of sentences near the end:

> It will be seen that some of the matters of complaint brought home to the Commissioner were the outcome of too much zeal on his part: some arose from mistakes of the law or from misapprehension of his power. These mistakes and misapprehensions are such as any person in his position might be likely to make, and do not strike my mind as being of such a character as to amount to misconduct in office.[21]

The government refused to clear up the ambiguity by either dismissing Herchmer or giving him a public expression of confidence, although the minister now in charge of the NWMP, W.B. Ives, sent officers a memo in the summer of 1893 indicating that Herchmer would not be fired. Mounted Police historians William Beahen and Stan Horrall claim that, although the episode shook public confidence in the Mounted Police, internally it cleared the air and improved relations between the commissioner and his officers.[22] That may have been true for some or even most of the officers, but it certainly was not for Sam Steele. Commissioner Herchmer was not in a strong enough position to fire him, but there were many ways he could make Steele's life miserable. To make matters worse, Steele's friend and best man at his wedding, Inspector Albert Huot, died suddenly in March. Steele's diary for 1893 is one of the sparsest of his adult life; from May to the end of the year there are only a few short entries. He was clearly deeply depressed.

Even had Steele's relations with his superior been better, there was not much reason to be optimistic about his future in the Mounted Police since the Force itself was in jeopardy. Ever since the defeat of the Rebellion in 1885, the Liberal Party had questioned why the government should pay for a police force in the North-West Territories, when it did not do so for any of the provinces.[23] John A. Macdonald had always been able to fend off their demands, even while admitting that the NWMP were intended to be a temporary measure, but after his death his successors found the Liberal arguments more compelling. In May 1892, James McMullen, an Ontario Liberal MP, introduced a motion calling for the government to annually reduce the numbers of the NWMP (the unstated implication being that it would shortly cease to exist).[24] In the debate that followed the government spokesman, Interior Minister Edgar Dewdney, argued that the Mounted Police were still necessary, but added that a hundred men had already been eliminated. Prime Minister Sir John Thompson followed up by re-emphasizing the cuts and then stated, "It is the intention of the Government gradually to reduce that force as circumstances permit." Opposition leader Wilfrid Laurier found the undertaking satisfactory and McMullen was persuaded to withdraw the motion.

Steele and other Mounted Police officers read these debates carefully and assessed their career prospects accordingly. The government had always stressed concerns about the stability of relations with the First Nations as the principal reason for the continued existence of the Force. The commissioner was instructed to maintain a large presence at Regina, Fort Macleod, and Calgary, and to make the required staff cuts in places deemed more secure. These were mainly in the eastern districts of the North-West Territories, places like Qu'Appelle, Prince Albert, Battleford, and Maple Creek, which were more densely settled than the District of Alberta. By the end of 1893 it was clear to Steele that Commissioner Herchmer was not going to fire him or transfer him to a less desirable post. His diary resumes in January 1894 with a much more positive tone, although he grumbles that Herchmer is sending him all the drunkards and incompetents in the Force to be reformed.[25]

The cutbacks in the Force were gradual at Fort Macleod through 1894, mainly the result of men retiring and not being replaced. Many who left did so because the commissioner stopped giving permission to marry. Married men did not get any extra pay but officers and some senior NCOs received accommodation, rations, and other supplies for their families—expenses the government was determined to eliminate.[26] A bigger change for Steele came at beginning of 1895 when the two divisions at Fort Macleod, "D" and "H," were amalgamated. This meant that three senior officers were out of a job, including his closest friend, Superintendent Macdonell.[27] The Macdonells began ranching near Fort Macleod that spring with Steele as an investing partner. Alex also invested with Sam in a number of mining ventures and they remained close friends, but it was a blow to Marie not to have Minnie next door.[28] Apart from the personal side of the cuts, fewer officers meant a lot more work for those who were left. Mounted Police inspectors and superintendents acting as justices of the peace tried the majority of minor criminal cases in the North-West Territories. The growing settler population around Fort Macleod meant more of this work.[29]

The Liberals in Parliament who were determined to eliminate the Mounted Police professed to be confident that all the problems of the First Nations in the North-West Territories had been solved. As one of them put it in 1892, in an assertion of breathtaking smugness:

> *They are undoubtedly well fed: I do not know that we are providing for them as amply as He that provides for all living, did before, but since we have banished the buffalo from that country the Government, I dare say, is making the best provision they possibly can for the Indians.*[30]

In fact, the penny-pinching that was affecting the police was having much more dire consequences for the Indigenous population. The Indian Affairs Department had for two decades been implementing a policy of reducing rations on the reserves to force the First Nations to learn farming as a means of self-sufficiency. The "one size fits all" policy ignored very different local circumstances and the vagaries of weather. By the mid-1890s rations, even on the most fortunate reserves, were barely adequate to sustain life. In some places incompetence and occasional corruption on the part of Indian Affairs officials left those on reserves with a grim choice between killing settlers' cattle or starving.[31] The residential school system was also just coming into full operation on the prairies. In 1894, new regulations were passed giving Indian agents the power to compel attendance and the police, to their great distress, had to take children away from their parents and, not infrequently, return them to the schools when they ran away. Indian Affairs backed off somewhat after a couple of years but not before a lot of the trust between the First Nations and the government had been eroded.[32]

In 1882, Indian Affairs first suggested that First Nations who wished to leave their reserves be required to obtain a pass from an Indian agent.[33] The western treaties signed only a few years before explicitly gave First Nations the right to leave reserves for hunting and other purposes, so the idea got little traction at first, but after the defeat of the Rebellion in 1885, Hayter Reed persuaded the government to introduce a requirement for passes for those bands believed to have actively resisted. By the 1890s, Indian Affairs was trying to make passes universal. The only significant resistance to the policy came from the Mounted Police, who objected on both legal and practical grounds. In 1892, Superintendent A.B. Perry, one of the few NWMP officers of the time with legal training, pointed out that the pass system had no basis in law.[34] The commissioner issued a circular memorandum to officers warning them they could only persuade recalcitrants to return and not use any kind of coercion. Some Mounted Police officers, such as Superintendent R. Burton Deane, commanding "K" Division in Lethbridge, strongly favoured the pass system and pushed it as far as they could, although as Deane admitted, "they (the Indians) know as well as we do that we have no right to interfere with them."[35] Steele, in contrast, ignored the pass system as much as possible. He rarely mentioned it in his annual reports and it appears only twice in his diaries.[36]

Steele's district took in the Blood (Kainai) and Peigan (Piikani) reserves; two of the largest in Canada. They suffered the same general problems as the other western First Nations of the period. The population on the Blood Reserve dropped by half, from 3,560 in 1881 to 1,703 ten years later due to disease and malnutrition.[37] Steele spent a considerable amount of time on the reserves and was on good terms with leaders like Chief Red Crow. He was also fortunate in that the Indian agents on both reserves were very competent. Blood agent William Pocklington, a former mounted policeman, worked to help the Kainai develop haying and coal mining, with a good deal of success. When Pocklington moved

Steele on his horse "Black Prince" at Fort Macleod, circa 1894.
[BPSC, 2008.1.2.1.6.1.11]

to the Peigan Reserve at the end of 1891 his successors, especially James Wilson, continued his policies.[38] Even so, life for most people on the reserves was harsh. Almost inevitably, there was a series of violent incidents across the prairies in the mid-1890s, one of which directly affected Sam Steele.

In April 1895, to the north on the Siksika Reserve, a ration issuer who refused extra meat for a sick child was shot and killed by the child's father, who was subsequently shot by the police. In October of the same year a Cree man named Almighty Voice, who was under arrest for cattle killing, escaped from the NWMP lockup at Duck Lake. A few days later, on October 26, he shot and killed Sergeant Colin Colebrook who had tracked him down and was attempting to arrest him. The killing set off an epic pursuit lasting a year and a half during which Almighty Voice was aided by sympathizers on reserves around northern Saskatchewan. He was finally spotted at the end of May 1897, and killed two more policemen, two civilian volunteers, and wounded several others before finally being killed himself by a NWMP field gun brought up to shell the grove of poplars where he had barricaded himself.

Almost exactly a year after the Almighty Voice tragedy began, a somewhat similar series of events took place in Steele's district. The central figure in this case was a forty-year-old Blood warrior named Charcoal. Charcoal was a prominent member of a Blood sub-band known as Shooting Up, for what the rest of the people on the reserve considered their overly aggressive behaviour.[39] In 1883, when the Indian agent discovered that Charcoal had been drawing rations for a family of eight, rather than his actual five, and reduced them accordingly, Charcoal killed a cow on a ranch near the reserve and spent a year in jail. By the time he got out, one of his wives had deserted him and the other had died. He quickly took another wife but she too left him after a few years. In 1891 he married a widow named Pretty Wolverine Woman who, although just twenty-six, had already been married four times. In the spring of 1896 he added another wife, an attractive eighteen-year-old named Sleeping Woman. This family arrangement was normal among the Kainai, but whether or not Pretty Wolverine Woman resented the new wife, she shortly began an affair with a young man named Medicine Pipe Stem. That was bad enough, but Medicine Pipe Stem was also her cousin, thus violating one of the most serious prohibitions in the Kainai belief system. The relationship threatened not merely Charcoal's self-respect but his prominent position in several of the Kainai religious societies, especially the Horn Society.

It was impossible to keep this kind of affair secret in such a closely knit society and when word reached Charcoal he ordered the two lovers to end it at once. At the end of September, however, he caught them in the act in a shed in a remote part of the reserve. He shot Medicine Pipe Stem and took his wife away to wait for the inevitable reaction from the police when the body was discovered, telling her that they would then die together. To his surprise, nothing happened for two weeks because the body was not discovered for eleven days, and then the cause of death was not immediately apparent because Medicine Pipe Stem had been shot through the eye and the bullet had not exited. The shooting was not confirmed until an autopsy was done on October 14, but as soon as the body was discovered, Charcoal made an attempt on the life of Chief Red Crow and then shot and wounded farm instructor Edward McNeil. These actions make no sense for someone seeking to evade punishment but have been explained plausibly by Hugh Dempsey as arising from Charcoal's traditional beliefs about the appropriate death for a Blood warrior. Dempsey argues that Charcoal knew he would die and that killing a high status enemy to precede him to the land of the dead would assure his own standing in the afterlife.[40]

The Mounted Police had at first been unaware that a murder had been committed, then had no idea who might have done it, but the day of the autopsy, Pretty Wolverine Woman's brother, Little Pine, came forward and told them that Charcoal was not only the killer, but the one who had attacked Red Crow and McNeil. He also informed them that Charcoal had taken his two wives, his mother-in-law, his daughter Owl Woman, and Pretty Wolverine Woman's two sons from a previous marriage and left the reserve. None of these six wanted to accompany him but Charcoal threatened to kill the children if they refused. The unhappy group moved west and south up the valley of Lee's Creek toward the mountains, then crossed over to the Belly River and made camp in the Blood Reserve timber limit.

As soon as he heard that Charcoal had departed, Steele took steps to try to capture him. He guessed, correctly, the direction that Charcoal would travel and ordered the detachments at Lee's Creek and Big Bend at the southern end of the reserve to mount patrols to prevent the fugitives from crossing the border into the United States, and on October 16 went to Big Bend himself to take charge of the pursuit. The police quickly recruited about forty Bloods who were willing to act as scouts for 50¢ a day, food, and the provision of rifles and ammunition.[41] Charcoal's extended family aside, the Bloods were just as anxious as the police to stop him before he killed more people. Their first chance came when a man named James Henderson reported that a man matching Charcoal's description had stolen his coat, which he had taken off while loading timber near the Belly River. Thence, there was a single trail into the mountains. The scouts lost no time following it up and in the early morning of October 17 discovered Charcoal's camp, which they reported to Inspector A.M. Jarvis at Big Bend.

Jarvis and a party of police and scouts moved up the heavily wooded valley to make the arrest, but as they approached the camp someone stepped on a dry stick and the noise alerted Charcoal. As he came out of his tipi, a scout named Green Grass shot at him and the rest of the patrol opened up as well. Amazingly, neither Charcoal nor any of the women and children was hit by the hail of bullets. Inspector Jarvis, whose head was grazed by a bullet from one of his own men, was the only casualty. In the general chaos Charcoal got away with his rifle, his two wives, and one stepson. The police rescued the others and confiscated Charcoal's horses and food supplies. It seemed that his capture must be only hours away, but Charcoal's luck, which had kept the bullets away, was still holding. It was easy enough to hide in the dense bush until dark but he needed horses to break free from the pursuit. He and his diminished party headed back toward Lee's Creek where there were some ranches. Here two of the search party, Inspector H.J.A. Davidson and Constable Basil Nettleship, decided to leave their tired horses to rest at an abandoned stable while they continued to look on foot. When they returned to the stable, horses and saddles were gone and there could be no doubt who had taken them.

Steele was annoyed by this embarrassing display of carelessness but not in any way alarmed. All the trails across the border were sealed off, winter was coming on, and soon Charcoal would be forced to show himself. Charcoal this time headed north to the Peigan Reserve where his mother and other relatives lived. On the way he abandoned the exhausted Mounted Police horses and stopped to steal some food from a ranch on the trail between Fort Macleod and Pincher Creek. Steele quickly shifted the search from near the international boundary north, but not fast enough. Charcoal made his way into the Porcupine Hills west of the Peigan Reserve where he was able to steal more horses and visit the reserve to get food and clothing from family members. On his trips to the reserve he tied up his wives at the camp and took his stepson with him, but on October 19 the boy managed to escape and make his way to the Indian agent. The next day the boy led the police to the camp, which Charcoal had by then abandoned to head back south to the Blood Reserve.

Here he found help from relatives for the next ten days but on October 30 his wives, left in camp as usual, managed to untie their bonds and escape. They told the police where Charcoal's camp was located and a patrol was immediately sent off. The day after the women's escape, Sergeant Hilliard arrested Charcoal's brothers Bear Back Bone and Left Hand, who had been supplying him with food, arms, and ammunition, along with two dozen other members of their family at Lee's Creek. They were brought to the guardhouse at Fort Macleod and held for trial. The legality of this mass arrest was dubious at best, since it included a number of children, but Steele recognized that unless his family support was cut off, Charcoal could remain at large indefinitely. The country was too big and too sparsely populated to corner him with the handful of police and scouts available because of the diminished size of the Force. All the adults of Charcoal's family had been complicit in giving him aid, and separating them from the children was not practical under the circumstances.

Charcoal was still in the area four days later, as the police discovered when he shot and slightly wounded Corporal William Armer at Lee's Creek. When further searches of the area turned up nothing,

Steele approached Bear Back Bone and offered him a deal. All the family would be released if the two brothers would cooperate in bringing Charcoal in. Steele even threw in an offer to stay the prosecution of Bear Back Bone's son, Crane Chief, who was under arrest for cattle theft. The deal was quickly accepted and the families were allowed to return to their homes. Charcoal, meanwhile, had gone back to the Porcupine Hills. He cautiously avoided the Peigan Reserve for several days, but on November 8 he found the young wife of a man named Cross Chief gathering firewood by herself and raped her. The Peigans had been looking for Charcoal and this new crime stirred them to greater activity.

They quickly found a trail leading back toward the Blood Reserve and notified the police detachment. Constable James Hatfield joined the group in pursuit and sent a message to Pincher Creek to send a patrol to cut off a possible escape route to the mountains. The patrol left at once under Sergeant William Brock Wilde, who told his men not to take any chances if they found Charcoal; they should not try to approach closer than fifty metres, but shoot him if he refused to surrender immediately.[42] Wilde's patrol met Hatfield's group about twenty kilometres south of Pincher Creek and they quickly spotted Charcoal cooking food near a branch of the Waterton River. He jumped on his horse and fled but the pursuers quickly followed with the Peigans in the lead. Their horses, tired from a long ride, quickly slowed, but Sergeant Wilde, mounted on a large and powerful horse, moved ahead. Ignoring his own very sensible instructions, Wilde grabbed a pistol from a scout named Tail Feathers and closed in on Charcoal who turned and shot him off his horse. Charcoal then stopped, went over to the wounded policeman, and finished him off with a shot to the stomach. Taking Wilde's horse, he rode off.

The pursuers could not catch him but picked up his trail the following day and got close enough late on November 11 to fire some shots, but none hit the fugitive. Charcoal now headed back to the Blood Reserve, hoping for support from his family, as Steele had expected. His brothers immediately upheld their end of the bargain by tackling Charcoal, disarming him and calling the police. He attempted to commit suicide by slashing his wrists with an awl, but family members stopped the bleeding and a police surgeon treated the wounds so that he could be taken to the Fort Macleod guardhouse to await trial. The federal Liberals had campaigned in the spring 1896 election—which brought them to power—on getting rid of the Mounted Police because they were no longer needed. As such, the new government was understandably anxious to put the episode behind it as quickly as possible and put some pressure on Steele to try to arrange for the trial to be held immediately.[43] Judge David Lynch Scott, who was to preside over the trial, wisely decided that no corners would be cut.

The trial date was set for January 6, 1897, and actually began a week later. Charcoal was represented by Horace Harvey of Calgary, one of the leading lawyers in the North-West Territories and later chief justice of Alberta. Charcoal was tried first for the murder of Medicine Pipe Stem. He had admitted to the killing in a conversation with Indian Agent Wilson and Harvey tried to have the latter's testimony excluded. He lost the point but it did not really matter since the evidence from other witnesses was overwhelming. During the second trial, for the murder of Sergeant Wilde, Harvey tried to get Left Hand to admit that Steele offered him money to betray his brother, which he denied. Then Harvey asked, "Do you want to see your brother hung?" Left Hand replied, "All the white men and all the Indians knew that Charcoal was crazy. Yes, you might as well hang him."[44] Charcoal himself testified at some length, making numerous false statements. Among other things, he claimed that Wilde had fired his revolver first, that he did not recognize Wilde as a policeman, and that the killing was therefore done in self-defence. It was easily proved that Wilde's pistol had not been fired and the assertion that Charcoal did not know Wilde was a policeman was, under the circumstances, so absurd that the jury took only eight minutes to come back with a verdict of guilty.

Steele's handling of the Charcoal case was not entirely beyond reproach, but it is hard to imagine what choices he might have made that would have resulted in less damage. Correctly interpreting the implications of the killing of Medicine Pipe Stem would have required a knowledge of Kainai religious beliefs that was far beyond the grasp of Steele or anyone else outside the Kainai at that time. In any case, because of the cuts to the NWMP and the fact that men were being pulled out of Fort Macleod and sent to the Yukon, Steele did not have the manpower to mount an all-out search for Charcoal. His bargain with Charcoal's brothers likely saved lives. During his testimony at the trial, Left Hand commented, "He thought Charcoal was a lunatic. People as crazy as Charcoal were not worth bothering about. He had no brains, and no heart."[45] Steele was sufficiently in tune with the people on the Blood Reserve to understand what he could and could not do. The contrast with the handling of Almighty Voice, who killed four men and seriously wounded three more while evading capture for a year and a half, is instructive.

Charcoal was sentenced to hang at Lethbridge on March 16. In the month and a half before the execution, Steele visited him almost every day, coming, if not to admire him, at least to respect his skills at evading capture. At the same time he had to adjudicate an unseemly squabble between the local Anglican and Roman Catholic clergy about which church would act as Charcoal's spiritual advisor and conduct his funeral. After talking to the family, Indian Agent Wilson, both priests, and at length with Charcoal himself, Steele came down on side of the Catholics.[46] A few days before the execution Steele went to Lethbridge to supervise construction of the gallows and arrange for crowd control (at the time executions were still public spectacles in Canada). Steele did not attend the hanging; perhaps an indication of his ambivalent feelings about the whole episode.[47]

Steele had many other things on his mind at this point in his life. His daughter Gertrude nearly died while Charcoal's trial was going on and his third child and only son, Harwood, was born a few months later. The prospects of supporting his growing family as a police officer seemed to be in grave doubt with Laurier's victory in the federal election of June 1896. Steele could see the change coming long in advance and he began to make moves to find alternative sources of income. Steele had for many years made relatively small investments in both urban and homestead land, oil, and cattle. In the middle of the 1890s a new prospect beckoned that was on quite a different scale. Prospectors in southeastern British Columbia discovered and began to develop silver, zinc, and lead deposits. The first and largest was the massive mine and smelter complex that grew up around the town of Rossland in the early 1890s.[48] With the building of railway branch lines into the region from the United States and the CPR planning its line through the Crowsnest Pass, large-scale investment from New York and London began to flow into mining prospects. Fortunes were apparently being made by foreigners and it seemed to many people in southern Alberta that there was no reason why they should not do the same. It was almost a patriotic duty.[49]

Once he decided that the British Columbia mines offered the best prospect of an alternative career, it was almost inevitable that Steele would become a central figure in a series of local investment schemes. He knew the southern interior of British Columbia, had many friends there from his days building the CPR and later at Fort Steele, and with them he began to stake claims starting in 1893.[50] These claims at Sand Creek near Fort Steele developed into a company called the Empire mine. Steele had no experience in mining, or for that matter any other business, but his reputation for integrity was solid. His fellow police officers, and the local ranchers and businessmen he knew, had no hesitation in trusting him with their money. In the latter category, two men were particularly important. Fred Steele (no relation) owned a thriving photography business in Winnipeg and was intent on expanding westward with that and other enterprises. Frederick William Godsal came from a wealthy English family and ran a huge cattle ranch at Pincher Creek.

Steele's first large-scale public mining venture came in the fall of 1896, when he launched the Ibex Mining and Development Company with claims near Slocan, British Columbia. He was the company president and Fred Steele was the treasurer.[51] In December the company published a prospectus and offered 200,000 of its 1,200,000 shares for sale at 25¢ each. Steele initially retained 135,000 of the shares. About the same time he and a group that included Godsal and the Fort Macleod banker John Cowdry formed the Macleod Company to exploit some claims farther up the valley near Ainsworth, British Columbia. Steele was not an officer of this company but he invested $900 for 30,000 shares. By far his largest investment came in July 1897 when he paid the astonishing sum of $22,667.50 for 45,335 shares of the Black Diamond Mining Company, which had a mine at Ainsworth. Historical money values are notoriously difficult to calculate but today that sum would be the equivalent of at least $500,000 and probably closer to a million. Steele's total earnings in his twenty-five years in the NWMP, by comparison, came to about $30,000.

Steele had nothing like that amount of money to invest in 1897 (or at any other time in his life), so the question is, where did it come from? The answer is that almost the entire sum was loaned to him by his friend Godsal.[52] The more fundamental question is why both of them, and the others who joined in these ventures, were prepared to take such huge risks? Although they contained other metals, the ores in the British Columbia mines were almost entirely dependent for their value on the world price of silver. That price in the 1890s was largely determined by the American political situation. The rapid expansion of the United States economy in the late 19th century was hindered by the supply of gold, which in turn restricted credit. The solution favoured by the Democratic Party was buy silver to back the dollar and it managed to push through the *Sherman Silver Purchase Act* of 1890 that committed the government to purchase 4.5 million ounces a month. Because this was done with treasury notes that could be redeemed for either silver or gold—most people opted for the latter—it had the paradoxical effect of decreasing the money supply and was a major factor in the financial crisis of 1893. The repeal of the *Sherman Act* that year drove the price of silver down further, but with economic recovery and Democratic presidential nominee William Jennings Bryan campaigning in the 1896 election on a platform of a silver-backed dollar, the prospects looked brighter.

Unfortunately for Steele and his fellow investors, Bryan lost the election and 1896 proved to be the high water mark for the "free silver" movement. This was by no means obvious at the time, however, and optimism prevailed. Serious work started in the spring of 1897 on the various properties and when Steele and others visited the diggings in July, consulting engineer William Tretheway told them that the ore samples from the Ibex mine predicted a value of $400,000.[53] Shortly after the party got back from British Columbia, things began to fall apart. It became apparent that Fred Steele, a key figure in the Ibex, Empire, and Black Diamond projects, was both incompetent and dishonest. The details of Fred Steele's misdeeds are obscure, but it appears that he and the other investors drastically underestimated the very large amounts of money required to get mines into production. When the public sale of shares failed to produce the necessary funds, Fred Steele tried to disguise the shortfall by moving money around from company to company. A decade later, Sam Steele recounted to a friend that Fred Steele

> *finally came over and saw me in my Orderly room one night, and confessed that he had embezzled the amounts, and that one Gibson employed by the Companies had been the cause of his undoing, by getting a hold on him, in the first place, in the alleged payment of ten per cent on the Black Diamond Bond $4,000.00 four thousand, which they pretended they had to pay to the owner of that mine.*[54]

Fred Steele tried to atone by transferring all his mining investments to Sam, but they did not cover all the losses.55 Sam Steele unhesitatingly agreed to cover the amount owing to the Bank of British Columbia, which seems to have been about $2,500. He also reduced some of his obligations by transferring a quarter of his interest in the Empire mine to Godsal. Any plans he might have had for a business career outside the Mounted Police were now in ruins. He had little choice but to make the best of his career in the Force as long as it might last, while making plans to pay off his debts and salvaging what he could of his investments. His diary for 1897 ends abruptly in mid-August and remains blank for the rest of the year, perhaps a reflection of his unhappy state of mind. When it resumes in January 1898, he is still involved in trying to secure financing for the mining operations. On January 5 he comments, "My birthday today. I hope the next if I live to see it will be a happier one than the present one."56

The future of the Mounted Police was, in fact, looking a little brighter in the fall of 1897. The Almighty Voice and Charcoal episodes had weakened the argument that the police were no longer needed on the prairies. The Liberal Party had done well in the North-West Territories in the 1896 election and their MPs in this fastest growing region of the country were unanimous in demanding that plans to dissolve the Force be dropped. Ultimately the decisive factor came from the remote north. The enormous area east of Alaska and north of British Columbia along the Yukon River had come under Canadian control in 1870, but the government had paid no attention to it over the next quarter century. There was a small HBC presence and a handful of Roman Catholic and Anglican missionaries, but it was not until 1894 that two mounted policemen, Inspector Charles Constantine and Staff Sergeant Charles Brown, were sent in to investigate the need for a government presence and to report on American prospectors working on the Yukon River just on the Canadian side of the border with Alaska.

None of the miners had found significant quantities of gold yet, but Constantine's reports convinced the government to send him back in 1895 with twenty men. He set about acting as Indian agent, magistrate, gold commissioner, collector of customs, and generally asserting Canadian sovereignty over the territory. The timing was good since in August 1896, four men made a discovery on a tributary of the Klondike River that was rich enough to set off the last great North American gold rush. The government set about organizing an army unit called the Yukon Field Force to reinforce its authority in the north, but the Canadian army was so tiny that only 200 men could be spared and they would not be ready to go until 1898. The Mounted Police were the only realistic means of maintaining control. The number of police in the Yukon was doubled to forty in the spring of 1897 with plans to have almost 200 there by the end of the year. This was the biggest change in the distribution of the NWMP since the creation of the Force and it had important implications for senior officers like Steele.

The Yukon contingent would quickly replace Fort Macleod as the largest command outside the Regina headquarters and its remoteness meant that whoever took it over would be very much on his own. The only serious candidates for the job were thus the most experienced officers in the Force. The choice quickly came down to three: Assistant Commissioner J.H McIlree, Superintendent A. Bowen Perry, and Steele. In September 1897 Steele received a letter from the commissioner that said,

> *I received a wire yesterday that McIlree had dislocated his ankle, and would be laid up for some time, consequently I had to wire you to be in readiness to take his place. I have notified the Department but have not yet received orders, and they may send Perry. Whoever goes will be there two months at least, as it will take that time to get the supplies over the pass. McIlree will hand over his instructions and his credit. You will sail I presume on the "Quadra" about the 20th inst.*[57]

The fact that no decision was actually made for another four months makes it clear that Steele was third choice for the job.

Assistant Commissioner McIlree's ankle must have healed by the new year, so he apparently turned down the job. McIlree was comfortable with his administrative work at Regina and his favourite recreations of golf and curling, and the prospect of moving to the frozen frontier of the Yukon had little appeal. Superintendent Perry (commissioner of the NWMP and Royal Canadian Mounted Police 1900–1923) was the rising star of the Mounted Police in 1897. A graduate of the first class at the Royal Military College at Kingston, Perry served briefly in the Royal Engineers before joining the NWMP. He was in charge of training at headquarters in Regina 1889–1897 and, while there, studied law and was called to the bar. He was one of the few officers in the Force who had Liberal political connections. He was chosen to lead the NWMP contingent to London for Queen Victoria's Diamond Jubilee celebrations in the spring of 1897, a clear indication that he enjoyed government favour. When he returned from England, Perry was given the job of establishing an office in Vancouver to provide support for the expanded operations in the Yukon. He travelled north in the fall and spent some time making arrangements with the American authorities at Skagway.

Perry could certainly have had the job of commanding the Mounted Police in the Yukon but did not seize the opportunity. Sam Steele did. On January 28, 1898, he recorded in his diary, "Received orders at night to leave to-morrow for Yukon duty. Set to work and got things in shape for that country."[58] Three days later he was in Vancouver waiting to get on a boat to Skagway. Steele's diary entries for the weeks leading up to his departure are filled with his continuing efforts to clear up his failed investments. Staying at Fort Macleod would have made it much easier to do so. Going to the Yukon also meant that he would be separated from his family, whom he adored, for an indefinite period, but he did not hesitate. Steele recognized an opportunity in the Yukon that both McIlree and Perry missed. If the gold strikes turned out as rich as they promised to be, the Yukon would be a centre of world attention. The job meant isolation and the professional risks involved in handling an enormous responsibility with very limited resources, but these were the kind of challenges Steele always found irresistible.

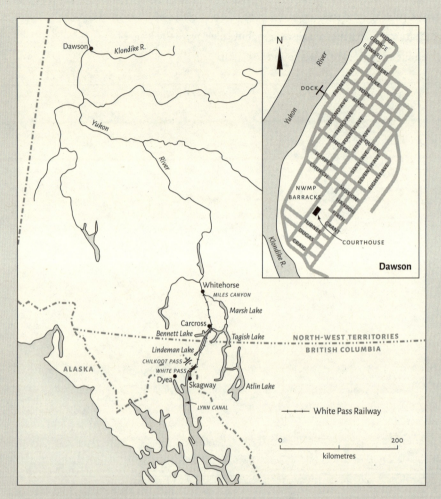

The Gold Rush.

# 7 ‖ The Klondike Gold Rush
## 1898-1899

STEELE GOT ON THE TRAIN for Vancouver after three hours in Calgary with little idea of what he would be doing when he got there. In a letter to Marie written en route he said, "I may not be sent up to the Yukon but I cannot see what they can want with me anywhere else."[1] His uncertainty reflected Canadian government policy, or lack of policy at that time. The cabinet member in charge of the Yukon, Minister of the Interior Clifford Sifton, was competent and decisive but lacking in experience. To make matters worse, the Laurier government had inherited a complex international situation concerning the Yukon–Alaska boundary. When the Americans purchased Alaska from Russia in 1867, they took over an Anglo-Russian treaty of 1825 that established the 141st meridian as the boundary north to the Arctic Ocean, except for the coastal panhandle strip as far south as 54°40' (just north of present-day Prince Rupert). Exactly how far inland the boundary ran in the lower area had never been determined. The towns of Dyea and Skagway at the head of the long inlet called Lynn Canal controlled access to the shortest route to the Yukon through the Chilkoot and White passes. Canada claimed that territory but since the Americans did as well and were in possession, the chances of successfully asserting Canadian ownership were very slim.

The Liberals were much more disposed to believe that reasonable accommodations could be made with the United States over the boundary and related issues than their predecessors in office— naïvely, as it turned out. They were well aware, however, that most Canadians believed the Americans had one set of rules for themselves and a different one for everyone else. They had, after all, briskly expelled the HBC from Alaska as soon as they took over from the Russians, and excluded Canadians from conducting business on American soil. The Treaty of Washington (1871) gave Canada navigation rights on the Yukon and other Alaskan rivers, but these were being interpreted in the most restrictive possible ways. Sifton could not afford to appear to be giving in to the Americans, so he made strenuous efforts to find a route into the Yukon that avoided American territory as much as possible, even travelling personally over the Chilkoot and White passes and investigating the Stikine River route farther south. He decided on the latter, but a bill to charter a railway there was defeated by the Conservative-dominated Senate in March 1898.[2]

Steele was only dimly aware of these developments, although they would affect his immediate future. In Vancouver, waiting for his orders and the boat to Skagway, he had a little time to explore that burgeoning city. When he had been here a mere thirteen years before to mark the completion of the CPR, Vancouver had not existed, now it was a thriving modern port. He reported to Marie, "I have been all over the city. It is very pretty and well paved, electric cars etc. etc. run on all the principal streets. It is a very expensive place to live in but *very* Canadian."[3] In fact, the place was full of so many old friends and acquaintances from Ontario and the prairies that he had insufficient time to visit them all.[4] On February 6 he boarded the SS *Thistle*, which departed up Georgia Strait the following day. He had never been on an ocean-going vessel and his first impression that the boat was "wretched" and overcrowded reflects some nervousness, but his mood picked up when he found that he was one of the few passengers not bothered by seasickness.⁵ After stopping at Wrangell, Alaska, to drop off soldiers of the Yukon Field Force bound for the Stikine River, the Thistle made its way through cold and stormy seas to Skagway. It was anything but a pleasure cruise, as Sam noted to Marie:

> We had very rough weather, a heavy sea running most of the time and at night thick snow storms compelling good and careful navigation. In fact none of us felt quite sure of getting through alive. Standing on ones head in the berth is not suggestive of safety.⁶

Steele had been handed his orders in Vancouver by Superintendent Perry, who left for Skagway on an earlier boat. Perry's instructions were to establish customs posts at the border on the Chilkoot and White passes. The police already knew that it would be just as practical, and infinitely more comfortable, to collect duties a little inland at Lake Bennett and Perry's visit was made in hopes of persuading Ottawa to make the change. On arriving in Skagway, Steele found that Perry had left instructions for him to wait there until he (Perry) returned from a trip over the Chilkoot to investigate the situation. Steele introduced himself to the ranking American in Skagway, a United States Army captain named Rucker, whom he described as very kind and cooperative, which was all very well, but neither Rucker nor any other American authorities seemed to have much control over either the town or the routes inland. Steele described Perry's trip back to Skagway from Lake Bennett in a letter to Marie:

> Major Perry in coming down from the summit of the Dyea which is not far from here had a strange experience. He had to sit on the legs of a corpse all the way from Sheep Camp, which is in the US. Two men were caught stealing and the citizens condemned one to death and the other to flogging. One was not willing to die by the rope but fought the crowd

with his pistol and was shot dead. It was on his remains Major Perry had to ride down. Horrible is it not?[7]

Steele was to have more opportunity to observe conditions in Skagway than he had expected. The collapse of the government's Stikine railway scheme meant that police reinforcements had to be sent over the Chilkoot and Steele was ordered to wait for them at Skagway, so he spent an uncomfortable but interesting six weeks in the town. The police had an office where they both worked and slept, when it was possible to do so. He complained to Marie:

> The whole night long as I lie in my bed without a soul to speak to in any part of the building I hear outside the howling of dogs, women, pistol shots, shrieks, yells and curses until four (4) AM, then a number of working people get up so you can well imagine what it is like.[8]

Sometimes it got worse:

> We had quite a little experience a few nights or mornings ago. Wood (Inspector Z.T.) and I had not yet risen it was about 6:30 AM when we heard firing in the street, oaths, curses, etc and finally it was all around the house. We could hear the bullets strike certain buildings. We got up. It turned out to be three men firing and trying to kill two others. The two took shelter behind our shack and were dodging in and out firing back two were wounded, none killed. If a stray bullet came our way it would have gone through the shack and we were in as much danger as the men fired at.[9]

Steele quickly grasped the logistical problems the Mounted Police were about to face in supporting upwards of 200 men scattered along 700 kilometres of wilderness river. Everything from food and clothing to government forms and stationery had to be imported from southern Canada. Many tons of supplies had to be ordered, shipped to Skagway, and carried over the passes in time for the trip downriver to Dawson when the ice melted. Once the arrangements for ordering the essentials were in hand, Steele decided to see how the customs posts at the tops of the passes were doing. He and a constable set off in mid-March and ran into a ferocious blizzard as they tried to climb the Chilkoot, with blinding snow and winds so strong they were repeatedly blown off their feet and rolled down the slope.[10] They were forced to give up and take refuge with a construction crew working on a tramway over the pass. They had to crawl down a tunnel to reach tents buried deeply in the snow, where they stayed for three days until the storm blew itself out.

The weeks at Skagway gave Steele the opportunity to consider the other challenges he would be facing in the Yukon. There was good news and bad news. On the positive side, he was very pleased with the men under his command. The officers—Z.T. Wood, Robert Belcher, W.D. Jarvis and D'Arcy Strickland—were all individuals he liked and respected, while the men seem to have been the cream of the Mounted Police, chosen by the commissioner and comptroller with an eye to changing the government's mind about carrying through with the plan to eliminate the Force. The bad news was that the administration of the Yukon was in the hands of political appointees of dubious competence. As Sam put it in a letter to Marie, "The country is full of Grits, chums of Siftons."[11] The trouble started at the top with James Morrow Walsh, the man appointed commissioner, in charge of both civil administration and the police. Steele had served under Walsh fifteen years earlier (see chapter 3) and their relationship had been uneasy at best. After Walsh was forced to resign from the Mounted Police he went into business in Manitoba, became active in the Liberal Party, and befriended Clifford Sifton. After the Liberal victory in 1896, Walsh wrote a lengthy memorandum to Laurier urging him to carry through with the elimination of the Mounted Police.[12] Instead, he was appointed to command them in the Yukon.

Nothing could have better illustrated the Liberal government's distrust of the Mounted Police than this move, which effectively removed the Yukon contingent from the NWMP chain of command. Walsh, however, did not play the part expected of him. He agreed to take the job only for a year and, when he got to the territory, stayed at Lake Bennett, refusing to go to the principal scene of the action at Dawson. Walsh's reluctance, combined with the growing realization that the Klondike gold strike was much bigger than anyone expected, pushed Ottawa to make changes. In January 1898, William Ogilvie was named to replace Walsh. Ogilvie was a surveyor who had explored and mapped the Yukon, and set out the first mining regulations there for the Canadian government a decade earlier. He was in England at the time of his appointment and could not reach the Yukon before summer. Ogilvie knew the country but had no administrative experience; he was appointed in large part because he was Clifford Sifton's uncle by marriage. As it turned out, Ogilvie would be a good choice, but in the spring of 1898 that remained to be seen.

Walsh was in control until Ogilvie made his way north and Steele was well aware that until that happened, Walsh would have many opportunities to make life difficult for him, perhaps even to wreck his career. Walsh had quarreled with the first mounted policeman in the Yukon, Inspector Charles Constantine, which led to that officer being moved back to southern Canada. Steele was understandably concerned about how Walsh would react to his appointment, but he was even more worried by the commissioner's failure to exercise any control over the civil administration. He wrote to Marie:

> *I find things in a frightful muddle...and that two serious sums of money have been expended in a way that will make the hair of our legislators stand on end. With all his faults it would have been well for the government if they had LW Herchmer as administrator instead of that mountebank Walsh, who seems to think he is responsible to nobody.*[13]

By mid-March at least one concern had been overcome, because Steele found he had no difficulty working out his personal relationship with Walsh. "Major Walsh has evidently let 'bygones be bygones' and has spoken in high terms of me to people," he reported to Marie.[14] When he finally moved to Lake Bennett and met with Walsh in person, he was "most heartily received."[15]

A severe attack of bronchitis in late March delayed Steele's move and when he finally felt ready, he decided to go inland through the White Pass where he could ride a horse. It was not much better than the Chilkoot, as he wrote to Marie:

> I left Skagway on the 27th on horseback and after a desperate and rapid ride of two and a half hours reached the summit of the dreadful White Pass where I found Strickland suffering from a most severe attack of chronic bronchitis. I had Cartwright with me so I sent Strickland on to Tagish to his family. He was delighted and deserved the change. He is a Trojan and had done so well. I stayed two days with Cartwright to see him properly started and finding he was quite up to the work I pushed on on the 30th as far as the "log cabin" camp. [As] I was passing through Mr Macaulay a wealthy man and a native of Orillia hailed us and insisted on my staying the night. I was glad of the rest for I was tired and weak after my illness. I came on next day but as I was too sick to eat breakfast I had a hard time of it for the ten miles of mountain trail. We had a dreadful time of it going down some enormous hills. Our horses frequently fell and mine rolled over me several times. Once he fell over with horn in the pit of my stomach but all who saw us thought we were wonderful horsemen for our lives were in our hands and few would have dared to ride over it as it is now very different from what it was a month ago. When I got here I was tired but Dr. Bowman a fine man about my own age gave me immediate relief.[16]

Steele immediately met with Walsh, who was more than happy to rely on his competence as a means of avoiding further trouble before he could depart the scene; Steele, in turn, was left with a free hand at a crucial time. In a nutshell, Steele's job was to collect customs duties and generally exercise some sort of control over the thousands of gold seekers who were beginning to struggle over the Chilkoot and White passes. By the end of March, when he moved his base of operations from Skagway to Lake Bennett, the Canadian government still had little idea of the potential crisis taking shape there. It remained focused on the important but nebulous goal of asserting Canadian political and economic sovereignty. Steele saw no real difficulties in those areas; 200 policemen and the latest in military technology, a Maxim machine gun, gave him far more firepower than the Americans had on hand in Alaska. Nor was he concerned that the soldiers of the Yukon Field Force were months away from reaching the scene of the action.[17] What Steele instantly grasped was that, unless immediate steps were taken to control the influx of prospectors, hundreds of lives would be lost over the next year. If he waited for instructions from Ottawa, nothing could prevent badly constructed boats from dumping their passengers into the Yukon's icy waters, while many of those who survived the journey would face starvation if they did not bring food supplies for the year with them.

Steele unhesitatingly made up his own regulations to avert the humanitarian tragedy.[18] The first priority was food, and travellers were informed that they would not be allowed to proceed beyond Lake Bennett without six months' supply. This amounted to about a ton per person, all of which had to be hauled over the passes at the expense of immense labour. Even carrying 100 pounds at a time, which only strongest and fittest could manage, meant a minimum of twenty trips over the passes. There was some grumbling, but few people relished the prospect of starving to death in the icy wilderness. The regulations had the unplanned side effect of giving the local First Nations one of their few opportunities to benefit from the rush by hiring out as packers at high rates. Once the prospective miners got to Lake Bennett, they set about building boats to take them down to the diggings when the ice melted in May. The police required all boats and passengers to be registered and the boats inspected for safety.

This was no small task. In his diary for May 21, Steele noted that 1,420 boats had been registered, only about a fifth of the final number.[19] The mood of the boat builders was not improved by the discovery that Lake Lindeman and the part of Lake Bennett closest to the passes, the only logical places to build boats, were actually in British Columbia and that the police necessarily enforced a requirement to purchase a British Columbia government permit to cut timber for their vessels.[20] Steele's headquarters were at the main boat-building site on Lake Bennett, which had blossomed into an enormous tent city. Steele estimated that in April there were nearly 30,000 people there, which made it the largest community on the west coast north of Seattle.[21] Boat building paused for a day on May 24 to celebrate Queen Victoria's birthday with games (including a tug-of-war, which Steele noted with satisfaction that the police won), and a salute fired by the Maxim.[22] Lakes Lindeman and Bennett were part of the drainage system that made up the headwaters of the Yukon River. From there the route to the Klondike led into the much larger Tagish Lake, to Marsh Lake, and through Miles Canyon into the Yukon River itself near what became the town of Whitehorse. There was a police post at Tagish by April and Steele planned to move his headquarters there as soon as possible.

In the spring of 1898 Steele's initial orders were to extend the line of police posts downriver as soon as navigation opened, but he expected to be stationed at Tagish for as long as two years. He liked the place for its natural beauty and relatively benign climate, "said to be like Edmonton but I think it is milder."[23] It was, he thought, a place where some or all of his family might come to live with him once the warm weather came. "How would you like to come up to Tagish for the summer and let Flora go to school!...I should not suggest it but two years without my Maye. Oh God—and life so short."[24] Unfortunately for these plans, there were complications at both ends. The personal mail for the Mounted Police was held up for over a month at Skagway, so it was not until mid-April that Steele heard how things were going back at Fort Macleod. When it finally arrived, the word from Marie was anything but reassuring. Harwood, just approaching his first birthday, was seriously ill. The replacement commanding officer at Fort Macleod had informed Marie that since her husband was not living at the post, she was no longer entitled to rations. Without Sam's support she felt lonely and unwanted.

Steele was outraged about the rations issue and immediately wrote to both Commissioner Herchmer and Minister Sifton demanding they be restored. Although Steele's political ties and preferences lay with the Conservative Party, Marie's family also had some useful Liberal connections. Her uncle Henry Harwood was the Liberal MP for Vaudreuil and a distant cousin, Henri-Gustave Joly de Lotbinière, had recently been added to Laurier's cabinet as minister of Inland Revenue. The letter to Sifton mentioned these connections and Steele sent Marie a draft letter to Uncle Henry enlisting his support.[25] The rations were promptly restored and the episode undoubtedly had significant consequences for Steele's position in the Yukon. Sifton was not only the minister in charge of the Mounted Police, but the Liberal Party's political manager for all of Canada west of Ontario. In Canadian politics of the 1890s patronage was considered a normal and natural part of the system; in fact, in 1898 Sifton was facing a minor revolt within the Liberal Party for not handing out enough jobs to supporters.[26] With Walsh's imminent departure from the Yukon, a decision had to be made about who would get the second most important job in the NWMP, and Uncle Henry and Cousin Henri made it much easier for Sifton to appoint Steele.

Restoration of the rations helped Marie's situation but did nothing to provide the emotional support she needed. Joining Sam at Tagish had definite attractions but getting there with three young children was a daunting prospect. Flora was now school age and there were no prospects of any educational facilities in the north for years to come. Marie was also handling Sam's British Columbia mining affairs, which would be much more difficult to do from the Yukon. The other possibility was to move back to Montreal to be near her family. That offered good schools and lower living expenses. Montreal, on the other hand, had a dreadful infant mortality rate in the 1890s that worried both parents. Sam kept hoping through the spring and early summer of 1898 that Marie would decide to come north. His letters contain repeated assertions that she should make whatever decision that would be best for her and the children, but it is very clear which option he preferred. After a sentence or two assuring Marie that moving the family to Montreal would be fine, a typical letter contained pages of detailed plans about what clothing, linens, dishes, bedding, and even a portable rubber bathtub she should bring to the Yukon. There was advice about where to shop for these items in Vancouver and which steamboat she should take to Skagway. One letter contained a sketch of the quarters being constructed at Tagish.[27]

In mid-June Marie decided to join her husband, but childhood illnesses affecting both "little Dubbie," as Harwood was now known, and then Flora, put the trip off for a few weeks. In July, Sam was sending Marie's letters to Vancouver in case she should already be on her way, but before she could bring herself to make the final decision, events intervened. As late as July 7, Steele was still uncertain about whether or not he would stay in the Yukon. He feared that Superintendent Perry was angling for the top job in the territory and urged Marie to write her uncle and cousin again on his behalf.[28] The earlier assurances about Steele's political credentials seem to have made that unnecessary. In any case, Sifton was under pressure to at least appear to be taking steps to clean up the Yukon administration because of a series of scathing articles in the *London Times* by its correspondent, Flora Shaw.[29] Two weeks later Steele's friend, Superintendent Zach Wood, sent him a clipping from an Ontario newspaper announcing that he would get overall command of the police and be stationed in Dawson.[30] Confirmation came a few days later with official letters from Sifton and Comptroller Fred White.

The full details were even better than Steele had hoped. Ottawa praised the work he had done so far and confirmed all his decisions about imposing regulations on those travelling to the diggings. He would report only to the commissioner of the Yukon and to White in Ottawa, bypassing the NWMP commissioner in Regina and giving him control of what amounted to a separate police force. For the added responsibility he would receive the magnificent sum of an extra two dollars a day. He was appointed a member of the Yukon Council and promoted to lieutenant-colonel in the militia so that he would not be outranked by the commanding officer of the Yukon Field Force.

By this time, Marie had reluctantly decided to move to Montreal, as Sam heard indirectly in a letter from her brother. He wrote her plaintively, "I get so mixed up with sometimes one decision and sometimes another that I scarcely know what to expect."[31] As soon as he did know for sure, he sent a telegram: "Very glad you have decided to go to Montreal do not think of coming to Yukon."[32] He followed up with letters urging her to consult doctors about the healthiest places to live in the city and to have the children vaccinated as soon as possible. He also reassured her that his move to Dawson meant that she had made the right decision:

> *Dawson of course would not do for you or the children, it is unhealthy and I would not like to see you there suffering. It is orderly but apart from that simply a hell upon earth, gamblers, thieves, and the worst of womankind. One of the latter went through to the south a few days ago with $25,000.00 that she had earned, a coloured woman, and a dance hall girl had eight thousand. It is a tough place indeed and although our laws prevail these people would be worse mischief if they were not permitted to gamble and carry on.*[33]

Once the family decision was made, Steele could turn his full attention to the job. In early August word came in of a gold strike on Atlin Lake. The lake straddles the British Columbia–Yukon border and no one was quite sure which side the gold strike was on, so Steele spent a week on a small steamboat called the *Kilbourne* travelling to the lake. He found it "a fine lake little known 100 miles or so long with beautiful islands, mountains, trees and grassy slopes,"[34] but definitely in British Columbia. As soon as he got back from Atlin, he began making preparations to move to Dawson. He was receiving many reports, from *London Times* correspondent Flora Shaw, among others, that Dawson was riddled with corruption and administrative chaos. Steele could hardly wait to get started on cleaning it up, but on August 12 he got a telegram from Ottawa instructing him to wait for Commissioner Ogilvie, who was expected to arrive from England in a couple of weeks. Steele knew next to nothing about Ogilvie except that he was a surveyor who had spent time in the Yukon. How the two men got along would be crucial for both and for the territory they would jointly govern.

On August 25, Ogilvie's ship arrived at Skagway and the following day Steele used the newly installed telephone line from the Chilkoot summit to find out the commissioner's travel plans. Although Ogilvie brought with him an entourage of about twenty officials, he moved with encouraging briskness, reaching Bennett on August 30. In a meeting the following day, Steele took advantage of Ogilvie's knowledge of the country to make final decisions about the location of police posts in the interior. He asked Ogilvie to set aside land for an Indian reserve at Tagish, which the commissioner immediately agreed to do.[35] Not only did the two agree on matters of business and how it should be conducted, but, he reported to Marie with relief, there was an immediate personal connection. "Mr Ogilvie arrived here with his party of nineteen people all nice fellows and I have found him to be all that can be desired. He is pleasant, unassuming, a good story teller, and deeply read."[36] On September 2, Steele and Ogilvie boarded a steamer for Dawson, determined to change both the image and the reality of Canadian administration in the Yukon.

It did not take long to find out that the reports of lax administration were true. The first stop on the trip downriver was the police post at Whitehorse Rapids, where Steele found all the men still in bed, and the sergeant in charge "under the influence of liquor."[37] He placed the NCO under arrest to be tried at Tagish and pushed on. After several stops to choose locations for police posts along the way, the party arrived at Dawson on September 6. The next day Steele was in his office early, sending off urgent orders for the supplies necessary to sustain his men, horses, and dog teams through the coming winter. Construction was underway on completing the Mounted Police quarters, a hospital, and building accommodations for the Yukon Field Force next door. Most of the work was being done by prisoners serving time in the police guard room, although not fast enough to suit Steele. "Saw that the prisoners worked harder," he commented in his diary.[38]

Nobody in Dawson worked harder than Steele. He found seven of his already overworked men down with typhoid fever.[39] The typhoid was only the most obvious consequence of the failure of the Canadian administration to this point. Steele had made sure that most of the 30,000 gold seekers made the journey safely from Bennett to Dawson with sufficient food, but nothing else had been done to prepare for their arrival. The population explosion meant that the cramped river flat where Dawson was located turned immediately into a large open sewer. The senior government officials, Crown Prosecutor and Land Commissioner Frederick Coates Wade, and Gold Commissioner Thomas Fawcett, were far too busy lining their pockets to bother themselves with such mundane matters as sewage disposal and Walsh, of course, had abdicated any responsibility for holding them to account by failing even to visit Dawson. Ogilvie quickly appointed Steele to two key positions, chairman of the licence commission (in charge of regulating all businesses in the town) and health commissioner, which allowed him to introduce basic sanitary arrangements. These jobs, of course, were in addition to commanding the police, serving as one of the four members of the Territorial Council and trying cases as a magistrate. Mountains of paperwork accompanied each position and Steele routinely worked until 2 or 3 A.M. to keep it under control and leave time to write his lengthy biweekly letters to Marie.

He thrived on the work. At the end of September his comfortable new quarters were ready and he moved in. Before that, he and Ogilvie had roomed next to each other in rented space. This arrangement was fine for transacting business but the walls were thin and Ogilvie played music constantly on a music box and a "Graphophone," one of the early machines that used wax cylinders to reproduce sound. Steele was generally fascinated by new technology but found the music repetitive and distracting after a time.

Plowing through the work was easily accomplished, but navigating the political minefields that abounded in Dawson was more difficult. Those who hoped to make their fortunes by providing services to the actual gold diggers, "mining the miners" as the phrase went, needed at minimum the cooperation, preferably the connivance, of the government officials. Some of these people were providing legitimate services by legitimate means; others sought unfair advantage by getting inside information or favours from those who made and enforced the rules. Most of these people turned up at Steele's door within days of his arrival in Dawson and sorting them out was his first priority.

Steele decided at once that the only way he could maintain his personal integrity and the reputation of the police was to keep his distance from all who stood to benefit from his decisions. The head of the police force could not afford to have social relations with any of them, regardless of his opinions about their legitimacy. His attitude toward the young Irish-American, Belinda Mulrooney, one of the most interesting entrepreneurs of the gold rush in Dawson, is a good example. Mulrooney was well on her way to making a fortune, opening a restaurant, building and selling houses, and eventually constructing the biggest and best hotel in Dawson. Belinda avoided direct involvement in the seamier side of town life, gambling and

Steele as commanding officer of the Yukon NWMP during the gold rush.
[BPSC, 2008.1.2.1.6.1.12.4]

prostitution, but some of her early property deals might not have stood close examination. When she invited Steele and other notables to Thanksgiving dinner, he chose to stay away, for reasons he explained to Marie:

> I was asked to dine at the hotel of Miss Mulroon[e]y her own hotel but did not go (Thanksgiving) I was then asked by her to go on Sunday yesterday but managed to get out of it. She is sharp, is mixed up with miners and has been mixed up with certain officials in the way of money making. I am not going to make myself cheap. She can get others if she likes to do so, but after what I know she can't get my legs under her mahogany. She asked Ogilvie, Fawcett, Judge Dugas, Giraud and a couple of other people and they all went. I suppose they will think me unsociable.[40]

There was certainly an element of snobbery in Steele's attitude. Much as he liked Ogilvie, he thought the commissioner did not have high enough social standards:

> Ogilvie is too simple in his habits dines with a trashy lot of clubs and with a poor cook eats anything just the same as if in the survey party and this has a bad effect. He is a good officer but that style does Canada a great deal of harm. He goes to the dinner of any Tom, Dick and Harry in the country who are only common people. Thank goodness we hold up our end and are as particular as if in Ottawa or London.[41]

Steele's friends were thus confined to fellow police officers, the officers of the Yukon Field Force, those government officials who were untainted from the Walsh regime, and H.T. Wills, manager of the Bank of Commerce. The banker was the government agent and therefore semi-official.

This was a large enough social circle to meet Steele's needs, given his crushing burden of work. The mess was congenial and relieved occasionally by dinners at the home of Inspector Cortlandt Starnes, whose wife had accompanied him to Dawson. As he told Marie:

> I breakfast at nine and there is not an objectionable one at the mess table so that we all mess together at every meal. Harper is president and feeds us well, and I sit on the side of the table as is customary at meals for the C.O. to do. Capt. Burstall of the Yukon Field Force sits opposite Captain Ogilvie is at the right of me, Scarth is at the foot of the table Belcher on his left and the Dr is in the middle of that side.[42]

He was very grateful for the family hens, which Marie had insisted on sending with him from Fort Macleod. They supplied the mess with eggs that were rare and expensive items in Dawson. By the New Year he had established a daily routine that he carried out even when the temperature plunged to −45°C:

> I have been busy all day and have carried out my daily routine which is as follows—up at 7:00 walk one mile to the town station inquire if anything had transpired during the night, signed the book, walk up the long hill and then down the short steep one then breakfast, 9 AM. Then inspect the cells and prisoners, sign the book. Then—office and busy seeing people on business of all sorts until one o'clock. Then lunch—then the office until four o'clock, then three miles up the Klondyke on the ice, then up a long hill which takes ten minutes to ascend, then over the Mt through the upper town two miles to the top of the high hill behind the barracks, then down to quarters this in 1¼ hrs so you see I walk—then orderly room work until six o'clock then dinner—then letters to friends etc etc and my dearest wife and babies. This is varied by Council meetings and when it is I walk the five miles either before breakfast or after dinner.[43]

Steele's aloof attitude to Dawson society did not mean that he was unaware of what was going on in the town and in the larger territory. Quite the contrary, he was acutely conscious of what the population found most irritating about the government. At the top of the list was mail service. In July 1898 the government had contracted with an American company to carry the mail but the first shipment only got as far as Skagway before the company went bankrupt. This was a problem that Steele felt personally since his letters from Marie were held up. He could also do something about it. The Mounted Police had from the start operated what amounted to a courier service between Skagway and Dawson for their internal communications. With winter coming on, Steele proposed a dog team service every two weeks and Ogilvie quickly accepted.[44] The first mail run left Dawson on November 15, too early as it turned out. The sleds broke through the river ice, and while the drivers managed to escape, all the mail, including $500 Sam was sending to Marie, was lost.[45] After this nearly disastrous start the service worked well.

Another major grievance was the 10 per cent royalty charged by the government on gold produced. Steele had no sympathy whatsoever for those who complained about it. He confided to Marie:

*The miners are all howling about the royalties on the gold output, but it is all right. What on earth right have a few thousand foreigners to take out of the country that there is in it for nothing? We provide them with officers, peace, order and law and must the rest of the people of Canada pay for that? I should think not. It must be, if possible, raised in the country as long as we do not charge them with more than they can pay and make a good profit out of their work. Perhaps ten percent is too much, but judging from the fact that all who are willing to work come out with sacks of gold more money than they could earn in forty years or even in a hundred, they are not so much oppressed by the royalty.*[46]

There was nothing Steele could do about the royalty rate even had he wished to, but he could do his best to make sure that the government kept its side of the bargain. He knew that there were well-founded suspicions that the collection of the royalties was not as honest as it might be; some miners were able to evade it and some of the gold stuck to the hands of the collectors. In February 1899, Steele wrote to Ogilvie requesting that the collection of royalties be transferred to the police and he agreed. In both his autobiography and in a letter to Marie, Steele claimed that he set up a network of undercover detectives in all the mining camps to make sure the royalty was paid.[47] Just who these people were is a mystery. Steele does not mention them in his annual report, so they were certainly not on the government payroll. In any case, the system seems to have worked.

Once Steele's changes were in place there was general agreement that the police were administering the system according to the law, but in the public mind there was a sizeable loophole in the system. Government employees, including the police, were not prohibited from taking out claims and engaging in mining themselves. Constables and NCOs rarely had the money to invest, but officers did. Steele mounted an ingenious defence of the system in his annual report:

> The mining laws do not prohibit any one from locating mining property, and I do not believe the few claims that have been staked by members of the force have been the means of causing injury to the public; in fact, quite the contrary, besides it would be well to note that the members of the force are British subjects, and anything that they may make in their honest efforts will contribute to the prosperity of the Dominion.[48]

Steele was, of course, one of those making an "honest effort" to contribute to his country's prosperity by investing in claims and he was uneasily aware that, although it was within the letter of the law, it did not look good.

Sifton had instructed Commissioner Ogilvie to conduct an official inquiry into the charges of corruption against the Walsh administration, but the terms of reference were too narrow to stem the rising tide of criticism. Prohibiting government employees from mining would cost the government nothing and might help appease the critics. Early in 1899 Steele was busy trying to liquidate his mining investments in British Columbia so that he could invest in gold claims. He bought a quarter interest in two claims on Bonanza and Sulphur creeks with a small group of friends. This was done before the expected ban on government employees buying claims came down in May, so it was quite legal, but Steele thought it prudent to transfer ownership of his shares to Marie.[49] He even suggested that his mother-in-law should take out a Yukon miner's licence so that he could invest on her behalf. All of this seems at odds with Steele's rather self-righteous stand on refusing to accept a salary for serving on the Territorial Council, but several things were happening that shaped his attitudes.

By 1899, experience had shown that the extra pay for Yukon service was not nearly enough to compensate for the living costs in Dawson. Steele found that his duties as magistrate provided some help. The Canadian Criminal Code of the period provided that a portion of the court costs for each case tried went to the presiding judge if he was not a stipendiary (salaried) magistrate. There was no shortage of mostly minor cases to try, as he reported to Marie in July: "I made $190.00 yesterday in costs of cases and including that in the whole month I made $411.00 four hundred and eleven dollars exclusive of pay."[50] One, at least, of the cases, involving the crew of the steamship *Yukoner*, had complexities that would have baffled a Supreme Court justice. The *Yukoner* was originally owned by an American company which operated it from the Bering Sea port of St. Michael upriver to Dawson. The boat was purchased in the fall of 1898 by Pat Galvin, an American living in Dawson who had struck it rich on the creeks. A boiler explosion on her first trip under new ownership resulted in the *Yukoner* being iced in part way to Dawson for the winter. The owner and passengers went on to Dawson in another boat but the crew had to stay for the entire winter. When the ice finally melted in the spring they had not been paid for months and were in an understandably testy mood. A fight broke out between the captain and a crew member. The crew restrained the captain and put him aboard the next passing boat, but that was the extent of the violence involved.

The captain arrived in Dawson before the crew and went immediately before Steele's court to charge the crew with mutiny and piracy. Steele's experience as justice of the peace in the North-West Territories had, needless to say, included no cases of these exotic crimes. The alleged offences had probably been committed by Americans, probably in American territory, on board a Canadian boat owned by an American citizen. After consulting the chief justice and talking over the case with the American consul, Steele decided that he did have jurisdiction and committed the men for trial. He could quite easily have ducked the controversy that went with the case, but the mutiny offended his sense of order and discipline. "The case is important," he wrote to Marie, "for so many piratical acts have been done on the river in American territory that it is time something was done in the matter."[51] Owner Pat Galvin, on the other hand, sided with the crew. He hired the best available lawyers and posted their bail. The case dragged on for months after Steele had left the Yukon, by which time the accused had long since disappeared.

Steele's example of stern rectitude in his private life was generally followed by his officers and men. Many of them became lifelong friends and several later joined Lord Strathcona's Horse to follow him to South Africa. The only one who gave him serious trouble was one of his favourites, Inspector Frank Harper. Harper had joined the Mounted Police directly from England in 1880, enlisting as a constable and quickly rising through the ranks to become an inspector in 1887. Harper undoubtedly had some military experience in England and seems to have been an engaging and popular young man. In the spring of 1899, although he had a wife and children in the North-West Territories, Harper fell hard for a dance hall girl with the evocative name of "Diamond Tooth Gertie."⁵² He appeared with her frequently in public and spent all his pay on her. Worse still, as far as Steele was concerned, he began failing to show up for work and neglected his duties. Steele read him the riot act, reluctantly reported his unbecoming conduct to Ottawa, and sent him off on a lengthy tour of inspection upriver in hopes that absence from temptation might bring him to his senses. It seemed to work for a while but Harper absented himself again for four days in early August. In September there was worse news, as Steele recorded in his diary: "Judge tells me that Harper is $5000.00 short in his Sheriffs account etc I sent for him but up to the present no sign of him to be found. What a great pity a fool, wine and women."⁵³

Steele seems to have been quite unaware in the summer of 1899 that his enemies were working actively for his downfall. He spent July and most of August planning the winter work for his command and telling Marie that he hoped to be able to travel south for a visit the following summer. But at the end of August he received a disturbing report from Ottawa and he wrote with unaccustomed anxiety to Marie:

> Mr. White states that someone to whom I wrote has said that I gave them a statement re the maladministration in the Yukon and that I made charges against some of the officers in it, and I write to you to ask you dear if by any chance anyone got hold of anything I wrote you and if anyone else did. I wish you would ask Richard if I did write anything I have been so busy etc etc that I have not had time to copy my letters but I have been under the impression that I have been very guarded indeed. I do not think Auguste or Richard being lawyers would make such mistakes as to repeat anything written in confidence.⁵⁴

Steele knew the rules of the political game as well as anyone; opinions that might embarrass the government might be privately held and communicated but any criticisms that could be publicly attributed were fatal.

Paradoxically, Steele's very success in cleaning up the administration of the territory and silencing the critics of the government left him vulnerable. The drama of the trail of 1898 was receding in the public mind, the country was in the early stages of a prolonged economic boom, and there was a new issue—Britain's war in South Africa and whether Canada should become involved—to feed the headlines. Steele's tenuous Liberal connections had been enough to get him the command in the Yukon when the government's back was to the wall, but his position was always precarious. He had, in fact, been quite surprised that Superintendent Perry, who had much better Liberal credentials, was not appointed. Viewed through the cold lens of Ottawa politics, however, it made sense to let Steele do the heavy lifting in Dawson. If he failed, Perry could be sent in. If he succeeded, as in fact happened, Ottawa could take the credit. Either way, Steele was no longer the indispensable man. It is impossible to say for certain who was responsible for Steele's recall from the Yukon but the most likely candidate is Sir Charles Hibbert Tupper, son of the former prime minister. Tupper was the Conservative Party's point man on Yukon matters and there is a brief reference to him in Steele's diary in July 1899. Steele's friend, T.D. "Duff" Patullo, Ogilvie's secretary, Liberal insider and later premier of British Columbia, showed him a letter from Tupper to Major Morgan of the Yukon Field Force, asking for "all particulars of the mismanagement of the Yukon."[55]

Whether or not these were the details linked to Steele's name, sometime in August the damage was done. On September 7 the blow fell and it was crushing. That day he mailed his usual lengthy letter to Marie full of chatty gossip about events in Dawson.[56] Hours after the letter was mailed, a telegram arrived for him over the newly opened line. He wrote tersely in his diary, "Got orders to leave for the NWTy the first chance."[57] Word got out quickly and most residents of Dawson were outraged. All three of Dawson's newspapers, which never agreed on any other subject, united in demanding that the order be rescinded. Steele knew that any kind of effort in this direction would be futile and would in all probability damage his career further. He noted, "Great signs of dissatisfaction in the District owing to my move in to the NW Territories. I am told steps taken. Hope not."[58]

It took almost three weeks to make the necessary arrangements to turn over command of the Yukon. All accounts had to be finalized, not just for the NWMP operations, but for Steele's judicial work, his duties as a member of the Territorial Council, and other offices. He was working harder than ever, constantly interrupted by well-wishers dropping in to say goodbye and expressing their unhappiness at his firing. Finally it was all done and he made arrangements to leave on a steamboat departing upriver on September 26. When Steele got on board, several thousand people turned out at the dock and a deputation presented him with a bag of gold dust, not for himself but for his wife. The organizers must have been well aware that Steele would have refused it if the distinction had not been made. As the boat made its way toward Whitehorse, the men at the police posts along the river lined the banks to salute and cheer their former commander and flew the flags at half mast. It was these spontaneous expressions of respect that brought the first outburst of bitterness in Steele's diary: "Bad thing this cursed *strange* for one to be treated in this shameful way after working hard and honorably for the people of the Dominion and the honour of the government of our country. Curse the day I ever served such a country."[59]

After ten days on the river, the boat passed Whitehorse and near Carcross the passengers got on the new Yukon and White Pass railway that whisked them to Skagway in less than a day. Steele found Skagway little improved from his time there in 1898 but fortunately was able to get on board the SS *Humboldt* for Seattle after only one night in the town. The trip down the coast was uneventful and the company on board congenial. Steele was even able to play whist for the first time since he left Fort Macleod. He was in charge of a party of mentally ill individuals, "lunatics" in the official language of the period, who were being sent to southern Canada for treatment since there was no mental hospital in the Yukon, but they caused him no trouble. The *Humboldt* arrived in Seattle on October 11 and Steele and his charges sailed to Vancouver the following day. He spent several days in the city meeting with friends and, among other things, buying a civilian suit, perhaps an indication of how uncertain he was about his future in the Mounted Police. Then it was off to Montreal for the joyous reunion with his family.

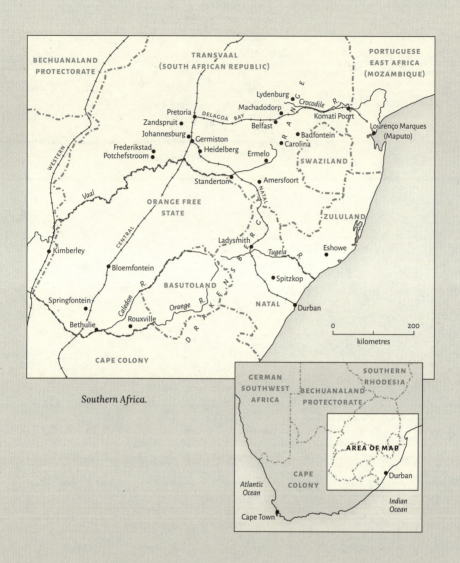

*Southern Africa.*

# 8 ‖ Fighting for Queen and Country
*Lord Strathcona's Horse*
1899–1901

WHEN SAM STEELE GOT BACK from the Yukon in October 1899, he was angry, frustrated, and worried about his future. The only thing he was certain of was that he did not want to return to commanding a Mounted Police post in the North-West Territories. The future of the NWMP was still very much in doubt and even if it survived, his damaged relations with the Liberal government made promotion unlikely. On the other hand, he had to find a way to support his young family, and staying in the Force, even under those circumstances, might be the only realistic alternative. He asked for and received leave until the end of the year to think about his future. As he had done at earlier turning points in his life, he returned to Orillia to spend time with family and friends. He did not ask their advice but re-establishing contact with his roots seemed to help him make his decision.

While Steele was in Orillia, things were happening in Ottawa that would change his life. Gold had taken him to the Yukon and it was another gold strike that would, indirectly, take him to Africa. The area that is now the Republic of South Africa had, by the last decade of the 19th century, an extraordinarily complex history of European colonialism going back 250 years. The Dutch first recognized the strategic importance of the southern tip of the continent for the seaborne trade with Asia when they established a colony at the Cape of Good Hope in the 1650s. After a century and a half, the descendants of the Dutch settlers, with the addition of a few French Huguenots in the 1690s, had developed an agricultural society based on slavery and the sternly Calvinist Dutch Reformed Church. By the time the British arrived to take over the colony during the Napoleonic Wars, the settlers had come to refer to themselves as "Boers" (farmers), a people whose way of life, and even their spoken language, was no longer entirely European but "Afrikaans" (African).[1]

After the British government decided to keep the territory, it managed to attract some English-speaking settlers to the Cape Colony but never enough to form a majority. Most of the Boers did not care much for the English but it was easy enough to avoid them at first. The Boers constantly pushed north and east against increasing resistance from the Bantu-speaking people who, like the Boers, lived by raising cattle. The Boers developed their own militia system, called a "commando," under which all able-bodied men had to have rifles and horses in readiness to be called out at a moment's notice to attack or defend. For many years, this organization, along with superior weaponry, provided land for growing Boer families, captured cattle to be incorporated into their herds, and captured Bantu to be enslaved. By the 1820s, however, resistance to Boer expansion was becoming fiercer and there were demands that the British authorities provide protection for the indigenous peoples. However, in the aftermath of the Napoleonic Wars the British government was in a cost-cutting mood, and rather than intervene militarily, endeavoured to reduce conflict in southern Africa by prohibiting frontier expansion and negotiating treaties with the Xhosa[2] and other African peoples—policies which were resented by the Boers.

In 1834, slavery was abolished throughout the British Empire. To many Boers, whose way of life was based upon slavery, and who were already unhappy under British rule, this was the final straw. A mass migration of as many as 15,000 people left the Cape in what was known as the Great Trek, to establish new states beyond the reach of British control.[3] The first of these, Natal, on the east coast was annexed by the British shortly thereafter, but the Orange Free State and the South African Republic (Transvaal) in the arid interior were left largely to themselves. As long as the British controlled the coastal areas, and therefore access to the interior, no one worried too much about the small, impoverished Boer republics, although powerful British anti-slavery groups like the London Missionary Society continued to press for intervention to protect the indigenous population.

The situation began to deteriorate in the late 1860s when the world's largest diamond deposits were discovered at Kimberley on the western edge of the Orange Free State. The diamond mining areas were quickly annexed by the British, but hints of further discoveries of diamonds and gold in the Boer republics sharpened the appetite of some people in London and Cape Town for more. In 1877 the British, buoyed by the success of Confederation in Canada, decided to impose a similar union on the Cape, Natal, Orange Free State, and Transvaal, whether they wished it or not. The two Boer republics were annexed as part of the process, but four years later rebelled and declared their independence, inflicting several stinging defeats on the British forces. The British backed off and saved face with a vague claim of a right to supervise the external relations of the republics. Just as things seemed to be settling down, there was a massive gold discovery at Johannesburg in the centre of the Transvaal.

At first, it seemed to the British that the influx of non-Boers to work the Rand mines meant that "the Transvaal would become British by default, pulling the Afrikaners of the interior into the British orbit, and making South Africa another Canada."[4] The president of the Transvaal, Paul Kruger, had other ideas and used his newfound wealth to bolster his country's independent status, buying arms from Germany and France, and negotiating with the Portuguese to build a railway through their territory of Portuguese East Africa (now Mozambique) to the port of Lourenço Marques (now Maputo) on the Indian Ocean. In the late 1890s the aggressive British Colonial Secretary Joseph Chamberlain—urged on by Cecil Rhodes, controller of the diamond industry and prime minister of the Cape Colony, whose British South Africa Company was moving north into what became Southern and Northern Rhodesia (now Zimbabwe and Zambia)—was determined to assert imperial power. The Jameson Raid, an attempted invasion from Rhodesia over the 1895–1896 New Year weekend, failed disastrously and only caused Kruger to step up his arms buying. In 1898 the British found an issue that they thought could be used to control the Boers. Thousands of miners had poured into the Transvaal with the gold strikes. These "Uitlanders" (foreigners), as the Boers called them, were not numerous enough to swamp the Afrikaner population, but since they were overwhelmingly adult males, if given the vote, might threaten the political control of hard-liners like Kruger. As a result, the Boer republics imposed a residency requirement of ten years, thereby denying the vote to the Uitlanders. The British, in turn, pressured the Transvaal to make changes and began strengthening their military forces in South Africa.[5]

Negotiations broke down in the summer of 1899 and the Boer military leaders decided that it would be better to attack while their fighters still had a numerical advantage before British reinforcements arrived. When they opened the fighting on October 11, the Boers were clearly hoping that a series of quick defeats would force the British to recognize their independence as they had in 1881, and at that time it seemed like a reasonable hope. The Boers could put about 35,000 tough, well-organized fighters who knew the country into the field, as opposed to the 27,000 British soldiers available in South Africa at the time.[6] The Afrikaner forces were exceptionally well armed with the latest in German Mauser rifles, machine guns, and Krupp field artillery. The first encounters, culminating in the Boer victories of "Black Week" in early December, seemed to validate the strategy. But this was not the 1880s. Britain was on an imperialist high in 1899, having celebrated Queen Victoria's Diamond Jubilee two years earlier, with representatives from every corner of the greatest empire the world had ever seen. The country was not about to let a few early defeats stand in the way this time.

Canadians were largely innocent of any detailed knowledge of the complexities of the South African situation, but that did not stop them from holding strong opinions, either for or against the British position. Opposition to any Canadian involvement was centred in Quebec and, as Carman Miller points out in *Painting the Map Red: Canada and the South African War, 1899–1902*, enthusiasm for the war was strongest in the large cities of Anglophone Canada.[7] Prime Minister Wilfrid Laurier, with an election due in 1900, did his best to avoid the divisive issue. The English commanding officer of the Canadian militia, General E.T.H. Hutton, lobbied openly for Canada to send troops, which infuriated Laurier and his minister of Militia, Frederick Borden. Relations between the general and the government quickly became toxic. By the time the fighting began, pressure from the majority of the electorate in favour of Canadian participation became irresistible. Just two days after the start of the war, Ottawa announced that an infantry force of a thousand men, the Royal Canadian Regiment (RCR), would go. The other branches of the militia, cavalry and artillery, felt slighted and campaigned vigorously for a second contingent. Having given in to the principle, and since the British government was paying most of the shot, the government decided on November 1 to send a force of mounted infantry and field artillery. The British government was, at this point, more interested in the political gesture of imperial solidarity that the first contingent had supplied and deferred accepting the offer. It hastened to change its mind on December 16 after the defeats of "Black Week."

Steele was an interested observer of these manoeuvres. Even before the announcement of a second contingent in mid-December, rumours flew that mounted troops were to be sent and few Canadians knew as much about commanding such units under fire as he did. The prospect of seeing real action was far more appealing than going back to a police post in the North-West Territories. On the other hand, leaving Marie and the children so soon after his sojourn in the Yukon would be wrenching. For the month of November, at least, he was content to wait and see how things developed. The wait was not long. Steele was called to Ottawa in late December where Hutton offered him the position of second in command of the mounted unit he was planning. Steele's political sense had been honed by his Yukon experience and he quickly realized that Hutton was on his way out as general officer commanding of the Canadian militia, so he turned the offer down.[8] Hutton's plan was rejected in favour of two mounted units—the Royal Canadian Dragoons recruited in central and eastern Canada, and the Canadian Mounted Rifles (CMR) in the west.

Steele claims in his autobiography that he was offered and accepted command of the CMR, but that "I was on the point of proceeding west to organize the corps, when of my own accord and for reasons of my own I gave up the command and was appointed second."[9] The top spot went instead to NWMP Commissioner L.W. Herchmer. This was, on the face of it, an extraordinary decision. Steele was accepting the position of second in command of a smaller unit than the one he had just turned down, to work under a man with whom he had had a difficult relationship. As he so often did, he explained the "reasons of my own" in his letters to Marie. The CMR were to be recruited and officered largely from the Mounted Police and that bore heavily on his hopes of becoming commissioner: "I am very unhappy at leaving you and would not go if no police were going but if others went it would give them a claim on me for promotion when they came back and that would not do."[10] If Herchmer wanted the job, which he did, politics dictated

that he must have it, at least for the time being. Steele was told
confidentially that when the CMR got to South Africa, Herchmer
would be moved to a staff job so that Steele could command in the
field.[11]

Something like this in fact happened to Herchmer in South Africa,
but by that time Steele's career had taken a different direction.
On the last day of 1899, Lord Strathcona, the immensely wealthy
Canadian high commissioner in London, offered to pay for the
recruiting and equipment of another mounted unit to be raised in
western Canada. Unlike the earlier Canadian contingents, Lord
Strathcona's Horse, as it was quickly named, would be a temporary
unit of the British Army. Strathcona, unaware of the tensions in the
Militia Department, asked that Hutton choose the officers, but
when Laurier demurred, he agreed to let Militia minister Borden do
it. Steele, in spite of his anger over being pulled out of the Yukon,
had been busily mending fences with the Liberal government since
his return. He was working through Marie's uncle Henry but he now
added something new. One of his officers from the Yukon, Inspector
Francis Cartwright, son of Laurier's minister of Trade and Commerce,
Sir Richard Cartwright, had sent him a letter recommending Steele
to his father. The cabinet could now be sure that Steele would not
make political trouble about the Yukon and it would be safe to give
him a high-profile military command. Borden suggested Steele's
name as commanding officer and Strathcona unhesitatingly agreed.

While these negotiations were going on, Steele was very busy
recruiting and organizing the CMR. When the news of Strathcona's
Horse became public on January 15, he was on a train from Fort
Macleod with most of the CMR bound for Halifax. Although his
autobiography states that he was not offered command until he
was in Halifax ready to sail January 30, his diary tells a slightly
different story.[12] When the CMR train passed through Montreal on
January 21, Steele heard from his family that he was being considered for command of the new regiment. The rumour was confirmed
by General Hutton when the train reached Halifax the following

day.[13] On January 25, Steele was headed back to Ottawa to organize Lord Strathcona's Horse, elated at the opportunity to shape the new regiment as he wanted. Within a few days he had ordered all the equipment for the unit and was ready to find the men he needed. No detail was too small to escape his attention. He reported to Marie that he had persuaded the authorities to issue four pairs of socks to the men instead of two.[14] Strathcona arranged for McGill veterinary professor Duncan McEachran to buy the horses, so Steele did not need to worry about that. Steele knew that most of the best available recruits from the Mounted Police had already gone with the CMR—after all he had picked them out himself—but he was confident he could find enough men with the right stuff outside the Force to supplement the core of NWMP officers and NCOs. He left Ottawa for the west on January 31 and before he reached Regina, he had more than a thousand applicants for the 500 places available.[15]

Whenever possible Steele personally selected recruits, making sure they could ride and shoot and that they were to be, as he instructed his recruiting officer in Winnipeg, "men of the most respectable character...such as would pass into the North West Mounted Police."[16] Some of the earlier contingents had found that unfit men managed to make their way to South Africa so Steele arranged that all were to have two medical examinations, one at recruitment and another when the regiment assembled. There would be no extended period of training to bring the regiment together, so Steele attempted to recruit the troops of thirty-eight men (each of the regiment's three squadrons had four troops) from the same districts and keep them together. Major Robert Belcher, Steele's choice as second in command, was sent east with instructions that, "On arrival in Ottawa he is to place the troops from different localities under an Officer and Non-Commissioned Officer both to be if possible from the same district as the men."[17] Several officers and men from the Yukon were making their way by dogsled to join and a few more, "buglers, batmen and shoeing smiths," would be found in the east.[18] The Strathconas were allotted a

Vickers-Maxim machine gun to each squadron, the crews to be provided by the artillery.[19]

Recruiting was complete by February 9 and two trainloads of men left for Ottawa. The regiment was quartered in the Lansdowne Park agricultural exhibition buildings, which, although meant to accommodate farm animals, were comfortable enough. That was just as well, since they spent the next month in the capital waiting for the earlier contingents to depart Halifax. Horses, clothing, and equipment arrived over the next two weeks and Steele used the time to work on the training of his men. The Strathconas, as a body, had significantly less military experience than the earlier units so discipline might have been a problem. Steele's long experience told him that attempts to impose traditional strict military discipline would not work in these circumstances. Discipline there must be, but the officers were ordered to see that there was to be no "harshness or ungentlemanly conduct towards the men."[20] Steele would find experienced leadership, even if it meant bucking the British Army. Lieutenant E.C. Parker, who had served in the Royal Munster Fusiliers, had recruited one of the British Columbia troops and seemed to Steele to have the badly needed military credentials. When the British Army refused to grant him a commission, on the grounds of some alleged misdeed, Steele appealed to Borden to overturn the decision. When that failed, Parker offered to enlist as a private. Steele agreed and immediately promoted him to senior sergeant.[21]

The month in Ottawa meant that Marie could come up to spend some time with Sam. He wrote her warning that work would take precedence: "I do not think you need bring up a low necked dress. Everyone is so busy that it is impossible to do anything in the way of entertaining."[22] Marie undoubtedly ignored her husband's fashion advice since they did dine with family members, with Fred White, and with senior Militia Department staff while in the capital. By the end of the first week in March the regiment had acquired all of its equipment and horses and the last few men from the Yukon

*Officers and men of "B" squadron, Lord Strathcona's Horse, at Ottawa before leaving for South Africa. [BPSC, 2008.1.3.2.6.1.4]*

were trickling in. Through Borden, Steele arranged a ceremonial presentation of guidons on Parliament Hill. He noted in the Lord Strathcona's Horse War Diary that "The Minister and Lady Borden take a great interest in the regiment," an interest that he cultivated at every opportunity.[23] The British defeats in December had the paradoxical effect of increasing enthusiasm for Canadian participation, even in Quebec.[24] Thousands of people showed up for the guidon ceremony and heard speeches by Laurier, Borden, and the leader of the opposition, Sir Charles Tupper. When the Strathconas marched to the station to board the train for Halifax on March 12, the crowds were so dense the troops could hardly make their way through to board. In Montreal the crowds were even bigger. Steele estimated there were 30,000 people, including students from McGill and Laval, lining the route as the men marched to a civic banquet. They were finally able to get away by 10 P.M.[25]

The train trip to Halifax, with Marie and her mother aboard, was an extended triumphal procession, with presentations of flags and speeches at all stops along the way. Lord Strathcona had astutely associated his unit in the public mind with Teddy Roosevelt's Rough Riders, who had garnered huge publicity for their exploits in Cuba during the Spanish-American War a year earlier. Steele built on this image by equipping his men with Stetson hats and California stock saddles; adding an essential British touch by recruiting a few privates from the Alberta ranching community with aristocratic connections, notably Lord Edward Seymour and Robert Cochrane.[26] This image of the Strathconas as a unit that combined the toughness of the western frontier with social exclusiveness was irresistible to the press of the day. Steele knew that it had benefits that went far beyond ephemeral publicity: it helped create the *esprit de corps* he regarded as essential and it made the regiment difficult for the military leadership in South Africa to ignore. Some of the other Canadian units spent a lot of time on boring lines-of-communication assignments. Steele was determined this would not happen to Lord Strathcona's Horse.

The train pulled into Halifax early on March 15 and the men immediately loaded the horses aboard the SS *Monterey*, which had been chartered to take them to South Africa. Dr. McEachern was worried, correctly as it turned out, that they might contract disease from the stables ashore.[27] The men had to endure another round of parades, ceremonies—including the reading of a telegram from Queen Victoria—and speeches before they got on board the following day. Steele, in typical fashion, had everything organized for them. Training routines began immediately and continued daily until the ship reached Cape Town, although in hot weather near the equator, Steele moved the exercises to the cooler temperatures of the early morning.[28] The men thrived on the routine but the voyage turned out to be disastrous for the horses. They started getting sick the first day out of Halifax. At first it was thought the animals were suffering from seasickness because the ship rolled a lot, but efforts to make them more comfortable, even to the point of giving them a shot of whiskey, failed to help and they began to die: two on March 18, eleven on March 19, and seven on March 20, with no signs of stopping.[29] Pneumonia was the cause and Steele and his veterinary officers could only wait helplessly for the epidemic to run its course. Before it did, 162 horses were dead, more than a quarter of the number loaded at Halifax.

The close quarters on the ship and the lack of distractions apart from the horses meant that Steele could concentrate on assessing his officers and NCOs. The War Diary gives the impression that there were few problems, but Steele was, as usual, more frank in his letters to Marie. "Some of the officers," he noted, "are green yet in looking after the health and comfort of their men."[30] The most important NCO, the regimental sergeant major, Frank Elliot, had been taken on with strong recommendations from General Hutton, but Steele had only given him an acting appointment until he proved himself. Elliot evidently came to the Strathconas with a healthy sense of entitlement, which he demonstrated by being insolent to Major Belcher. If he expected Hutton's sponsorship to protect him, he was sorely mistaken. Steele immediately reduced his rank to private and replaced him as regimental sergeant major with his nephew, Elmes Steele.[31] This bit of nepotism might easily have backfired, but Elmes, who had served in the 90th Battalion in Winnipeg and the NWMP, had the necessary experience to command respect.[32] He had been Sam's clerk since the formation of the regiment and had demonstrated his administrative abilities in that position.[33]

There were the usual minor disciplinary issues to be dealt with. The month in Ottawa had given the men time to connect with the local prostitutes and the results made themselves apparent for some. "Gave orders that no men of the few with private diseases wash where

*Lord Strathcona's Horse rifle drill on the way to South Africa. [BPSC, 2008.1.3.2.6.2.3.11]*

the others do," Steele noted in his diary.[34] Beer was available to the men on board and a few overindulged, including some senior NCOs, so Steele ordered the canteen to stop serving it.[35]

As the crisis with the horses began to recede and Steele was satisfied that he was shaping his regiment into something that would live up to the high expectations of both its sponsor and the Canadian public, he allowed himself to relax a little. That brought an immediate attack of longing for the family he left behind: "Oh my darling how I miss you and the dear little ones. I hope God may bring me back safe to you my pet. God bless you, Love to all and thousands of kisses to you the children."[36] A week later, he was still in a deeply homesick mood. "I am very lonely dear but I know you are too my pet and I must be cheerful and write cheerfully. I hope we will not be long parted and that I will do my duty well. I am trying hard to do so my own dearest. God bless you all."[37] As the boat neared Cape Town, Steele's thoughts turned increasingly to what would face the Strathconas once they reached land.

Uppermost was the question of horses. He confided to Marie:

> Lost 160 horses by pneumonia. This has been an unfortunate my dear and although it is through no fault of mine that the horses have been lost, yet no doubt it may injure my reputation very much. No doubt a great many men tried to get the command and some of them will be envious and ready to damage me. We will most likely have to remain in camp for a couple of weeks whether the war is over or not.[38]

To his relief, upon arrival he quickly discovered that many other units had suffered similar losses and that remounts were available, although their quality left much to be desired.[39] His concern that the war might be over before the Strathconas could get into action was allayed at once by a rather enigmatic telegram from the commander in chief, Lord Roberts: "Bloemfontein No C1065 12th April 1900. The Officer Commanding Strathcona's Horse not to be disappointed at not being brought here. There is very important work for his corps to do for which I have specially selected it. Ends."[40]

Newly arrived units at Cape Town were vulnerable to having their pockets picked in various ways by those already there. The transport officers immediately confiscated Lord Strathcona's Horse's draft horses and wagons, replacing them with inferior animals and equipment before Steele could make the necessary personal connections that would allow him to protect his regiment.[41] Poaching could even extend to men. General Hutton, now in South Africa and organizing a scouting unit, asked for volunteers from the Strathconas. The War Diary laconically recorded: "A number of men paraded under the impression that they were really required, but upon the facts being stated, withdrew their names, preferring to serve with the regiment. Informed Major General Hutton by wire of the result."[42]

There were a few of his men that he might happily have sent on to Hutton. Several ignored orders and left the Green Point camp to sample the charms of Cape Town. Steele was obliged to deal firmly with some repeat offenders and admitted to Marie that the hasty recruiting had turned up undesirables in the ranks: "Wilson and a few more have broken out of camp two or three times and been brought in by the military police. These men have been tried by court martial and several sent to cells. They should not have been engaged but barring about 20 men the rest are first class chaps."[43] There was time for Steele to deal with these personnel problems because it took more than a month in camp to sort out the horse situation. The Cape Town camp turned out to be infected with an equine respiratory disease called glanders, which was endemic in South Africa. More horses died or were shot to prevent the spread of the disease and had to be replaced.

The delay allowed Steele to learn about the kind of war his men would have to fight and train them accordingly. All members of the regiment were armed and mounted, including clerks. He quickly realized that mobile firepower was vitally important and he worked his three Maxim machine guns hard. He was delighted when the Strathconas received one of the new Vickers-Maxim 37mm quick-firing guns, known as "pom poms," that the British rushed in when it was realized the Boers were making good use of them. The pom poms were very large machine guns that fired exploding shells at a rate of 300 rounds per minute. They had, Steele noted with satisfaction, "a very discouraging effect on the enemy."[44]

The time in Cape Town also brought a number of Canadian visitors. L.W. Herchmer, on medical leave from the CMR, dropped by, shortly before he was relieved of his command. Most important for Steele's future were several visits from the Conservative MP and militia colonel, Sam Hughes. Hughes was the most vocal member of the "colonels' lobby," the group of Canadian MPs in the late 19th century who did their best to promote the interests of the militia. He despised regular soldiers and fervently believed that enthusiastic amateurs, like himself, were far superior. In the months leading up to the war Hughes campaigned relentlessly for Canadian participation, infuriating Laurier and his cabinet, while at the

*Green Point Camp near Cape Town, the Strathconas' first experience of South Africa. The obsolete cannon cannot have been reassuring. [BPSC, 2008.1.3.2.6.2.5.2]*

same time alienating General Hutton by his insistence that Hughes should be allowed to personally recruit and lead a Canadian contingent. When this met a brusque refusal, he managed to sail to South Africa as a civilian on the same ship as the RCR and spent the next two months pleading with the British military authorities for a job. A shortage of British officers led to an appointment as supply officer, then as a scout for Brigadier Herbert Settle's small force suppressing a rebellion in the northern Cape Colony.

The Cape rebels were lightly armed with obsolete Martini-Henry rifles and badly organized, a situation made to order for the impetuous Hughes who led the way in recapturing several towns.[45] The lack of serious opposition (the rebels, unlike the soldiers of the Free State and the Transvaal, had no machine guns or artillery) confirmed all Hughes's prejudices about British regular soldiers. In late April Hughes was back in Cape Town, awaiting reassignment and telling anyone who would listen about his exploits. Steele saw him several times and his reaction was noncommittal at first. "Lt Col Sam Hughes called to see the officers of the regiment. He says the Boers are cowards and not good shots," he wrote in his diary.[46] After a few days his opinion had deteriorated: "Dined with Sam Hughes. Sam as usual vulgar and egotistical."[47] In a letter to Marie two weeks later he was even more scathing. He and some other officers had met the group of Canadian nurses leaving for the front: "Col. Hughes (Sam) was with them. He is a blowhard and a nuisance. Does not have sense enough to keep his tongue quiet and makes a show of Canada among the modest but brave soldiers of all parts here. I avoid his company the fool."[48] Hughes had been offered a captaincy in Lord Strathcona's Horse when it was forming in Canada and scornfully turned it down. Steele was very grateful he had been spared that burden but Hughes would return to his life a decade later.

Finally, in the last week in May, the promised assignment materialized. It was the brainchild of one of the most interesting people ever to enter Sam Steele's life—the Anglo-Irish diplomat (later to be executed for treason during the First World War) Roger Casement. In 1899 Casement was British Consul in Portuguese West Africa (now Angola) but he had earlier served in Lourenço Marques. The only railway line into the Boer republics from the outside world not controlled by the British ran from Lourenço Marques into the Transvaal, crossing the Crocodile River which formed the border at a place called Komati Poort. Casement discovered that the bridge there was lightly defended by the Boers and pushed hard for a quick surprise attack by a small force that would march through Swaziland, blow up the bridge, and hold off the Boers until reinforcements arrived. The plan was daring and risky but might have succeeded if it had been carried out when it was first proposed in early April. After two months of ponderous negotiations involving Casement, British High Commissioner Sir Alfred Milner, and the army command, it finally got under way.

On May 24 the first ship with "A" and "C" squadrons left for Natal. Four days later the ss *Wakool* with "B" squadron, Steele and Casement followed. As soon as they were at sea, Steele opened his sealed orders outlining the raid. In the War Diary Steele wrote—at a date before they left—that "There is too much talk of this move. The Army people do not seem to be sufficiently discreet."[49] But that was probably wisdom after the fact; his personal diary of those days shows no sign of concern. In any case, when the ship arrived at Kosi Bay near the border of Portuguese East Africa on June 3, a dispatch from Lourenço Marques was waiting with Admiral Sir Robert Harris, the British naval commander in charge of the operation, that word of the operation had leaked and the Boers had strongly reinforced the bridge garrison. Harris, showing more sense than most of the British land commanders at this stage of the war, wisely called the mission off.[50] As Casement's biographer admits, the scheme had "a Wild West aura" about it that reflected his romanticism.[51]

Steele and "B" squadron rejoined the rest of the regiment at Durban and discovered that the plan was not quite dead. Understanding its revival requires a brief foray into the politics of the British Army high command in South Africa. The commander in chief of the British forces there at the outbreak of the war was General Sir Redvers Buller, a man who knew the country well and, having fought the Boers in the 1881 war, recognized them as a tough and capable enemy.[52] Buller's pre-war warnings were ignored, and he was sent to South Africa with a completely inadequate number of men and insufficient equipment. Several of his subordinates compounded the situation by disregarding explicit instructions and getting themselves trapped in the towns of Kimberley, Mafeking, and Ladysmith. The situation at Ladysmith in Natal was particularly serious because the Boers made good use of the formidable barrier of the Tugela River to turn back four bloody attempts by Buller's forces to relieve the town. They also adapted their tactics much more quickly than the British did to take advantage of the long-range, magazine rifles firing smokeless powder that were now the standard weapons of both sides. Buller's early failures allowed his enemies to have him demoted to command only of the Natal front and replaced in overall command by the team of Field Marshall Lord Roberts and his chief of staff, Lord Kitchener. Buller had opposed the Casement operation, while Roberts approved it.

The result was confusion. Steele's diary recorded: "B Squadron disembarked today after some delay caused by conflicting telegrams. Had great trouble in getting matters settled Lord Roberts and Sir R Buller being on different lines. Got telegram from Lord Roberts through Military Secretary to say that he approved of the operation and asked me to carry it out at once."[53] Steele with "B" squadron went by train to join the rest of the regiment who were waiting on the Tugela River. On June 10 the united force moved north to the town of Eshowe in Zululand, which would be the departure point for the raid. After two days of pleasant marching through country that Steele thought resembled the foothills west of Calgary, the Strathconas were informed by telegram first that the operation had been postponed, and then that it had once again been cancelled.[54] Rather disconsolately, they marched back to Durban. The war seemed as if it might be ending with Roberts's forces marching into Pretoria and Transvaal President Kruger fleeing his capital, but Steele and his men were cheered by the news that many of the younger Boer generals and political leaders were vowing to continue the fight. As Buller had predicted, the conflict would soon devolve into a guerilla war, which meant that mobile forces like the Strathconas would be more necessary than ever.

On June 16 the regiment boarded eight trains at Durban and spent the next four days travelling to Zandspruit in the Transvaal, where Buller was organizing his army to pursue some of the remaining Boer forces. Once there they became part of Lord Dundonald's 3rd Mounted Brigade. Buller had been part of the Red River Expedition as a young officer and Robert Cochrane, Dundonald's son, was serving in the Strathconas, so both greeted Steele warmly. They inspected the regiment and complimented Steele on it. This was all very well but neither seemed in any hurry to get on with the war and Steele chafed at the delay. "All we want is one fight," he wrote wistfully to Marie.[55] In fact, Steele was lucky to have had a slow introduction to the fighting. At this point, like so many others before encountering the Boers in the field, he was still inclined to underestimate the enemy. On the train trip from Durban he noted the trenches along the Tugela River with their carefully constructed stone breastworks that had enabled General Botha's men to hold off Buller's much larger force so easily: "Passed Ladysmith covered with breastworks of stone made carefully and evidently designed by foreign engineers."[56] Like most of the British officers in South Africa, Steele's only actual fighting experience was on a small scale against poorly armed opponents and he found it hard to believe that the Boers were a sophisticated enemy. Steele, however, picked up the lessons to be learned very quickly and saved the lives of many of his men.

Buller's large force moved up the railway toward the town of Standerton against light opposition, which allowed the Strathconas to get some scouting experience. The retreating Boers blew up the railway bridge at Standerton, bringing the advance to a halt until it could be repaired. While they waited, the Canadians were sent out on patrols into the countryside. Steele thought their work inexcusably sloppy at first, tore a strip off several officers, and reduced one sergeant to the ranks for looting.[57] One of the other mounted units in Dundonald's brigade was the South African Light Horse (SALH), a regiment recruited entirely from Uitlanders driven out of the Transvaal at the start of the war, who were inclined to take revenge on the Boers by looting whenever the opportunity offered. Some of the Strathconas had picked up on these ideas but Steele was determined that his regiment would not loot. Once the bridge was repaired, Buller sent a strong force up the railway to Heidelberg, while the mounted units protected the flanks by patrolling. On one of these patrols, the Strathconas suffered their first battle casualties on July 1.

When a section of the troop under Lieutenant Seymour Tobin came under fire, three men were sent to investigate a farmhouse with a white flag and Private Angus Jenkins from Red Deer was shot and killed. After a quick funeral attended by Lord Dundonald and his staff, Steele had him buried on the farm, ordered the farmer to respect the grave, and took a couple of snapshots of it to ensure that he did.[58] Captain Donald Howard and Private Jonathan Hobson were captured the same day, although both were released a month later, when Buller's forces overran the main Boer prisoner of war camp. A few days later "A" squadron was escorting a supply convoy under the command of the 10th Hussars. When they were attacked by a party of 300 Boers, the British officer in charge, Major Rycroft, ordered a troop under Lieutenant Ketchen to occupy one of the small rocky hills known as *kopjes*. The commander of "A" squadron, Major Snyder, thought it was too far away to be supported but obeyed orders. He was quickly proved right as the six Strathconas were surrounded, at which point Rycroft compounded the error by refusing to go to their rescue. A battery of horse artillery arrived and drove the Boers off, but by that time the Boers had killed one of the party and captured the rest.[59]

Knowing that his regiment would suffer losses, more in fact from illness and accident than from enemy action, Lord Strathcona had arranged for fifty replacements to follow the main group. They arrived in Cape Town under the command of Lieutenant Agar Adamson just after the regiment left for Natal. Adamson was an Ottawa civil servant and militia officer who had tried unsuccessfully to join the earlier Canadian contingents. His wealthy and politically well-connected wife pulled strings to get him the appointment this time around.[60] In the first week of July the reinforcement party moved up from Durban with the SALH. On a patrol on July 5, Adamson's men were lured into a pursuit of some retreating Boers that turned out to be a trap. Several were severely wounded and two captured. The only redeeming feature of the incident came when Sergeant Arthur Richardson rode out under heavy fire and rescued one of the wounded men. He received Canada's first Victoria Cross for his heroism.

The episode marked the beginning of a rapid deterioration of relations between Steele and Adamson. One of Adamson's goals was to obtain a commission in the British Army, something that was only likely to happen if he distinguished himself in some way. Adamson had courage in abundance but Steele knew that a "death or glory" attitude would only get his soldiers needlessly killed. He remarked in a letter to Marie: "The Anglo Saxon when young has to be taught caution by a severe lesson. I hope they will be more careful in future."[61] Steele would have wholeheartedly agreed with General George Patton's comment that "the object of war is not to die for your country, but to make the other bastard die for his."[62] The personalities of the two men were so different that a clash was almost inevitable. Adamson came from a prominent Ottawa family and had attended Cambridge. Before he left for South Africa he paid a visit to his future commanding officer's wife. Marie, always acutely conscious about social slights, was not charmed by her visitor: "I must confess I was not much impressed with Lt. Adamson. He is *too English* for me with all his airs & capers—he spoke as if he had a hot boiled potato in his mouth & made such foolish speeches."[63] Adamson seems to have considered Steele as an Ontario backwoodsman who would never have made it in Ottawa. Steele "lacked polish," he told his wife. It irritated Adamson that Steele, in spite of his social deficiencies, was a very successful commander who unaccountably had attracted the patronage of Lord Strathcona. There was never a direct confrontation; instead Adamson poured out his frustrations in letters his wife, full of half-truths and outright fabrications about Steele that found their way into Ottawa gossip.[64]

On July 7, a squadron of the Strathconas escorted General Buller to Heidelberg where he met Roberts and travelled with him to Pretoria to consult on the future direction of the war. To ensure that the Strathconas got what Steele considered an appropriate part in that direction he wrote to Dundonald, requesting that they be employed as a unit on scouting duties and not broken up into small parties guarding the railroad. While Buller was conferring the regiment got some rest, remounts, baths, and new clothing—even haircuts.[65] When the general returned, the news was good. Buller's force would pursue Botha's army into the very difficult country of the Drakensberg Mountains in the northeastern Transvaal. Steele's men would be very much a part of the advance. The first step was to escort a large supply convoy back down the railway line to the jumping off point at Paardekop.

On August 7 the push to the north began against serious opposition from Botha's estimated 7,000 men, who had thirteen long-range field guns positioned on the *kopjes* to dominate the road. Buller's infantry attacked the Boer positions while the Strathconas, leading the 3rd Mounted Brigade on the left front of the column, were given the job of working around to outflank the enemy. They did so very successfully, advancing about thirty kilometres and driving the Boers out of the town of Amersfoort. After a delay of two days caused by heavy fog, the force moved out for Ermelo forty kilometres north with the Strathconas again in the van. In spite of a dust storm that lasted all day and often reduced visibility to less than a hundred metres, Steele used his pom pom and machine guns to overcome pockets of resistance. Major Jarvis and "B" squadron were first into the town, taking it over and capturing several Boer fighters and quantities of arms.[66] The advance resumed August 13 against light opposition with the Strathconas given a break acting as rear guard. The next day Lord Dundonald ordered Steele to investigate the town of Carolina a few kilometres off the line of march. Major Belcher with "C" squadron ran into heavy fire from the town but the men were able to dismount and drive the Boers out.

This was the first time that the Strathconas came under heavy fire that threatened to cause large numbers of casualties. Steele responded quickly by moving his men into a convenient hollow, which gave them some protection. The incident was recorded by Trooper R.P. Rooke:

> *While we were standing in the hollow, one of the* S.A.L.H. *scouts on the ridge in front of us was struck by a pom pom shell, right in full view of us all, the shell striking him in the leg, & entered his horse's side & bursting made a fearful sight & unnerved us all. But the Colonel kept us in hand & by keep us moving around in a square enabled us to keep our horses under control & calm our own nerves.*[67]

They held the town while Lieutenant-Colonel George Henderson, Buller's chief intelligence officer, searched for letters and papers that might reveal the Boers' intentions, then blew up the magazine and pulled out. Two men who had become separated from the main group rode into town to find the Strathconas gone and the enemy back in control. They managed to bluff them by claiming to be an advance patrol of a much larger force and after a tense night made their escape in the early morning with an angry group of Boers hot on their heels. The following day, as the advance resumed, there may have occurred an incident similar to the war crime that led to the court martial and execution of the Australian officer Harry "Breaker" Morant a year later.[68] The story was that a group of Strathconas were scouting with a party of the SALH. Checking out a farmhouse displaying a white flag, the SALH were fired upon and one or two of their men killed. The Canadians then allegedly joined the surviving members of the SALH, captured half a dozen Boers, and hanged them from a tree in the farmyard.[69] The men involved were supposedly taken before General Buller and severely reprimanded, then released.

The story is not beyond the realm of possibility. Certainly there were numerous recorded incidents of the Boers firing from locations displaying white flags. The problem is that there are no eyewitness accounts of the event. The most detailed version came from a Strathcona trooper, R.P. Rooke, who wrote it down in a memoir seven years after the war. He did not witness the incident but heard about it from others and was "a mile or two" away from the farm when it was supposed to have happened. There is no official record of any soldiers being reprimanded by Buller. The War Diary is silent on the subject, but while Steele had ample opportunity to sanitize that document, his personal diary and the very detailed letters to his wife written immediately after the hangings were supposed to have happened contain not a word that would support the allegations. Agar Adamson, who in his letters to his wife never missed an opportunity to pass on in great detail anything that might discredit Steele, and who was close by at the time, makes only an enigmatic reference to rumours circulating.[70]

General Botha retreated north to the town of Belfast where he decided to make a stand, constructing trenches on a long ridge just to the south of the town. This set the stage for the last large-scale conventional battle of the war. Buller waited a week for Roberts's army to join up then launched his attack on August 22. For the first few days it was largely an infantry and artillery battle, with little for the Strathconas to do. On August 26 they entered the fight, protecting the flank of Buller's advance against the centre of the Boer line. The position was exposed and under enemy observation but the Strathconas held them off all day, retiring under fire after the main force got into position to attack the key to the Boer position, Bergendal Farm, the following day. In the course of that day the regiment fired more than 12,000 rounds of rifle and machine gun ammunition and 500 rounds from their pom pom.[71]

The following day an intense artillery bombardment, followed by a bayonet charge, captured the farm and collapsed the defence line, forcing Botha to retreat again. Machadodorp, the next town just fifteen kilometres north, was not just a major supply centre but the place where President Kruger had retreated from Pretoria and established his temporary capital. He now left the country and made his way to Lourenço Marques where a Dutch warship took him to Europe. Buller's force pushed on against stiff resistance. The Strathconas came under heavy artillery fire and were lucky to escape with only a few wounded. One of the enemy shells exploded near Steele while he was conferring with Buller and Lord Dundonald, wounding one of Dundonald's staff officers and two Strathcona privates.[72] The Strathconas dismounted and drove the Boers out, capturing the town.

Most people on the British side expected that Botha's defeat and the departure of Kruger would mean a quick end to the war. Botha, however, although down to about 2,500 men, showed no signs of giving up. In fact, he and the other Boer military leaders were planning a different kind of war.[73] He still had plenty of room to move in the rugged terrain, as the historian Thomas Pakenham described it, "God-given country for Boer tactics."[74] In September he moved sixty kilometres north to base himself on the town of Lydenburg. His rear guard contested the British advance every step of the way and on September 1, one of them came close to putting Steele's war to an end. The Strathconas had pushed the enemy across the Crocodile River but one of them stayed behind hiding beneath a bridge. As Steele and Captain George Cameron trotted across he fired three shots through the bridge deck.[75] The narrow escape did not bother Steele, but another incident involving Lieutenant Adamson did. As he noted in his diary, "Our men did good scouting except Adamson who foolishly pushed on five miles and crossed our front losing a man."[76] Steele and Colonel Julian Byng, commanding the SALH, both thought he was lucky not to lose his entire troop. Adamson undoubtedly got the rough edge of Steele's tongue for this episode.[77]

Dundonald decided that they should stop for the night at Badfontein, about a dozen kilometres short of Lydenburg. Charged with protecting the right of the camp, Steele's men found a large *kopje* about 6,000 metres away, well out of rifle shot, but with roads on the hillside away from the British that would allow artillery to be brought up. Steele set up an outpost on the hill to prevent this but soon after one of Dundonald's staff officers decided it was too far from the camp to be a threat and ordered it withdrawn. Steele complied, "with misgivings."[78] Attempts to resume the advance over the next couple of days ran into fierce resistance from the Boer artillery. The Strathconas protecting a Royal Horse Artillery battery came under heavy fire but luckily they were on soft ground and most of the shells buried harmlessly before exploding. Steele realized this was too good to last and ordered his men to move forward into the shelter of a creek bed: "Shrapnel was fired as we galloped across but it burst high and fell harmlessly on our broad brimmed Stetsons, our horses however were nearly frantic with the bullets which fell like hail."[79]

With Buller's force pushed back to the Badfontein camp, Steele was still concerned about the hill to the right and sent out scouts to confirm his earlier opinion. They reported again that the enemy could easily bring guns up to threaten the camp and Steele was finally ordered to occupy the hilltop. He sent out a troop under Lieutenant John Leckie, who did so, but when he in turn sent a section under Sergeant Archibald Logan forward, they ran into a much larger Boer force. Refusing to surrender, Logan and two privates fought until their ammunition ran out and died there. Steele examined the location of the fight when the position was retaken and wrote to Marie: "Some of them had been murdered when wounded as the Boer shells were only a few feet off and the men had each three bullet wounds."[80] A fourth man, Private Albert Garner, was severely wounded but was rescued by one of the surgeons. Leckie's remaining men were now in trouble and when he requested help, Steele sent two troops forward. They were instructed to follow the route taken by Leckie and come in behind his position, but ignored orders and rode straight at the enemy who waited until they were close and opened fire, killing Sergeant John Brothers and Private Charles Cruickshank.[81] The Boers promptly moved their guns into position and shelled the camp until they were dislodged by a large-scale infantry attack.

Going to the top of the hill to arrange for the burial of his men, Steele could see General Ian Hamilton's column moving in from the left to outflank Botha.[82] The Boers were forced to abandon Lydenburg and move through a narrow mountain gap into the adjoining river valley, making for the town of Spitzkop. The route was bordered by a line of *kopjes* called the Devil's Knuckles. General Neville Lyttleton's 4th Division was given the job of leading the pursuit and the Strathconas were ordered to protect Lyttleton's right flank, facing the *kopjes*. As soon as the artillery silenced the Boer guns, the Canadians raced to the top and, with the enthusiastic assistance of the Gordon Highlanders, who caught hold of the Strathconas' stirrups to pull them up the hills, drove the enemy off a succession of *kopjes*. General Buller was delighted with the "dashing and capable" work of the regiment but ignored Steele's request that they be allowed to push on and possibly capture part or all of Botha's force.[83] Steele admired Buller more than any of the other British generals, but he believed that his excessive caution was preventing an early end to the war.

Buller's column spent the last half of September resting at Spitzkop. This was just as well since even with the replenishment there, when the rather leisurely pursuit resumed, seventy of the Strathconas were reduced to walking because their horses had been killed or died of exhaustion.[84] The column made its way back to the railway at Lydenburg in the first week of October, where it was broken up. Lord Roberts now claimed victory, formally annexing the Transvaal and declaring that the remaining Boers under arms were rebels who could be dealt with by policing. General Buller was ordered home, where he was fired, essentially for being in the wrong faction of the vicious internal politics of the British Army at the time.[85] Steele and his soldiers began preparations for packing up and going home. The Boers, however, were far from finished. Botha's army in Natal had been reduced to scattered bands but in the vast, arid spaces of the western Free State and the northern Cape Colony, De la Rey, Smuts, and De Wet were very much in the fight.

In mid-October the Strathconas turned over their remaining horses to a British cavalry unit and boarded trains for Pretoria, where the men began to celebrate the end of their war, while Steele, ensconced in the Grand Hotel, caught up on his paperwork and correspondence. Thirty men from the regiment had decided to join the police force being organized by Lord Baden-Powell and another eight were going to work for the South African railway system.[86] A day after he arrived in Pretoria, Steele learned that the high command had no intention of dispensing with the services of the Strathconas. Their one-year term of enlistment still had over two months to run and Steele had to break the bad news to Marie:

> *I fear I must give you a disappointment for I have today been informed that we are to be employed for another two months on an expedition to the north of here and then go home. I am getting the regiment fully equipped from the boots up, and hope that we may be able to add some laurels to ours already won.*[87]

Most of Steele's men were as unhappy about the situation as Marie undoubtedly was. As they marched out of Pretoria to help protect the railway line at Germiston, south of Johannesburg, Steele left 100 men behind who had reported sick, almost a quarter of his force.[88] On the march he had to discipline ten men for drunkenness and insubordination.[89]

Fortunately, the tedium of patrolling the railway had no time to set in and make things worse. General De Wet had surrounded General G. Barton's 6th Brigade, now nearly out of ammunition, near the town of Frederikstad ninety kilometres southwest of Johannesburg. The Strathconas were loaded on trains and arrived to join the rescue column commanded by Colonel H.T. Hicks of the Dublin Fusiliers at Welverdiend on October 24. They moved up the next day with the Strathconas protecting the left flank. The column fought through just as the Boers were launching a full-scale attack. The reinforcements and ammunition they brought with them enabled Barton to turn the tables and drive the enemy out of their trenches, inflicting forty-three casualties and taking thirty-six prisoners.[90] The rest of the Boer force of about 1,500 melted away into the countryside. This was the beginning of a miserable month for the Strathconas. They patrolled out of Frederikstad and the nearby town of Potchefstroom. Steele described Frederikstad as "A beautiful place with apricots, quinces, oranges, lemons and other fruits. Wheat oats and barley ripening, and streams of water on sides of streets and all around."[91]

What made it unpleasant was, first of all, the weather. It rained heavily most days, dragging down the spirits and making it impossible to maintain a clean camp. Dysentery and what was called at the time enteric fever (typhoid) ravaged the Strathconas; even Steele's usually iron constitution succumbed. For about ten days he was too sick to mount his horse and was reduced to riding ignominiously in the ambulance.[92] He put it down to drinking "bad milk" but it was certainly more serious than that. De Wet's commando had broken up into small bands, conducting raids on the railway and then disappearing. The only counter that Kitchener could come up with was the brutal one of laying waste to the countryside until it could no longer support the rebels. Women and children were rounded up and moved to concentration camps where they died by the thousands due to incompetent administration. Although the Black population generally supported the British side, they were collateral damage in this process, with more than 14,000 dying in the camps.[93] Farms were burned, livestock were rounded up and slaughtered, and wells were poisoned. The Strathconas hated it, as the War Diary reported:

> "B" Squadron shifting Boer families from their farms on the river to town. The work did not suit the men at all. The cries and lamentations of the women and children had a most depressing effect upon them. It will be useless to keep such a regiment employed in that way.[94]

By early December De Wet had shifted his operations almost 500 kilometres to the south, on the northern border of the Cape Colony. When he succeeded in capturing a British garrison there, General Charles Knox, who had been pursuing him, was given more troops. They included the Strathconas who boarded a train on November 30 for a four-day journey to Springfontein Junction. A month of intense action followed, the only such period during the war that Steele was unable to keep up his personal diary and write any letters to Marie. From Springfontein it was a short ride on another line to Bethulie, where the Strathconas got off the train and went immediately into action. Knox had De Wet cornered but in a position that allowed the latter to observe all approaches. Steele's men found an approach that ran through a *donga* (ravine) and gave them some cover. They were held up briefly while cutting their way through a fence, but pushed on after losing several horses. The attack broke the Boer line as night was falling. A heavy rain started about the same time and De Wet was able to take advantage of the near zero visibility to get away.

The pursuit continued in heavy rain for three days with the Strathconas and the 9th Lancers in the lead. The Boers evaded the pursuit at first but they would have to cross the Caledon River, swollen by the downpour, in order to get away. On December 7, Steele and his men came to a fork in the road, the left leading to a bridge over the Caledon, the right to the town of Rouxville. Steele sent half of his force a few kilometres down each road and waited for the rest of the column to catch up. He could hear artillery firing from the direction of the bridge, which told him that De Wet was trying to capture it from the British defenders, but he could not persuade his commanding officer:

> *General Knox stated that Rouxville was in danger of attack and ordered the advance to take the Rouxville road, this was done at once much to the disgust of all concerned, for with two strong columns close on his rear it was quite unlikely that De Wet would attack the town,*

*which proved to be the case when after a toilsome and useless march, we arrived on the ridge overlooking the town.*[95]

In the War Diary he added an editorial comment: "In General Knox's failure to pursue De Wet on the Commissie Bridge road he has missed the chance of his life, for if he had done so, De Wet could not have escaped."[96]

The balance of December was a repetition of the frustration at Commissie Bridge. The mounted units would push aggressively forward, in spite of dismal weather and short rations. They would come close to bringing De Wet to battle, only to have General Knox fail to follow up. Steele's anger was shared by Colonel J.S. Barker, the officer in command of the column that included the Strathconas. He appreciated the willingness of the Canadians to challenge the Boer's light rear guard screen, in contrast to the British cavalry who were trained to stop and wait for support as soon as they came under fire. On December 21, the 9th Lancers did just that and Steele described Barker's reaction when he and his men were ordered up to support them:

*Colonel Barker seemed disturbed, said that the cavalry training was such that in duties of this kind when shots were exchanged their work ceased and others had to fight it out. He also said distinctly and loud enough for all to hear that Strathcona's Horse would have moved over the ground at front whether there was an enemy or not, and would not have delayed the column in its march for one moment.*[97]

After a month in which they travelled more than 600 kilometres in the saddle, under fire most days with little to show for it, Steele's men were more than ready to go home. He wrote to Kitchener informing him that the regiment's one-year term of enlistment was nearly up and requesting that they be permitted to leave. A telegram arrived on January 9 ordering them to Cape Town and home.[98] As they were getting ready to board the train at Elandsfontein,

Photo by William Notman of Marie and children while Sam was in South Africa with Lord Strathcona's Horse. [BPSC, 2008.1.1.5.1.5]

Kitchener appeared unannounced and inspected the troops and showered them with praise, saying that generals all over the country had been asking for them and that if he had had twenty regiments like Strathcona's Horse, the war would have been over much sooner.[99] Steele was delighted with the praise, but like his men, he was anxious to get home. He had signed on as one of the divisional commanders of Lord Baden-Powell's South African Constabulary and would be coming back so he was anxious to spend as much time as possible in Canada with his wife and family before that happened.

Much as Steele admired the fighting qualities of his men, he had no illusions about how they might behave once the discipline imposed by being shot at disappeared. He arranged that there would be no stopover in Cape Town; the men would go directly from the train to the boat and sail at once.[100] Most of the men would have preferred to go directly back to Canada but Lord Strathcona wanted them to stop in London, a request that could not be denied. Once at sea, Steele cracked down hard to make sure that there would be no unfortunate incidents while they were in London. The men were issued new uniforms, given haircuts, and had their beards shaved off. Two privates were court-martialed for indiscipline as an example that no disorderly conduct would be tolerated. When Steele noticed some men talking during a lifeboat drill, he gave them a tongue-lashing and promised daily repetitions of the parade until the talking stopped.[101]

The Strathconas arrived in London to an almost overwhelming round of honours and celebrations. The men were housed in the Kensington and St. John's Wood barracks and the officers in the Kensington Palace Hotel but, before they even had time to unpack, they were marched off to be one of the military units lining the parade route for King Edward VII's opening of Parliament (Queen Victoria had died on January 22, 1901, while their ship was at sea). The next day, February 15, the band of the Coldstream Guards led the regiment to Buckingham Palace where the King presented them

all with South Africa medals and Steele with the Royal Victorian
Order. Then Steele and his officers were inundated with invitations.
As Sam described it in a rather breathless letter to Marie:

> I lunched with the Duke of Argyle and Princess Louise yesterday
> and dine with Becton tonight, Duke of Abercorn tomorrow night.
> Lunch with Joe Colmer and his family tomorrow 1:30. Dine with
> Lord Dundonald on Tuesday. I dine with Secy of State for War on
> Wednesday to meet Lord Roberts. Thursday dine with Lord Strathcona
> and tomorrow 5 o'clock tea with Lord Strathcona.[102]

London society could not get enough of Lord Strathcona's Horse.

The most elaborate occasion came on February 18 when Lord Strathcona gave a vast banquet for his regiment. There were the usual gargantuan Edwardian quantities of food and a full quart of champagne at each place. In addition to Strathcona, the head table included "the Secretary of State for War, Lord Derby, Lord Aberdeen, Lord Dundonald, General Laurie, M.P. and many other general and field officers of the army, prominent Colonial statesmen and gentlemen interested in the colonies."[103] Britain by 1901 was feeling isolated and unloved because of the negative international reaction to the war, so the loyalty demonstrated by the dominions was very welcome. Lord Strathcona's Horse happened to be the first colonial unit to arrive in London from the fighting and they were the beneficiaries of this emotional reaction. The other Canadian contingents had gone straight back to Canada and, while they were greeted with warmth and enthusiasm, their welcome could not compare to what Steele and his men experienced in the great capital of the Empire. When they got back to Canada there was more. Steele received a CB (Companion of the Order of the Bath) and was promoted to full colonel in the Canadian militia, while several of his officers were appointed as Companions of the Order of St. Michael and St. George. Lord Strathcona's Horse had performed very well and deserved the tributes but, not surprisingly, the lavish praise heaped on the Strathconas aroused intense jealousy among many in Canada's little military establishment, as Steele would discover.

For the moment, he was happy to bask in the spotlight until it was time to head for Liverpool and board the ss *Numidian* for home. Two weeks on the rough North Atlantic brought Steele and his men to Halifax on March 8, where a Bank of Montreal representative was waiting to pay the men the difference between British Army rates of pay and the higher amounts of the Canadian contingents. Steele had a severe case of bronchitis by this time, due no doubt to exhaustion from the social whirlwind in London and an overwhelmed digestive system, but he roused himself to make a stirring speech to his men. "Boys," he said, "never forget that you are Canadians and that Canada, as a country, has no superior in the wide world."[104] He told them that they had demonstrated an essential Canadian characteristic by becoming soldiers when needed and now by returning to civilian life. The regiment formally disbanded in Halifax that day, but the men travelled together as far as Montreal, where they began to disperse. Steele had a joyful reunion with his family, and then spent a tedious month in Ottawa attending to the details of winding up the regiment.

# 9 | Imperial Interlude
## The South African Constabulary
## 1901–1907

WHEN SAM STEELE ACCEPTED THE COMMAND of Lord Strathcona's Horse and went off to fight the Boers in 1900, he calculated that this would open up the road to the position he had coveted for so many years, commissioner of the NWMP. He knew that Commissioner L.W. Herchmer was unpopular with the Laurier government and would likely be eased out when he returned from his tour of duty commanding the Canadian Mounted Rifles in South Africa. The assistant commissioner, J.H. McIlree, was competent but uninspiring. That left two likely candidates for the job, Steele and the man who had replaced him in the Yukon, Superintendent Aylesworth Bowen Perry. Born near Napanee, Ontario, Perry was the outstanding member of the first class of Canada's Royal Military College, winning the governor general's gold medal in his graduating year. His evident talents got him a commission in the Royal Engineers where he served briefly before returning to Canada in 1881, joining the NWMP the following year. He and Steele both served with distinction during the 1885 Rebellion and were promoted to superintendent soon after. Perry was just as ambitious as Steele and improved his qualifications by studying law and being called to the bar of the North-West Territories.

In the 1890s, while Steele was at Fort Macleod, Perry commanded Depot Division at Regina. This meant he was in charge of training for the Force and the posting put him in daily contact with the administrative and political issues and figures of the day. Steele knew that his rival had an edge in terms of education and political connections, but he thought that if he could add success in South Africa to his own outstanding record during the gold rush, he should get the job. In June, as the Strathconas were in the thick of the action against Louis Botha, there were rumours in the Canadian press that Perry might be appointed NWMP commissioner. Marie passed them along but Steele's first reaction was dismissive:

> *The enclosures re Perry do not disturb me in the least for I cannot see how they can legally make him Commissioner of the Force, and Lt Col Herchmer still Commissioner, and we do well in Africa. I am sure our people will object to anything of that sort and particularly the NWTy people.*[1]

There was more riding on Steele's chances of becoming commissioner than just ambition. To say that Marie was unhappy about her husband going off to South Africa with Lord Strathcona's Horse just a few months after getting back from the Yukon would be a very large understatement. She made her feelings clear in every letter she wrote. This one from May 1900 is typical:

> *I try to bear up but I can assure you, you have fully made up my mind that if you come back safe & sound, that you will not leave me again, for no matter what reason—neither Queen, country or anything else will part us. We have our little ones to bring up & educate. I need your helping hand to do my duty well. Life is too short & its pleasures too few to live away from the one you love best for years at a time. You*

must not ask me to submit to another separation, for I cannot & will not do it.²

Steele responded reassuringly: "I hope we shall get something desperate to do for the men want it and if we get through with honour you may rest assured that I will not ask to leave you. I had to go or I would have had no place in Canada any more."³

By August 1900, however, doubts were beginning to creep in:

> If Perry is promoted to the Commissionership you must wire. It cannot be possible that they would do so in the face of our work here. I could I think get an appointment out here from Sir Alfred [Milner] but would prefer to get the Comrship of our force until my time is up but of that I must not speak for there is many a slip between the cup and the lip.⁴

By the end of August Steele's worst fears were realized. Herchmer was forced to retire on August 1 and Perry was appointed commissioner, and although the appointment did not become public until he returned from the Yukon, Steele heard from his sources in the Force that it was planned. He was still reluctant to believe it and bitterly disappointed, but he had a family to support so his thoughts immediately turned to alternatives. Going back to the Mounted Police with Perry as commissioner was not one of them, he wrote to Marie: "I could stand anyone else but him. I daresay one could get three or four thousand dollars per annum here and I find the Transvaal a good climate, but I love my own country and would hate to leave it."⁵ One of the other rumours making the rounds at the time was that, because of the exceptional performance of Lord Strathcona's Horse, the Canadian government would make it a permanent unit of the army when it returned, with Steele as commanding officer.

The possibility of employment in South Africa that Steele mentioned in his letter grew out of the end game that was emerging as the guerilla war showed every sign of dragging on. Kitchener's policy of destroying the farms the commandos depended on for food and sending the women and children to concentration camps would eventually bring about a Boer surrender, but at a tremendous humanitarian cost. Of the 110,000 Boers in the camps, 27,997, mostly children, died of disease as a result of incompetence and neglect.[6] The British government might not have been averse to a little ethnic cleansing to get rid of the troublesome Boers but, having ostensibly started the war in defence of the democratic rights of Transvaal residents, it was in no position to do so. The emerging Boer leadership, especially the brilliant young Jan Christiaan Smuts, a Cambridge-trained lawyer, proved so adept at using the British and international press that some more humane solution seemed urgently necessary. In any case, South African gold was crucial to the City of London's domination of world finances and the stability of the pound as a world currency.[7] Successful gold extraction in the mines of the Witwatersrand, in turn, required a stable political environment.

British High Commissioner Alfred Milner had a plan to achieve that. Order would be restored, limited self-government would be gradually introduced, English-speaking settlers would be attracted to outnumber the Afrikaners, and the final outcome would be a federation of the Cape Colony, Natal, Orange Free State, and the Transvaal on the model of Canada. Step one, the imposition of order on a recalcitrant population, was something the British had considerable experience with in Ireland, India, and elsewhere. The key institution was a semi-military police force, prepared to fight if necessary but whose main responsibility was to enforce British law. Milner and the military commander, Lord Roberts, began discussing the formation of the police in July 1900 and it began taking shape in September. The task of setting it up was given to Major General Robert Baden-Powell, the hero of the siege of Mafeking in the early part of the war. Recruiting and organization started in October with an initial establishment of 6,000 men. With fighting still going on, Roberts insisted on 10,000 men, with the army picking up the tab for the additional 4,000.[8] The police were to be organized into four territorial divisions of 2,000 each with a reserve division of the same size.⁹

Baden-Powell immediately identified Steele as one of the people he wanted for his police force and asked Kitchener if he could be released from duty with Lord Strathcona's Horse.¹⁰ Kitchener, who was desperately short of experienced commanders of mounted troops, refused to let Steele go before the Strathconas' term of enlistment ran out at the end of January 1901. Baden-Powell met Steele on October 19 when some of the Strathcona officers were applying for positions with the South African Constabulary (SAC).¹¹ The meeting evidently confirmed Baden-Powell's opinion of Steele because he made him a very tempting offer and agreed to wait for him to take his regiment back to Canada. Steele thought he might be appointed second in command of one of the divisions with the rank of lieutenant-colonel at a salary of £1,000. Instead, Baden-Powell offered him command of a division as a full colonel with a salary of £1,200. The idea of a reserve division was dropped and Steele would be assigned to the Northern Transvaal district, the area that included the Rand mines and was therefore a crucially important element in Milner's grand design.¹² Given what had happened with the NWMP, the offer was too good to pass up. Steele's division of the SAC was roughly three times the size of the entire NWMP and the salary, the equivalent of $6,000 Canadian, was more than double that of the NWMP commissioner. Steele asked for a few months' leave in Canada before he took up the job, and when this was granted, he accepted.¹³

The trip from the heat of a South African summer to a damp, cold London winter, combined with the stress of making a life-changing decision, brought Steele down with a severe case of bronchitis. It lasted through the trip back to Canada, for the month it took to wind up the affairs of Lord Strathcona's Horse in Ottawa, and several weeks beyond that. The work seemed endless. There were all the various accounts to reconcile, dozens of letters to write on behalf of troopers seeking employment, and other details. It took two long days just to write out the discharge certificates on parchment.¹⁴ At the same time, Steele was trying to assert some control over the development of his new job. Milner and Baden-Powell wanted to recruit 2,000 men in Canada and the Canadian government had agreed in November to an initial 1,000. Steele wanted to oversee that process himself, as he had done with the Strathconas, but that did not work out since Lord Kitchener refused to let him go before the regiment's term of enlistment was up in mid-January. By the time Steele got to Ottawa in March, the situation had started to unravel.

The governor general, Lord Minto, was charged with supervising the recruitment for the SAC on behalf of the Colonial Office. Minto was in the midst of a lengthy feud with the senior officers of the Canadian militia and was determined to keep the appointment of officers in his own hands.¹⁵ Recruiting was supervised in western Canada by Lieutenant Percy Fall, a Strathcona's Horse officer who had signed up with the SAC when it formed. In the Atlantic Provinces the task was given to a militia officer, Lieutenant C.W.W. McLean. Fall was not one of Steele's best officers in the Strathcona's Horse and would not have been his choice for the job, but he seems to have ingratiated himself with Minto.¹⁶ McLean, for his part, had no knowledge of which candidates might make good policemen in South Africa, nor did he have any stake in finding out. The eastern recruits were already in Halifax waiting to board ship when Steele got to Ottawa, and he had only a week or so to look over the western group before they departed. He was not very impressed with them and was even less happy with how Fall was organizing their training. He commented in a letter to Marie from Ottawa:

> *There are as yet no more recruits to be got and a good thing too. They are as a body a disgrace to Canada. I may have to stay and see them off. The officers are fools as a rule and the lot not to be compared to any that went before them (in any shape or form).*¹⁷

This was not a good start and there was worse to come.

Steele had been told by Milner and Baden-Powell that he would have full authority to appoint officers for the contingent. On the strength of that assurance he had promised commissions to several of the Strathconas, including two experienced NWMP officers, A.M. Jarvis and M.H. White-Fraser, who were ideally suited for the SAC. When he visited the governor general as soon as he arrived in Ottawa, he discovered that Minto had already appointed half the officers and had decided who he wanted for the rest. Steele demanded that his nominees be accepted and that Fall be removed. He then announced to the newspapers that Jarvis, White-Fraser and others would be given commissions.[18] Steele knew that Minto's instructions from the Colonial Office only allowed him to recommend appointments but, not for the first nor the last time in his life, he found that being right was not enough to overcome political considerations. Minto rejected all Steele's nominations except Jarvis and, although Steele appealed for support from Lord Strathcona, there was no chance that the Colonial Office would back a mere Canadian colonel against the governor general, however unwise his actions. The original plan had been for Steele to recruit an additional 1,000 men when he reached Canada, but when the press discovered that Milner planned to try to keep them in South Africa as settlers, there was a strong public backlash and Ottawa quickly cancelled permission. Since Canada was doing everything possible to attract immigrants, it made no sense to allow young fit men to be siphoned off to Africa.

Steele spent April and May in Montreal with his family, getting ready to return to South Africa and trying to shake off the remnants of his bronchitis.[19] He was technically still on leave from the NWMP and tried to resign and start collecting his pension. He found out from NWMP Comptroller Fred White that the pension regulations did not permit him to do that, but that the legislation would soon be changed to make it possible, so he applied for and was granted a year's extension of his leave.[20] He indulged himself in one of his favourite activities, having his photograph taken, this time with his older daughter as he noted in his diary: "Up early went to Notman to get photo. Flora with me and much pleased."[21] Steele had planned to bring his family with him to South Africa but within a week or so at home he began to reconsider because of conditions in the country and the realization that his job would be more difficult than he expected.[22] There was still considerable danger from the guerilla fighting and the disruptions of the war had made typhoid endemic. When Steele boarded his ship in Montreal on June 8 and waved goodbye to his family until they were out of sight, he did not expect to see them soon. His diary entry reads: "Felt very blue. Have year of separation."[23]

His sadness was mild compared to Marie's. She poured out her feelings in a letter a few days after he left:

> I cannot tell you of the awful fit of loneliness which has been over me for the last three days. I would give a great deal to be able to have a good cry for I feel sure it would afford me relief. Why is it, my darling, that I have to submit to these heartbreaking separations when we could live so happily together with our three little ones? Fate is hard on me & if there are any more such trials in store, I think I shall give up entirely, as I cannot keep my courage up any longer. I have tried hard to be as brave a little woman as possible under all circumstances, but I feel that I really cannot do so any longer & if these partings are to go on any longer, you will come back some day & find my place vacant. I would far rather go through any trouble & be near you, than have this awful distance between us all the time. There is no more telling me to be courageous, there is not the right kind of stuff in me for a true soldier's wife. I am of too affectionate a nature, while apparently cold, to be able to stand all I have been compelled to undergo for the past three years. To think that a fourth year is only just beginning & of the risks you will run before we meet again drives me almost wild![24]

Steele arrived in Liverpool June 20 and took the train to London. He had sailed on a different ship than the recruits, on his doctor's orders that he have a complete rest without any responsibilities. After arriving in London he spent a weekend at Lord Strathcona's estate north of the city. When that visit was over, he was annoyed to find that his ship's departure to South Africa had been delayed, so he moved to a less expensive hotel. With the extra time at his disposal he took the opportunity to visit relatives in Wales. These were people he had never met, but he immediately bonded with them and delighted in finding the grave of a previous Sam Steele who had fought in the Battle of Waterloo.[25] The remaining days in London were spent in a constant round of lunches and dinners. He got on board ship for South Africa on July 6, pleased to know he could sleep as long as he liked. The trip was calm and pleasant until the last few days before reaching Cape Town on July 27; by that time Steele was thoroughly rested, bored, and eager to start his new job.[26]

There was a short delay in Cape Town because Baden-Powell had returned to England to recover from a bout of typhoid. On August 2 Steele was on his way to Johannesburg to report to Kitchener and organize "B" Division of the SAC. The division was to consist of 1,900 officers and men with 300 native auxiliaries. Until it was fully organized the division was based at SAC headquarters in Modderfontein, then a town, now a suburb of Johannesburg. Steele was favourably impressed by the chief of staff, Colonel J.S. Nicholson, and the others at headquarters. Steele was the only non-English senior officer and he was relieved to find that the others, several of whom had served in Canada, were friendly and helpful.[27] A major named Cantan was in temporary charge of the division and after quickly sizing him up, Steele arranged for his permanent appointment as second in command. Once in South Africa and away from Governor General Minto's influence, Steele was able to repair some of the damage by getting Lieutenant Fall assigned to another division and arranging commissions for most of those rejected in Canada.

Getting his division up and running put Steele in a more buoyant mood and he immediately began to think of ways to spend his salary. Typically, he counted on sources of income that were not yet there; in this case his Yukon mining investments and his NWMP pension. Although his salary appeared generous by Canadian standards, several people on the ship from London had told him that living expenses in South Africa were very high, a warning he ignored. He would need to buy two horses for his personal use, he wrote to Marie, and she should buy a four-horse spring wagon to be shipped over.[28] When the family came, Flora must go to a convent school in England as there were none he considered suitable in South Africa. On a lesser note, he sent an urgent request home for some bottles of his preferred hair dye, to be mailed with the labels removed and marked "poison."[29] Steele was now fifty-three years old and evidently his hair was beginning to grey. He was as vigorous as ever, but from this point on in his life, he was very concerned that others perceive him as being as young as he felt. It worked well enough while he was at headquarters and able to renew the dye daily, but one of his officers, Captain M.M. Hartigan, a great admirer of Steele, noted in his memoirs, "it could not have been a good dye because after he had been away on trek for a few days his hair would gradually assume a definite blue shade."[30] Steele was also concerned about putting on weight and now discovered the writings of Eugen Sandow, the Austrian physical culturist known as "the father of body-building." Steele read his 1897 book, *Strength and How to Attain It*, and was an immediate convert. He faithfully did the prescribed exercises, rarely missing a day for the rest of his life.[31]

A month after he assumed command, Steele's "B" Division, while not completely up to strength, was ready to start work. Steele had expected that the 1,200 Canadians recruited for the force would be under his command, but Baden-Powell and the imperial authorities decided they would be more likely to remain as settlers if they were distributed among the other divisions, although Steele was able to retain a few officers.[32] Most of Steele's command came from

Steele in Pretoria, 1902. The house on the right was that of Transvaal president Paul Kruger, where Steele lived before his family arrived from Canada. [BPSC, 2008.1.2.2.6.1.19]

the breaking up of the reserve division or were recruited directly from England. On September 2 he went to Pretoria to find out how Kitchener proposed to use his force. After what he described as an "easy, pleasant" discussion with the commander in chief, Steele was ordered to move his headquarters to Pretoria and start extending his network of posts to the northwest.[33] Offices were found for the division in the city and Steele was given the house of the former Transvaal president, Paul Kruger, as a residence.[34] The pacification process did not always go smoothly. Two of Steele's men were killed and two captured in a Boer raid early in October.[35] He attributed the losses to inexperience and travelled constantly, inspecting the posts to make sure they were properly organized for defence.

Extending control over the northern Transvaal was a slow, methodical process. Posts were usually under the command of a lieutenant with enough men to hold off an attack until help could arrive. They were spaced about ten kilometres apart for that purpose.³⁶ Once the line of stations was firmly established the police could begin the distasteful task of removing all the women and children and either capturing or killing the livestock, giving the Boer commandos no means of support. Then the line of posts could be extended further. It was a grim and ruthless strategy of control that seemed to many observers, even in Britain, more suited to medieval times than the opening years of the 20th century. Caution was always an essential part of the process, which most of Steele's officers found frustrating. In one of the forward pushes, Steele and his men had caught up with a group of the enemy attempting to drive some cattle away. However, a Boer ambush cost Steele the life of one of his most promising Canadian officers, Major J.H.C. Ogilvy, who had transferred to the SAC from the Royal Canadian Artillery. Steele described the encounter in a letter to Marie:

> *Major Ogilvy with the advance charged when he sighted the cattle. I was about one hundred yards from him or I would not have allowed it but being with the support a little to the right of where he was I could not have reached him in time. I threw part of my force to the right to outflank the donga and fifty to the left to take them on that flank and held part in reserve in front. I personally led the party who attacked the right and superintended the whole. The enemy opened fire at once and Major Ogilvy was mortally wounded by a Martini Henry bullet which went through his horses head and then went through his stomach and liver lodging in his thigh. It was too bad, he was a gallant officer and had a fine career before him, but he should not have gone at them that way.*³⁷

By mid-January 1902, Steele's line of posts stretched for 160 kilometres from Pretoria. The countryside was reminiscent of that in western Canada: "This is the high veldt and looks like the Macleod country, hardly any sign of a tree except at the houses."³⁸ By this time it was becoming clear that the Boers could not hold out much longer. Steele spent more time at his Pretoria office as the year wore on. The SAC officers' mess was congenial, although Steele thought his English subalterns should be more professional and less concerned with sport. "They are just what Kipling called them," he complained to Marie, "'muddied oafs and flannelled fools.' They are all for games and neglect the great game."[39] (The quote is from a poem Kipling published a year after this in 1903, but he had visited Lord Strathcona's Horse and dined with Steele in 1900, so he must have used the phrase at the time in conversation.) Having lost Ogilvy, whom he was grooming as second in command, Steele was now saddled with an English officer named Wilberforce. He quickly decided that Wilberforce was not up to the job and would have to go. He wrote to Baden-Powell, making his position clear, but was in some doubt about the outcome. "I do not know which of us the General will wish to dispose of, me I suppose."[40] He need not have worried. A few days later Baden-Powell came to lunch with him, confirmed all his recommendations for promotion, and shipped Wilberforce off to another division.[41]

With the fighting drawing to an end, the work of the SAC would be very different. It would have to be transformed from an auxiliary force of the army to a police force and Steele was the only divisional commander who had police experience. He knew exactly what to do, although he knew it would not be easy. As he commented to Marie, "Our work will be harder as you know in peacetime for we shall have to put the returned Boers on their farms and get them properly settled."[42] The first step was arranging that each troop had at least one colonial officer (Australian, New Zealander, or Canadian) in joint command with a British officer. All officers were required to take a course in the controllers and quartermasters' department to give them the necessary administrative skills for running a police post. All NCOs would be put through examinations before being confirmed in their ranks.[43] To learn the work, constables at headquarters were assigned to policing duties in Pretoria under the tutelage of two former NWMP sergeants who had been in the Yukon with Steele.⁴⁴ They were also given instruction in veterinary care and in the Dutch language. The latter was intended to give the police at least a rudimentary ability to communicate with the rural population, but had little effect. Dutch was still the written language of government in the Transvaal, but the spoken language of the population had evolved into Afrikaans. Steele and the rest of the British authorities dismissed Afrikaans as not a "real" language, but speaking to Boer farmers in Dutch was roughly comparable to trying to communicate with a British farmer in Shakespeare's English.

Negotiations for a final end to the war began in mid-April and continued for six weeks, culminating in the signing of the Treaty of Vereeniging on May 31, 1902. Under the terms of the treaty, the two former Boer republics would become British colonies with a promise that they would move fairly quickly to self-government. A general amnesty was extended to all who had fought against the British and a resettlement fund of £3 million established. Boer farmers would be allowed to have guns, provided they were registered with the police. The most contentious clause of the treaty provided that no decision about voting rights for the non-white population, then as now the overwhelming majority, would be made until after self-government was granted. This was the crucial concession that persuaded the die-hard Afrikaner leaders to sign the treaty.⁴⁵ Lord Milner, who became the governor of both colonies, was quite prepared to sacrifice the future rights of the majority population to conciliate the Boers. Steele would soon become deeply involved in the working out of the details of the treaty with all the complications it entailed, but at the time it was signed the only thing on his mind was getting his family to South Africa as soon as possible.

Even before the formal end to the fighting, regulations were relaxed and Steele received a letter authorizing families to come out. He cabled Marie on May 24, telling her to make arrangements as soon as possible.⁴⁶ In typical fashion, Steele assumed that she

*Marie and Sam reunited in Pretoria.* [BPSC, 2008.1.1.5.1.2]

had saved sufficient money to book passage immediately. Even though the government was paying the fare for the trip there were many other costs associated with the move and Marie had not been able to put much aside. Large sums were still going to the Yukon mining venture, they were paying support for Marie's brother Frank, who was at dentistry school in Philadelphia, money was going to Sam's half-brother John, and there were occasional payments to other relatives. In any case, a couple of months previously Marie and her mother had signed a year's lease on the house in Montreal. It was late in 1902 before all the arrangements were made and the family—including Marie's mother and her brother Antoine, a recent medical graduate who hoped to set up a practice in Pretoria—arrived on November 22.

In the months after peace returned, Steele was preoccupied with the task of completely reorganizing his division. Instead of large posts with up to 100 men each, much of the force would now be widely distributed in small units of six to ten, very similar to the NWMP system in western Canada. There were still concerns that fighting might break out, since many of the Boers had accepted the treaty with great reluctance and half a dozen of the sixty delegates had voted against it, so a substantial number of Steele's men were assigned to larger mobile units that could reinforce the smaller outposts if necessary. As early as July 1902, the SAC began to recruit former Boer fighters, as Steele noted: "Two hundred more men will be sent to me all burghers half of whom fought against us and a few for us. This will make the command 2,300 men exclusive of officers."[47] No more recruits were available from Canada and many in the force were leaving because they could not make the transition to peacetime conditions. The same was true of the English troopers in Steele's division.

The decision to recruit Afrikaners was a clear sign that government policy was aimed at reconciliation with them, at least in the short term. Milner's gamble was that over a period of a few years enough English-speaking settlers could be attracted to form a majority of the voting population.⁴⁸ The political situation was fluid and confusing. For Steele and his police force on the ground there were major contradictions. He spent the second half of 1902 energetically attempting to repeat in the Transvaal the experience of the NWMP on the Canadian prairies. The Mounted Police had succeeded there in large part because of the range of services, beyond basic law enforcement, that they rendered to ranchers and farmers. Similar opportunities existed in South Africa. Agriculture in the former Boer republics was primitive and undeveloped and Steele's men could help with veterinary and crop advice and by acting as game wardens to control wild animals. These activities seem to have been quite successful in promoting good relations between the SAC and the rural population, but there were other things that mattered more.

During the war, any Boers not active as commandos were comprehensively disarmed. At the same time, while there were no Black combat units, the British recruited and armed thousands of Black people, employing them as scouts and in other auxiliary roles.⁴⁹ At the end of the fighting they retained the weapons. The Afrikaners found this situation intolerable and lobbied to have the situation reversed. This was a telling test of racial attitudes and there was no doubt that the English feared giving the indigenous population any kind of power every bit as much as the Afrikaners. In a speech in Johannesburg in May 1903, Lord Milner put it plainly: "The white man must rule, because he is elevated by many, many steps above the black man; steps which it will take the latter centuries to climb, and which it is quite possible that the vast bulk of the black population may never be able to climb at all."⁵⁰ The governing council quickly passed the necessary regulations and in August 1902 Steele's men began collecting rifles from the non-whites. It went smoothly, partly because they were paid compensation for giving up the arms.

There is no doubt that Steele's attitudes differed little from those of Lord Milner. The views he expressed in *Forty Years in Canada* were quite stridently racist. In his view, the Blacks were lazy, untruthful and not "capable of gratitude for any kind act."[51] As was often the case with Steele, he reflected generalities that he absorbed from the society around him, while making exceptions about the people he actually knew. He had a driver named Hendrick whom he liked and respected. When he found his batman, Jack Kerr, beating Hendrick for some alleged transgression, he dismissed Kerr from the SAC even though he was the son of one of his oldest friends.[52] He had several hundred Black troopers in his division and they, too, were different—hard working and trustworthy. He talked to them when he made his tours of inspection and paid attention to what they told him: "Native Const. complain that their clothing does not last and as the block house in which they are is also the lock up they need a tent. They object very properly to sleep in the same place with the prisoners."[53] Steele put their good qualities down to their being Zulus and therefore warriors.

Steele began to push immediately for the introduction of the NWMP system whereby senior officers had the powers of justices of the peace to try minor cases. Although Lord Milner liked the idea, the legal department of the government managed to block it until shortly before Steele left. The ability to deal directly with minor cases cut the workload of the police dramatically and it also worked to cement relations with the Afrikaner farmers. Steele fully supported the policy of conciliation that returned power to the white minority and if he had been given a freer hand in areas like this, the SAC might have survived. Steele only commanded a fifth of the force and the other divisions were less successful than his in coming to terms with the Boers. The result was that the Afrikaner political leadership in the former republics, embodied in the Het Volk party led by the former generals Botha and Smuts, was able to portray the SAC as an alien imposition.[54] Getting rid of it was high on their list of priorities as soon as self-government was granted.

At the beginning of 1903, Baden-Powell left the SAC to return to England as inspector general of cavalry. He and Steele remained friends until the end of Steele's life and Steele greatly missed his

*Steele (fifth from right), Baden-Powell (sixth from right), with officers of the South African Constabulary. [BPSC, 2008.1.2.2.6.2.10]*

leadership. Some Canadians thought that Steele might be his replacement, but there was no chance of the appointment going to a colonial. The new head of the force, Colonel J.S. Nicholson, was competent and Steele got along well with him. Part of the funding for the SAC had come from the army, and since the fighting was now definitely a thing of the past that money was cut at the end of March 1903, reducing the size of the force by 4,000 men. Nicholson decided to make the cuts by getting rid of men he considered troublesome, many of whom happened to be Canadians who were much less reticent about airing their grievances than the British troops. Several Canadians were dismissed and contacted newspapers with stories of unfair treatment as soon as they got home. Baden-Powell and Nicholson dismissed the stories as the work of malcontents and they might have been ignored had it not been that Kate Massiah, the mother of a trooper in "A" Division, took the complaints directly to the top.

Mrs. Massiah, the first woman reporter accredited to the Quebec legislature, wrote Prime Minister Laurier, Lord Strathcona, and King Edward VII. Only Buckingham Palace responded, but that was certainly enough to get everyone's attention. The first item in her lengthy list of grievances was that the Canadians had been promised that they would serve under Steele, but were put under British officers who "failed to understand that our Canadians are accustomed to being treated as intelligent men, not as an automatic body." Steele, on the other hand, "understands Canadian men and their conditions."[55] Probably because of Mrs. Massiah's efforts, two troops of Canadians were transferred to Steele's "B" Division. He blamed the Canadian officers who had been recruited by Lord Minto, commenting to Marie: "They take a course at the school and think they are fit to command and are not. I have none of them thank goodness except young St George and Moore. Their troops when handed over to me were in rags and tatters poor chaps."[56]

As the SAC was being cut back, the government was facing a serious labour shortage in the mines of the Witwatersrand, the engine of the economy. Approximately 129,000 miners were needed but only about half that number of Black workers, denied citizenship rights under the peace settlement, could be recruited to do the hard and dangerous work for the low wages offered.[57] Lord Milner attempted to solve the problem by the importation of large numbers of Chinese labourers. Almost everyone except the mine owners thought this was a bad idea, but it went ahead anyway. Starting in 1904, more than 40,000 were brought in and put to work under conditions of indentured servitude that looked more like something from the 18th century than the 20th.

The Chinese worked long hours for little pay and were often brutally mistreated by their white overseers in the mines. When not working, they were supposed to be confined to residential compounds built for them near the mines. The compounds had no walls or gates and naturally some of the labourers ignored the prohibitions and wandered around the countryside, to the distress of the rural population. There were robberies, murders, and even incidents in which the Chinese had stolen dynamite from the mines and used it to blow up farmhouses, although it is hard to imagine what the motivation for this might have been.[58] Steele's "B" Division of the SAC was responsible for the northern Transvaal where the mines were, and had the job of rounding up the Chinese and returning them to their compounds, as many as 150 a week. With the reduced numbers of police at his disposal, Steele's response was to urge the rearming of the rural Afrikaner population with shotguns as a measure of protection. This was popular but was not enough to prevent the Het Volk party from launching a Royal Commission to investigate the SAC in 1905. Most of the discontent with the force was in the Orange Free State and Steele was not called to testify, but that did not prevent major changes to the force. In the reorganization that followed at the end of 1905, into one division each for of the Transvaal and the Orange Free State, Steele was offered command of the police in the latter in the hope that he could restore the situation there, but by that time he had decided to return to Canada. He and his family quite liked Pretoria and had no desire to move before they left the country, so Steele took a staff job at headquarters.

The political situation in South Africa was changing rapidly in 1905. In April Milner, exhausted by his unsuccessful efforts to ensure British supremacy, resigned as high commissioner and governor. His replacement was the Earl of Selborne, an experienced administrator who came without the wartime baggage of his predecessor.[59] He inherited Milner's senior officials and his policies, but a British election early in 1906 brought in a Liberal government which immediately granted full self-government to the former republics. It was clear to Steele that there would be no future for him in the SAC under governments dominated by Afrikaner nationalists. He had never felt fully at home in South Africa in any case. As he repeatedly told Marie in his letters, it was only the money that kept him there. He had subscriptions to the Montreal *Star*, the Toronto

*Globe* and the Toronto *Star*, as well as the local weeklies from the area where he grew up, the Orillia *Packet* and the Barrie *Advance*, because, he said, "I want to keep posted on my country."[60] From time to time he mused about buying a farm in Ontario and living on what it could produce, supplemented by his NWMP pension. Until Laurier's Liberals won a third term in 1904, with no sign they might be defeated any time soon, he still clung to the faint hope that a Conservative government might make him commissioner of the NWMP.[61] Before the fighting ended and there were still numbers of Canadian troops in South Africa, Steele was happy to help any who needed it. He wrote to Marie: "You would be very much surprised and I am sure, gratified, to know that on all sides I am recognized as the Canadian Champion not in the Corps but out of it. Every Canadian who wants advice and assistance to get anything turns to me and I hope not in vain."[62]

Steele had remained on very good terms with Laurier's minister of Militia, Sir Frederick Borden. Borden's son had been killed while fighting with the Royal Canadian Dragoons in 1900 and Steele arranged for the placing of his gravestone as the war came to an end.[63] It was to Borden that he turned in December 1905 for a job in the Canadian militia. The timing was good, since the Canadian economy was booming and the thousands of settlers pouring into the prairie provinces meant that the army was expanding its organization there. The government also had to replace the British garrisons at Halifax and Esquimalt when they were withdrawn that year. Borden offered Steele an appointment in the militia, which Steele thought would probably be a staff position at militia headquarters in Ottawa. He quickly accepted and arranged for letters of reference from Milner, Baden-Powell, and Colonel Nicholson.[64] He told Lord Selborne of his decision and originally planned to leave at the end of March, but Selborne asked him to stay another six months so it was agreed that his departure date would be October 1, 1906.[65] Until that time, he was given the job of setting up a ring of police posts around the mining area where the Chinese were housed. It was not until two weeks before he left that he actually saw one of the compounds where they lived.[66] By that time the company had greatly improved housing, food, and recreational facilities for the workers, which led Steele to claim in his autobiography that they had nothing to complain about.

By far the biggest part of the work of the Canadian army Steele was returning to consisted of training the thousands of weekend soldiers in the militia. In order to bring himself up to date on training methods and standards in the British Army, Steele arranged to go back by way of England and spend a few months at the training centre at Aldershot.[67] It was close enough to London that the family could live in the city and enjoy all it had to offer. In September the family started packing and making arrangements for the move. Most of their furniture would be sold, with only the two pianos shipped back to Canada. Marie had never found moving easy and now had a severe reaction. As Steele recorded in his diary, "She is much worried about it and suffering from the most severe headaches. I told her she must not worry about the quantity we have to take home to Canada as it cannot be helped."[68] Marie's anxiety was understandable. After three years of a relatively stable life in Pretoria, she was now confronted with months in the world's largest city followed by a return to some as yet unknown location in Canada, if, in fact, Borden kept his word.

On October 2, the family got on the train to Durban, where they boarded the White Star liner SS *Suevic* on its regular run between Australia and England. After a brief stop at Cape Town they headed out into the Atlantic. Steele immediately started on the reading program he had set for himself with Archibald Forbes's translation of Helmuth von Moltke's history of the Franco-Prussian War.[69] He had always read military history, but during the South African War he met and became friends with the brilliant historian of the American Civil War, Colonel G.F.R. Henderson, who was serving as Kitchener's director of intelligence.[70] It seems likely that Henderson influenced Steele's reading list since he specifically mentions

"Skinner's Court," the Steele family house in Pretoria. [BPSC, 2008.1.2.2.6.3.6]

several of Henderson's works. Steele had hoped that Marie would recover once they were at sea, but if anything she became worse. A doctor on board examined her and told the family that the condition was not life threatening but could last for months. She showed some signs of improvement when the ship got into cooler conditions north of the equator, but worsened as they neared England. The ship docked in London on November 1 and Marie was bundled into an ambulance and taken directly to a hospital for women called the Nursing Institute. A doctor there diagnosed her condition as a "nervous collapse and almost a cataleptic attack."[71] He prescribed a prolonged period of complete rest.

Marie's illness forced Steele to cancel his plans to spend time at Aldershot. Instead he busied himself finding a flat for the family in a building called Playfair Mansions in Kensington. Schools had to be arranged for the children; Sacred Heart Convent for the girls and the Froebel Institute for Harwood.[72] All three started piano and dancing lessons as well, which pleased Steele but not the family's upstairs neighbour, who complained to the landlord that the children spent too much time practicing. He noted in his diary, "The children practicing at the piano were interrupted by the people upstairs who kept knocking on the floor to stop the practice. Those people are a nuisance. They would soon be in trouble in Canada if they carried on such capers."[73] He visited Marie daily as her condition improved. At the end of the first week in January she was allowed to see the children and go on brief outings and finally, on January 26, was released from hospital. Steele kept up with his reading program, which included classics such as Alfred Thayer Mahan's *The Influence of Sea Power upon History*, as well as more technical works on tactics. When Marie rejoined the family he began attending a military college run by Colonel William Bosworth for a course in tactics and strategy. The curriculum was typical of such institutions of the period, with a heavy emphasis on the campaigns of the Napoleonic Wars, but they also spent time on the American Civil War, the Franco-Prussian War, and even the recently concluded Russo-Japanese War in which trenches, machine guns, and artillery produced massive casualties that prefigured the First World War.[74] He also obtained documents from Generals Barton, Buller and Kitchener certifying his tactical fitness to command.

Once Marie returned from hospital, the family enjoyed an active social life, attending the theatre, ballet, and opera. For the children there were pantomimes and variety shows at the Hippodrome. Steele lunched often with friends from the South African War and regularly spent time with Lord Strathcona. In March he satisfied a long-held wish to visit the home of his mother's family and spent two weeks touring Scotland. In mid-April political leaders from the self-governing dominions arrived in London for an Imperial War Conference. The Canadian delegation included Sir Frederick Borden and Steele quickly arranged an interview. From Borden he learned that he would not be on the staff in Ottawa but would be district officer commanding of the newly created Military District No. 13,

*Steele in London on his way back to Canada, 1907. [BPSC, 2008.1.3.3.6.1.22]*

which took in Alberta and parts of western Saskatchewan with headquarters in Calgary.[75] A week later he met with Major General Percy Lake, the chief of the general staff, who was also in England. Lake confirmed his appointment and told Steele that he must be in Calgary by the end of June to command the annual militia summer training camp.[76]

Travel arrangements were hastily made and a round of farewells began. He visited Sandhurst with his old friend from 1885, General Strange. Steele went to Dublin for a week at the end of April to visit Baden-Powell and observe the cavalry training there. Then he and Marie spent a week in Wales with the Steele relatives. After Marie had recovered, the time in London had been great fun for all, but as Steele noted in his diary, "This is a terrible country to run away with money. Travel with a family is no joke."[77] On May 30 the family boarded the train to Liverpool and hastened aboard the SS *Tunisian* for the Atlantic crossing and the next stage in their lives.

# 10 ∥ Preparing for War
## 1907–1914

THE STEELES ARRIVED in Montreal on June 8, 1907, to a warm welcome. "All the family called to see us and we were happy," Steele noted in his diary.[1] Steele went immediately to Ottawa where the official reception was just as enthusiastic. He met with General Lake and Sir Frederick Borden, and with old friends like Fred White of the Mounted Police. The editor of the Ottawa *Free Press* organized a welcome home banquet and Steele brought Marie up for the occasion. He only had a few days before leaving to supervise the summer cavalry training camp at Calgary, so Marie and the children planned to stay in Montreal until he had time to find suitable accommodation for them. While Steele was still in Montreal, Governor General Earl Grey happened to be passing through and asked to meet him: "Went to the station at the request of Earl Grey the Governor General who wished to see me. I met him, he introduced me to the Countess Her Excellency, and he said that he merely wished to shake hands and welcome me back to Canada."[2]

It had been eight years since Steele had seen the prairies and on the train trip west he was amazed by the rapid growth of every city and town they passed through. Arriving in Calgary at 3:30 in the morning of June 27, he grabbed a couple of hours sleep at his hotel and then rose to attend the opening of the camp. The militiamen at the camp gave him a rousing welcome, helped no doubt by the fact that the senior militia officer, Lt. Col. James Walker, was one of his oldest friends. They had both served at the Gunnery School at Kingston and joined the NWMP at the same time.[3] Walker had left the NWMP in the 1880s to manage the Cochrane Ranch and then became one of Calgary's most successful businessmen and civic leaders. The site for the camp, Steele found, was "bad and dusty," but the officers and men were "a fine lot," keen and hard working.[4] The camp wrapped up with a parade and speeches by various dignitaries, including Steele, on July 1. A few days later he presided at the opening of the Agricultural Fair (the predecessor of the Calgary Stampede) with the mayor, the lieutenant governor, and two cabinet ministers.

As the initial enthusiasm surrounding his homecoming died down, the realities of Steele's job began to set in. His appointment was part of a far-reaching series of changes Sir Frederick Borden was trying to make to the Canadian army. These involved increasing the size of the permanent force and creating the various branches needed to sustain a functional military organization in the field: a medical corps, engineers, signals, intelligence, ordnance, and army service corps.[5] These changes would permit the organization of the dozens of militia regiments into larger units, brigades, and divisions, at least on paper. They would also allow for more realistic training of the part-time soldiers who made up the militia regiments across the country. One of the many organizational gaps in the system was in the new provinces of Alberta and Saskatchewan, where the rapid increase in population meant a growing demand for new militia regiments. Before 1907, all three prairie provinces were part of Military District No. 10 with headquarters in Winnipeg. Now Alberta (and the adjoining North-West Territories all the way to the Arctic Ocean) was split off as Military District No. 13.[6]

The west and particularly the prairie region was the most neglected part of the country in terms of military organization. There were numerous militia units, some dating back to the 1880s, but the four military districts west of Thunder Bay were not organized into commands like the rest of the country, which would have allowed the creation of brigade and divisional structures. Fewer than 200 of the 2,500 or so permanent force soldiers were stationed in the west, eighty-four members of the Royal Canadian Mounted Rifles in Winnipeg and 100 gunners at the west coast naval base at Esquimalt.[7] This meant that carrying out the main responsibility of the permanent force of training the volunteers was next to impossible. Since no training schools had been conducted in the vast area between Winnipeg and Esquimalt before 1907, the enthusiasm with which Steele was greeted at the Calgary camp was not surprising. Just what Steele had been led to believe about future prospects for his military district is not entirely clear, but he seems to have expected that a new permanent mounted infantry unit, a revived Lord Strathcona's Horse, would be created to be stationed in Alberta.[8]

In the summer of 1907 all of this was in the future; for the moment, the permanent force component of Military District No. 13 consisted of Steele himself. As he reported to Marie in mid-July: "I have no clerk, no staff, and have to hunt up a clerk, staff adjutant will come some time I suppose."[9] Calgary was not even confirmed as the final choice for the headquarters of the district. Edmonton and Medicine Hat were both lobbying for it, although their chances were not good. Steele met with Minister of the Interior Frank Oliver in August who, although an Edmontonian, made it clear he preferred Calgary: "Had a chat with Frank Oliver about the site of the barracks. He is in favour of Calgary and says he will wire the Minister."[10] An election was due in 1908 and Calgarians were still outraged that the federal government had chosen Edmonton as the provincial capital, especially since the new provincial government had decided to locate the university there as well. Steele nevertheless made a show of visiting all the possible locations in the province, a tour that took up much of August.

Calgary was growing fast in 1907, and houses for rent were expensive and hard to find, especially those, as Steele explained to Marie, "suitable for our station."[11] He did manage to find one before the end of July and immediately began deluging Marie with letters urging her to move as soon as possible. As always, there were complications. Both parents wanted to put Flora and Gertie in St. Urbain's Academy, a boarding school in Montreal, but there was determined resistance from both daughters. It seemed easier to deal with this from Calgary. "You must be firm my dear. You can if you like you know," was one piece of no doubt irritating advice, followed a few lines later by this rather contradictory line: "Of course the tuition is all in your hands my dear. It is important that they should speak and write French though and well."[12] In the end a compromise was reached. Flora (age sixteen) stayed in Montreal, while Gertie (age twelve) went to Calgary. Marie remained in Montreal through September to get her first-born settled in school.

The Steeles had hired servants while in England, a man and wife named Bagnall who came with them to Canada and also decided to move with the Steeles to Calgary. Also in the summer of 1907, Marie's aunt and close friend Minnie Macdonell, whose husband had died the previous year, was swindled out of the ranch they owned near Lethbridge and was invited to live with the Steeles. The extra people meant that the house leased in July was no longer big enough. Steele was able to sublet it and find a larger place a few blocks from where the Calgary Stampede grounds are now located.[13] The family arrived on October 3, but the joy of the reunion was overshadowed by Steele's discovery that his expected promotion to full colonel would not happen. His initial appointment on returning to Canada was at the rank of lieutenant-colonel, but since he had been given colonel's rank in the militia after returning with Lord Strathcona's Horse, and since his appointment in the SAC was at the same level, he expected that he would shortly be given what he considered his due. Two things prevented this. The impending election meant that the Militia Department's budget was even tighter than usual. Even more important was the fact that advice to the minister on promotions was in the hands of the senior permanent force officers in Ottawa. He had some friends there, notably the adjutant general, Brigadier D.A. Macdonald, but many regarded Steele with a jealous eye because of the publicity Lord Strathcona's Horse had attracted in South Africa.

Steele reacted badly: "I bitterly regret having accepted the position and would not have done so had it not been for the life insurance I have to pay."[14] Steele knew that he would be taking a large pay cut when he returned from South Africa. Still, he had his NWMP pension and while in London he had made arrangements with a broker named John A. Macdonald to sell his shares in the southern British Columbia mines. Macdonald looked at the assay reports that Steele had and told him that, if they were confirmed, he could sell the properties for the enormous sum of $120,000 (the equivalent of more than $2.5 million in 2018 dollars).[15] There were a couple of other investors but Steele's share seems to have been approximately half, and with that he could easily have afforded to retire to the life of a gentleman farmer that he sometimes fantasized about. However, until the deal was confirmed he had a cash flow problem, so he put his disappointment aside and turned to the military task at hand. Building an organization from scratch was something he had done several times before and he welcomed the opportunity of putting his personal stamp on it. Military District No. 13 needed almost everything—equipment, new or expanded militia units, rifle ranges, and drill halls. All of these things were subject to the requirements of government patronage, something that Steele understood very well from his Mounted Police days. The volunteer militia had also been plagued since its inception with political interference in the naming and promotion of officers. Sir Frederick Borden was attempting to reduce, if not eliminate, these practices and Steele was determined to push that policy as far as he could.

Early in 1908 there was devastating financial news:

> *Got letters from John A Macdonald and the report of the* M.E. *[mining examiner] on Empire also directions re coal to be sold. The report of* M.E. *is most unfavourable, and if correct shows that the property has been lied about and that the people concerned in working and floating it are either knaves or fools. It is reported as being iron instead of copper, copper pyrites nodules were all that could be seen.*[16]

The property was worth next to nothing and Steele's dreams of financial security evaporated. He would have been well advised to cut his losses at this point, but he refused to sell until the end of his life. Steele's relative penury over the next few years prevented him from dispensing the hospitality he thought his position demanded. It also created some social awkwardness since many of the volunteer officers and even some of his permanent force subordinates had extensive private means. His heirs finally disposed of the mining property in the 1920s for a few thousand dollars.

Perhaps it was as well that Steele was busy with the work of organization. He rented office accommodation within easy walking distance of his house, bought furniture for it, and found a clerk. He was assigned an adjutant, Captain Ernest Mackie, who had been with the Strathconas in South Africa. As spring approached he began planning for a second and larger training camp at Calgary. That went off in mid-June with just as much enthusiasm as the previous year. There was a large celebration in the summer of 1908 to mark the 300th anniversary of the founding of Quebec City and a mounted contingent had to be organized to send down. At the beginning of August, a disastrous forest fire burned down almost the entire town of Fernie, just across the border in southeastern British Columbia, leaving 100 dead and 7,000 homeless.[17] Steele immediately sent 200 tents to help house the survivors. A few days later Steele received word that Colonel Thomas Evans, the commanding officer of Military District No. 10 at Winnipeg, was seriously ill. Steele was ordered there to fill in for him and manage both districts. He was informed that he might be there for as long as three months.[18] Just a week after he got to Winnipeg, however, Evans died, and one of the first things Steele had to do was to organize a memorial service. Steele believed that Evans was one of the permanent force officers who had blocked his promotion to full colonel and he commented rather sourly on the eulogy in a letter to Marie: "The Minister laid it on 'too thick.' I would hate to be as good as Evans. No one, even amongst the Twelve Apostles has ever been so good."[19]

The death of Evans immediately opened the possibility that Steele might be offered the position in Winnipeg, but he had decidedly mixed feelings about the prospect. The district was much larger, taking in all of Saskatchewan and Manitoba as well as northern Ontario as far east as Thunder Bay. It had an established base, Fort Osborne Barracks, and the Royal Canadian Mounted Rifles, a small permanent force unit. The city was definitely more attractive. Winnipeg was three times the size of Calgary and much wealthier. He described it to Marie: "The city is fine 'knocks the spots off Montreal.' Beautiful homes, good cars, and beautifully planted streets, fine buildings and in fact all that can be desired in that way."[20] On the other hand, the job involved more work and greater responsibility without any increase in pay. Most of all it would mean moving again just as Marie and the family were getting settled in Calgary:

> I do not want to leave Calgary, and the only thing that would induce me to change would be if this were made into a "command," that is a group of districts under a full color brigadier general with an increase of one thousand dols per annum. As for the move I would prefer that someone else got the change to this district. You should not have to

*move this winter as it would be a terrible bother and I assure you dear one, nobody could appreciate more than I the trouble you have in moving, and have had poor darling.*[21]

Marie was non-committal at first. She was experienced enough at reading Sam's letters to know that, whatever his protestations, he would follow his ambitions. His competitive spirit was aroused by the fact that one of the officers at Winnipeg, Lt.-Col. D.C.F. Bliss, wanted the job badly and mounted a vigorous lobbying campaign. Among other things, Bliss spread rumours that Steele preferred Calgary, leading him to send indignant letters to the minister and the chief of staff saying that, as a good soldier, he would go where ordered. He got an immediate telegram, followed by a letter from Adjutant General Macdonald:

*I am writing you at the earliest moment at my disposal, however, my wire would have relieved you of any anxiety in regard to the subject of your two letters—at all events it was intended to convey that meaning—and you need not have the slightest worry over the situation—our friend B. may as well save his powder, he is not in it in any shape, you can rest assured of this. When the time comes for discussing the changes which may follow the death of poor Evans your interests will be carefully looked after—I can say no more.*[22]

A letter from Borden followed saying much the same thing, but adding that no decision would be made until after the general election at the end of October.[23]

Steele spent all of October on an extensive inspection tour of all the militia units between Winnipeg and the Rockies, ending with a week in Calgary with his family. In early November he got a letter from General Lake, formally offering him the choice of Calgary or Winnipeg. He and Marie must have discussed it when he was with her the previous month but, taking nothing for granted, he sent a lengthy analysis of the relative costs of both cities, "much in favour of Winnipeg."²⁴ She replied immediately by telegram that she would go wherever he wanted. His hope that a larger command might be created encompassing all of the prairies and perhaps even including British Columbia came to nothing. As he heard in a private letter from his friend Lt.-Col. François-Louis Lessard, a staff officer in Ottawa, the Quebec celebrations in the summer had eaten up too much of the budget. The Steeles decided that the family would not move until Flora finished school in Montreal at the end of June 1909. She came home for Christmas in December 1908 and Steele was able to accompany her from Winnipeg to Calgary.

Once the decision was made to take over Military District No. 10, Steele set about organizing it to his satisfaction. He quickly discovered why Lt.-Col. Bliss, who had lobbied strenuously for the job, was not considered for the command by Ottawa. His wife came to see Steele in early December to plead for help. Bliss was an alcoholic and had failed to give his family money or food for weeks. Colonel Evans had known about the problem and had pressured Bliss to give them money but that stopped after his death.²⁵ A court of enquiry found that Bliss had been passing bad cheques and was frequently absent from his duties without leave. All this was reported to Ottawa by Steele and the Militia Council decided that, in view of the fact that Bliss had served with some distinction in South Africa, he would given the choice between a court martial or immediate resignation.²⁶ He chose the latter. The rest of Steele's officers at Winnipeg were much more satisfactory. Three of them, A.C. Macdonell, Louis Lipsett and H.D.B. Ketchen, would become generals during the First World War.

As he settled in, Steele found Winnipeg a welcoming environment. One old friend from the Red River Expedition, Sir Daniel McMillan, was now Manitoba's lieutenant governor, and there were many others like him. When the legislature opened in February 1909, Steele escorted McMillan and afterwards attended a dinner with "all the swells of the place."²⁷ Many of these people were stalwarts of the Historical Society of Manitoba and Steele was quickly drawn into giving talks at their meetings and dinners about his life. These were very well received and many people urged him to consider writing his memoirs. The idea appealed and he wrote the London publisher, John Murray, to get his reaction. Murray liked the idea and encouraged Steele to go ahead.[28] Steele even had an idea for a title. He wrote Marie that he had been reading Lord Roberts's autobiography, *Forty-one Years in India: From Subaltern to Commander in Chief*, and his own book would eventually be called *Forty Years in Canada*.[29] He started writing down his memories using his own diaries and began collecting others from his friends to supplement them.[30]

At the end of April, the Militia Department appointed a new commanding officer for Alberta, relieving Steele of that extra responsibility. He was happy for the excuse to go to Calgary to officially turn over the command to his successor and spend a week with the family. They decided that the commanding officer's residence in Winnipeg was too small for their purposes since Flora would finish school in June, and all three children as well as Minnie Macdonell and two servants would be living with them. The army house was turned over to Steele's second in command, Major A.C. Macdonell, and he began the search for a larger one. Two weeks before the family was due to arrive, he finally found one at 353 Broadway and signed a lease.[31]

June was always a busy month with the organization of the annual summer training camps but this year there was more work than usual. The militia unit at Thunder Bay, the 96th Regiment (later the Lake Superior Regiment), was in a disorganized state and one of its lieutenants was being blackmailed for an alleged "unnatural offence."[32] In early June Steele travelled to Port Arthur to meet with General William Otter to decide if the unit would have to be disbanded. After inspecting the regiment and meeting with the commanding officer and the lieutenant, they decided it could be salvaged. The unfortunate lieutenant was dismissed, an experienced sergeant major was summoned from Winnipeg to show them how to maintain their records and accounts, and Steele left with stern warnings that improvements must be thorough and immediate.

The family arrived at the end of June but a burst pipe and some needed electrical repairs kept them in a hotel for two weeks. They were just settling in when Steele was once again at Thunder Bay dealing with a different kind of emergency. He had gone back to see if the 96th Battalion was carrying through its improvements; while he was there, the CPR workers at Fort William went on strike and violence threatened. The city police were unable to contain the situation and the mayor, Louis Pelletier, although sympathetic to labour, gave Steele a requisition for troops to be called out to protect life and property. Steele had no option in this case, since the *Militia Act* mandated that district commanders must provide "aid to the civil power" when requested, and in fact this was one of seventeen occasions in the decade between 1905 and 1914 when it happened in various parts of Canada.[33] The required aid would be permanent force troops if available and volunteer militia as needed. The closest permanent force unit was at Winnipeg, but since it was the CPR's property that was at risk, the railway was happy to provide a special train to bring the Canadian Mounted Rifles to Fort William.[34] In the meantime, all available men from the 96th were put on duty.

The CPR had initially brought in a few special constables who were now surrounded by angry strikers in one of the dockyard buildings. The 500 or so strikers, "Finns, Poles, Italians, Galicians and Greeks," according to Steele, were threatening the constables and were determined to prevent the railway from bringing in strikebreakers. Once his soldiers were in place on August 12, Steele informed the mayor that it was time to read the *Riot Act*, ordering the strikers to disperse. With some satisfaction, he told the mayor that reading the act would give him the authority to open fire if necessary. When the mayor declined to do it, Steele had him repeat his refusal before witnesses and read the *Riot Act* himself.[35] He had provided himself with all the necessary interpreters and explained that the men must leave now but could return the following day to negotiate with the company. They went away without trouble. The next day the soldiers conducted a search and found quantities of arms and ammunition cached at the Finnish Hall and in a bush outside town. A few of the strike leaders were arrested and that brought an end to the incident. On August 13 all was quiet and the following day Steele dismissed the volunteers and sent the Canadian Mounted Rifles back to Winnipeg. By August 16 the CPR had reached an agreement with its employees and all were back at work.

Steele's reaction to this incident clearly prevented a dangerous situation from getting out of hand. Elsewhere in Canada, many of the other "aid to the civil power" situations in this period resulted in violence and death, while some dragged on for months.[36] The government in Ottawa and the CPR were both understandably delighted with the outcome.[37] The dock workers were certainly less enthusiastic, but the labour laws of the period gave them little support. There were ambiguities in the events at the port that Steele, typically, ignored in favour of positive action based on his own reading of the situation. The mayor could have declined to read the *Riot Act* until shooting started, as indeed he seemed inclined to do. By taking the responsibility himself, Steele undoubtedly prevented the shedding of blood that would have been in no one's interest.

Back in Winnipeg, Steele began serious work on his autobiography. He had written to Lord Strathcona asking permission to dedicate the book to him and was delighted with the reply: "Got a letter from Lord Strathcona to the effect that he would allow me to dedicate the book I hope (DV) to write this winter to him. It is very good of him and will mean a great deal to me."[38] Sometimes the writing went well, as on November 18 when he recorded completing twenty-five legal size pages, or a few days later when he noted: "Wrote all afternoon until I almost got writers cramp."[39] The family was all together now since Flora had finished school. Steele was now discovering at first hand both sides of family life. Flora, age seventeen, was becoming an adult, but Gertrude at fourteen and Harwood at twelve were inclined to be troublesome. Gertie and her mother had differences of opinion about clothes, while Harwood was habitually late, driving his father to write, "he needs a good lambasting," although there is no indication that any of the children were ever subjected to physical punishment.[40] When Steele introduced his friend Baden-Powell's Boy Scout organization to Winnipeg, Harwood quickly became an enthusiastic member, easing relations somewhat, but Steele noted that it was always easier to get him to a Scout meeting than to church.[41] The children walked and rode with their father, sang with their mother at home and Steele even built them a backyard skating rink when cold weather came.

In 1909 the government finally decided to revive the Lord Strathcona's Horse name for a permanent force unit. The Royal Canadian Mounted Rifles at Winnipeg, many of whom had served with the original Strathcona's Horse in South Africa, would inherit the name. Steele was asked his opinion of how it should be designated and noted rather gloomily in his diary, "I wired the minister in council (secry) rc the new regiments name suggested Lord Strathconas Horse, Royal Canadians. It will not go though."[42] He was wrong. The government accepted the new name with the single change of putting parentheses around Royal Canadians and so it remains to this day. Steele was appointed commanding officer, probably because the government thought it would be a cheaper form of compensation than giving him the promotion to full colonel that he believed he had been promised. He appreciated the gesture, although he was aware that it meant more work and no extra money. It also created a serious rift with Major A.C. Macdonell, his most senior and competent subordinate, who had been commanding officer of the Mounted Rifles and expected to remain in command of what was essentially the same unit.

Macdonell was a peppery former mounted policeman (his soldiers in the First World War, during which he rose to command the 1st Canadian Division, nicknamed him "Batty Mac") who had served in South Africa with distinction.⁴³ Macdonell's resentment simmered away for a few months until he finally sent a letter to Steele complaining that by accepting the appointment, Steele was holding up the promotion of all the officers below him. Steele called him and all the other officers in and told them that his appointment was only temporary and that a commander for the Strathconas would have to chosen on the basis of seniority from all the permanent force majors across the country. He was not holding up anyone, he told them: "I was simply holding the place until a regular C.O. was appointed, that it gave me more duty and no more pay, in fact was the opposite of advancement."⁴⁴ This was more than a little disingenuous since Steele was thoroughly enjoying himself, designing the dress uniform, crest, and motto for the regiment. Macdonell insisted on having his letter forwarded to Ottawa. It ground its way through the military bureaucracy there for several months and finally Macdonell was informed by the Militia Council that he had no case and was given a formal reprimand.⁴⁵ Relations between the two men gradually thawed in the fall of 1910, and in the spring of 1911 Steele supported Macdonell's application for promotion to lieutenant-colonel.⁴⁶ Macdonell settled in as second in command of the Strathconas and finally took over as commanding officer in March 1912.⁴⁷

The strained relations between Steele and Macdonell were a symptom of the general state of unhappiness in the permanent force in the years before the First World War. All ranks were badly paid, from privates at 50¢ a day to the senior officer levels. Steele estimated that his pay left him about $1,000 a year short, if he did the kind of socializing and entertaining expected of a commanding officer.⁴⁸ The Steeles survived by cutting back where possible, selling off small pieces of property and taking out loans on Sam's insurance policies. Steele's autobiography project was motivated at least in part by the hope that it would make some money. Promotion was glacially slow and there was little opportunity for professional growth. In the world outside, a military revolution that had started in South Africa, with machine guns and quick-firing artillery, was rapidly gathering momentum. The Canadian military had next to no resources to comprehend or react to these changes. Without any help or encouragement from Ottawa, Steele did his best to keep up on his own, studying the tactics of the Russo-Japanese War of 1904–1905 which, even more than South Africa, prefigured the trenches and massive casualties of the First World War.[49] On a visit to Fort William in 1911, Steele was interviewed by the local paper: "The reporter of the *News* met me and asked silly questions, silly because I cannot answer them. Asked if war was imminent between Gt. Britain and Germany. I said that I could not give anything for publication."[50] Steele, at least, was aware that this kind of war would be much bloodier than South Africa, even if he could do little to prepare his soldiers for it.

The only small move in bringing the Canadian army into the new century came in 1911, when a few British officers were seconded to help improve training standards. Military District No. 10 got Captain Louis Lipsett, who had served in South Africa as a staff officer, although Steele seems not to have encountered him there. He was favourably impressed by Lipsett, although he worried that he might not have the necessary sensitivity to work well with Canadians: "These people always come with the impression that we do not know anything and as that is just not the sort of thing I can swallow I shall make a point of seeing that the staff officer sent here does not get such a notion in his head."[51] The concerns proved unfounded. Lipsett settled in as one of Steele's most competent and reliable officers. They remained good friends until Lipsett's tragic death while commanding the British 4th Division in October 1918, just days before the end of the First World War.

A federal election was held in 1911 and military policy played some part in the campaign, although more on naval than army matters. The Conservatives returned to power after a decade and a half in opposition. As someone whose Tory connections went back to Sir John A. Macdonald and who had strong personal ties to the ruling Conservative regime in Manitoba, Steele was pleased with the outcome, although he had always worked well with Sir Frederick Borden. "I am sorry for Sir Frederick Borden's defeat," he noted in his diary, "as he had the interests of the Militia at heart."[52] The new minister of Militia and Defence was Sam Hughes, who would turn out to be, by any measure, the most controversial individual to hold that office in Canadian history. Steele had disliked Hughes when he first met him in South Africa, but now he hoped that Hughes might have mellowed over the years. The early indications were positive. On his first trip west after the election, Hughes told Steele he would get his long-awaited promotion to full colonel.[53] When Steele was in Ottawa at the end of November, Hughes repeated the promise in a meeting with Steele and the judge advocate general.

The promotion finally came through in the spring of 1912. That meant a little more pay and at about the same time Steele got an official car with his servant, Corporal Martin, as driver. The allowance for rent was also increased, which was just as well, since the house Steele was renting was sold and he had to find a new one. In May 1912 the Steeles moved to 236 Roslyn Road, in a pleasant neighbourhood just south of the Assiniboine River, across from the Manitoba legislature. The other house had been somewhat cramped with the growing children and their visiting friends, as well as Minnie Macdonell and a servant. Steele noted with satisfaction in his diary that the new house had more room to accommodate his daily Sandow exercises. It also had that modern innovation, a garage to house his automobile. When Minnie remarried in 1913 the Steeles moved once again, this time to an apartment. The Pasadena Block, at 220 Hugo Street North, had opened the previous year. The building embodied "luxurious and spacious" apartment living and is now a historic site, the only one of Steele's Canadian residences still standing.[54]

Steele had been following Eugen Sandow's regimen faithfully for a decade now. At first the motivation had largely been vanity, but now in his sixties he was increasingly worried about his health. His weight often went up to more than 240 pounds and Steele, who loved to eat, struggled mightily to bring it under control. From 1912 onward he complained frequently about heart palpitations but what really worried him was the possibility of diabetes. There was no treatment for the disease at that time beyond diet and rest. His doctor ordered both and they seemed to help: "Went to Dr. Davidson and he examined me telling me that I had improved, that there is little or no trace of sugar and that my pulse is better."[55] Resting was something Steele found very hard to do. In August 1911, he spent four days at Gimli on Lake Winnipeg with Harwood. "My only holiday for years," he noted in his diary.[56] In fact, it seems to have been the only holiday he ever took, apart from brief visits to family. Health concerns and increasing political conflicts with Sam Hughes led to the following outburst in 1912:

> Wish I could retire this year. This life with its wretched politics and the resulting sneaking and lying is detestable, making the members of one of the noblest professions a mean contemptable [sic] lot self-seeking, toadying with every decent man in doubt every day of his life and compelled to "fight the devil with fire."[57]

The fact that he was turning sixty-five in January 1913 led to more thoughts of retirement. "Wrote Major Christie Victoria B.C. re cost of living there," he noted in December 1912.[58]

Steele's finances, however, were in no shape to allow him to retire. Some of his health issues might have been the result of stress. His diary is full of entries about the necessity to cut expenses and sell property to pay bills. Early in 1913 he noted in his diary: "Wrote Lord Strathcona re a private matter between him and me."[59] There are earlier indications that Strathcona had offered to lend him money, and now he seems to have accepted. A year later, after Strathcona's death, he wrote: "Letter from Lord Strathcona's executors in Edinburgh re a loan his Lordship had made to me. Will not be able to pay it yet. He never intended me to pay it I am sure but it cannot be helped."[60] Steele was deeply affected by Strathcona's death, regarding him almost as a surrogate father. When he had donated $500,000 to create the Strathcona Trust in 1909 for the support of physical education through the schools and the cadet movement in Canada, Steele had happily agreed to serve on the executive, devoting much time to it up to the start of the First World War. The relationship remained close and cordial to the end. Writing his memoirs had revived painful memories of the stories circulated accusing Steele of drunkenness at the London banquet in 1901. The day before he died, Strathcona sent a letter to Steele confirming that the allegations were entirely unfounded.[61] The story was to be revived yet again at the outbreak of the First World War (see below).

Steele's work with the militia, arranging for the construction of armouries and rifle ranges to accommodate the new units being organized from the rapidly expanding population of the west, usually went smoothly, except when Sam Hughes decided to intervene on political grounds. In May 1913, without consulting Steele or any of the officers in the community, Hughes ordered that the annual summer camp at Battleford be moved from the south side of the river to a new location on the north side. The reasons given were that the old site was too small and lacked a sufficient water supply, but Steele suspected that one of Hughes's political cronies on the north side owned the land there. All the officers from the units in South Battleford promptly sent in their resignations.[62] Steele hurried out to try to salvage the situation. A quick inspection showed that there was nothing wrong with the original site, which Steele thought had room for 10,000 cavalry to manoeuvre. After lengthy negotiations, Steele managed to persuade most of the officers to withdraw their resignations but he felt that he had been forced to betray their interests: "The feeling in this town and all over at the action of the minister is intense and the task assigned to me the dirtiest and meanest I have met."[63]

There was a similar incident at Prince Albert a week later involving the location of a cadet camp. Steele noted in his diary, "The force here is disgusted with the dept and fear that they have

*Steele and his staff during summer militia training exercises at Camp Sewell, Manitoba. [BPSC, 2008.1.3.3.6.2.39]*

made a great mistake. I agree with them heartily."[64] Steele detested political interference of this kind because it undermined discipline and the authority of officers, which he rightly regarded as the foundation of military effectiveness. The largest annual training camp in Military District No. 10, at Camp Sewell east of Brandon, went more smoothly, with Hughes and General Sir Ian Hamilton in attendance. Numbers of volunteers and their ability to fire their rifles accurately at targets was all that really interested Hughes. Logistics, medical services and even the artillery were ignored as much as possible. One year before the beginning of the First World War, Steele's soldiers were borrowing farm wagons to use as makeshift ambulances.[65] Nevertheless, both Hamilton and Hughes assured him that the camp was the best they had observed in Canada that year. This was high praise from Hamilton, who was considered the British Army's leading authority on training. Steele was picking up rumours around this time that he might be appointed the next inspector general of the Canadian forces. "It would," he noted, "be nice to have it to wind up the service."[66]

Historians have long noted the popular enthusiasm for the war on both sides when it broke out in Europe in the summer of

1914.⁶⁷ Nationalist militarism everywhere in Europe easily trumped socialist denunciations of the conflict as a capitalist war. The mood in Canada, especially in the west, was somewhat different. Steele's efforts to introduce military drill in the schools of western Canada through the Strathcona Trust often ran into anti-war opposition.⁶⁸ The cadet program encountered similar difficulties. Tiny as the regular force was, it was difficult to keep up numbers. The pay was so low, Steele noted, "None but loafers offer to serve with us."⁶⁹ The homestead system on the prairies under the *Dominion Lands* Act required farmers to live on their land for specified periods of time, making them vulnerable to losing their farms if they were reported away while attending annual militia camps. It was not until 1912 that Steele persuaded Minister of the Interior Robert Rogers to publish an order exempting them from the rules while at camp.⁷⁰ In September 1913 Steele noted:

> *Colonel Mitchell called to see me at 8:00 and spent the evening. He thinks that as the people are clamouring for peace it may be a mistake to have maneuvres on Thanksgiving day and he suggests the 24th of May. When he says this he means that the 100 years of peace celebrations is on the way between Britain and the U.S.*⁷¹

Steele finished writing his memoirs in April and sent the draft off for editing. "It has been a weary task," was his comment.⁷² In May, the Imperial Order Daughters of the Empire at Portage la Prairie asked permission to name their group the "Sam Steele Chapter." He agreed, sent them a photo and went out with Marie to give them a talk on the history of western Canada.⁷³ The annual training at Camp Sewell in late June went off as usual but the heat of a Manitoba summer took its toll and Steele was ordered by his doctor to take a few weeks' complete rest, "not even riding in a motor car."⁷⁴ He obeyed the instructions for a week before going off to observe the cadet camp at Fort Qu'Appelle. Harwood was one of the cadets and Steele could not bring himself to stay away.

In the early months of 1914 the only troubles on the horizon for Britain seemed to be within the boundaries of the Empire, with the possibility of violence over Home Rule in Ireland. However, just after father and son returned to Winnipeg, the European situation made itself felt: "War cloud in Europe. Austria-Hun. has declared war on Servia as a result of the murder of the Archduke and Archduchess in Belgrade [actually Sarajevo]. The Servians not accepting in full the Austrian ultimatum."[75] It still seemed very far away. Even when the *London Times* came out in favour of Britain supporting France and Russia, Steele, like many others, expected the Royal Navy to be the decisive factor: it would quickly crush the German fleet and force an abrupt end to the fighting. Many professional soldiers rejoiced at the prospect of fighting when the British declared war on August 4. Steele was not among them. His diary entry reads: "Terrible state of affairs this. The whole world at war except America."[76]

Unlikely as overseas conflict had seemed for Canada in the years before 1914, the army had a plan in place. If, as expected, Britain requested help, a Canadian division would be sent overseas. An infantry division in 1914 consisted of sixteen infantry battalions of approximately 1,000 men each, organized into four brigades, as well as artillery, medical units, army service corps for supply, engineers, signallers, some cavalry for scouting, and staff officers. The plan envisioned that the permanent force units would be brought up to strength to form the core of the division. The best trained volunteer militia units from across the country would be selected, reinforced if necessary, and designated to fill out the brigades. The same applied to the other kinds of soldiers in the division. Commanders of the military districts, such as Steele—who had spent years recruiting, training, and observing volunteers and knew their strengths and weaknesses—would advise Ottawa on the choices. None of the military district commanders expected that all or even most of their advice would be followed, but no one was prepared for what actually happened.

Sam Hughes threw out the plan altogether, and sent telegrams directly to the commanding officers of militia units ordering them to disregard the mobilization plan, asking for the names of volunteers willing to serve in Europe, and directing them to report immediately to the new camp which was being rushed to completion at Valcartier near Quebec City. The only permanent force infantry unit, the RCR, was sent off to Bermuda to do garrison duty. Canadian military historians have almost unanimously agreed that the result was a chaotic mess that resulted in a division far from ready to go to war, and which had unfortunate consequences for recruiting later in the war.77 Sam Steele was definitely of this opinion:

> I was entirely ignored as were all the staff in Canada. Never in the history of the Canadian militia has there been such a madman in charge of the portfolio. Every rule or custom of either civil or military life has been utterly smashed and the whole fabric which has been built up has been destroyed.78

On August 18 Steele received a telegram from Hughes, ordering him to Valcartier to help with organizing the western contingents. Steele was not happy with the summons:

> The camp will be the very devil with its politics and its "pull."... All of the officers got excited when they heard that I had to go to Val Cartier [sic] and they wish to go too thinking that I am to take the contingent to war, and nothing will persuade them that I cannot go I am not in good enough health to go.79

In spite of his forebodings, he boarded the train to Valcartier as soon as the Winnipeg troops had been sent off. The situation was as bad as expected but at least a competent regular soldier, Colonel Victor Williams, whom he knew from the Mounted Police and South Africa, was in command of the camp and doing his best to keep Hughes under control: "Colonel Williams also stated that the minister [Sam Hughes] also wished to communicate direct with the captains of companies over the heads of their commanding officers, and that he, Williams, had said for God's sake Colonel do not centralize any more it is bad enough now."[80] Steele spent a week and a half helping to select officers for the western battalions. He pushed hard to have his friend, Henry Burstall, given command of the divisional artillery and for Macdonell to be named one of the four brigadiers; successfully in the first case, not so in the second.

Once the divisional organization was complete Steele went to Montreal for a few days to visit Marie's family. While he was there a telegram arrived from Sam Hughes offering him command of Military District No. 11 in Victoria. He immediately suspected, correctly as it turned out, that Hughes was trying to put him in this military backwater and that the reason was that someone had brought up the old story about him being drunk at Lord Strathcona's dinner in London in 1901. Hughes, a teetotaler, would give no senior appointment to anyone tainted by drink. Steele arranged for copies of Strathcona's final letter clearing him of the charge to be sent to headquarters and to Winnipeg cabinet minister Robert Rogers.[81] Then he was off to Toronto with Harwood, who was starting at Highfield School in Hamilton. By the end of September, Steele was back in Winnipeg. There was a growing expectation by this time that a second division would be sent, so Steele began preparing for more recruiting. There were the usual rumours that he might be chosen to command it, but he was inclined to dismiss them, as there were many other candidates.[82]

The second division was confirmed on October 7. This time the constituent units were to be organized in the military districts before proceeding to Valcartier. This avoided much of the chaos that had dogged the first division, but it left plenty of opportunity for Sam Hughes to insist on the appointment of officers whose main qualification was support of the Conservative Party. Steele complained frequently about this in his diary, while at the same time missing no opportunity to use his own political connections to advance his cause. This lobbying had some effect. In late October, Robert Rogers contacted Steele and offered him command of a brigade. Steele might have been inclined to accept if Sam Hughes had not a few days before had himself promoted from colonel to major general. Steele was apoplectic: "An alienist [psychiatrist] ought to be in the govt to warn the premier when one of his ministers is insane as that fraud Sam Hughes is."[83] In the space of a month, Steele was instructed to recruit and organize two battalions from his district. Then he was told it would be three, and days later only one. By mid-November he had organized all the units requested by Ottawa and was satisfied with the state of their training. The expectation of a short war was fading fast by this time, an eventually that Steele was anticipating as he started to recruit a third contingent.

The rapidly increasing scale of the Canadian military effort made Steele realize how different the situation was from the South African excursion, when volunteers signed up for a year and then hastened back to their homes and jobs. Now there were many more Canadian soldiers and they would be gone indefinitely, with serious consequences for those left behind. In December the Winnipeg YMCA offered $5,000 for a Christmas dinner for the soldiers in the city, something that Steele would have welcomed fifteen years earlier. This time he told them that "the money would be better spent in assisting the poor who could not go to the front and had wives and children to support and that there are widows whose occupations as keeper of boarding houses has gone through their lodgers going to the front, and who need help."[84] Western Canada had been suffering through a sharp economic downturn for a year or so before the beginning of the war, and Steele issued orders to his recruiters to ensure that every second applicant accepted was an unemployed man.[85]

On December 12 Steele received a telegram informing him that he was to be promoted to major general and appointed inspector general for western Canada. Hundreds of congratulations poured in from across the country and all walks of life, from Prime Minister Robert Borden and all three premiers of the prairie provinces to Steele's barber.[86] The reaction was a reminder to those in power—especially Sam Hughes—that Steele remained, in the public mind, one of Canada's most respected soldiers. A handful of others had successfully commanded battalion-sized units in South Africa, but Strathcona's Horse and its commander were widely perceived as the most competent. Steele was naturally very pleased at the expressions of support. For one thing, his new rank and status allowed him to push the promotion of some of his officers whom he believed were deserving, such as Macdonell and Ketchen. It also encouraged Steele to revise his earlier conviction that he had no chance of a senior command in the war zone. The complaints about his health problems dropped off in his diary and he stepped up his efforts to mobilize political support.

There had not been an inspector general for western Canada previously, so it was not immediately clear what Steele's new duties would be. He had to wait for his replacement as district officer commanding to be named, so in January 1915 his preoccupation remained getting the contingents for the 2nd Division ready to leave for England. Kitchener had informed the Canadian authorities that he would not accept a Canadian officer in command of the division. Steele received a letter from Milner confirming this, while assuring Steele that Kitchener thought highly of him: "Lord Milner's letter is rather a disappointing one to me. I was in hopes that I could get a look in at the war, but of course there is a lot to do here—and I may be allowed to go to the front later."[87] Hughes came out to Winnipeg on January 18 to look over the 2nd Division troops. According to Steele's own account, "Upon completing our inspection the Minister went back to the Royal Alexandra addressed the Canadian club. He mentioned my name in connection with training and organization and the vast assemblage gave me an ovation clapping and cheering to a tremendous extent."[88]

By mid-February, Steele was ready to begin his first tour of western Canada as inspector general, starting at Regina and moving on to Calgary, Vancouver, and Victoria. He enjoyed the work, not least because his new rank entitled him to stay in the best hotels. The Palliser in Calgary, he recorded, was "a palace, fire proof and a credit to the C.P. RY."[89] Making sure that men and equipment were up to standard and that officers knew their business was something that he knew well. As soon as he was appointed inspector general he had written to Baden-Powell, asking him to send copies of the latest British training manuals. On the return trip he visited Medicine Hat and Brandon. Back in Winnipeg he busied himself setting up his new office and dealing with "an enormous mass of correspondence."[90] He was making the final corrections to the proofs of his memoirs and worrying about Harwood, who had decided he would rather go to the Royal Military College than his school in Hamilton, and was behaving badly when he was refused. On March 15 a telegram arrived from Sam Hughes, ordering him to Ottawa for unspecified consultations. When he arrived, Hughes offered him command of the 2nd Division. Even though he knew that Kitchener would probably overrule the appointment, Steele accepted immediately, partly from a sense of duty and partly because he could not resist an opportunity, however faint, to be in on the action. At age sixty-seven, Sam Steele was off to his last war.

< *General Sam Steele on his promotion, December 1914.* [BPSC, 2008.1.3.3.6.1.42]

# 11 ‖ An Old Soldier Fades Away
### General Steele
### 1914–1919

WHEN HE ACCEPTED COMMAND of the 2nd Canadian Division, Steele was ordered to Toronto where the troops were concentrating. Things started to go badly at once. Arriving at 7 A.M. on March 20 after an overnight trip from Ottawa, Steele had a quick breakfast and went to the exhibition grounds to review the soldiers. The horse he was given for the occasion reared, throwing him off and partially falling on him. He suffered a broken collarbone, bruised ribs and a badly dislocated shoulder that kept him in hospital for two weeks. On April 6, he was sufficiently recovered to take the train to Ottawa and meet with Hughes the following day. Steele's diary record of the meeting stated:

> With Minister of Militia. He says that Kitchener does not want Canadians. I told him that although I had been offered and accepted the command of the Second division for the war I did not wish to embarrass the government. In reply he stated that the govt would not back down for Kitchener.[1]

Steele could easily have used his accident to back away from what could only be a difficult and possibly humiliating confrontation with Kitchener. This was his third opportunity since the outbreak of the conflict to make a useful and honourable contribution to the war effort by staying in Canada, but like a gambler who responds to losses by raising the stakes, he ignored the risks.

Steele had made naïve political choices in the past and suffered for it, but this time he badly underestimated the duplicity of Sam Hughes. Hughes had written a letter the previous fall to the British authorities. In it he declared Steele unfit to command the 1st Division on the grounds of age and "a lack of the faculty of thinking and acting rapidly when occasion might demand it."[2] The latter comment was on a par with Hughes's other judgements of the military abilities of Canadian officers, based as they were on loyalty to the Conservative Party and Hughes personally, but it clearly shows that he had no intention of keeping Steele in command of the 2nd Division once it got to England. Hughes had failed to convince Kitchener to appoint a Canadian commander for the 1st Division, which went to the British General, E.A.H. Alderson. He was determined not to lose the next round and the plan was, not to insist on Steele's appointment, but to use his considerable public reputation as a lever to get a different Canadian general appointed to the command. None of this was clear in the early spring of 1915, and Steele returned to Winnipeg to prepare for taking the division to war.

Steele was not without his doubts about the situation. He asked his friend, the Winnipeg cabinet representative, Minister of the Interior Rogers, "if they are going to confirm me in command of the Second Contingent and he replied yes!"[3] Steele was encouraged by this conversation, although he was unaware that, at this stage of the war, the cabinet rarely knew what Sam Hughes was doing. There was also an intense struggle for power and influence in the cabinet with Hughes and Rogers on opposite sides. Reassured, Steele began taking electrotherapy treatments for his shoulder injury, which seemed to help. Harwood, now eighteen, had joined the militia and

Steele planned to take him along as one of his aides-de-camp. Steele, as he usually did in these circumstances, applied for a $5,000 life insurance policy, noting "I put my date of birth at 5th Jan 49."[4] Steele knew this was incorrect, but it was clearly part of the process of convincing himself and others that he was young and fit enough for an active command. The insurance company required a urine test for diabetes, and that news was not so encouraging. "Dr. Gardner says that sugar not much was found in my urine, and that the Ins. Co. are strict about that. I gave him another bottle of urine."[5] That one was apparently satisfactory.

Steele left for Ottawa on May 11, and on arriving Hughes showed him the testy correspondence with Kitchener. It seemed to rule out his continuing to command the 2nd Division in action but now there was another possibility: "It was stated by Major Gen Gwatkin Chief of the Staff that I am to command all the Canadian troops at Shorncliffe. Brig Gen McDougall to command the depot under me."[6] Shorncliffe was the camp near the port of Folkestone, on the Strait of Dover, that had replaced Salisbury Plain as the principal Canadian training base in England. On May 15 Steele, accompanied by Harwood, boarded the ss *Megantic* at Montreal for the trip across the Atlantic. He travelled separately from most of his division on doctor's orders to rest and let his shoulder mend. Arriving ten days later, he went immediately to Shorncliffe to check in at his headquarters, and the following day to London where he talked briefly with Colonel John Carson, Hughes's representative in England.

Then he went to see Kitchener, who tried to persuade him as one old soldier to another (they were almost the same age), that he was too old for this war. Steele's response as recorded in his diary is worth quoting in full:

> *Called on Lord Kitchener He received me pleasantly but it is evident that he does not want a Canadian in command of the division at the front. He wants a British officer to take it and suggested my being on his staff to arrange difficulties with Canadians, and finally settled*

> that I would go to France next week and see the Canadians there, and assured me that I would say when I returned that he was right in his conclusions that it was a young mans war. Bosh! I say. Now of course the rank and file must be in their prime.[7]

Joining Kitchener's staff was not a bad offer under the circumstances and raised the possibility that it might lead to better things, but Steele knew that the phrase, "to arrange difficulties with Canadians," meant running interference for Kitchener with Hughes, and he wanted no part of that. Kitchener was as good as his word concerning the visit to the fighting and a week later Steele and his aide-de-camp, Captain Cochrane, went across and spent two days visiting the 1st Canadian Division, talking to Alderson and his staff as well as all the brigade commanders.

The war that Steele found in late May 1915 was unlike anything he had experienced or studied in his extensive reading in military history. For that matter, the fighting on the Western Front was unlike anything that the soldiers on both sides, from privates to generals, had ever encountered. The continuous line of trenches that ran for hundreds of kilometres from the English Channel to Switzerland completely ruled out the possibility of manoeuvre. The kind of scouting that Lord Strathcona's Horse did in South Africa had disappeared altogether from military practice, replaced by aerial observation and photography. The trenches were no longer hastily dug ditches but complex systems of field fortifications with multiple lines of defence that were kilometres in depth. Deep bunkers protected defenders from artillery fire and masses of barbed wire funneled attackers into the firing zones of machine guns. The 1st Division had already experienced the first poison gas attack of the war in April. The fact that it failed to produce the kind of breakthrough that the high command on both sides longed for did not prevent gas from becoming a regular weapon until the end of the war.[8] Strategic thinking, such as it was in 1915 and 1916, consisted of trying to concentrate more men and guns in one section of the line in the hope of punching a hole big enough to allow the cavalry to pour through and create a war of movement.

Back at Shorncliffe, supervising training for his division, Steele did his best to make it as realistic as possible. He had been a horse soldier for his entire military career and still loved to ride, but rather remarkably, Steele showed no indications of nostalgia for the good old days of the cavalry at any time during the war. He learned from his observations and from constant conversations with officers and men returning from the fighting and tried to prepare his men to fight the war as it was. Front-line soldiers in the 1st Division had already discovered that their Ross rifles were prone to jam, reports that were briskly dismissed by Sam Hughes who loved the Ross for its accuracy as a target rifle. Steele now began to hear that Ross rifles were jamming even during target practice on the range and instructed the musketry officer to report every incident at once. Most of the instructors were officers who had seen action at the front and knew the conditions there. They taught the men the backbreaking but life-saving art of trench construction and maintenance:

> I then accompanied by Captain Cochrane climbed the high hill to where the 19th 20th and engineers were busy digging trenches and completing them. They are doing very well indeed, all hands working with a will but I thought what an awful thing it is to be obliged to do this for the sake of our freedom, and to enable us to kill other men.[9]

|| The chain of command for the Canadians in England was now confused, to say the least. Hughes had appointed his friend, Colonel John Carson, as his personal representative in England. In spite of what Steele had been promised in Ottawa, when he arrived he found Brigadier J.C. Macdougall in charge of training Canadians and commanding the camp at Shorncliffe. Steele, as a major general, outranked both of them and was temporarily at least in command of the 2nd Canadian division. Steele was understandably

anxious to sort things out but on June 16, Hughes cabled that he was coming over to resolve the situation. While he waited, Steele found a house to rent in Folkestone so that he could move out of his hotel. He even managed a long weekend visit to his relatives in Wales. Hughes arrived in mid-July, accompanying Prime Minister Sir Robert Borden, and met with Kitchener to settle the question of command of the 2nd Division. In the negotiations, both men got something. Kitchener agreed to appoint Richard Turner, who had commanded the 3rd Infantry brigade. He thus got a younger man (Turner was fifty-four) with recent experience, while Hughes got a Canadian who, as a close friend of his son Garnet, he considered politically reliable. Turner had in fact not performed as well in the 1st Division's first full-scale battle at Ypres in April as the other brigadiers. He was a man of exceptional personal courage, having won the Victoria Cross in South Africa, but proved indecisive as a brigade commander when he was confronted with the first German gas attack of the war at Ypres.[10] Garnet dismissed criticism of his friend from Alderson as mere jealousy, and Hughes insisted on his appointment.

Sending Steele home at this point would have had serious political consequences and it was Kitchener, who liked Steele and perhaps felt badly about how he was being used as a bargaining chip by Hughes, who came up with a solution. Shorncliffe came under the administrative control of the British Army's Eastern District. The general in command of the district was leaving to take over a division in France, so Steele was offered that position. On July 26, Steele and Hughes went to see Kitchener again:

> Both Hughes and Kitchener said that the Command of the Shorncliffe district was more important and in every way better than the 2nd Division. I was very straight with K and said I would take it on condition that I had a free hand could appoint my own Staff and that I could go to France when I liked see the Canadians and arrange the

>   *reliefs to suit me, viz western men to western regts eastern men to the eastern regiments etc etc and he consented to it.*[11]

It was easy enough for Kitchener to accept those conditions, since he had no control over them. Steele probably recognized this as a face-saving gesture but had little option to accepting, although he did not for a moment believe the job more important. Hughes came to Shorncliffe and announced the change in command of the division and Steele's new appointment: "After the speech I met many who congratulated me on the apt to the command of the district. I said to all that I should be condoled with it."[12]

In early August Andrew Bonar Law, the Canadian who had gone into British politics and was now secretary of state for the colonies, came to Shorncliffe with Hughes and addressed the 1,500 officers of the 2nd Division. Steele chaired the occasion and the officers made it clear what they thought of his replacement as divisional commander by giving him a four-minute standing ovation.[13] On August 17, he formally turned over command to Richard Turner. Steele was happy that the command had gone to a Canadian:

> *I handed over command of the second division to Brig. Gen. Turner. I am glad he is getting it. He is a good officer, has the v.c. and d.s.o. Behaved well at the battles of Ypres, St. Julian etc. He is a gentleman in his manners and the division is lucky to have him.*[14]

Turner was unquestionably courageous and well mannered but it seems from these comments that word of his deficiencies at the senior command level had not yet penetrated beyond army headquarters. He was a permanent force officer who had served with great distinction in South Africa and that was good enough for Steele at this point.

Although he now had a new job, Steele's position could hardly have been more confusing. He was a Canadian general, in command

Reviewing Canadian troops at Shorncliffe, August 17, 1915. Front row: Prime Minister Borden and Sam Hughes. Second row: Sir George Perley, Steele, and Major General John Carson. [BPSC, 2008.1.3.3.6.2.18]

King George V, accompanied by Lord Kitchener and Steele, reviews the 2nd Canadian Division at Shorncliffe, September 1, 1915. [BPSC, 2008.1.3.3.6.2.5]

of a British Army military district that was occupied almost entirely by Canadian troops. The British Army was responsible for training, but the training base at Shorncliffe was commanded by a Canadian, Brigadier Macdougall. To make matters worse, Hughes told the cabinet and the Canadian chief of staff in Ottawa, General Gwatkin, that Steele had superseded Macdougall as commander of all Canadians in England. This would have made some sense, since Steele outranked Macdougall, but Hughes failed to tell anyone in England. The historian of the Canadian command structure in England during the war, Desmond Morton, believes that Hughes deliberately created administrative chaos so that he could personally retain control of officer appointments.[15] Colonel Carson in particular claimed the authority to make appointments, even though he was based in London and knew little about what was happening on the ground at Shorncliffe. When he visited the base at the end of August, Steele attempted to discuss the appointment of a commanding officer for the howitzer brigade but found to his astonishment that "Carson admits that he never heard of the artillery howitzer brigade."[16]

Things looked up a little in September when Steele organized a review of the 2nd Division by King George V and Kitchener. As soon as it was settled that he would remain in England, Marie, Flora, and Gertie decided to join him, sailing from New York on September 4. They arrived in Liverpool a week later and Steele met them and brought them to Folkestone, where they had a brief reunion with Harwood before he left for France as an aide to General Turner. An important part of Steele's job commanding the military district was overseeing medical care for wounded Canadian soldiers. He regularly inspected all the army hospitals in his district and while doing so noticed a new group of nurses called Voluntary Aid Detachments. These were mainly upper class women who trained on the job and worked without pay. Flora was immediately attracted by the idea and began training for hospital work, passing the required examinations in October.[17] The family liked the house at Folkestone and

Steele's position allowed him time to take them to London for shopping and visits to the theatre in his "new Cadillac motor."[18]

In mid-September the 2nd Division began moving some units across to France, but much still remained to be done to prepare it for action. One of its infantry units, the 20th Battalion, was found to be in a state of disarray. The only pre-war permanent force infantry battalion, the RCR, had been assigned to garrison duty in the Caribbean by Hughes to make sure that his favoured volunteers got first crack at combat. They had at last been allowed to come to England and Steele and Turner hoped to be able to use the RCR to replace the 20th. The RCR proved to need additional training, so they conducted a major housecleaning on the 20th, replacing a captain and nine lieutenants. Steele's diary recorded the root of the problem: "The 20th battalion of the 2nd had been nearly ruined by Lt Colonel Allan a political hack, who is desirous of being elected to Parliament and had many of his constituents in his Corps, consequently was afraid to do anything to them when they were guilty of any breaches of discipline."[19] Steele had worked out a rather uneasy *modus vivendi* with Carson and Macdougall for dealing with this kind of situation, under which the three consulted on officer appointments and usually managed to agree. The process absorbed a great deal of time and was always subject to direct interference from Sam Hughes. Steele believed that the system prevented Macdougall, in particular, from concentrating on his primary task of training the new divisions and replacements for France.

Steele thought that Macdougall and his staff were inexperienced and tried to assist them in organizing the training program for the 3rd Division, now also getting ready to join the fighting. This was a delicate situation since Steele, though he outranked Macdougall and had far more experience training soldiers, held a British appointment and could therefore not issue orders but only make suggestions. Sometimes that worked. Steele recognized that the officers coming over from Canada would have as little idea of the new kind of war going on in France as the rank and file, so he persuaded Macdougall to subject them to the same training courses: "Arranged with him and his G.S.O.1 to have all senior officers put through the bombing, signalling, musketry, bayonet fighting and machine gun work and then examined, so that those who are all right can go to France and spend some time in the trenches."[20] After a couple of weeks under fire, the colonels and majors would come back to England to take over their units before the division moved to France. This was a good idea but was quickly undermined by the situation created by Sam Hughes's insistence on recruiting new battalions in Canada and sending them over to England.

More than double the number of infantry battalions were recruited than could be absorbed into the four divisions of the Canadian Corps. Those not chosen were broken up for reinforcements. The meat grinder of the Western Front created an inexhaustible demand for privates, NCOs, and lieutenants but not as much for the senior ranks. Surplus majors and lieutenant-colonels piled up in England, many of them with political connections at home. As a way of solving the problem, Macdougall shipped many over to France on temporary assignments so that they could be sent home with the face-saving claim that they had served at the front. When Generals Alderson and Arthur Currie, the new commander of the 1st Division, complained that unsuitable officers were being sent over, Steele noted in his diary: "Some of them had stated that they only went over for a holiday trip and did not mean to go back. I had already warned Macdougall to be careful to send none but the best trained men to the front."[21]

One of Hughes's hasty appointments at the beginning of the war was that of Major C.D. Spittal of the Canadian Army Service Corps, which was responsible for organizing supply for the Canadian Expeditionary Force.[22] He proved unequal to the job and was moved to a training school for army service corps officers at Shorncliffe. He was no more successful in that role but Hughes, as always, was unwilling to admit his misjudgement and instructed Carson to send him to command the Canadian ammunition park in France. This was a vitally important position since it was responsible for maintaining a smooth flow of shells and other warlike stores to the front-line troops. Steele was apoplectic when he found out that Spittal and his assistant had been ordered overseas: "Too inefficient to work out of range of the guns but are considered by the amateur soldiers under whom we work good enough to take charge where they may be under fire and the lives of our men depend upon to a great extent the efficiency of their officers."[23] Steele's protests stopped the transfer and started an investigation into Spittal's conduct. Spittal was sent on leave, apparently in the hope that he would resign his commission. Instead, he tried to use his political support by requesting that his case be brought before the army council, where Hughes would be able to protect him.

Unlike the case with appointments and promotions, Steele had unambiguous authority over serious disciplinary cases and he had no intention of letting that happen: "Lt Col Spittal is evidently a very sharp man but a fool to fight this matter."[24] The investigation turned up numerous instances of "gross neglect of duty" and Steele ordered court martial proceedings, although he asked General Macdougall to delay them until he was sure of his ground: "Our Ministers representative in London seems so inclined to run the military affairs on political lines that we are likely to have some foolish complications arise."[25] He referred the case to the judge advocate general's office in London, which approved proceeding on three charges. In December Spittal was found guilty on two of the three. Hughes made one last effort to save Spittal's reputation by requesting that the charges be dropped and he be shipped back to Canada, but since he had already been convicted it was too late.[26]

Not all Steele's attention focused on his relations within the Canadian army. He spent much of his time managing the interactions between his soldiers and the surrounding British population. This meant everything from trying to keep venereal disease and drunkenness to acceptable levels to meeting King George V and the Archbishop of Canterbury. In between those poles, there was a constant stream of social contacts:

> Went to the hotel the Metropole at night and saw one of my paymasters that of the 32nd along with a lot of people and a Mrs. Dance who is not supposed to be an angel. This must be stopped at once and nipped in the bud. Paymasters cannot afford to go with fast women.[27]

A Mrs. Davies, who was helping to raise funds for the care of wounded soldiers, was convinced that German agents were everywhere and regularly reported the individuals she suspected to Steele. He listened politely and ignored the accusations, but that did not deter her. After almost a year of denunciations that included, among others, a British Army colonel, Steele noted, "The lady is still very keen on spies."[28] The Steeles met and became close friends with the member of Parliament for the area, Francis Bennett-Goldney.

Steele admired Secretary of State for the Colonies Bonar Law, but did not get along as well with the other prominent Canadian transplant to British politics of the time, Sir Max Aitken (later Lord Beaverbrook). He thought Aitken and his friend Sam Hughes were only interested in power, and when the former approached him about the possibility of a knighthood at the end of December 1915, he turned the offer down. He saw it, probably correctly, as a step toward easing him out of army, but he also believed that honours of this kind should wait until after the war.[29] Aitken's ambiguous presence in the Canadian command structure created, if that was possible, further confusion in the early months of 1916. Hughes had committed his country to provide four divisions and a total of half a million soldiers by that time. The 3rd and 4th Divisions, unlike the first two, would be assembled in England from the infantry battalions and other units at Shorncliffe and the new Canadian camp at Bramshott, recently opened to accommodate the overflow. It was clear to almost everyone that the ramshackle organization in place was not going to be able to handle the task. There were growing complaints from the divisions in France that reinforcements were inadequate in both numbers and training.

The British Army authorities became so concerned about the confusion in the Canadian command in January 1916 that they tried to do an end run around Sam Hughes. Steele received a secret letter from the War Office directing him to select the four best battalions undergoing training and organize them into a brigade for the 4th Division. He realized that this would cause an immediate explosion from Hughes:

> *Had a talk with Brig. Gen. Macdougall about the organization and I decided not to organize any brigade until further orders I therefore wrote the War Office through the proper channel and if the army council read between the lines as they can easily do they will see that if I carried out their orders there stood to be a bad time between them and our Mil Department as the latter will not be satisfied to have battalions selected on their merits. They will always do so either for political reasons, nepotism or favouritism all sorts, and I am not going to get mixed up with it.*[30]

This bizarre incident was a direct result of the failure of Sam Hughes to clarify the command structure in England. Steele was told that, although he was not in command of all Canadians in England, he was responsible for their training. This responsibility included the 4th Division camp at Bramshott—which was located in Aldershot Command, not in Steele's Eastern Command. Steele consulted his superior at the War Office, General Sir Leslie Rundle, who told him that his authority did indeed include Bramshott.[31] This was confirmed in April at a conference in London.[32] Steele was effectively inspector general of Canadian troops without actually being appointed to the position.

Sam Hughes was under increasing attack for his management of the war by early 1916, at home as well as overseas. In particular, the contracts he had handed out to friends and supporters for producing artillery shells had turned out to be expensive failures. The term of office of Borden's Conservative government expired in the fall of 1916 and there would have to be an election unless the Liberals agreed to an extension because of the wartime emergency. Borden wanted Hughes in Ottawa to defend himself on the shell contracts, but in March Hughes persuaded him that it was more urgent to let him go to England to sort out the command situation there. Borden was preparing his own plan at the same time, based on the advice of the Canadian high commissioner, Sir George Perley, and the chief of staff, General Gwatkin.[33] It essentially involved setting up a "Canadian Overseas Council" under Perley with General F.-L. Lessard replacing Steele as the senior military officer. But Borden seems to have lost his nerve and agreed to let Hughes go to England in March.

Steele knew that changes were certain to be made in the Canadian command in England but he was quite uncomprehending of the complex political machinations on both sides of the Atlantic. His uncertainty led him to make one of the worst political miscalculations of his career, and perhaps the only time in his life when ambition completely overrode what he knew to be the right course of action. When Hughes arrived in London on March 20 and summoned the senior officers to a meeting, his first goal was to save the Ross rifle, now under open attack by the Canadian Corps commander, General Alderson, and the 1st Division CO, General Arthur Currie. Soldiers' lives were being thrown away when the Ross jammed in action, a fact that Steele knew very well. But when Hughes raised the question at the meeting, Steele unhesitatingly supported the Ross: "General Hughes received us and we had a long talk from him. He devoted himself to me a good deal and asked my opinion on matters and about the men, the Ross Rifle, the officers, their messes their behaviour. I said the men who had the Ross would not exchange it for the Lee Enfield."[34] Steele knew very well that this was nonsense but it was what Hughes wanted to hear. He then immediately asked Hughes for the appointment as inspector general of Canadian troops in England.

It was bad enough that Steele had compromised his principles to seek a job from a man he despised; it was even more damaging that he did not get it. As inspector general or as commanding officer of all Canadian troops in England, Steele could have redeemed himself by sorting out the confusion of training in England, something he was well qualified to do, but that opportunity would not come his way. The politics that surrounded these appointments were too complex for Steele to understand, much less influence, although that did not stop him from trying. Hughes offered the post that Steele coveted, of commanding officer of Canadian troops in England, to General David Watson, who turned it down and was given command of the 4th Division instead. Command of the newly enlarged Canadian Corps in France was taken from General Alderson, who was given the post of inspector general, although apparently the official appointment was never made and he made his way back to the British Army after a few months. Alderson's position as corps commander went to General Sir Julian Byng, whom Steele knew well since Byng had commanded the South African Light Horse against the Boers, fighting alongside Lord Strathcona's Horse. Steele wrote congratulating him and received a chatty letter in return.[35] These appointments absorbed most of Hughes's time in England and he tried to paper over the command situation there by creating a temporary council with Aitken, Carson, Macdougall, Steele, and a few others. It met only twice in April and achieved nothing, leaving Steele and the others to carry on as best they could.

By the time Hughes returned to Canada, Prime Minister Borden's patience with him was running out. Any illusions Borden had about Hughes's competence had been dissipated and only his political support in rural Ontario kept him from being fired.

Borden had relieved Hughes of all his administrative responsibilities in the area of munitions and supplies and was now listening more and more to Sir George Perley about the leadership morass in England. Perley thought that the only way to solve the command problem was to fire Carson, Macdougall, and Steele and start fresh.[36] Perley came to Ottawa in July 1916 to discuss the situation and it was decided to send Hughes back to England for one more try, with strict instructions to submit any reorganization plan to Ottawa before implementation. For Borden, this was Hughes's last chance, but the minister of Militia was as oblivious to any threat to his power as he appeared to be to the massive casualties of the disastrous Somme offensive then underway. He ignored a stream of telegrams from Borden asking about the reorganization plans, while his behaviour became steadily stranger. Among other things he insisted on personally demonstrating his version of how to use a bayonet to a bewildered group of privates.

Although Hughes ignored queries from Ottawa for a month, he was moving to create what he called a "Sub-Militia Council" in London. Steele heard rumours that he was to be part of this new body on August 17.[37] Two weeks later Hughes leaked the news to the *Ottawa Journal*, giving the impression that the new organization was already in place and named its members, including Steele. When he read in the newspaper what his repeated requests for information had failed to elicit, the prime minister was astonished and outraged. He told Hughes to return to Canada at once, an order he blithely ignored, calling two meetings of the council to make sure it was functioning as he wished before he left England. According to Steele's diary, Hughes spent most of the first meeting browbeating Carson and Macdougall to ensure they would continue to do his bidding: "The Minister then read a report he was sending to Sir Robert Borden Prime Minister, all self glorification and lies."[38] Worse was to come. When Hughes inspected the troops in training at Shorncliffe, Steele wrote:

> [Hughes] told the men that the instructors knew nothing, that they knew more than their instructors attacked the instructors in the presence of the men, made a fool of himself generally, and displayed the most colossal ignorance possible. Wrestled with one of the instructors and both fell on their backs.³⁹

By the time Hughes left England at the end of September, Borden had made his decision. Sir George Perley would be appointed as minister of the Overseas Military Forces of Canada, leaving Hughes as minister of Militia in Canada with few remaining powers. Most people would have resigned at this point but Hughes clung desperately to the remaining shreds of his political career until Borden dismissed him from the cabinet on November 9.⁴⁰ Steele found out about the new regime at a meeting of the sub-militia council on November 3, attended by Perley and the Finance minister, Sir Thomas White. After the session, which dealt largely with routine matters, Steele met with the two ministers privately at their request:

> I went to see Sir George Perley at Five P.M. by request and met there Sir Thos White Finance Minister of Canada. Sir George and he catechised me on the situation asking me what kind of council they should have and I said, a chief of the General Staff, Adjutant General, Quarter Master General, Master General ordnance Chief Paymaster Gen.⁴¹

Steele was given no indication about what, if anything, his role might be, but it was obvious that Perley intended to proceed much more deliberately than his predecessor.

While all the high political drama was going on in the summer of 1916, Steele had other things on his mind. Lord Kitchener's death when the warship he was travelling on was torpedoed in early June affected Steele deeply. He liked and respected Kitchener and with his death lost his connection to the very top of the British military hierarchy. In mid-June he was astounded to receive a letter from the paymaster general in Ottawa, informing him that because his appointment was in the British Army, he should have been receiving British rates of pay, not the higher Canadian scale. Would he please repay the $2,500 owing as a result of the mistake?[42] This set off a dispute that lasted for months before Steele finally won his point. He continued his Sandow exercises faithfully, and as soon as he was settled in Shorncliffe he added French lessons from a refugee Belgian diplomat, Monsieur Serruys, to his routine. The French army was the senior allied partner in the war and Steele believed it was his professional responsibility to learn the language. He had the same difficulties that most adult learners encountered: "French lesson. I was not good at verbs and must study more."[43]

Two of Steele's children were directly involved in the war by this time and while he was proud of them, he also worried as a parent. Flora had taken up nursing and worked in one of the military hospitals near Shorncliffe but sought wider horizons: "Flora is anxious to go to Egypt to nurse. Poor little girl she does not know what it means but I will not oppose her in the least. I hope she will succeed."[44] This did not happen, but in July 1916, Flora moved to a hospital in France near the front lines: "She departed with 25 other girls, none of whom she has met. She was quite cheerful but it is a sad blow to her mother."[45] Harwood also went to France as aide-de-camp to General Richard Turner in September 1915. He had vision problems that kept him out of the trenches at that stage of the war, but by the summer of 1916 he became restless running errands for the general and took a staff course at Cambridge. When he returned to the fighting in November, his commanding officer told him that any hope for promotion meant spending time in the front lines. Relaxed standards because of the massive casualties of the Somme battles, combined with some gentle pressure from Steele on Harwood's brigade commander, H.D.B. Ketchen, who was one of his pre-war subordinates at Winnipeg, got Harwood into the trenches.[46] Only Gertie, to Steele's considerable annoyance, showed no interest in work of any kind.

The Steele family at Folkestone, 1916. [BPSC, 2008.1.1.5.1.6]

Problems with training and the flow of reinforcements grew steadily worse in the summer of 1916. The generals in France and, increasingly, the press at home wondered why there were thousands of unemployed officers in England and constant shortages in the fighting battalions. Steele knew the reasons, but could do little in the face of Hughes's micromanaging. By June 1916 the 1st, 2nd, and 3rd Canadian Divisions were in action in France, leaving only the 4th Division organizing in England. Once it left for France, the main job in England would be training reinforcements. To do that, there were thirty-two infantry battalions at Shorncliffe and Bramshott, along with artillery, cavalry, engineers, medical corps, and army service corps—a total of about 42,000 men that summer. Steele put forward a plan to streamline the training system by reducing the number of infantry training battalions to nineteen and sending fourteen extra officers with each of the 4th Division battalions to make up for anticipated casualties. Carson and Macdougall approved the plan and the War Office quickly agreed.[47] Hughes agreed to send the additional officers but vetoed the reduction in training battalions. He would need them for the fifth division he was planning. He was talking of as many as eight Canadian divisions, but the professional soldiers regarded even five as unsustainable.[48] Steele commented in his diary: "It is reported that a fifth divn is being formed Canada with General Leckie in Command of it. This is absurd. Four divisions will keep us going all the time to reinforce them."[49]

The pressure to keep up the flow of reinforcements mounted steadily. Steele worried that the public and government did not understand that recruits arriving from Canada could not be sent directly into battle: "Much worried on account of the delay in sending troops here in time to be fully trained A large draft went to-day and at least three thousand were not fully trained."[50] He estimated that it took at least two and a half months to train an infantryman, considerably longer for artillery and engineers.[51] A communication from General Byng in August provided him with support for his training plans: "Got a syllabus of work for training the troops from Lt Gen J.H.G. Byng. It is good and coincides with what I have already directed to be done here, but as it is direct over his own signature it will have more weight."[52] One of the ideas he managed to put into effect was to arrange for the promotion of 150 experienced NCOs to commissioned rank: "This is a great satisfaction to me as it is my own recommendation, that the rank and file be recognized instead of appointing to commission a lot of young men who have never seen a guard mounted or belonged to a unit for ten minutes."[53]

Following his meeting with Perley and White at the beginning of November, Steele's hopes for an unambiguous role revived and he wrote Perley asking for the appointment as inspector general.[54] Two weeks later he met again with Perley:

> I went to Perley at 3. P.M. he said that he wanted a Canadian on his staff and he had evidently changed his mind about Gen Gwatkin. He said he was going to France on the 16th and would see about the staff when he got back. He talked over the staff and he suggested Insp Gen for me.[55]

Steele now ramped up his lobbying efforts, soliciting support from Sir Thomas White, Lord Shaughnessy, Bonar Law, and Robert Rogers. Unfortunately for Steele, these had the opposite of the desired effect. The last thing Perley wanted was another political general and Shaughnessy's intervention in particular caused Perley to delete Steele from consideration for the job.[56] There were other political considerations involved. Byng wanted to replace Turner as commanding officer of the 2nd Division and a job would have to be found for him as he had a significant following among Quebec Conservatives.[57] Within a week Macdougall was ordered back to Canada, Carson was informed that his services were no longer required, and Steele waited for his turn to hear the bad news.

Through the unhappy Christmas of 1916 and the first week of the New Year, Steele was in limbo, expecting to be fired at any time. He consoled himself by riding his horse daily, something he had not done since he had arrived in England. On January 9 he was summoned to meet again with Perley and went off armed with an extensive documentation of his work. Somewhat to his surprise, he was not dismissed: "He is satisfied he states for me to carry on in the same as usual, and said that he had never blamed me for any mistakes in the training."[58] This was a relief but, when he thought about it, not terribly helpful, since his status had been unclear ever since he left the 2nd Division eighteen months previously. The stress and uncertainty he had laboured under since the summer of 1915 were beginning to take their toll. He was sleeping badly and feeling generally unwell, to the point that he decided to consult Sir Henry Morris, an eminent Harley Street kidney specialist. The doctor found no abnormalities in his urine, pronounced him generally healthy, and prescribed some medicine.[59]

Although Steele did not know it at the time, one of the reasons Perley did not remove him, as he had done with Macdougall and Carson, was that he discovered that the policies Steele had either proposed or put into place were the correct ones. Steele's plan for dealing with the senior officer surplus by offering them the chance to take a reduction in rank so they could join the fighting was reaffirmed. A standard training syllabus of fourteen weeks like the one Steele advocated was finally introduced, and the number of battalions at the camps in England was reduced from fifty-seven to twenty-six.[60] The doubts about his future and concerns about his health in the early months of 1917 were offset by having all his family around him once again. Flora had applied for a transfer to a military hospital in Serbia but he had managed to talk her out of it and she was now back in England for a rest.[61] Harwood was safely out of the trenches for the moment and home on leave. The presence of the children attracted many visitors to the Steele household,

*Flora Steele in her nursing uniform, 1918. [BPSC, 2008.1.1.5.1.11]*

among them a young officer named Dudley: "Stewart Dudley son of my old friend Captain Dudley A.S.C. came to spend the week end with us. He has grown into a fine lad."[62] Gertrude evidently thought so too, since she later married him.

In March 1917, Prime Minister Borden arrived in London for a two-month stay to attend the Imperial War Conference, bringing with him several cabinet ministers including Steele's supporter, Robert Rogers. His presence raised Steele's hopes once again and he lost no time trying to make his case. At first he got little encouragement. Shortly after they arrived, Borden and Rogers toured the military hospitals and training establishments at Shorncliffe with him, but showed no signs of being prepared to give Steele the kind of appointment he wanted. Several weeks later, when he finally got a one-on-one meeting with Rogers, the response was much warmer:

"The minister then said that I would be put all right. I had only to wait patiently. The London 'Bunch' were in a mess which had to be put right at once or he would know the reason why."[63] After a month of waiting, as the Canadian delegation was about to depart, Steele went to London for a final interview with an obviously reluctant Rogers, who had not been able to make good on his promises. The United States had recently declared war on Germany and Rogers offered to send Steele to Washington to advise the United States Army on organization and training, a proposal that did not interest him in the least.[64]

Earlier in his career that kind of challenge would have appealed to him, and the fact that he dismissed it so unhesitatingly suggests that he had made some basic decisions about his future. For one thing he was increasingly concerned about his health. Although Dr. Morris had been reassuring, the symptoms of the diabetes that he had feared for many years continued to accumulate. His weight, which had ranged between 230 and 240 pounds for all of his adult life, had started to drop, to 210 pounds in March 1917, and 199 in June.[65] He weighed himself obsessively several times a day, sometimes with his full uniform on as if to convince himself that he was not losing ground. For the months of March and April he kept a daily log of the amounts and frequency of his urination. In September he openly admitted to himself in his diary that something serious was going on: "Weight 202, much thinner than last year. I weighed 210 lbs in 1916, a great change from last year when I was 224 in clothing, and two or three years ago when I was 240 lbs in plain clothes, seventeen stone, but that was my heaviest."[66] He was also experiencing skin problems with severe itching that prevented him from sleeping.

Although he never entirely gave up hope that he might assemble enough political influence to get the kind of senior Canadian army appointment he believed he deserved, it was clear to him that Robert Rogers, his voice in the cabinet, could no longer be counted on. Rogers was in political trouble over accusations of profiting from war contracts and did not run in the 1917 election. The clearest indication that Steele recognized the way the political winds were blowing was his request in April to make a visit to France. He wanted at least a chance to see how the war was changing at first hand. Permission was granted and on June 1 he crossed to Boulogne and called in at Canadian headquarters to talk to Byng. Then it was on to generals Currie at the 1st Division and Watson at the 4th near Vimy Ridge. Steele was intensely proud of the army he had helped train: "The Canadian soldiers shew by their bearing very good discipline. They have had a hard time but are brilliant fighters."[67] He spent a day with his friend and former subordinate, Brigadier H.D.B. Ketchen, and presented medals to the men of his 6th Brigade.

Steele's visit to the front came shortly after the great Canadian victory at Vimy Ridge. In the two years since his first visit to the fighting the Canadian Corps had evolved into a highly professional fighting force that took full advantage of the new technology of war. Training was a crucial part of the process and, as the historian of that process, Bill Rawling, noted, "The Canadians eventually became adept because they were well trained for the task."[68] Kenneth Radley, whose two books on Canadians in the Great War pay more attention to training than any others, agrees.[69] Steele, working under very difficult conditions, had much to do with the quality of the Canadian training, but the administrative chaos Hughes produced has obscured the importance of his work.

The second half of Steele's tour was with the French army. In Paris he met General Philippe Pétain, the hero of Verdun and French chief of staff. Pétain spoke no English and Steele lost his nerve about using his recently acquired French, but he had been assigned a Captain Serot as translator, so there were no awkward moments:

> After that I called on General Petain. He is very alert and although he does not speak English he assured me that there is nothing that I cannot see. I can go anywhere. I told him that I wished to see as much as

*possible in the time allowed but did not like to give him unnecessary trouble. He assured me in his graceful French way that it was a pleasure. I thanked him through Captain Serot as I did not care to use my French which would not be so clear. I understood every word but speaking is different.*[70]

Steele visited the training facilities of the French 3rd and 4th armies, observing everything from the latest techniques in trench construction and artillery observation to air squadrons. He hit it off particularly well with the commander of the 4th Army, General Henri Gouraud, who was fascinated by Steele's tales of the First Nations of western Canada and quizzed him about why more French Canadians were not represented in the war. Visiting a front-line dugout, Steele was astonished to find that the colonel commanding the battalion had his own chef there and provided lunch complete with champagne.[71] The French were equally surprised when Steele insisted on drinking water.

Back in England, he reported on his visit to Perley and heard the news that Arthur Currie had succeeded Byng as commanding officer of the Canadian Corps. He was delighted, partly because he respected Currie's abilities but also because he knew that Perley and Max Aitken had been pushing Richard Turner for the job. "Thank God," he confided to his diary, "It [Turner's appointment] would have been the ruin of the Canadian Corps."[72] If Steele needed any confirmation that his own military career was jeopardy, it came when a cable he sent to Rogers urging the promotion of Ketchen was intercepted by the censor and ended up on Perley's desk.[73] This was in direct contradiction to Perley's efforts to reduce the kind of political infighting that had crippled the Hughes regime. Steele pretended not to care, but he must have known that it diminished further his already slim chances of a meaningful appointment.

In the summer of 1917 all attention in the Canadian government and military was focused on the growing manpower crisis in the army. Successful battles like Vimy Ridge and Hill 70 were just as bloody as defeats. Although the Americans were in the war at last, it would be many months before they made an effective contribution and the shaky Kerensky government in Russia was looking less and less able to keep that country in the war. Voluntary enlistments had fallen drastically and the Borden government decided that conscription was the only way to carry the war effort forward. Imposing the draft would require broader political support but opposition Liberal leader Sir Wilfrid Laurier rejected a coalition in May. The decision to go ahead put a severe strain on the unity of the country, especially in Quebec, where anti-conscription riots in the spring of 1918 saw five killed when soldiers fired on crowds in Quebec City. In an effort to hold things together, Borden spent the summer of 1917 recruiting pro-conscription Liberals for a Unionist Party and rigging the electoral system with two pieces of legislation, the *Military Voters Act* and the *Wartime Elections Act*, which biased the vote strongly in favour of the government in power. The *Military Voters Act* gave the vote to all serving members of the military and, if the individual did not specify the constituency where the vote was to be counted, allowed the government to assign it. The *Wartime Elections Act* took the vote away from immigrants from Germany and Austria-Hungary who had been naturalized since 1902 and gave it to women who were wives, widows, mothers, or sisters of soldiers.

The manipulation was so blatant that many senior Canadian officers, including the man at the top, Sir Arthur Currie, refused involvement with organizing the soldier vote. Steele had no such doubts. He saw support for conscription as a patriotic duty and was quite willing to do whatever he could to forward the cause. In July he began writing letters to western Canadian newspapers in favour of conscription.[74] Steele's support was very welcome to the government, given his popularity in the west, where support for conscription was at best shaky among the farm population. The opposition clearly thought so too; a Calgary Liberal candidate wrote Steele, objecting to his actions.[75] However, both of his children who were involved in war effort reinforced Steele's position and he considered them representative of the opinion in the ranks. When Borden formed his Union cabinet, taking in some Liberals, he commented in his diary, "This is the only government which will stand a chance of winning the war from the Canadian point of view."[76]

At the same time, Steele expected that his political support for the Union government would be rewarded, so it was a shock when he was summoned to London in mid-November:

> *Saw Sir George Perley. He was affable and told me that the Canadian Militia Department wish to retire me. I protested that it was a humiliation undeserved. Told him that if I was retired, I must have full allowance of Major General holding the Staff appt of Inspector General of western Canada, and that I should not be retired here. I should go back and resume duty, in Canada and then retire.*[77]

Perley agreed to pass the request along to Ottawa. In spite of his indignation, Steele, ever the good soldier, spent much of the next two weeks helping Hector McInnes, the organizer Borden had sent over to manage the military vote.[78] That vote went overwhelmingly to the Unionist side and, judiciously distributed where it would do the most good, produced a landslide victory in seats except in Quebec. The government had a different kind of reward in mind for Steele's political work. The day before the election, Steele got a letter offering him the consolation prize of a knighthood:

> *Received a letter from the Secy of State for the Colonies Mr Walter Long asking me to accept a K.C.M.G. [Knight Commander of the Order of St. Michael and St. George] This is the second time. I refused it two years ago but may as well accept this time for if I do not people will think that I am doing nothing, otherwise I would prefer not to accept it.*[79]

He did accept it, becoming Sir Samuel Steele on January 1, 1918. This did not mean that he had given up trying to stave off retirement.

Perley had been replaced as minister of the Overseas Military Forces by Sir Edward Kemp and when he arrived in London in January, Steele quickly made an appointment to see him. His mood was combative, as he wrote in a letter to Hugh John Macdonald: "The epistle is to the effect that I will not take the treatment lying down."[80] Kemp tried to spread oil on troubled waters: "After a few minutes he asked me if I felt hurt at the order for return to Canada to be retired I replied that was very much annoyed and humiliated and that it was a wrong and improper proceeding to do it and especially when it was done."[81] Steele was not at all mollified and subjected Kemp to a lengthy review of all the injustices of his time in England:

> [Kemp] kept on trying to impress upon me that I was not looked upon unfavourably, quite the contrary. I replied what kind of treatment is it that superannuated an officer capable of hard work and sends him back to his native town to dangle about clubs when other men and women are working to win a great war and where he will be regarded as a has been.[82]

It is hard to see this outburst as anything but venting by a man who realized deep down that his career was over. It certainly confirmed Kemp's view that retiring Steele was the right thing to do.

This became clear with what Steele regarded as unseemly haste. On February 5 he received a telegram from a General Cuthbert, asking if he could take over command of the district a week later.[83] In London a few days later he called at Eastern Command and discovered that the pressure to change had come from Canadian headquarters: "Lord French and all the rest expressed great distress at the wicked way I have been treated by being given such short notice to quit and an apology will come to me."[84] The turnover was put back to the end of the month. On February 11 a cable from Canada formally announced his retirement, but even before that took effect he was saved from an ignominious trip back to Canada to "dangle around clubs." His rescuer was an Ontario lawyer and

*Steele's friend and benefactor William Perkins Bull with nurses at Bull's hospital in London. [BPSC, 2008.1.3.3.6.2.53]*

businessman named William Perkins Bull, who had made a huge fortune in oil and real estate in Alberta and British Columbia. In 1916 he moved to London for the duration of the war and established a convalescent hospital for Canadian soldiers. It was through the hospital that he met Steele.

The two men immediately hit it off and before long Steele and his family were frequent dinner guests of Bull and his wife. Bull had a lifelong fascination for Canadian history; among other things, he wrote the first history of Canadian sport with the odd title *From*

*Rattlesnake Hunt to Hockey* and sponsored a series of other historical publications.[85] Bull was entranced by Steele's tales of the early west. At a Masonic meeting in London on February 20, when he heard of Steele's retirement, Bull offered Steele a position with a company he owned. One of Bull's enterprises, Red Deer Investments, owned half a million acres of land around the Alberta town. Steele was offered a directorship with a salary of £1,000 a year and a £500 share in the company. This was extremely generous, in fact more than his army salary, and Steele gratefully accepted the offer. In June Perkins Bull set up another company, Overseas Estates Ltd., to market his land holdings in Britain. Steele was made a director of that company as well at a salary of £500. He had once again been trying to sell his mining interests in British Columbia but now the pressure was off. With the money from the Perkins Bull enterprises added to his Mounted Police and army pensions, for the first time in twenty years he had no money worries.

As the end of February and the turnover of his command approached, there were several farewell parades where Steele presented medals and said a reluctant goodbye. The first batches of conscripts were arriving from Canada and Steele noted with satisfaction that they were a fine-looking body of men:

> Colonel Smart has seen that they are treated with the greatest kindness, and of course Colonel Leckie commander of the brigade will carry out that intention well. Two officers were heard on the train from London saying that they would make it hot for the conscripts Colonel Smart heard this and assembled the senior officers and told them that if he knew what or which officers had stated such stupid sentiments he would have them sent back to Canada.[86]

Steele cleaned out his office and handed the command over to his successor on March 1, commenting in his diary: "First day in twelve years in which I have had no responsibility except for myself."[87] The

Canadian Club at Folkestone gave him a farewell banquet and then it was off to London to find a house.

He and Marie were able to rent a house owned by a retired Indian civil servant at 22 Gwendolen Avenue in the pleasant suburb of Putney. It was comfortable and readily accessible to Steele's new office and to central London by bus. The successful move gave Steele some temporary relief from the eczema that had been bothering him since the previous fall. It quickly returned, however, and his weight kept on dropping, to 196 pounds in March.[88] Eczema and weight loss are both symptoms of diabetes and it seems clear that Steele was suffering from it in 1918, although he fought against admitting this. He blamed his weight loss on his inability to sleep because of the eczema and tried to treat it, using many bottles of the medication that Sir Henry Morris prescribed and having daily medicinal shampoos from his barber to treat his scalp. His mood was not improved by a notification from the army that he would have to return to Canada to collect his military pension. Fortunately, he was able to see Sir Robert Borden when he came to London in June and Borden immediately cabled the Militia Department to reverse the order.[89]

Steele's duties with the Perkins Bull companies were anything but onerous, consisting largely of using his vast network of friends throughout western Canada to send him information about land qualities and prices. Most of this correspondence could be drafted at home. By July he was only managing to go into the city for special occasions, as when he and Bull had lunch with the federal minister of Immigration, Alexander Calder, and the premiers of Alberta and Manitoba.[90] He was finding it increasingly difficult to get out of bed for any reason, even when Harwood came home on leave in June from his new job as staff captain with the 63rd Division of the British Army. He had his civilian suits altered to take account of his decreasing weight and began wearing them, noting in his diary: "Plain clothes for the first time since war declared."[91] He had started taking sleeping pills but they did little for him. In August his weight was down to 182 pounds and the eczema was severe.

Steele had discovered that Eugen Sandow, whose exercises he continued to do, was in London operating a business as a consultant in physical culture. In desperation, he went to see him and began a new course of exercises at Sandow's office. After ten days he admitted it was not working and that he was more exhausted than ever: "I think it is too much for me while I am sick."[92] His doctor and Sandow both agreed. He stopped the exercises and spent the first two weeks of September in bed, getting up only to shave. The lease on the house at 22 Gwendolen Avenue ran out at the end of September and Steele summoned enough energy to find a new one nearby, at 101 Howard's Lane. The need to exert himself for the move on September 20 seemed to give him a respite. On September 23 he went into the office and had lunch with Perkins Bull, who told him he should not worry about the job, but go back to bed.[93]

Steele took the advice, returned to his bed, and never really left it. An army doctor named McCoy took over his care but was able to do little to help him or make him comfortable. He was in constant discomfort, unable to sleep more than a few hours at a time. When he did manage to summon enough energy to write in his diary, it was with terse entries like this: "Still in bed miserable night. Perspiration all day and night."[94] The end of the fighting with the allied victory in November roused his interest: "The terms of the Armistice with the Central Powers proclaimed at 10:30 AM, all wild with joy, Foch is a great soldier."[95] The final diary entry of his life came on November 30. "Still sick. 3rd month in bed. Took a hot bath very uncomfortable. Harwood very busy at his book."[96] The book, the first of a dozen Harwood would write, was *The Canadians in France* (London: T.F. Unwin Ltd., 1920). Steele hung on for two more months and died, a few weeks after his 71st birthday, on January 30, 1919.

Although he ended his life bitter and resentful about how he had been treated by the Canadian government, there was no question about being buried in England. He asked that he be interred

Steele in early 1918. The last photograph of him in the uniform he loved.
[BPSC, 2008.1.3.3.6.1.15]

in Winnipeg, the place where he had begun his western career and where he had spent some of the happiest days of his family life. There was a military funeral in England but the shortage of shipping meant that his body could not be returned to Canada until June. Steele's funeral in Winnipeg on July 3, even in the aftermath of the Winnipeg General Strike that had ended a few days before, was a major event. Thousands lined the streets to watch the funeral procession. Steele's coffin was borne by eight members of the Royal North-West Mounted Police (the new name of the NWMP since 1904) and an honour guard of twenty others, with General Ketchen and four other brigadiers as honorary pallbearers. The premier of Manitoba, the mayor and Assistant Commissioner Starnes of the Mounted Police, Steele's friend from his Yukon days, all attended, as did the board of trade, several veterans groups, all the military units based in Winnipeg, the cadets, and boy scouts.

Archbishop Matheson conducted the funeral service at All Saints. His voice, "shaking with emotion," according to the *Winnipeg Free Press* reporter, the archbishop noted that while it was not customary to have a eulogy as part of the Anglican funeral service, Steele was an exception: "It is meet and right, therefore, that this afternoon we should honour a man of the greatness of General Steele, one of those pioneers and empire builders who have paved the way to national greatness."[97] He gave a lengthy and laudatory account of Steele's career, starting with the particularly appropriate line that Steele was "a soldier by the ordination of his nature." No single sentence could have better summed up Steele's life. After a firing party from the Fort Garry Horse fired a salute, Steele was laid to rest in St. John's cemetery.

No word could describe Sam Steele better than "patriot." He would have agreed with Stephen Decatur's famous line, "my country, right or wrong." This is often superficially interpreted to mean "my country is always right," but that was never Steele's conception. As this book demonstrates, he frequently thought his country was wrong, but his response was always to try to make it better. He believed that he owed his country loyalty and service to the best of his abilities, but never blind obedience.

Before Steele's body left England, some friends had a death mask made with the intention of putting up a statue, but it somehow got lost. Many years later it turned up in the possession of the wealthy Calgarian, Eric Harvey, who founded the Glenbow Museum in that city. Harvey was fascinated by Steele and spent a considerable amount of money on genealogical research, attempting to find out if they were related. Harwood tried to get the mask back from Harvey, threatening legal action before an agreement was reached under which Harvey kept the mask but agreed never to put it on display.[98] It resides in the Glenbow Museum vaults to this day.

The fate of the death mask is symbolic of how Steele's public profile, so high for so many years before the war, suddenly dropped out of sight. He died at a time of extraordinary confusion, with hundreds of thousands of Canadians returning from the war. It was also a time when Steele's brand of patriotism was devalued by the mass slaughter of the Great War. Public attention was absorbed by the negotiations for the Treaty of Versailles, and most people wanted to forget the conflict as quickly as possible. The other institution that had shaped Steele's life, the Mounted Police, was also in a state of rapid transition. In the year of Steele's death the Royal North-West Mounted Police merged with the Dominion Police to become the Royal Canadian Mounted Police, a prelude, many thought, to its disappearance. Steele was a figure of major importance in the history of both the Mounted Police and the Canadian army, but until at least the 1950s neither institution seemed interested in claiming him as part of their story. Even his son Harwood, who wrote numerous books on both the Mounted Police and the Canadian army and who planned to write his father's biography, never managed to do it. But Archbishop Matheson in his eulogy appropriately summed up Steele's life and achievements: Canada would have been a different place in the half century after Confederation without Sam Steele.

# ‖ Epilogue

AFTER THE FUNERAL IN WINNIPEG, Marie moved to Montreal where she lived, near her extended family, for the remainder of her life. Throughout his life, Sam Steele worried about his wife's health. To some degree this was rooted in Victorian notions of women as the weaker sex, but although Marie did suffer some fairly serious illnesses, she outlived her husband by more than thirty years, dying in 1951. Flora took over the primary responsibility for looking after her mother, living with her until her own death late in 1948. It is not clear what their source of income was, since Flora was not employed outside the home. Some of Sam's investments seem to have finally achieved a modest success in the 1920s and 1930s. Marie had half his Mounted Police pension and presumably some part of his military pension. Gertrude was part of the household until her marriage to Stewart Dudley early in the 1920s. They moved to South Africa later in the decade, where their three children were born.

Harwood Steele was twenty-two years old when the war ended and his father died. He had served with both the Canadian and British armies, rising to the rank of captain. Most of his service was in various staff positions, but he did spend enough time in the trenches to receive the Military Cross, an award given to junior officers for "acts of gallantry," not administrative efficiency. After the war, Harwood remained an active member of the Canadian militia as a captain in the Winnipeg Grenadiers until 1926. He hoped to make a living as a writer, publishing his first book in 1920, a history of the Canadian army in the First World War.[1] Three novels followed, in 1923, 1926, and 1927.[2] The last of these, *The Ninth Circle*, was aimed at the children's market. Making a living as a writer has never been easy in Canada, and in the 1920s only a handful of people were able to do it. Harwood, not surprisingly, found it necessary to sustain his livelihood in other ways.

From 1923 to 1925 he did public relations work for the CPR. In 1925 he was appointed by the federal government as historian to Vilhjalmur Stefansson's Canadian Arctic Expedition of 1913–1918. Presumably this meant organizing the records of the expedition and perhaps producing a narrative that would sustain Canadian claims to the northern territories, but nothing was ever published with Harwood's name on it. The job did bring him to Montreal where he switched his militia interests to the Duke of York's Royal Canadian Hussars. With that regiment he was promoted major in 1929 and lieutenant-colonel and officer commanding in 1938. Beginning in 1928 he began touring Canada and the United States as a lecturer on the history of the Mounted Police. His work with the Canadian Arctic Expedition led to one of his most successful books, *Policing the Arctic*, published in 1936.[3]

When the Second World War broke out in 1939, Harwood immediately volunteered for the British Army. After a short refresher course at the Staff College, he served in Northern Ireland, at Kohat in what is now Pakistan near the Afghan border, and with the 14th Army in Burma. Following the war, he returned to his lecture tours and writing. There was considerable public interest in the Indian independence movement and he added his wartime experiences there to his repertoire. In the postwar period he wrote several more works of fiction, the most successful being a collection of stories.[4]

Harwood remained in awe of his father for the rest of his life. With the help of his sister Flora, he devoted much time and effort to making sure that Sam's memory was kept alive exactly as he wanted it to be at the end of his life. This was heavily conditioned by the fact that because the war ended when it did, Harwood spent the last three months of his father's life at his side, listening to the well-developed narrative Sam had constructed about why he was denied an active command in the conflict. Harwood and Flora kept a close eye out for anything written about their father and insisted, threatening legal action when necessary, on three key points. The first was that his birth date was 1851, not 1848. The second was that he only rarely drank, and never to excess. The final one was that the cause of Sam's death was the great influenza epidemic at the end of the war. None of these things was true. The evidence in Steele's papers in each case is overwhelming, but each had an important bearing on Sam's state of mind at the end of the war.

Steele had convinced himself in his final days that his enemies had sabotaged his chances by circulating stories about his drinking, particularly the alleged incident at Lord Strathcona's banquet in 1901. Steele knew that his age was an issue and changed his birthdate on various documents to make himself appear younger. He denied to the end that he had diabetes, maintaining even when he was bedridden that he was capable of doing a full-time job, although there are prescriptions for the side effects of the illness and special diabetic diets in his papers. To uphold the fiction that a healthy Sam was prematurely and unjustly retired, Harwood and Flora fastened on the great flu epidemic as a fitting end to their father's life—struck down suddenly in his prime rather than wasting away from a lengthy and debilitating illness.

The interesting question is why Harwood did not take the ultimate step in preserving his father's memory by writing a biography. He clearly intended to do so. The diaries, letters, and other documents in the Steele Collection contain extensive pencilled annotations in his handwriting identifying things he wanted to include. As this writer is well aware, the massive extent of the Steele archive makes it a daunting prospect, but there was no lack of time for Harwood to do it since he lived for more than thirty years after the end of the Second World War, dying at age eighty-one in 1978. Harwood's notes show that he was perfectly capable of sorting out relevant details from the records, but the only attempt he made at writing his father's life came in 1956 when he published *The Marching Call*.[5] It can only be described as a truly wretched book. It has many factual errors, lacks any historical context, vastly overestimates Steele's importance in some events, treats Indigenous people in an entirely negative fashion, and is filled with invented dialogue straight out of the *Boy's Own Annual* of the 1920s.

The imperialist caricature of Sam Steele that emerges from pages of *The Marching Call* is nothing like the real human being but it undoubtedly represents Harwood's idea of his father. The book begins with Steele joining the NWMP in 1873, thus enabling Harwood to bypass the potentially embarrassing facts about his birth date. It ends with the Rebellion in 1885. The absence of Steele diaries and letters for that period, along with the fact that very few NWMP records before 1885 survived the Parliament Hill fire of 1916, meant that Harwood could shape the story as he wanted it without fear of contradiction. Before and after that narrow slice of Sam Steele's life, his son could never bring himself to go. The emotional price of altering his father's flawless image was too great.

# Notes

### Introduction

1. University of Alberta, Bruce Peel Special Collections, Sir Samuel Steele Collection (hereafter BPSC), Steele Diary, Orillia, November 16, 1899 (2008.1 Box 3, Folder 17).
2. The Battle of Stormberg, December 10, 1899; the Battle of Magersfontein, December 11, 1899; the Battle of Colenso, December 15, 1899.
3. The first mention in Steele's diary of the appointment is Sunday, January 21, 1899, when he was on the train for Halifax with the CMR: "Left Montreal at noon. All the family saw us off. All feeling I would be back to take charge of Lord Strathconas horse—although I go ostensibly to join the ____ CMR to S Africa."
4. Steele felt quite strongly about avoiding any public criticism of former colleagues. His contemporary, Superintendent R. Burton Deane, published his memoirs, *Mounted Police Life in Canada* (London: Cassel) in 1916 and was outspoken in his opinions. In his diary on April 23, 1917, Steele expressed his disapproval:

    > Received a nice letter from Colonel Fortescue in reply to mine. He has been very ill. He is reading my book and gives it praise for modesty and interest Compares Deanes book with it to the detriment of the latter. He says Deane has forgotten the Latin motto, Dei Mortuus Nil Nici Bonum. This is true. Many have told

me that I have been too modest in my book, but I prefer that to being so very boastful. Deane could have done better but was wrongly constituted. What a chance he had to make a place for himself a clever man but without the knowledge of men.

Steele's Latin is a little shaky but the sentiment is clear.

5. BPSC, Steele Diary, March 20, 1908.
6. BPSC, Letters to Marie, December 15, 1901.
7. BPSC, 2008.1.1.3.2.3. This draft of *Forty Years in Canada*, for example, refers to "details taken from my own diary," 3.

## 1 || Early Life

1. There are several sources for the life of Elmes Steele, the best and most recent of which is Ronald J. Stagg, "Elmes Yelverton Steele," *Dictionary of Canadian Biography*, vol. IX. Harwood Steele and his sister Flora collected a large quantity of materials relating to family history and gave copies to the DCB. Most of the originals of these items are now housed in Bruce Peel Special Collections at the University of Alberta. Stagg's article has a comprehensive bibliography.
2. Susanna Moodie (née Strickland) wrote *Roughing It in the Bush: or, Forest Life in Canada* (London: 1852), while her sister, Catharine Parr Traill (née Strickland) wrote *The Backwoods of Canada: Being Letters From the Wife of an Emigrant Officer* (London: 1836). In the books, the sisters recount various aspects of the difficult lives faced by pioneering families in Upper Canada. See also, Charlotte Gray, *Sisters in the Wilderness: The Lives of Susanna Moodie and Catharine Parr Traill* (London: Duckworth, 2001).
3. J.R. Miller, *Compact, Contract, Covenant: Aboriginal Treaty Making in Canada* (Toronto: University of Toronto Press, 2009), chapter 4.
4. Edward G. Rogers, "The Algonquian Farmers of Southern Ontario, 1830–1945," in Donald B. Smith and Edward G. Rogers, *Aboriginal Ontario: Historical Perspectives on the First Nations* (Toronto: Dundurn Press, 1994).
5. BPSC, 2008.1.1.3.3.7. Manuscript draft of *Forty Years in Canada*, 6.
6. John C. Steele, "Reminiscences of a Pioneer" (originally published in the *Orillia Packet* 1893–1894), *Simcoe County Pioneer and Historical Society: Pioneer Papers*, No. 4 (1911; Canadiana Reprint 1974).
7. A.F. Hunter, *A History of Simcoe County*, vol. 1 (Barrie, ON: County Council, 1909), 220.

8. Lt. Col. W.E. O'Brien, "Early Days in Oro," *Simcoe County Pioneer and Historical Society: Pioneer Papers* No. 1 (1908); *Simcoe County Pioneer and Historical Society: Pioneer Papers* No. 4 (1911).
9. BPSC, Sam to Marie, April 22, 1889.
10. BPSC, Sam to Marie, February 26, 1902, 2008.2.1.1.1.504.
11. Steele, *Forty Years in Canada*, 3.
12. BPSC, Sam to Marie, February 23, 1902, 2008.2.1.1.1.502.
13. Peter Vronsky, *Ridgeway: The American Fenian Invasion and the 1866 Battle of Ridgeway that Made Canada* (Toronto: Allen Lane, 2011).
14. BPSC, S.F. Wise, Director of History, Department of National Defence, to Harwood Steele, October 29, 1968.
15. Steele, *Forty Years in Canada*, 5.
16. Garnet Joseph Wolseley was at this time well into a career that took him to the rank of Field Marshal and Commander in Chief of the army. He had served with distinction in Burma, India and the Crimean War. He observed and wrote about the American Civil War. Wolseley was one of the small group of military intellectuals who worked to modernize the British Army in the late 19th century. His efforts to overcome the complacency of the period made him a controversial public figure and the pattern for Gilbert and Sullivan's "Model of a Modern Major General."
17. The best account of the expedition is George F.G. Stanley, *Toil and Trouble: Military Expeditions to Red River* (Toronto and Oxford: Canadian War Museum and Dundurn Press, 1996).
18. BPSC, Mulvey Diary. Although identified as the diary of Ensign Stewart Mulvey, it seems clear from internal evidence that Mulvey wrote the diary at the dictation of another officer, probably McMillan.
19. Alvin Gluek, *Minnesota and the Manifest Destiny of the Canadian Northwest: A Study in Canadian-American Relations* (Toronto: University of Toronto Press, 1965)
20. Steele, *Forty Years in Canada*, 18.
21. BPSC, Mulvey Diary, July 8, 1870.
22. BPSC, Mulvey Diary, September 9, 1870.
23. BPSC, Mulvey Diary, September 9, 1870.
24. Steele, *Forty Years in Canada*, 34.
25. Stanley, *Toil and Trouble*, 189.
26. Steele describes the incident in *Forty Years in Canada*, 38–39. John Kerr's memoirs recount it with a few minor differences. Kerr served briefly in the Manitoba Mounted Police after leaving the Ontario Rifles. He spent six

years wandering around the North-West Territories, befriending, among others, Gabriel Dumont. Then he returned to his home in Perth, Ontario, where he was town clerk for forty years. His niece, Constance Kerr Sissons, compiled an account of his western adventures from his diaries and other writings. C.K. Sissons, *John Kerr* (Toronto: Oxford University Press, 1946), 60–62.

27. Thomas Bland Strange, *Gunner Jingo's Jubilee* (1893; repr., Edmonton: University of Alberta Press, 1988), 347–80.
28. BPSC, Sam to Marie, April 22, 1889.
29. William Francis Butler, *The Great Lone Land: A Narrative of Travel and Adventure in the North-West of America* (London: Sampson Low, Marston, Low and Searle, 1872). The book went through seventeen editions before the First World War and is still in print.
30. Peter Cozzens, *The Earth is Weeping: The Epic Story of the Indian Wars for the American West* (New York: Alfred A. Knopf, 2016).
31. S.W. Horrall, "Sir John A. Macdonald and the Police Force for the Northwest Territories," *Canadian Historical Review* (June 1972); R.C. Macleod, *The North-West Mounted Police and Law Enforcement 1873–1905* (Toronto: University of Toronto Press, 1976), chapter 2.
32. Steele, *Forty Years in Canada*, 52.

## 2 ‖ The North-West Mounted Police

1. R.C. Macleod, *The North-West Mounted Police and Law Enforcement 1873–1905* (Toronto: University of Toronto Press, 1976), 16.
2. The best history of the episode is still Philip Goldring, "Whisky, Horses and Death: The Cypress Hills Massacre and its Sequel" in *Canadian Historic Sites: Occasional Papers in Archaeology and History No. 21* (Ottawa: National Historic Parks and Sites Branch, Parks Canada, 1979). These Canadian Historic Sites publications are not always easy to find, but this one is available at http://parkscanadahistory.com/series/chs/21/chs21-2a.htm. The wonderful novel by Guy Vanderhaeghe, *The Englishman's Boy* (Toronto: McClelland and Stewart, 1996), conveys the atmosphere of the time and place better than any historical study.
3. For the impact of disease, see James Daschuk, *Clearing the Plains: Disease, Politics of Starvation, and the Loss of Aboriginal Life* (Regina: University of Regina Press, 2013).
4. The end of European colonial rivalries in North America by the middle of the 19th century effectively eliminated the bargaining power of the

Indigenous peoples and thus any prospect that they might retain some degree of autonomy. See Jeremy Adelman and Stephen Aron, "From Borderlands to Borders: Empires, Nation-States, and the Peoples in Between in North American History," *American Historical Review* (June 1999): 814–41.

5. Robert M. Utley, *The Indian Frontier, 1846–1890*, rev. ed. (1984; Albuquerque: University of New Mexico Press, 2003), 4. For a more up-to-date perspective, see Theodore Binnema, *Common and Contested Ground: A Human and Environmental History of the Northwestern Plains* (Toronto: University of Toronto Press, 2004).

6. A recent account of that sad history is Peter Cozzens, *The Earth is Weeping: The Epic Story of the Indian Wars for the American West* (New York: Alfred A. Knopf, 2016). The exception was Texas, which relied on its own paramilitary Texas Rangers to do the job. See Andrew R. Graybill, *Policing the Great Plains: Rangers, Mounties, and the North American Frontier, 1875–1910* (Lincoln: University of Nebraska Press, 2007).

7. John Peter Turner, *The North-West Mounted Police 1873–1893*, vol. 1 (Ottawa: King's Printer, 1950), 112.

8. Macleod, *The North-West Mounted Police and Law Enforcement*, 17–18.

9. Steele, *Forty Years in Canada*, 61.

10. Library and Archives Canada (LAC), North-West Mounted Police Personnel Records 1873–1904. Steele to Commissioner French, April 17, 1874, and French to Minister of Justice, July 10, 1874.

11. Steele, *Forty Years in Canada*, 62.

12. Fur traders had been travelling west as far as the Pacific coast for half a century but their routes ran several hundred kilometres north of the boundary.

13. Steele, *Forty Years in Canada*, 67.

14. The account of the trip to Edmonton is drawn from Turner, *The North-West Mounted Police 1873–1893*, vol. 1, 170–80 and Steele, *Forty Years in Canada*, 68–75. It seems probable that both were based on a diary kept by Steele, now lost. Turner's version gives a daily diary of the journey that is considerably longer but which is identical to Steele's in several places.

15. *Report of the North West Mounted Police*, 1874.

16. Steele, *Forty Years in Canada*, 87.

17. John Foster, "The Metis and the End of the Plains Buffalo in Alberta," in *Buffalo*, ed. John Foster, Dick Harrison, and I.S. MacLaren (Edmonton: University of Alberta Press, 1992); R.F. Beal, J.E. Foster, and Louise Zuk,

*The Métis Hivernement Settlement at Buffalo Lake, 1872–1877: An Historical Report* (Edmonton: Alberta Department of Culture, Historic Sites and Provincial Museums Division, 1987).

18. LAC, NWMP Personnel Records 1873–1904, Steele to French, April 1, 1875.
19. Steele, *Forty Years in Canada*, 88. There are several versions of the dispute that resulted in the placement of Fort Saskatchewan. One story is that HBC Factor Richard Hardisty made the demand that the post be located at Edmonton. This version is detailed in Peter T. Ream, *The Fort on the Saskatchewan: A Resource Book on Fort Saskatchewan and District* (Fort Saskatchewan, AB: Metropolitan Printing, 1974). It seems to be based on a story in the *Edmonton Bulletin* in 1886, eleven years after the event. The context of that report was another acrimonious set-to between the citizens of Edmonton and Ottawa over plans to move the federal Land Office to the south side of the river. The HBC had no vital interests to protect in keeping the police post in Edmonton. The settlers in the town, on the other hand, did. I am inclined to accept Steele's account.
20. Steele, *Forty Years in Canada*, 88.
21. Steele, *Forty Years in Canada*, 91. John Peter Turner, who is usually very accurate on details of this kind, has Steele moving to Swan River in 1876 (Turner, *The North-West Mounted Police 1873–1893*, vol. 1, 256) but the correct year is 1875.
22. Steele, *Forty Years in Canada*, 92.
23. S.W. Horrall, *A Chronicle of the Canadian West: North-West Mounted Police Report for 1875* (Calgary: Historical Society of Alberta, 1975), 8–10.
24. Turner, *The North-West Mounted Police 1873–1893*, vol. 1, 212.
25. Canada, *Sessional Papers*, 1876, No. 7, Report on the State of the Militia of the Dominion of Canada for the Year 1875. Appendix B, "Report on the North West Mounted Police," xliv. This comment motivated Steele to have another try at getting himself sent to England for cavalry training. Again, he did not succeed. LAC, NWMP Personnel Records, Steele to Commissioner, November 4, 1875.
26. Steele, *Forty Years in Canada*, 101.
27. There is a large and growing literature on the negotiation of the western numbered treaties, centred mainly on what each party understood, or failed to understand, about the documents being signed. The literature to date is admirably summed up in David J. Hall, *From Treaties to Reserves: The Federal Government and Native Peoples in Territorial Alberta, 1870–1905* (Montreal and Kingston: McGill-Queen's University Press, 2015), chapter 2,

"The Paradox of Agreement and Mutual Incomprehension: Treaties 6 and 7."
28. BPSC, A.R. Macdonell Diary, July 27, 1876, 2008.1.1.3.1.6.
29. LAC, NWMP Personnel Records, S.B. Steele Certificate of Engagement, September 20, 1876. Steele's brother Richard left the police at this time and homesteaded near Fort Saskatchewan.
30. BPSC, A.R. Macdonell Diary, February 19, 1877, 2008.1.1.3.1.6.
31. LAC, Governor General Sir John Douglas Sutherland Campbell, Marquis of Lorne Fonds, Macdonald to Lorne, January 25, 1881.
32. Hugh A. Dempsey, *Crowfoot: Chief of the Blackfeet* (Norman: University of Oklahoma Press, 1972), 86.
33. Dempsey, *Crowfoot*, chapter 9.
34. Joseph Manzione, *"I am Looking to the North for My Life": Sitting Bull, 1876–1881* (Salt Lake City: University of Utah Press, 1994), 51–66.
35. Steele, *Forty Years in Canada*, 127.
36. Steele, *Forty Years in Canada*, 130.
37. Steele, *Forty Years in Canada*, 146.
38. Nearly two years later a Kainai named Star Child was arrested and tried for the murder but the jury found insufficient evidence to convict.
39. Steele, *Forty Years in Canada*, 150.
40. Roderick C. Macleod, "James Morrow Walsh," *Dictionary of Canadian Biography*, vol. XIII.
41. Manzione, "I am Looking to the North for My Life," 64.
42. Cozzens, *The Earth is Weeping*.
43. Steele, *Forty Years in Canada*, 156.
44. Steele, *Forty Years in Canada*, 166.
45. Steele, *Forty Years in Canada*, 165.
46. Steele, *Forty Years in Canada*, 167.
47. Steele, *Forty Years in Canada*, 168.
48. Macleod, *The North-West Mounted Police and Law Enforcement*, 157–59. Sometimes the police sided openly with the navvies. In June 1884, fourteen navvies sued the CPR at Calgary for non-payment of wages. Inspector Dowling, sitting as a justice of the peace, ordered the company to pay in all cases. Canada, *Sessional Papers*, 1885, Report of the Commissioner of the North-West Mounted Police Force 1884, Appendix A, "Criminal and other Cases tried in the North-West Territories," 56.

49. Canada, *Sessional Papers*, 1885, Report of the Commissioner of the North-West Mounted Police Force 1884, 5, and Appendix A, 53; Steele, *Forty Years in Canada*, 177–79.
50. "I pointed out that the introduction of such a system would be tantamount to a breach of confidence with the Indians generally, inasmuch as from the outset the Indians had been led to believe that compulsory residence on reservations would not be required of them, and that they would be at liberty to travel about for legitimate hunting and trading purposes." Canada, *Sessional Papers*, 1885, Report of the Commissioner of the North-West Mounted Police Force 1884, 6.
51. Some Métis groups and the Saskatchewan government refuse to call the events of 1885 a rebellion, insisting on the word "resistance" instead. While this terminology is entirely correct for the actions of Riel and his followers at Red River in 1869–1870, the situation fifteen years later was quite different. All dictionary definitions of "rebellion" are clear and unambiguous, e.g., *Canadian Oxford Dictionary*, "organized armed resistance to an established government." There was arguably no "established government" at Red River in 1869 but by 1885 Canadian authority had been firmly in place for a decade and a half. Riel himself in conversations in the days before the shooting started referred to his intended actions as a rebellion. Bob Beal and Rod Macleod, *Prairie Fire: The 1885 North-West Rebellion* (Toronto: McClelland and Stewart, 1996), 140 and 353, footnote 47.
52. Steele, *Forty Years in Canada*, 183.
53. *Calgary Herald*, June 18, 1884.
54. Dempsey, *Crowfoot*, 159–60.
55. The case is recorded in Canada, *Sessional Papers*, 1885, Report of the Commissioner of the North-West Mounted Police Force 1884, Appendix A, "Criminal and other Cases tried in the North-West Territories," 56. The defendant's name is recorded as "Bear's Hand," an error that appears in the *Calgary Herald* report as well. Mounted Police officers tried most criminal cases in the North-West Territories in this period and, rather remarkably, did not hesitate to acquit. See R.C. Macleod and Heather Rollason, "'Restrain the Lawless Savages': Native Defendants in the Criminal Courts of the North West Territories, 1878–1885," *Journal of Historical Sociology* (June 1997).
56. BPSC, Steele Diary, January 25, 1885.
57. BPSC, Steele Diary, January 31, 1885.

58. BPSC, Steele Diary, January 23, 1885.
59. BPSC, Steele Diary, January 25, 1885.
60. In Canadian law at the time, two justices of the peace sitting together could try quite serious crimes. See Rod Macleod and Nancy Parker, "Justices of the Peace in Alberta," in *Forging Alberta's Constitutional Framework*, ed. Richard Connors and John M. Law (Edmonton: University of Alberta Press, 2005).
61. Canada, *Sessional Papers*, 1886, Report of the Commissioner of the North-West Mounted Police Force 1885, 16–17.
62. Steele, *Forty Years in Canada*, 199.
63. The *Riot Act* became part of Canadian law when Britain acquired the colony from France in 1763 and was incorporated into the Criminal Code in 1891. It was used most recently in the 2011 Stanley Cup riot in Vancouver.
64. Steele's version in *Forty Years in Canada* is largely corroborated by the NWMP Annual Report for 1885, although the latter lacks some of the more colourful details. Steele's diary through February and March shows no indication that he was concerned about, or even aware of, the growing labour tension. Most of the March entries in the diary include the notation "nothing of importance." The diary ends abruptly on March 26, presumably the day he became ill, and does not resume until September, following the Rebellion. Another piece of evidence supporting Steele's account is to be found in a letter from his future wife in 1889 in which she mentions hearing about the incident from another police officer who was no friend of Steele's. BPSC, Marie to Sam, April 14, 1889.

## 3 || Steele's Scouts in the Rebellion

1. Bill Waiser, "Too Many Scared People: Alberta and the 1885 Rebellion," in *Alberta Formed—Alberta Transformed*, vol. 1, ed. Michael Payne, Donald Wetherell, and Catherine Cavanaugh (Edmonton and Calgary: University of Alberta Press and University of Calgary Press, 2006), 271–98. For the broader picture of First Nations during the Rebellion see Blair Stonechild and Bill Waiser, *Loyal Till Death: Indians and the North-West Rebellion* (Calgary: Fifth House, 1997).
2. Sarah Carter, *Lost Harvests: Prairie Indian Reserve Farmers and Government Policy* (Montreal and Kingston: McGill-Queen's University Press, 1990).
3. Bob Beal and Rod Macleod, *Prairie Fire: The 1885 North-West Rebellion* (Toronto: McClelland and Stewart, 1996), chapters 3–5.

4. The best interpretation of how Riel's religious and political ideas evolved and intersected is Thomas Flanagan, *Louis "David" Riel: Prophet of the New World* (Toronto: University of Toronto Press, 1996).
5. Brian Titley, "Hayter Reed and Indian Administration in the West," in *Swords and Plowshares: War and Agriculture in Western Canada*, ed. R.C. Macleod (Edmonton: University of Alberta Press, 1993). The general attitude of the Indian Affairs bureaucrats is well summed up by Titley in his biography of one of the later superintendents of the department, Duncan Campbell Scott, in which he is described as "an almost obsessive penny-pinching book-keeper." Brian Titley, *A Narrow Vision: Duncan Campbell Scott and the Administration of Indian Affairs in Canada* (Vancouver: University of British Columbia Press, 1986), 202. See by the same author, *The Indian Commissioners: Agents of the State and Indian Policy in Canada's Prairie West, 1873–1932* (Edmonton: University of Alberta Press, 2009).
6. Reed had been a militia officer who first went west with the Red River Expedition. Steele obviously knew him and occasionally mentions seeing him in his diary. He never refers to him as an old friend, as he does with others who shared that journey, suggesting that he disliked Reed.
7. Donald B. Smith, *Honoré Jaxon: Prairie Visionary* (Regina: Coteau Books, 2007), 44–50.
8. Canada, *Sessional Papers*, 1886, Report of the Commissioner of the North-West Mounted Police Force 1885, Part II, 21–27.
9. Strange's autobiography was entitled *Gunner Jingo's Jubilee* (London: Remington and Co., 1893).
10. Strange, *Gunner Jingo's Jubilee*, 430, says that Hatton had eighty men, but his book is incorrect on many details.
11. BPSC, 2008.1.1.3.1.3. J.K. Oswald Notebook, Steele's Scouts Standing Orders, Calgary, April 14, 1885. Civilian members of the Scouts were required to buy their horses and arms, if they did not already have them. All horses were purchased from General Strange's ranch and most were unbroken.
12. Steele, *Forty Years in Canada*, 213.
13. BPSC, Oswald, Steele's Scouts Standing Orders, Nominal Rolls of No. 1 and No. 2 Troops.
14. BPSC, 2008.1.1.3.1.4. J.K. Oswald Notebook, Standing Orders, After Order No. 1, April 16, 1885.
15. Waiser, "Too Many Scared People," 282.
16. *Edmonton Bulletin*, May 2, 1885.

17. BPSC, Oswald, Standing Orders, April 26, 1885.
18. Strange, *Gunner Jingo's Jubilee*, 443–44.
19. Steele wrote, "My three brothers, Richard, Godfrey and James, were at Edmonton, and were sworn in as scouts." Steele, *Forty Years in Canada*, 215. None of the three appears on the lists of men for Steele's Scouts. It is possible that the Steele brothers joined the Alberta Mounted Rifles or one of the local volunteer home defence units.
20. BPSC, Oswald, Squadron Orders, May 4, 1885.
21. *Edmonton Bulletin*, May 2, 1885.
22. BPSC, Oswald, Squadron Morning Orders, Camp Victoria, May 14, 1885.
23. BPSC, Oswald Notebook, May 24, 1885.
24. Steele, *Forty Years in Canada*, 223.
25. Steele claimed to have counted 300 rifle pits on the hilltop. This is certainly an exaggeration. Bob Beal and I walked over the position in 1984 when we were doing the research for *Prairie Fire*. The remains of the Cree positions were clearly visible after a century, even though the site is on private land and has had no preservation work done on it, but the hilltop is not large enough to accommodate the number Steele claims. It seems likely he was inflating the number to provide an excuse for the decision of his friend, General Strange, not to press the attack earlier.
26. Steele, *Forty Years in Canada*, 225.
27. Fury was put on light duties after he recovered, but in 1888 was given a medical discharge and a pension. LAC, NWMP Personnel Records 1873–1904, William Fury File.
28. Beal and Macleod, *Prairie Fire*, 290.
29. Steele, *Forty Years in Canada*, 228.
30. BPSC, Oswald Notebook, Camp Beaver River, June 16, 1885.
31. BPSC, Oswald Notebook, June 29, 1885.
32. *Edmonton Bulletin*, July 11, 1885.
33. *The Canadian Pictorial and Illustrated War News*, Saturday, July 11, 1885.
34. Roderick Charles Macleod, "Francis Jeffrey Dickens," *Dictionary of Canadian Biography*, vol. XI.
35. BPSC, Steele Diary, September 11 and 12, 1885. 2008.1.1.1.
36. Steele, *Forty Years in Canada*, 236.
37. Steele, *Forty Years in Canada*, 237.

## 4 || Frustrated Ambition

1. Canada, *Sessional Papers*, 1887, Report of the Commissioner of the North-West Mounted Police Force 1886, 47.
2. BPSC, Steele Diary, January 17, 1886.
3. BPSC, Steele Diary, 1886, Cash Accounts, January–July.
4. T. Morris Longstreth, *The Silent Force: Scenes from the Life of the Mounted Police of Canada* (New York: The Century, 1927).
5. LAC, NWMP Personnel Records, S.B. Steele File. Harwood also complained to the RCMP commissioner and copies of all the correspondence with Longstreth ended up in their records. Harwood Steele to Commissioner Cortlandt Starnes, October 28, 1927.
6. LAC, Steele Personnel File, T. Morris Longstreth to Harwood Steele, December 11, 1927.
7. BPSC, Steele Diary, 1886.
8. BPSC, Steele Diary, April 14, 1886.
9. BPSC, Steele Diary, September 1, 1886.
10. BPSC, Steele Diary, April 2, 1886.
11. Turner, *The North-West Mounted Police 1873–1893*, vol. 2, 273.
12. BPSC, Steele Diary, February 3 and 4, 1886.
13. BPSC, Steele Diary, February 16, 1886.
14. BPSC, Steele Diary, March 1, 1886.
15. *Saskatchewan Herald*, April 12, 1886.
16. *Saskatchewan Herald*, February 22, 1886.
17. LAC, NWMP Records, Commissioner's Office 1886, File, "Re Supt. Steele's allegations as to frauds in Q.M. Stores at Battleford." Memo, Inspector Allan to Commissioner Herchmer, December 2, 1886 enclosing report and correspondence with William Allan and Whitehead.
18. Steele's report is not in the file and there are no copies of it in his own personnel file, nor in those of Allan or Antrobus.
19. LAC, Steele allegations file, Commissioner L.W. Herchmer to Steele, November 26, 1886.
20. LAC, NWMP Personnel Records, W.D. Antrobus File. Investigation held at Swift Current, August 1884. Report of Surgeon Augustus Jukes.
21. LAC, Antrobus Personnel File, Comptroller Frederick White to Commissioner Irvine, September 13, 1884.
22. LAC, Antrobus Personnel File, assistant commissioner to commissioner, April 3, 1891.
23. LAC, Sir John A. Macdonald Papers, Pope to Macdonald, April 30, 1891.

24. The other was William J.S. Elliott, appointed in 2007. Nobody was surprised in 1886 when Commissioner Irvine was fired but most expected the job to go to a British officer. The job was, in fact, offered to Lord Melgund, who had served as General Middleton's chief of staff during the Rebellion, but he turned it down. Melgund returned to Canada in 1898 to become governor general after inheriting the title of Earl of Minto. Lawrence William Herchmer was the son of a Kingston clergyman whom John A. Macdonald described as "my school fellow and long life friend." LAC, Sir John A. Macdonald Papers, Macdonald to L.W. Herchmer, July 22, 1872. Herchmer served briefly in the British Army in Ireland and India. After returning to Canada, he served as commissariat officer for the international commission surveying the Canada–United States boundary across the prairies. He became an Indian agent and eventually inspector of Indian Agencies, the position he held at the time of his appointment to the Mounted Police.
25. LAC, Steele Personnel File, Alonzo Wright to Comptroller Fred White, August 20, 1886.
26. LAC, Steele Personnel File, McCarthy to Sir John A. Macdonald, September 9, 1886.
27. BPSC, Steele Diary, October 16, 1886.
28. The notes are dated, Calgary 10/11/1886.
29. BPSC, Sam to Marie, February 26, 1889. He also comments about this time, "I have been nearly two years a total abstainer." February 23, 1889.
30. William Beahen and Stan Horrall, *Red Coats on the Prairies: The North-West Mounted Police 1886–1900* (Regina: Centax Books, 1998), 8.
31. Robin Fisher, "Isadore," *Dictionary of Canadian Biography*, vol. XII.
32. Canada, *Sessional Papers*, 1888, Report of the Commissioner of the North-West Mounted Police Force 1887, 19–20.
33. Canada, *Sessional Papers*, 1888, Report of the Commissioner of the North-West Mounted Police Force 1887, 53.
34. Beahan and Horrall, *Red Coats on the Prairies*, 8.
35. Edward Lloyd Affleck, *Sternwheelers, Sandbars and Switchbacks: A Chronicle of Steam Transportation in the British Columbia Waterways of the Columbia River System 1865 to 1965* (Vancouver: Alexander Nicholls Press, 1973), 15.
36. NWMP *Annual Report 1887*, 53.
37. LAC, NWMP Personnel Records, Thomas Lake File.
38. NWMP *Annual Report 1887*, Appendix R, "Annual Report of Assistant Surgeon Powell," 120.

39. Margaret Whitehead, ed., *They Call Me Father: Memoirs of Father Nicolas Coccola* (Vancouver: University of British Columbia Press, 1988), 108.
40. Jacqueline Gresko, "Paul Durieu," *Dictionary of Canadian Biography*, vol. XII.
41. BPSC, Steele Diary, January 11, 1888.
42. Coccola, *Memoirs*, 106.
43. In 1886 he solicited the support of the bishop of Saint Boniface for his bid for the assistant commissionership. The bishop replied, "I beg to say that although, as you say, we are not personally acquainted, I am nevertheless happy to know you by the medium of our missionaries." LAC, Steele Personnel File, Bishop of Saint Boniface to Steele, August 27, 1886.
44. Naomi Miller, *Fort Steele: Gold Rush to Boom Town* (Surrey, BC: Heritage House, 2002), 52.
45. Steele, *Forty Years in Canada*, 250.
46. Miller, *Fort Steele: Gold Rush to Boom Town*, 52.
47. NWMP *Annual Report 1887*, Appendix F, "Annual Report of Superintendent Steele," 63–64.
48. NWMP *Annual Report 1887*, Appendix R, "Annual Report of Assistant Surgeon Powell," 120–21.
49. BPSC, Steele Diary, January 31, 1888.
50. BPSC, Steele Diary, March 2, 1888.
51. NWMP *Annual Report 1887*, Appendix F, "Annual Report of Superintendent Steele," 68.
52. BPSC, Steele Diary, April 20, 1888.
53. BPSC, Steele Diary, April 22, 1888. "Took exercise after returning and read life of Daniel Webster until 1.30." It was probably George Ticknor Curtis, *Life of Daniel Webster* (New York: Appleton, 1870).
54. BPSC, Steele Diary, March 3, 1888.
55. BPSC, Steele Diary, April 26, 1888.
56. BPSC, Steele Diary, May 28, 1888.
57. BPSC, Steele Diary, June 3, 1888.
58. BPSC, Steele Diary, June 10, 1888.
59. BPSC, Steele Diary, June 20, 1888.
60. BPSC, Steele Diary, July 3, 1888.
61. BPSC, Steele Diary, July 3, 1888.
62. BPSC, Steele Diary, July 22, 1888.
63. BPSC, Steele Diary, August 7, 1888.
64. BPSC, Steele Diary, August 13, 1888.
65. BPSC, Steele Diary, August 16, 1888.

## 5 ‖ The Love of His Life

1. The sole evidence for this is in a letter to his future wife, where he wrote, "I told you once that I was engaged to a lady. Well when it happened and after that I tried to force myself to think I liked [her] but I could not. She could not enter my mind except by accident. Poor girl she died a month or two ago and had an unhappy marriage, she went insane on account of it, and I do not wonder at it. He was a most uncouth fellow and left her ____ at a H.B.C. Co. fort in the far north." BPSC, Sam to Marie, July 9, 1889. There is no indication in the voluminous Steele papers about who this person was, or where or when it happened.
2. BPSC, Sam to Marie, December 18, 1888.
3. Marie Harwood bore a strong resemblance to the famous Canadian soprano of the time, Emma Albani. She mentions having attended her concerts several times and seems to have modelled herself on the singer. Marie was nevertheless somewhat self-conscious about her height. Almost all her photographs show her seated.
4. Robert Harwood won the seat of Vaudreuil in the elections of 1872 and 1874 but lost in 1878.
5. Marie referred to herself in one letter as "a penniless lass with a long pedigree." (This is a quote from Charles Kingsley's novel, *Alton Locke*.) BPSC, Marie to Sam, January 27, 1889.
6. BPSC, Marie to Sam, May 12, 1889.
7. Only one of these notes survives. "Dear Miss Harwood I suppose it 'goes without saying' that we cannot ride today? I have to visit hospital cases while on duty, and the weather is stormy. It is too bad." BPSC, Sam to Marie, October 16, 1888.
8. BPSC, Sam to Marie, December 30, 1888.
9. BPSC, Sam to Marie, February 2, 1889. After his complaint about being put off he commented, "thank goodness I made up for lost time afterwards."
10. BPSC, Steele Diary, October 19, 1888.
11. BPSC, Steele Diary, November 5, 1888.
12. Dan Horner, "'Shame Upon You as Men!': Contesting Authority in the Aftermath of Montreal's Gavazzi Riot," *Histoire Sociale/Social History* (May 2011); Brian Clarke, "Religious Riot as Pastime: Orange Young Britons, Parades and Public Life in Victorian Toronto," in *The Orange Order in Canada*, ed. David A. Wilson (Dublin: Four Courts Press, 2007), 114.
13. BPSC, Sam to Marie, January 18, 1889.
14. BPSC, Marie to Sam, January 23, 1889.

15. BPSC, Sam to Marie, January 3, 1889.
16. BPSC, Marie to Sam, January 27, 1889.
17. BPSC, Sam to Marie, February 2, 1889.
18. BPSC, Sam to Marie, January 23, 1889.
19. BPSC, Sam to Marie, February 14, 1889.
20. Canada, *Sessional Papers*, 1890, Report of the Commissioner of the North-West Mounted Police Force 1889, Appendix F, "Annual Report of Superintendent Steele Commanding Macleod District."
20. Canada, *Sessional Papers*, 1890, Report of the Commissioner of the North-West Mounted Police Force 1889, Appendix F, "Annual Report of Superintendent Steele Commanding Macleod District."
22. BPSC, Sam to Marie, June 23, 1889.
23. BPSC, Sam to Marie, May 17, 1889.
24. Canada, *Sessional Papers*, 1890, Report of the Commissioner of the North-West Mounted Police Force 1889, Appendix F, "Annual Report of Superintendent Steele Commanding Macleod District."
25. Hugh Dempsey, *Red Crow: Warrior Chief* (Saskatoon: Western Producer Prairie Books, 1980), 180.
26. Steele's sense of the correctness of his actions grew over the years. The account in his autobiography is much more dramatic than his letters or official reports at the time. It concludes, "my action was supported in every particular by Sir John Thompson, Minister of Justice, who held we could arrest an Indian at any time or place. They were wards and we were officers of the Crown, therefore there was no chance of a miscarriage of justice.!!" Steele, *Forty Years in Canada*, 264-65.
27. J.R. Miller, *Equal Rights: The Jesuit Estates Act Controversy* (Montreal and Kingston: McGill-Queen's University Press, 1979).
28. BPSC, Sam to Marie, July 8, 1889. "Do you remember my saying on the train to Winnipeg that Lex thought I was an Orangeman? ...What would *you* do if I had been one my dear? I suppose you would send me about my business at once would you not? Some of the people are awfully bigoted are they not and I suppose the society I mention is one of the worst."
29. BPSC, Sam to Marie, July 19, 1889.
30. BPSC, Sam to Marie, December 22, 1888, February 23, 1889, March 20, 1889.
31. Fred White was the deputy minister in charge of the NWMP. A confidant and former private secretary of Sir John A. Macdonald, White was a

consummate bureaucrat who managed the Force for thirty years. He and Steele developed a friendship that lasted long after Sam left the NWMP.
32. BPSC, Sam to Marie, July 30, 1889.
33. BPSC, Sam to Marie, October 6, 1889.
34. BPSC, Sam to Marie, October 14, 1889.
35. BPSC, Marie to Sam, April 2, 1889.
36. BPSC, Sam to Marie, May 29, 1889.
37. There is a full and balanced account of this episode in Beahen and Horrall, *Red Coats on the Prairies*, chapter 9, "The Herchmer Scandals."
38. BPSC, Steele Diary, August 12, 1889. "Const Craig arrested by order of the Commissioner which came in cipher telegram."
39. BPSC, Sam to Marie, December 11, 1889.
40. BPSC, Sam to Marie, December 19, 1889.
41. BPSC, Sam to Marie, October 14, 1889.
42. BPSC, Sam to Marie, September 25, 1889.
43. BPSC, Steele Diary, January 3–8, 1890.
44. BPSC, Steele Diary, January 8, 1890.
45. BPSC, Sam to Marie, October 29, 1889.
46. BPSC, Steele Diary, January 14, 1890.
47. Huot died a few years later of an unidentified illness. Starnes went on to serve with Steele in the Yukon and was RCMP commissioner 1923–1931.
48. BPSC, Steele Diary, January 15, 1890.
49. BPSC, Steele Diary, January 17, 1890.
50. BPSC, Steele Diary, January 19, 1890.
51. BPSC, Steele Diary, January 21, 1890.
52. BPSC, Steele Diary, February 6, 1890.
53. Steele, *Forty Years in Canada*, 268.
54. BPSC, Sam to Marie, December 11, 1889.
55. BPSC, Steele Diary, February 10, 1890.
56. BPSC, Steele Diary, February 21, 1890.
57. BPSC, Steele Diary, March 6, 1890.

## 6 || Fort Macleod and Family

1. Flora Macdonald Steele, "Happy Memories," *Scarlet and Gold* (1939): 56. Flora Steele wrote this account of her childhood at Fort Macleod when she was a teenager. It was published much later in the RCMP veterans' magazine.

2. BPSC, Steele Diary, 1891, Cash Accounts, August. Emily Palmer was paid $10 a month, Macdonald got $5.
3. BPSC, Steele Diary, April 9, 1891.
4. BPSC, Steele Diary, January 22, 1891.
5. BPSC, Steele Diary, January 24, 1892.
6. BPSC, Steele Diary, 1890, Cash Accounts, August.
7. BPSC, Sam to Marie, July 16, 1892.
8. BPSC, Steele Diary, August 2, 1895. "There was a little girl born at my quarters today." May 5, 1897, "My wife was delivered of a child this A.M. a boy both well."
9. BPSC, Steele Diary, September 11, 1895, for example.
10. BPSC, Steele Diary, January 19, 1897. "The child Gerty nearly died. I thought she was gone but both doctors succeeded in getting some pus out of her throat which has given her some relief and enabled her to sleep."
11. Beahen and Horrall, *Red Coats on the Prairies*, has an excellent chapter on the inquiry and its consequences for the NWMP.
12. BPSC, Steele Diary, July 29, 1890.
13. Abbott was a leading figure in the Montreal Anglophone business and political elite to which the Harwoods belonged. His estate at Sainte-Anne-de-Bellevue was directly across the river from Vaudreuil.
14. Beahen and Horrall, *Red Coats on the Prairies*, 137.
15. BPSC, Steele Diary, June 24, 1891. "The change of Sanders for Wood to take place on the 1st the letter arrived today I am informed by Sanders that he was hurried up so fast that he had not time to turn around as they the Herchmers wanted to give Insp Wood no time to have the change countermanded."
16. BPSC, Steele Diary, January 3, 1892.
17. BPSC, Steele Diary, February 7, 1892.
18. *Calgary Weekly Herald*, February 17, 1892.
19. BPSC, Sam to Marie, July 24, 1892.
20. BPSC, Steele Diary, March 26, 1893.
21. *Report of the Inquiry into the conduct of Commissioner L.W. Herchmer*, quoted in Beahen and Horrall, *Red Coats on the Prairies*, 140.
22. Beahen and Horrall, *Red Coats on the Prairies*, 140.
23. The *British North America Act* made law enforcement, and hence policing, a provincial responsibility.
24. Canada, House of Commons, *Debates*, May 16, 1892.
25. BPSC, Steele Diary, February 17, 1894.

26. Beahen and Horrall, *Red Coats on the Prairies*, 194–98.
27. BPSC, Steele Diary, February 14, 1895. "Supts Macdonell & Norman and Insprs Hopkins and Oliver got notice of superannuation on the grounds of their office having been abolished."
28. Steele and Macdonell had bought adjoining quarter sections of land in 1891. It is not clear if this is where Macdonell's ranch was or whether he acquired Steele's quarter as part of their later complex business dealings. BPSC, Steele Diary, 1891, back endpaper: "S.B.S. N.E. Qr. Sec. 24 Tp. 3 Range 30 West of 4th initial Mer. A.R.M. N.W. Qr. Of the same."
29. Shelley A.M. Gavigan, *Hunger, Horses, and Government Men: Criminal Law on the Aboriginal Plains, 1870–1905* (Vancouver: University of British Columbia Press and The Osgoode Society for Canadian Legal History, 2012), chapter 1, "Legally Framing the Plains and the First Nations"; R.C. Macleod and Heather Rollason-Driscoll, "'Restrain the Lawless Savages': Native Defendants in the Criminal Courts of the North West Territories, 1878–1885," *Journal of Historical Sociology* (June 1997); Rod Macleod and Nancy Parker, "Justices of the Peace in Alberta," in *Forging Alberta's Constitutional Framework*, ed. Richard Connors and John M. Law (Edmonton: University of Alberta Press, 2005), 267–88.
30. Canada, House of Commons, *Debates*, James McMullen, May 16, 1892.
31. These policies and their consequences have been extensively studied. See Sarah Carter, *Lost Harvests: Prairie Indian Reserve Farmers and Government Policy* (Montreal and Kingston: McGill-Queen's University Press, 1990); Helen Buckley, *From Wooden Plows to Welfare: Why Indian Policy Failed in the Prairie Provinces* (Montreal and Kingston: McGill-Queen's University Press, 1992); James Daschuk, *Clearing the Plains: Disease, Politics of Starvation, and the Loss of Aboriginal Life* (Regina: University of Regina Press, 2013).
32. The book that really brought the residential schools tragedy to public attention was J.R. Miller, *Shingwauk's Vision: A History of Native Residential Schools* (Toronto: University of Toronto Press, 1996). See also, John S. Milloy, *A National Crime: The Canadian Government and the Residential School System, 1879 to 1986* (Winnipeg: University of Manitoba Press, 1999); Bernard Schissel and Terry Wotherspoon, *The Legacy of School for Aboriginal People: Education, Oppression, and Emancipation* (Don Mills, ON: Oxford University Press, 2003).
33. The only detailed treatment of this issue is F. Laurie Barron, "The Indian Pass System in the Canadian West, 1882–1935," *Prairie Forum* 13, no. 1 (Spring 1988): 25–42. The article compares the system to South African

apartheid, to which it has some superficial resemblance. This assertion, a weak point in an otherwise excellent piece, has unfortunately been repeated by many others over the last thirty years. Canadian historians, however expert in their own areas of study, appear to know little about South Africa. None of them mention the fact that apartheid, strictly speaking, did not come into force until 1950. Even a quick look at the predecessor South African legislation, such as the *Native Lands Act* (1913) or the *Natives (Urban Areas) Act* (1923), would show how different both intentions and practice were in the two countries.

34. Canada, *Sessional Papers*, 1893, Report of the Commissioner of the North-West Mounted Police Force 1892, 49.
35. Canada, *Sessional Papers*, 1891, Report of the Commissioner of the North-West Mounted Police Force 1890, "Annual Report of Superintendent R. Burton Deane," 52.
36. BPSC, Steele Diary, May 31 and August 11, 1892.
37. Hugh Dempsey, *Red Crow: Warrior Chief* (Saskatoon: Western Producer Prairie Books, 1980), 191–92.
38. Dempsey, *Red Crow*, 198–200.
39. Hugh Dempsey, *Charcoal's World* (Saskatoon: Western Producer Prairie Books, 1978), 4.
40. This is the substance of Dempsey's book, *Charcoal's World*. It accounts for many of Charcoal's actions but does have some inconsistencies. Dempsey writes that warriors in Charcoal's circumstances would in the past have sought death by attacking against odds. He also notes that Charcoal possessed a religious object called a Bear Knife that was believed to give protection in battle. It is hard to see how his half-hearted attempt to kill Red Crow and shooting the unarmed farm instructor through a window in the dark squares with those beliefs. If Charcoal's overriding motivation was to kill an appropriate victim, why did he not make sure that McNeil was dead?
41. BPSC, Steele Diary, October 17, 1896.
42. *Macleod Gazette*, January 22, 1897. Charcoal Trial, testimony of police interpreter Charles Holloway.
43. BPSC, Steele Diary, November 22, 1896. "Wrote the Comr re Mr Whites letter suggesting all sorts of things re Charcoals trial. Wrote Mackenzie Crown Prosecutor re the speedy trial of Charcoal. He came up to see me and after a talk it was decided to wire the Comr in cipher and press matters re trial."

44. *Macleod Gazette*, January 22, 1897.
45. *Macleod Gazette*, January 22, 1897.
46. BPSC, Steele Diary, January 20–22, 1897.
47. BPSC, Steele Diary, March 16, 1897. "Charcoal hanged at 8:30 was not present. Had made all arrangements for the execution."
48. It eventually became Cominco. Jeremy Mouat, *Roaring Days: Rossland's Mines and the History of British Columbia* (Vancouver: University of British Columbia Press, 1995).
49. My research assistant, Dan Watson, spent several months sifting through the Steele papers to sort out Steele's often tangled business dealings. I am deeply indebted to his clear and comprehensive report.
50. BPSC, 2008.1.1.4.20 (82-23), Empire Claim Partnership Deed 21/06/1893.
51. *Fort Macleod Gazette*, December 11, 1896. The other company officers were: vice-president, R.W. Bryan, superintendent of the Kaslo and Slocan Railway; secretary, David King, publisher of the Kaslo newspaper; superintendent and consulting engineer, William J. Trethewey; solicitor, Chas. W. McAnn, QC.
52. BPSC, Steele to Godsal, April 10, 1907, 2008.1.1.4.18 (82-21).
53. BPSC, Steele Diary, July 10, 1897.
54. BPSC, Steele to Hugh John Macdonald, October 14, 1907, 2008.1.1.4.28 (83-4).
55. BPSC, Steele Diary, July 31, 1897. "Made Fred Steele transfer 45 000 forty five thousand shares Black Diamond Stock in security for money for which he drew upon ___ and ___ applied using it for the Ibex and for the Black Diamond Mines when it really belonged to the Macleod. Meeting of Ibex Co adjourned until its annual meeting. Made rules for the guidance of the company. All cheques to be signed by the treasurer and countersigned by the secretary." Steele often wrote numbers in both forms (numerically and written) in his diaries and letters, presumably to avoid confusion because of the necessity of keeping accurate accounts.
56. BPSC, Steele Diary, January 5, 1898.
57. BPSC, Herchmer to Steele, September 10, 1897.
58. BPSC, Steele Diary, January 28, 1898.

## 7 || The Klondike Gold Rush

1. BPSC, Sam to Marie, January 31, 1898.
2. David Hall, *Clifford Sifton*, vol. 1, *The Young Napoleon, 1861–1900* (Vancouver: University of British Columbia Press, 1981), 186.
3. BPSC, Sam to Marie, February 4, 1898.
4. BPSC, Steele Diary, January 31–February 5, 1898.
5. BPSC, Steele Diary, February 8–9, 1898.
6. BPSC, Sam to Marie, n.d. (probably February 16, 1898).
7. BPSC, Sam to Marie, February 17, 1898.
8. BPSC, Sam to Marie, March 15, 1898.
9. BPSC, Sam to Marie, March 26, 1898.
10. BPSC, Sam to Marie, n.d. (probably mid-March), 1898.
11. BPSC, Sam to Marie, n.d. (probably mid-March), 1898.
12. Walsh to Laurier, September 15, 1896, in Macleod, *North-West Mounted Police and Law Enforcement*, 58–59.
13. BPSC, Sam to Marie, February 17, 1898.
14. BPSC, Sam to Marie, March 20, 1898.
15. BPSC, Sam to Marie, April 4, 1898.
16. BPSC, Sam to Marie, April 4, 1898.
17. BPSC, Sam to Marie, April 29, 1898. "There is no need for them up here—extra expense for nothing."
18. As numerous authors have noted, this action was quite illegal. It is not clear whether Steele realized that this was the case or that, if he did, whether it bothered him. He lost his diary in late February and did not find it again until mid-April. "Diary found all right." BPSC, Steele Diary, April 13, 1898.
19. BPSC, Steele Diary, May 21, 1898.
20. BPSC, Steele Diary, May 18, 1898.
21. BPSC, Sam to Marie, April 17, 1898.
22. BPSC, Steele Diary, May 24, 1898.
23. BPSC, Sam to Marie, April 10, 1898.
24. BPSC, Sam to Marie, April 11, 1898.
25. BPSC, Sam to Marie, May 3, 1898.
26. Hall, *Clifford Sifton*, vol. 1, 223.
27. BPSC, Sam to Marie, April 30, 1898.
28. BPSC, Sam to Marie, July 7, 1898.

29. The best account of Shaw's Yukon visit and the impact of her articles is in Charlotte Gray, *Gold Diggers: Striking It Rich in the Klondike* (Toronto: HarperCollins, 2010).
30. BPSC, Steele Diary, July 20, 1898.
31. BPSC, Sam to Marie, July 25, 1898.
32. BPSC, Sam to Marie, August 9, 1898.
33. BPSC, Sam to Marie, August 20, 1898.
34. BPSC, Sam to Marie, August 4, 1898.
35. BPSC, Steele Diary, August 31, 1898.
36. BPSC, Sam to Marie, September 1, 1898.
37. BPSC, Steele Diary, September 2, 1898.
38. BPSC, Steele Diary, September 7, 1898.
39. BPSC, Sam to Marie, September 7, 1898.
40. BPSC, Sam to Marie, November 16, 1898.
41. BPSC, Sam to Marie, November 25, 1898.
42. BPSC, Sam to Marie, November 1, 1898.
43. BPSC, Sam to Marie, February 5, 1899.
44. Canada, *Sessional Papers*, 1899, vol. 12, no. 15, "Annual Report of Superintendent S.B. Steele," 11.
45. BPSC, Steele Diary, December 17, 1898.
46. BPSC, Sam to Marie, August 20, 1898.
47. Steele, *Forty Years in Canada*, 329.
48. Canada, *Sessional Papers*, 1899, vol. 12, no. 15, "Annual Report of Superintendent S.B. Steele," 19.
49. BPSC, Sam to Marie, May 24, 1899.
50. BPSC, Sam to Marie, July 7, 1899.
51. BPSC, Sam to Marie, July 5, 1899.
52. BPSC, Sam to Marie, July 14, 1899.
53. BPSC, Steele Diary, September 21, 1899.
54. BPSC, Sam to Marie, August 28, 1899.
55. BPSC, Steele Diary, July 25, 1899.
56. BPSC, Sam to Marie, September 7, 1899.
57. BPSC, Steele Diary, September 7, 1899.
58. BPSC, Steele Diary, September 11, 1899.
59. BPSC, Steele Diary, September 29, 1899.

## 8 || Fighting for Queen and Country

1. In the 1890s the small Boer educated class still clung to the use of Dutch, which remained the language of government records.
2. The Xhosa and their northern neighbours, the Zulu, make up about two-thirds of the Black population of South Africa.
3. T.R.H. Davenport and Christopher Saunders, *South Africa: A Modern History*, 5th ed. (London: Macmillan, 2000), chapter 3.
4. John Darwin, *The Empire Project: The Rise and Fall of the British World System, 1830–1970* (Cambridge: Cambridge University Press, 2009), 219.
5. Diana Cammack, *The Rand at War, 1899–1902: The Witwatersrand and the Anglo-Boer War* (London, Berkeley and Pietermaritzburg: James Currey, University of California Press and University of Natal Press, 1990).
6. Leopold Scholtz, *Why the Boers Lost the War* (New York: Palgrave Macmillan, 2005), 16–22. This book, originally published in Afrikaans as *Waarom die boere die oorlog verloor het*, is an excellent study of the planning and operations on both sides. Because the author uses records, correspondence, and unpublished accounts of Smuts, Botha, and other Boer military leaders, and does not rely on much later memoirs, the book has much greater explanatory power than most English-language histories of the South African War.
7. Carman Miller, *Painting the Map Red: Canada and the South African War, 1899–1902* (Montreal and Kingston: Canadian War Museum and McGill-Queen's University Press, 1993), chapter 2.
8. Steele, *Forty Years in Canada*, 338–39.
9. Steele, *Forty Years in Canada*, 339.
10. BPSC, Sam to Marie, January 11, 1900.
11. BPSC, Sam to Marie. "I was not to have been second in Cmd in S.A. in the last corps. Herchmer was to have been put on the Staff and I to take command but that would have caused soreness." The date on this letter is January 1, 1900, but this is certainly wrong. The letter was written from Chapleau, Ontario, on the train west to recruit for Lord Strathcona's Horse, which did not come into existence for another month. Steele's personal diary makes it clear that he was in Ottawa on January 1–4. From internal evidence the date must be January 31.
12. Carman Miller (*Painting the Map Red*, 291) accepts this date, probably because it conforms to the information in The Lord Strathcona's Horse War Diary (hereafter LSH War Diary), but Steele did not start working on the diary until well after the fighting was over and did not finish it until

1906. BPSC, Steele Diary, May 19, 1906: "Signed and mailed diary of Lord Strathcona's Corps." His personal diary recorded at the time seems more likely to be accurate.

13. BPSC, Steele Diary, January 21 and 22, 1900.
14. BPSC, Sam to Marie, January 31, 1900.
15. BPSC, Sam to Marie, February 4, 1900. In spite of his optimism, only thirty-eight of the original Lord Strathcona's Horse were from the NWMP, as opposed to 138 in the CMR. See Miller, *Painting the Map Red*, 295.
16. BPSC, LSH War Diary, February 2, 1900.
17. BPSC, LSH War Diary, February 8, 1900.
18. One of the buglers was Edward McCormick, aged not quite sixteen when he enlisted, the youngest Canadian to serve in the war. McCormick got his mother's written permission, lied about his age and knew very little about playing the bugle. When these facts were discovered on the boat to South Africa, Steele gave him the position of mounted orderly. LAC, Edward McCormick Papers, MG30 E396.
19. With unconscious irony, Steele always misspelled it in his diary and letters as "Vicars-Maxim."
20. BPSC, LSH War Diary, February 10, 1900.
21. BPSC, Steele Diary, March 6, 1900, and LSH War Diary, March 8, 1900.
22. BPSC, Sam to Marie, February n.d. (probably February 16), 1900.
23. BPSC, LSH War Diary, March 4, 1900.
24. Miller, *Painting the Map Red*, 154–55.
25. BPSC, LSH War Diary, March 12, 1900.
26. Douglas Cochrane, 12th Earl of Dundonald, was a prominent British Army officer of the period. Steele would serve under him in South Africa.
27. BPSC, LSH War Diary, March 15, 1900.
28. BPSC, LSH War Diary, March 29, 1900.
29. BPSC, Steele Diary, March 19, and LSH War Diary, March 18 ff. The daily numbers differ slightly in the two diaries. The War Diary figures probably come from veterinary reports.
30. BPSC, Sam to Marie, March 21, 1900.
31. BPSC, Steele Diary, March 22, 1900; BPSC, Sam to Marie, March 26, 1900. Elmes Steele was the son of Sam's older half-brother, Henry Edward Steele. Elmes was promoted to lieutenant in South Africa and acted as the regiment's paymaster.
32. LAC, NWMP Personnel Records 1873–1904, #58432, Elmes John Steele, Regt No. 3093. Served 1894–1897.

33. BPSC, Sam to Marie, March 9(?), 1900. "Elmes is splendid doing excellent work, and the corps is getting into good shape."
34. BPSC, Steele Diary, March 26, 1900.
35. BPSC, Steele Diary, April 3 and 4, 1900.
36. BPSC, Sam to Marie, March 26, 1900.
37. BPSC, Sam to Marie, April 1, 1900.
38. BPSC, Sam to Marie, April 10, 1900.
39. BPSC, Sam to Marie, May 1, 1900.
40. BPSC, LSH War Diary, April 14. 1900.
41. BPSC, LSH War Diary, April 23, 1900.
42. BPSC, LSH War Diary, April 19, 1900.
43. BPSC, Sam to Marie, April 26, 1900.
44. BPSC, Sam to Marie, May 6, 1900.
45. Scholtz, *Why the Boers Lost*, 95.
46. BPSC, Steele Diary, April 27, 1900.
47. BPSC, Steele Diary, April 30, 1900.
48. BPSC, Sam to Marie, May 11, 1900.
49. BPSC, LSH War Diary, May 20, 1900.
50. BPSC, LSH War Diary, June 3, 1900.
51. Brian Inglis, *Roger Casement* (London: Hodder and Stoughton, 1973), 52.
52. Thomas Pakenham, *The Boer War* (New York: Random House, 1979), provides the most sympathetic, and to my mind, convincing, view of Buller. Scholtz, *Why the Boers Lost*, is much less inclined to take account of Buller's difficulties.
53. BPSC, Steele Diary, June 7, 1900. Carman Miller states that Steele lobbied to revive the project and Roberts agreed (*Painting the Map Red*, 311). From the LSH War Diary, the only source available to Miller, it would be easy to reach that conclusion. This is another instance of Steele adjusting the narrative in light of later developments—in this case a later discovery that the bridge had not been reinforced. Steele's personal diary written at the time shows no communication with Roberts prior to receiving the orders to revive the plan. A letter written to Marie at the time is even more explicit. "I got to Durban, landed and delayed there by Gen Bullers desire to get us but Lord Roberts insisted upon it and we have to go ahead." BPSC, Sam to Marie, June 8, 1900. Steele was happy enough to proceed with the raid, but a regimental commander presuming to advise a Field Marshall on strategy would never have occurred even to someone as self-assured as Steele.

54. BPSC, Steele Diary, June 12, 1900.
55. BPSC, Sam to Marie, June 23, 1900.
56. BPSC, Sam to Marie, June 17, 1900.
57. BPSC, Steele Diary, June 27, 1900. "The extension and patrolling was done badly by C Squadron Howards fault Several officers did very well but on the whole the connections were badly kept I got a report from Major Belcher who was in cmd and sent to brigade ____ I also got one from him to send to the officers in chg and all present. Put in orders my objections to the way the work was done. Reduced a Sergt Morrison(?) for damaging the property of a farmer and for insubordinate language to Sgt Brothers who is a first class N.C.O."
58. BPSC, Sam to Marie, July 3, 1900.
59. BPSC, Steel Diary, July 5, 1900.
60. Sandra Gwyn, *The Private Capital: Ambition and Love in the Age of Macdonald and Laurier* (Toronto: McClelland and Stewart, 1984), 350–51.
61. BPSC, Sam to Marie, July 3, 1900.
62. Patton used several similar versions of this quote in addresses to his 3rd Army in England in 1943 and 1944. https:quoteinvestigator.com/2015/04/24/war/.
63. BPSC, Marie to Sam, October 18, 1900.
64. These charges are retailed in Gwyn, *The Private Capital*, chapter 24. They are entirely unsubstantiated and so at odds with all the other evidence about Steele that they have to be dismissed.
65. BPSC, Steele Diary, July 11, 1900.
66. BPSC, Steele Diary, August 11, 1900.
67. LAC, Robert Percy Rooke Papers, MG30 E357.
68. Morant and several other members of an Australian unit called the Bushveld Carbineers were tried by court martial for the killing of twenty Afrikaner civilians and found guilty of twelve. He and Lieutenant Peter Handcock were executed by firing squad. The incident is the basis of the 1980 film *Breaker Morant*.
69. Miller, *Painting the Map Red*, 323–24. Miller gives more credence to the report than I am prepared to do. He quotes Rooke but omits the first part of the sentence beginning the account: "An incident occurred, *or was reliably reported to have occurred*" (my emphasis). LAC, Robert Percy Rooke Papers. The rest of Rooke's narrative consists of actions that he personally witnessed. He gives no indication about when he heard the story or what the source was.

70. Gwyn, *The Private Capital*, 363.
71. BPSC, LSH War Diary, August 26, 1900.
72. BPSC, Steele Diary, August 27, 1900.
73. Scholtz, *Why the Boers Lost*, 85.
74. Pakenham, *The Boer War*, 484.
75. BPSC, Sam to Marie, September 3, 1900.
76. BPSC, Steele Diary, September 1, 1900.
77. BPSC, Sam to Marie, September 3, 1900.
78. BPSC, LSH War Diary, September 1, 1900.
79. BPSC, LSH War Diary, September 2, 1900.
80. BPSC, Sam to Marie, September 12, 1900.
81. BPSC, LSH War Diary, September 3, 1900.
82. BPSC, Steele Diary, September 6, 1900.
83. BPSC, LSH War Diary, September 10, 1900.
84. BPSC, LSH War Diary, October 6, 1900.
85. Pakenham, *The Boer War*, 484–85.
86. BPSC, Steele Diary, October 9, 1900.
87. BPSC, Sam to Marie, October 16, 1900.
88. BPSC, Sam to Marie, October 29, 1900.
89. BPSC, Steele Diary, October 22, 1900.
90. BPSC, LSH War Diary, October 25, 1900.
91. BPSC, Sam to Marie, November 4, 1900.
92. BPSC, Steele Diary, November 15–26, 1900.
93. Peter Warwick, *Black People and the South African War 1899–1902* (Cambridge: Cambridge University Press, 1983), 145; Bill Nasson, *Abraham Esau's War: A Black South African War in the Cape, 1899–1902* (Cambridge: Cambridge University Press, 1991), 179.
94. BPSC, LSH War Diary, November 27, 1900.
95. BPSC, LSH War Diary, December 7, 1900.
96. BPSC, LSH War Diary, December 7, 1900.
97. BPSC, LSH War Diary, December 21, 1900.
98. BPSC, LSH War Diary, January 9, 1901.
99. BPSC, Sam to Marie, January 26, 1901. Scholtz agrees with this assessment, pointing out that although the total British forces outnumbered the Boers by more than ten to one, they only had a third as many mounted men (*Why the Boers Lost*, 88).
100. BPSC, LSH War Diary, January 18, 1901.
101. BPSC, LSH War Diary, February 4, 1901.

102. BPSC, Sam to Marie, February 16, 1901.
103. BPSC, LSH War Diary, February 18, 1901.
104. *Montreal Gazette*, March 9, 1901.

## 9 || Imperial Interlude

1. BPSC, Sam to Marie, June 27, 1900.
2. BPSC, Marie to Sam, May 13, 1900.
3. BPSC, Sam to Marie, June 27, 1900.
4. BPSC, Sam to Marie, August 1, 1900.
5. BPSC, Sam to Marie, August 20, 1900. Steele and Perry had never served together, so there was no personal animosity, just wounded pride and frustrated ambition. Perry proved to be a highly successful commissioner, serving until 1923 and, with the creation of the Royal Canadian Mounted Police in 1919, starting the transformation to a national police force.
6. Leopold Scholtz, *Why the Boers Lost the War* (London: Palgrave Macmillan, 2005), 29; earlier works give considerably smaller numbers, e.g., Leonard Thompson, *The Unification of South Africa 1902–1910* (London: Oxford University Press, 1960), 12, says 21,200.
7. David E. Torrance, *The Strange Death of the Liberal Empire: Lord Selborne in South Africa* (Montreal and Kingston: McGill-Queen's University Press, 1996), 7.
8. Carman Miller, *Painting the Map Red: Canada and the South African War, 1899–1902* (Montreal and Kingston: McGill-Queen's University Press, 1993), 368.
9. National Army Museum (UK), Baden-Powell Papers, South African Constabulary Staff Diary, October 27, 1900.
10. BPSC, Sam to Marie, October 3, 1900. "Major General Baden Powell asked Col Biggar if I could be induced to stay in South Africa."
11. BPSC, Steele Diary, October 19, 1900.
12. BPSC, Sam to Marie, November 19, 1900.
13. BPSC, Steele Diary, November 18, 1900.
14. BPSC, Steele Diary, April 6 and 7, 1900.
15. Miller, *Painting the Map Red*, 370.
16. Miller, *Painting the Map Red*, 373. Fall apparently borrowed money from his troopers in South Africa and failed to repay it.
17. BPSC, Sam to Marie, March 16, 1901.
18. *Montreal Gazette*, March 12, 1901.
19. BPSC, Steele Diary, April 12, 1901.

20. LAC, NWMP Records, S.B. Steele File, Privy Council Order 1255, June 6, 1901.
21. BPSC, Steele Diary, April 11, 1901.
22. BPSC, Sam to Marie, March 19, 1901.
23. BPSC, Steele Diary, June 8, 1901.
24. BPSC, Marie to Sam, June 18, 1901.
25. BPSC, Sam to Marie, June 29, 1901.
26. BPSC, Steele Diary, July 23, 1901.
27. BPSC, Steele Diary, August 6, 1901.
28. BPSC, Sam to Marie, August 9, 1901.
29. BPSC, Sam to Marie, August 10, 1901.
30. Jim Wallace, *No Colours, No Drums: Canadians in the South African Constabulary* (n.p.: Bunker to Bunker Books, 2003), 241.
31. BPSC, Steele Diary, August 27, 1901.
32. BPSC, Sam to Marie, August 24, 1901.
33. BPSC, Sam to Marie, September 2, 1901.
34. The original house, restored with some later additions, including Kruger's private railway car, is now the Kruger Museum, 60 WK Nkomo Street, Pretoria.
35. BPSC, Sam to Marie, October 7, 1901.
36. BPSC, Sam to Marie, December 4, 1901.
37. BPSC, Sam to Marie, December 15, 1901. This was the original date of writing, but the incident occurred December 20 and the second half of the letter continues on that date.
38. BPSC, Sam to Marie, January 9, 1902.
39. BPSC, Sam to Marie, April 6, 1902.
40. BPSC, Sam to Marie, February 2, 1902.
41. BPSC, Sam to Marie, February 15, 1902.
42. BPSC, Sam to Marie, April 20, 1902.
43. BPSC, Sam to Marie, March 15, 1902.
44. BPSC, Sam to Marie, April 12, 1902.
45. L.M. Thompson, *The Unification of South Africa 1902–1910* (Oxford: Oxford University Press, 1960), 12.
46. BPSC, Sam to Marie, May 24, 1902.
47. BPSC, Sam to Marie, July 3, 1902.
48. Donald Denoon, *A Grand Illusion: The Failure of Imperial Policy in the Transvaal Colony during the Period of Reconstruction 1900–1905* (London: Longman Group, 1973), chapter 3.

49. Kitchener reported arming 10,053 Black auxiliaries. Bill Nasson believes there were many more and that Kitchener deliberately underreported the numbers to avoid alarming the white population of the Cape Colony. Bill Nasson, *Abraham Esau's War: A Black South African War in the Cape, 1899–1902* (Cambridge: Cambridge University Press, 1991), 22.
50. Thompson, *Unification of South Africa*, 6.
51. Thompson, *Unification of South Africa*, 386.
52. BPSC, Sam to Marie, February 9, 1902.
53. BPSC, Steele SAC Notebook, October 28, 1905.
54. Denoon, *A Grand Illusion*, chapter 3.
55. Wallace, *No Colours, No Drums*, 209.
56. BPSC, Sam to Marie, June 15, 1902.
57. Diana Cammack, *The Rand at War, 1899–1902: The Witwatersrand and the Anglo-Boer War* (James Currey, London: University of California Press and University of Natal Press), 204.
58. BPSC, Steele Diary, May 15, 1906; Wallace, *No Colours, No Drums*, 252–54.
59. See Torrance, *Strange Death of the Liberal Empire*.
60. BPSC, Sam to Marie, January 15, 1902.
61. BPSC, Sam to Marie, April 6, 1902.
62. BPSC, Sam to Marie, February 21, 1902.
63. BPSC, Sam to Marie, March 15, 1902.
64. BPSC, Steele Diary, January 8, 1906.
65. BPSC, Steele Diary, January 24, 1906.
66. BPSC, Steele Diary, September 19, 1906.
67. BPSC, Steele Diary, May 24, 1906.
68. BPSC, Steele Diary, September 17, 1906.
69. BPSC, Steele Diary, October 14, 1906.
70. BPSC, Sam to Marie, February 2, 1902. Jay Luvaas, *The Education of an Army: British Military Thought, 1815–1940* (London: Cassel, 1965), chapter 7, considers Henderson the most talented British military writer of the period. He was starting on a history of the war in South Africa when complications from malaria forced him to go to Egypt to try to restore his health. He died there in March 1903.
71. BPSC, Steele Diary, November 2, 1906.
72. BPSC, Steele Diary, January 16, 1907.
73. BPSC, Steele Diary, January 15, 1907.
74. BPSC, Steele Diary, February 6, 11, and 15, 1907.
75. BPSC, Steele Diary, April 19, 1907.

76. BPSC, Steele Diary, April 26, 1907.
77. BPSC, Steele Diary, May 25, 1907.

**10 ‖ Preparing for War**

1. BPSC, Steele Diary, June 8, 1907.
2. BPSC, Steele Diary, June 21, 1907. Grey was a friend of Lord Selborne, who wrote to him praising Steele.
3. BPSC, Sam to Marie, July 9, 1907.
4. BPSC, Sam to Marie, June 28, 1907.
5. J.L. Granatstein, *Canada's Army: Waging War and Keeping the Peace* (Toronto: University of Toronto Press, 2002), 45.
6. Canada, *Sessional Papers*, 1907–8 No. 35, "Annual Report of the Militia Council," 1.
7. Canada, *Sessional Papers*, 1907–8 No. 35, "Annual Report of the Militia Council," 10.
8. BPSC, Steele Diary, August 10, 1907.
9. BPSC, Sam to Marie, July 13, 1907.
10. BPSC, Steele Diary, August 8, 1907.
11. BPSC, Sam to Marie, July 8, 1907.
12. BPSC, Sam to Marie, July 15, 1907.
13. The address was 1531 – 1st St. W.
14. BPSC, Steele Diary, October 3, 1907.
15. BPSC, Steele Diary, May 10, 1907, and BPSC, Steele to Godsal, May 10, 1907, 2008.1.1.4.18 (82-21).
16. BPSC, Steele Diary, February 18, 1908.
17. *Calgary Daily Herald*, August 3, 1908.
18. BPSC, Steele Diary, August 7, 1908.
19. BPSC, Sam to Marie, August 31, 1908.
20. BPSC, Sam to Marie, August 14, 1908.
21. BPSC, Sam to Marie, August 28, 1908.
22. BPSC, Sam to Marie, September 15, 1908, enclosing letter from Brigadier Macdonald dated September 10, 1908.
23. BPSC, Sam to Marie, September 18, 1908.
24. BPSC, Steele Diary, December 1, 1908.
25. BPSC, Steele Diary, December 9, 1908.
26. BPSC, Steele Diary, February 1, 1909.
27. BPSC, Sam to Marie, February 5, 1909.
28. BPSC, Steele Diary, March 13, 1909.

29. BPSC, Sam to Marie, January 29, 1909. In the letter he gives Roberts's title as *Forty Years in India*.
30. Many of those diaries can be found in the Steele Collection at Bruce Peel Special Collections, University of Alberta.
31. BPSC, Steele Diary, June 10, 1909.
32. BPSC, Steele Diary, June 4, 1909.
33. Desmond Morton, "'Aid to the Civil Power:' The Canadian Militia in Support of Social Order, 1867–1914," *Canadian Historical Review* (December 1970).
34. BPSC, Steele Diary, August 12, 1909.
35. BPSC, Steele Diary, August 12, 1909.
36. Morton, "Aid to the Civil Power."
37. BPSC, Steele Diary, August 24, 1909, notes messages of congratulation from the Militia Council and the CPR vice-president.
38. BPSC, Steele Diary, September 28, 1909.
39. BPSC, Steele Diary, November 22, 1909.
40. BPSC, Steele Diary, October 16, 1909.
41. BPSC, Steele Diary, October 31, 1909.
42. BPSC, Steele Diary, March 9, 1909.
43. A.C. Macdonell was no relation of Steele's friend, Superintendent A.R. Macdonell.
44. BPSC, Steele Diary, March 18, 1910.
45. BPSC, Steele Diary, August 12, 1910.
46. BPSC, Steele Diary, March 7, 1911.
47. BPSC, Steele Diary, March 16, 1912.
48. BPSC, Steele Diary, April 25, 1910.
49. BPSC, Steele Diary, May 15, 1910.
50. BPSC, Steele Diary, July 26, 1911. This was at the time of the Agadir crisis in North Africa that threatened war between Germany and Britain's ally, France.
51. BPSC, Steele Diary, August 19, 1911.
52. BPSC, Steele Diary, September 22, 1911.
53. BPSC, Steele Diary, November 1, 1911.
54. "Pasadena Apartments," www.historicplaces.ca.
55. BPSC, Steele Diary, April 4, 1914.
56. BPSC, Steele Diary, August 15, 1911.
57. BPSC, Steele Diary, May 11, 1912.
58. BPSC, Steele Diary, December 15, 1912.

59. BPSC, Steele Diary, January 10, 1913.
60. BPSC, Steele Diary, May 19, 1914.
61. BPSC, Steele Diary, February 11, 1914.
62. BPSC, Steele Diary, May 22, 1913.
63. BPSC, Steele Diary, May 27, 1913.
64. BPSC, Steele Diary, May 31, 1913.
65. BPSC, Steele Diary, June 28, 1913.
66. BPSC, Steele Diary, April 21, 1913.
67. The best short account is Hew Strachan, *The First World War*, vol. 1, *To Arms* (Oxford: Oxford University Press, 2001), chapter 2, "Willingly to War."
68. See Mark Howard Moss, *Manliness and Militarism: Educating Young Boys in Ontario for War* (2001: Toronto: University of Toronto Press, 2015).
69. BPSC, Steele Diary, April 4, 1910.
70. BPSC, Steele Diary, June 15, 1912.
71. BPSC, Steele Diary, September 18, 1913.
72. BPSC, Steele Diary, April 14, 1914.
73. BPSC, Steele Diary, May 5, 1914.
74. BPSC, Steele Diary, July 6, 1914.
75. BPSC, Steele Diary, July 27, 1914.
76. BPSC, Steele Diary, August 4, 1914.
77. Granatstein, *Canada's Army*, is representative of the majority view. Ronald G. Haycock, *Sam Hughes: The Public Career of a Controversial Canadian, 1885–1916* (Waterloo, ON: Wilfrid Laurier University Press, 1986) is, not surprisingly, sympathetic to Hughes. Tim Cook, *At the Sharp End: Canadians Fighting the Great War, 1914–1916* (Toronto: Penguin, 2007), 33, calls the mobilization "surprisingly effective."
78. BPSC, Steele Diary, August 24, 1914.
79. BPSC, Steele Diary, August 18, 1914.
80. BPSC, Steele Diary, August 28, 1914.
81. BPSC, Steele Diary, September 21, 1914.
82. One of the leading possibilities was F.-L. Lessard, who had also commanded Canadian soldiers in South Africa. See John Macfarlane, "The Right Stuff? Evaluating the Performance of Lieutenant-Colonel F.-L. Lessard in South Africa and his Failure to Receive a Senior Command Position with the CEF in 1914," *Canadian Military History* 8, no. 3 (1999).
83. BPSC, Steele Diary, October 24, 1914.
84. BPSC, Steele Diary, December 5, 1914.
85. BPSC, Steele Diary, December 22, 1914.

86. BPSC, Steele Diary, December 13-20, 1914.
87. BPSC, Steele Diary, January 6, 1915.
88. BPSC, Steele Diary, January 18, 1915.
89. BPSC, Steele Diary, February 24, 1915.
90. BPSC, Steele Diary, March 10, 1915.

## 11 || An Old Soldier Fades Away

1. BPSC, Steele Diary, April 7, 1915.
2. G.W.L. Nicholson, *Official History of the Canadian Army in the First World War: Canadian Expeditionary Force, 1914-1919* (Ottawa: Queen's Printer, 1962), 112.
3. BPSC, Steele Diary, April 17, 1915.
4. BPSC, Steele Diary, April 30, 1915.
5. BPSC, Steele Diary, May 5, 1915.
6. BPSC, Steele Diary, May 14, 1915.
7. BPSC, Steele Diary, May 26, 1915.
8. The best account of the Canadian experience at this stage of the war, and one of the best on any army during the First World War is Tim Cook, *At the Sharp End*.
9. BPSC, Steele Diary, July 1, 1915.
10. Cook, *At the Sharp End*, 117-18.
11. BPSC, Steele Diary, July 26, 1915.
12. BPSC, Steele Diary, July 28, 1915.
13. BPSC, Steele Diary, August 4, 1915.
14. BPSC, Steele Diary, August 17, 1915.
15. Desmond Morton, *A Peculiar Kind of Politics: Canada's Overseas Ministry in the First World War* (Toronto: University of Toronto Press, 1982), 48.
16. BPSC, Steele Diary, August 29, 1915.
17. BPSC, Steele Diary, October 19, 1915.
18. BPSC, Steele Diary, October 5, 1915.
19. BPSC, Steele Diary, September 9, 1915.
20. BPSC, Steele Diary, December 1, 1915.
21. BPSC, Steele Diary, December 28, 1915.
22. Haycock, *Sam Hughes*, 259.
23. BPSC, Steele Diary, September 28, 1915.
24. BPSC, Steele Diary, October 25, 1915.
25. BPSC, Steele Diary, October 28, 1915.
26. BPSC, Steele Diary, December 18, 1915.

27. BPSC, Steele Diary, August 8, 1915.
28. BPSC, Steele Diary, April 21, 1916.
29. BPSC, Steele Diary, December 30, 1915.
30. BPSC, Steele Diary, January 5, 1916.
31. BPSC, Steele Diary, January 18, 1916.
32. BPSC, Steele Diary, April 28, 1916.
33. Morton, *A Peculiar Kind of Politics*, 68.
34. BPSC, Steele Diary, March 22, 1916.
35. BPSC, Steele Diary, June 6, 1916. Byng's biographer, Jeffery Williams, quotes him as writing to a friend on the appointment, "Why am I sent to the Canadians? I don't know a Canadian." See Jeffery Williams, *Byng of Vimy: General and Governor General* (London: Leo Cooper, 1983), 115. This is a very curious comment because he clearly knew Steele well, since they fought side by side in South Africa and dined together on several occasions, but that has not prevented every Canadian historian who has written on Byng's time commanding the Canadian Corps from repeating the quote as if it was fact, most recently by Tim Cook, *Vimy: The Battle and the Legend* (Toronto: Allen Lane, 2017), chapter 2.
36. Morton, *A Peculiar Kind of Politics*, 70.
37. BPSC, Steele Diary, August 17, 1916.
38. BPSC, Steele Diary, September 5, 1916.
39. BPSC, Steele Diary, September 20, 1916.
40. Haycock, *Sam Hughes*, 307.
41. BPSC, Steele Diary, November 3, 1916.
42. BPSC, Steele Diary, June 11, 1916.
43. BPSC, Steele Diary, April 16, 1917.
44. BPSC, Steele Diary, March 12, 1916.
45. BPSC, Steele Diary, August 6, 1916.
46. BPSC, Steele Diary, December 30, 1916.
47. BPSC, Steele Diary, June 24, 1916.
48. William Stewart, "Frustrated Belligerence: The Unhappy History of the 5th Canadian Division in the First World War," *Canadian Military History* (Spring 2013): 32.
49. BPSC, Steele Diary, July 10, 1916.
50. BPSC, Steele Diary, August 25, 1916.
51. BPSC, Steele Diary, August 31, 1916.
52. BPSC, Steele Diary, August 19, 1916.
53. BPSC, Steele Diary, August 26, 1916.

54. BPSC, Steele Diary, November 5, 1916.
55. BPSC, Steele Diary, November 15, 1916.
56. Morton, *A Peculiar Kind of Politics*, 98.
57. Morton, *A Peculiar Kind of Politics*, 98.
58. BPSC, Steele Diary, January 9, 1917.
59. BPSC, Steele Diary, January 31, 1917.
60. Morton, *A Peculiar Kind of Politics*, 100–103.
61. BPSC, Steele Diary, January 14, 1917.
62. BPSC, Steele Diary, March 9, 1917.
63. BPSC, Steele Diary, March 28, 1917.
64. BPSC, Steele Diary, April 27, 1917.
65. BPSC, Steele Diary, March 19 and June 28, 1917.
66. BPSC, Steele Diary, September 2, 1917.
67. BPSC, Steele Diary, June 3, 1917.
68. See Bill Rawling, *Surviving Trench Warfare: Technology and the Canadian Corps, 1914–1918*, 2nd ed. (Toronto: University of Toronto Press, 2014), 7.
69. Kenneth Radley, *We Lead, Others Follow: First Canadian Division 1914–1918* (St. Catharines, ON: Vanwell Publishing, 2006). "In *We Lead, Others Follow*, I attributed Canadian fighting effectiveness to sound command, good staff work and excellent training. My opinion has not changed." Kenneth Radley, *Get Tough, Stay Tough: Shaping the Canadian Corps, 1914–1918*, Wolverhampton Military Studies No. 4 (Birmingham, UK: Helion and Company, 2014), xvii.
70. BPSC, Steele Diary, June 8, 1917.
71. BPSC, Steele Diary, June 13, 1917.
72. BPSC, Steele Diary, June 21, 1917.
73. Morton, *A Peculiar Kind of Politics*, 123.
74. BPSC, Steele Diary, July 14, 1917.
75. BPSC, Steele Diary, October 9, 1917.
76. BPSC, Steele Diary, October 13, 1917.
77. BPSC, Steele Diary, November 13, 1917.
78. BPSC, Steele Diary, November 29, 1917.
79. BPSC, Steele Diary, December 16, 1917.
80. BPSC, Steele Diary, January 8, 1918. Macdonald was the son of the former prime minister, Sir John A. Macdonald.
81. BPSC, Steele Diary, January 8, 1918.
82. BPSC, Steele Diary, January 14, 1918.
83. BPSC, Steele Diary, February 5, 1918.

84. BPSC, Steele Diary, February 8, 1918.
85. William Perkins Bull, *From Rattlesnake Hunt to Hockey: The History of Sports in Canada and of the Sportsmen of Peel, 1798 to 1934* (Toronto: G.J. McLeod Ltd., 1934). William Perkins Bull Historical Series—Peel Information Network www.Pinet.on.ca.
86. BPSC, Steele Diary, February 26, 1918.
87. BPSC, Steele Diary, March 2, 1918.
88. BPSC, Steele Diary, March 9, 1918.
89. BPSC, Steele Diary, June 24, 1918.
90. BPSC, Steele Diary, July 7, 1918.
91. BPSC, Steele Diary, July 9, 1918.
92. BPSC, Steele Diary, August 28, 1918.
93. BPSC, Steele Diary, September 23, 1918.
94. BPSC, Steele Diary, October 23, 1918.
95. BPSC, Steele Diary, November 11, 1918.
96. BPSC, Steele Diary, November 30, 1918.
97. "Impressive Official Funeral is Accorded Soldier and Pioneer," *Winnipeg Free Press*, July 4, 1919. The previous day, Russell-Lang's Bookstore ran a prominent ad announcing that they had plenty of copies of *Forty Years in Canada* for sale. The book had not been available before Steele left in 1915, but he had signed autograph sheets which would be included in each purchase.
98. Glenbow Archives, Sam Steele Fonds, Harwood Steele to Eric L. Harvie, June 6, 1966.

## Epilogue

1. Harwood Steele, *The Canadians in France* (London: T.F. Unwin, 1920).
2. *Spirit of Iron (Manitou-Pewabic): An Authentic Novel of the North-West Mounted Police* (Toronto: McClelland and Stewart, 1923); *I Shall Arise* (London: Hodder and Stoughton, 1926); *The Ninth Circle* (New York, A.L. Burt, 1927).
3. Harwood Steele, *Policing the Arctic: The Story of the Conquest of the Arctic by the Royal Canadian (Formerly North-West) Mounted Police* (London: Jarrold's Publishing, 1936).
4. Harwood Steele, *To Effect an Arrest: Adventures of the Royal Canadian Mounted Police* (Toronto: Ryerson Press, 1947).
5. Harwood Steele, *The Marching Call* (London: Thomas Nelson, 1956).

# Bibliography

## Primary Sources

**BRUCE PEEL SPECIAL COLLECTIONS**

The Sir Samuel Steele Collection housed in Bruce Peel Special Collections at the University of Alberta is by far the most important source for Sam Steele's life. It contains his personal diaries for the years from 1885 until his death in 1919, except for 1887. Steele's correspondence in the collection is extraordinary. In addition to his business correspondence as a mounted policeman and an army officer, he wrote constantly to family and friends, sometimes as many as twenty letters a day. Once he met and married Marie Harwood, the letters between them, all of which seem to have survived, become the most important part of the archive, often providing more detail than the diaries and providing Steele with an outlet to express his emotions and opinions on social and political topics. The archive also contains official correspondence and reports, diaries of friends and associates that he collected while writing *Forty Years in Canada*, drafts of the memoir, and thousands of photographs.

**GLENBOW ARCHIVES**

The Sam Steele Fonds at the Glenbow Archives holds a small collection of Steele's papers, including some banking records from his time in Fort Macleod.

LIBRARY AND ARCHIVES CANADA

The Records of the North-West Mounted Police (RG-18) at Library and Archives Canada are a major source for Steele's life and career. The Comptroller's Office Official Correspondence Series is important because it deals with government policy decisions relating to the police and Steele's monthly reports as a divisional commanding officer. The comptroller, Fred White, was also a personal friend of Steele. The personnel records (available online at https://www.bac-lac.gc.ca/eng/discover/nwmp-personnel-records/Pages/north-west-mounted-police.aspx) are indispensable not only for Steele, but for the other members of the Force with whom he interacted. Steele's personnel file runs to several hundred pages.

Robert Percy Rooke Papers, (MG30 E357)
Governor General Sir John Douglas Sutherland Campbell, Marquis of Lorne Fonds
Sir John A. Macdonald Papers
Edward McCormick Papers, (MG30 E396)

NATIONAL ARMY MUSEUM (UK)

Baden-Powell Papers

SESSIONAL PAPERS OF CANADA

The Annual Reports of the Commissioner of the NWMP contain the yearly reports of divisional commanders. They are to be found in Canada, Parliament, *Sessional Papers* (House of Commons) for the years from 1876 until Steele left the NWMP. The report for 1875 was not printed at the time but was published a century later by the official historian of the RCMP: S.W. Horrall, A *Chronicle of the Canadian West: North-West Mounted Police Report for 1875* (Calgary: Historical Society of Alberta, 1975).

NEWSPAPERS

*Calgary Herald*
*Edmonton Bulletin*
*Fort Macleod Gazette*
*Montreal Gazette*
*Regina Leader*
*Saskatchewan Herald*
*Winnipeg Free Press*

## Secondary Sources

Adelman, Jeremy, and Stephen Aron. 1999. "From Borderlands to Borders: Empires, Nation-States, and the Peoples in Between in North American History," *American Historical Review* (June).

Affleck, Edward Lloyd. 1973. *Sternwheelers, Sandbars and Switchbacks: A Chronicle of Steam Transportation in the British Columbia Waterways of the Columbia River System 1865 to 1965*. Vancouver: Alexander Nicholls Press.

Barron, F. Laurie. 1988. "The Indian Pass System in the Canadian West, 1882–1935," *Prairie Forum* 13, no. 1 (Spring).

Beahen, William, and Stan Horrall. 1998. *Red Coats on the Prairies: The North-West Mounted Police 1886–1900*. Regina: Centax Books.

Beal, Bob, and Rod Macleod. 1996. *Prairie Fire: The 1885 North-West Rebellion*. Toronto: McClelland and Stewart.

Beal, R.F., J.E. Foster, and Louise Zuk. 1987. *The Métis Hivernement Settlement at Buffalo Lake, 1872–1877: An Historical Report*. Edmonton: Alberta Department of Culture, Historic Sites and Provincial Museums Division.

Beasley, Thomas F. 1989. "The 1909 Freight Handlers' Strike: Col. Sam Steele Searches Strikers for Guns," Thunder Bay Historical Museum Society, *Papers and Records* 17.

Binnema, Theodore. 2004. *Common and Contested Ground: A Human and Environmental History of the Northwestern Plains*. Toronto: University of Toronto Press.

Buckley, Helen. 1992. *From Wooden Plows to Welfare: Why Indian Policy Failed in the Prairie Provinces*. Montreal and Kingston: McGill-Queen's University Press.

Bull, William Perkins. 1934. *From Rattlesnake Hunt to Hockey: The History of Sports in Canada and of the Sportsmen of Peel 1798 to 1934*. Toronto: G.J. McLeod Ltd.

Butler, William Francis. 1872. *The Great Lone Land: A Narrative of Travel and Adventure in the North-West of America*. London: Sampson Low, Marston, Low and Searle.

Cammack, Diana. 1990. *The Rand at War, 1899–1902: The Witwatersrand and the Anglo-Boer War*. London, Berkeley, and Pietermaritzburg: James Currey, University of California Press and University of Natal Press.

Carter, Sarah. 1990. *Lost Harvests: Prairie Indian Reserve Farmers and Government Policy*. Montreal and Kingston: McGill-Queen's University Press.

Clarke, Brian. 2007. "Religious Riot as Pastime: Orange Young Britons, Parades and Public Life in Victorian Toronto." In *The Orange Order in Canada*, edited by David A. Wilson. Dublin: Four Courts Press.

Cook, Tim. 2007. *At the Sharp End: Canadians Fighting the Great War 1914–1916.* Toronto: Penguin.

———. 2008. *Shock Troops: Canadians Fighting in the Great War 1917–1918.* Toronto: Penguin.

———. 2017. *Vimy: The Battle and the Legend.* Toronto: Allen Lane.

Cozzens, Peter. 2016. *The Earth is Weeping: The Epic Story of the Indian Wars for the American West.* New York: Alfred A. Knopf.

Darwin, John. 2009. *The Empire Project: The Rise and Fall of the British World-System 1830–1970.* Cambridge: Cambridge University Press.

Daschuk, James. 2013. *Clearing the Plains: Disease, Politics of Starvation, and the Loss of Aboriginal Life.* Regina: University of Regina Press.

Davenport, T.R.H., and Christopher Saunders. 2000. *South Africa: A Modern History.* 5th ed. London: Macmillan.

Deane, R. Burton. 1916. *Mounted Police Life in Canada: A Record of Thirty-One Years' Service.* London: Cassel.

Dempsey, Hugh A. 1972. *Crowfoot: Chief of the Blackfeet.* Norman: University of Oklahoma Press.

———. 1979. *Charcoal's World: The True Story of a Canadian Indian's Last Stand.* Saskatoon: Western Producer Prairie Books.

———. 1981. *Red Crow, Warrior Chief.* Saskatoon: Western Producer Prairie Books.

Denoon, Donald. 1973. *A Grand Illusion: The Failure of Imperial Policy in the Transvaal Colony during the Period of Reconstruction 1900–1905.* London: Longman Group.

Fisher, Robin. n.d. "Isadore," *Dictionary of Canadian Biography,* vol. XII.

Flanagan, Thomas. 1996. *Louis "David" Riel: Prophet of the New World.* Toronto: University of Toronto Press.

Foster, John. 1992. "The Metis and the End of the Plains Buffalo in Alberta." In *Buffalo,* edited by John Foster, Dick Harrison, and I.S. MacLaren. Edmonton: University of Alberta Press.

Gavigan, Shelley A.M. 2012. *Hunger, Horses, and Government Men: Criminal Law on the Aboriginal Plains, 1870–1905.* Vancouver: University of British Columbia Press and The Osgoode Society for Canadian Legal History.

Gluek, Alvin. 1965. *Minnesota and the Manifest Destiny of the Canadian Northwest: A Study in Canadian-American Relations.* Toronto: University of Toronto Press.

Goldring, Philip. 1979. "Whisky, Horses and Death: The Cypress Hills Massacre and its Sequel." *Canadian Historic Sites: Occasional Papers in Archaeology and*

History No. 21. Ottawa: National Historic Parks and Sites Branch, Parks Canada.

Granatstein, J.L. 2002. *Canada's Army: Waging War and Keeping the Peace*. Toronto: University of Toronto Press.

Gray, Charlotte. 2010. *Gold Diggers: Striking It Rich in the Klondike*. Toronto: HarperCollins.

———. 2016. *The Promise of Canada: 150 Years–People and Ideas That Have Shaped Our Country*. Toronto: Simon and Schuster Canada.

Graybill, Andrew R. 2007. *Policing the Great Plains: Rangers, Mounties, and the North American Frontier, 1875–1910*. Lincoln: University of Nebraska Press.

Gresko, Jacqueline. n.d. "Paul Durieu," *Dictionary of Canadian Biography*, vol. XII.

Gwyn, Sandra. 1984. *The Private Capital: Ambition and Love in the Age of Macdonald and Laurier*. Toronto: McClelland and Stewart.

Hall, David J. 1981. *Clifford Sifton*. Vol. 1, *The Young Napoleon, 1861–1900*. Vancouver: University of British Columbia Press.

———. 2015. *From Treaties to Reserves: The Federal Government and Native Peoples in Territorial Alberta, 1870–1905*. Montreal and Kingston: McGill-Queen's University Press.

Haycock, Ronald G. 1986. *Sam Hughes: The Public Career of a Controversial Canadian, 1885–1916*. Waterloo, ON: Wilfrid Laurier University Press.

Horner, Dan. 2011. "'Shame Upon You as Men!': Contesting Authority in the Aftermath of Montreal's Gavazzi Riot," *Histoire Sociale/Social History* (May).

Horrall, S.W. 1972. "Sir John A. Macdonald and the Police Force for the Northwest Territories," *Canadian Historical Review* (June).

Hunter, A.F. 1909. *A History of Simcoe County*. Barrie, ON: County Council.

Inglis, Brian. 1973. *Roger Casement*. London: Hodder and Stoughton.

Leach, Norman S. 2015. *Sam Steele: An Officer and a Gentleman*. Toronto: Dundurn Press.

Longstreth, T. Morris. 1928. *The Silent Force: Scenes from the Life of the Mounted Police of Canada*. New York: The Century.

Luvaas, Jay. 1965. *The Education of an Army: British Military Thought, 1815–1940*. London: Cassel.

Macfarlane, John. 1999. "The Right Stuff? Evaluating the Performance of Lieutenant-Colonel F.-L. Lessard in South Africa and His Failure to Receive a Senior Command Position with the CEF in 1914," *Canadian Military History* 8, no. 3.

Macleod, R.C. 1976. *The North-West Mounted Police and Law Enforcement 1873–1905*. Toronto: University of Toronto Press.

———. n.d. "Francis Jeffrey Dickens," *Dictionary of Canadian Biography*, vol. XI.

———. n.d. "James Morrow Walsh," *Dictionary of Canadian Biography*, vol. XIII.

Macleod, R.C., and Heather Rollason. 1997. "'Restrain the Lawless Savages': Native Defendants in the Criminal Courts of the North West Territories, 1878-1885," *Journal of Historical Sociology* (June).

Macleod, Rod, and Nancy Parker. 2005. "Justices of the Peace in Alberta." In *Forging Alberta's Constitutional Framework*, edited by Richard Connors and John M. Law. Edmonton: University of Alberta Press.

Manzione, Joseph. 1991. *"I am Looking to the North for My Life": Sitting Bull, 1876-1881*. Salt Lake City: University of Utah Press.

Miller, Carman. 1993. *Painting the Map Red: Canada and the South African War, 1899-1902*. Montreal and Kingston: Canadian War Museum and McGill-Queen's University Press.

Miller, J.R. 1979. *Equal Rights: The Jesuit Estates Act Controversy*. Montreal and Kingston: McGill-Queens University Press.

———. 1996. *Shingwauk's Vision: A History of Native Residential Schools*. Toronto: University of Toronto Press.

———. 2009. *Compact, Contract, Covenant: Aboriginal Treaty Making in Canada*. Toronto: University of Toronto Press.

Miller, Naomi. 2002. *Fort Steele: Gold Rush to Boom Town*. Surrey, BC: Heritage House.

Milloy, John S. 1999. *A National Crime: The Canadian Government and the Residential School System, 1879 to 1986*. Winnipeg: University of Manitoba Press.

Morton, Desmond. 1970. "'Aid to the Civil Power': The Canadian Militia in Support of Social Order, 1867-1914," *Canadian Historical Review* (December).

———. 1982. *A Peculiar Kind of Politics: Canada's Overseas Ministry in the First World War*. Toronto: University of Toronto Press.

Moss, Mark Howard. 2015. *Manliness and Militarism: Educating Young Boys in Ontario for War*. Toronto: University of Toronto Press.

Mouat, Jeremy. 1995. *Roaring Days: Rossland's Mines and the History of British Columbia*. Vancouver: University of British Columbia Press.

Nasson, Bill. 1991. *Abraham Esau's War: A Black South African War in the Cape, 1899-1902*. Cambridge: Cambridge University Press.

Nicholson, G.W.L. 1962. *Canadian Expeditionary Force, 1914-1919: Official History of the Canadian Army in the First World War*. Ottawa: Queen's Printer.

O'Brien, Lt. Col. W.E. 1908/1911. "Early Days in Oro," *Simcoe County Pioneer and Historical Society: Pioneer Papers* No. 1; *Simcoe County Pioneer and Historical Society: Pioneer Papers* No. 4.

Pakenham, Thomas. 1979. *The Boer War*. New York: Random House.

Radley, Kenneth. 2006. *We Lead, Others Follow: First Canadian Division 1914–1918*. St. Catharines, ON: Vanwell Publishing.

———. 2014. *Get Tough, Stay Tough: Shaping the Canadian Corps, 1914–1918*. Wolverhampton Military Studies No. 4. Birmingham, UK: Solihull, Helion and Company.

Rawling, Bill. 2014. *Surviving Trench Warfare: Technology and the Canadian Corps, 1914–1918*, 2nd ed. Toronto: University of Toronto Press.

Ream, Peter T. 1974. *The Fort on the Saskatchewan: A Resource Book on Fort Saskatchewan and District*. Fort Saskatchewan, AB: Metropolitan Printing.

Rogers, Edward G. 1994. "The Algonquian Farmers of Southern Ontario, 1830–1945," in Donald B. Smith and Edward G. Rogers, *Aboriginal Ontario: Historical Perspectives on the First Nations*. Toronto: Dundurn Press.

Schissel, Bernard, and Terry Wotherspoon. 2003. *The Legacy of School for Aboriginal People: Education, Oppression, and Emancipation*. Don Mills, ON: Oxford University Press.

Scholtz, Leopold. 2005. *Why the Boers Lost the War*. New York: Palgrave Macmillan.

Sissons, C.K. 1946. *John Kerr*. Toronto: Oxford University Press.

Smith, Donald B. 2007. *Honoré Jaxon: Prairie Visionary*. Regina: Coteau Books.

Stagg, Ronald J. n.d. "Elmes Yelverton Steele," *Dictionary of Canadian Biography*, vol. IX.

Stanley, George F.G. 1989. *Toil and Trouble: Military Expeditions to Red River*. Toronto and Oxford: Canadian War Museum and Dundurn Press.

Steele, Flora Mcdonald. 1939. "Happy Memories," *Scarlet and Gold*.

Steele, Harwood. 1920. *The Canadians in France*. London: T.F. Unwin.

———. 1923. *Spirit of Iron (Manitou-Pewabic): An Authentic Novel of the North-West Mounted Police*. Toronto: McClelland and Stewart.

———. 1926. *I Shall Arise*. London: Hodder and Stoughton.

———. 1927. *The Ninth Circle*. New York, A.L. Burt.

———. 1936. *Policing the Arctic: The Story of the Conquest of the Arctic by the Royal Canadian (Formerly North-West) Mounted Police*. London: Jarrold's Publishing.

———. 1947. *To Effect an Arrest: Adventures of the Royal Canadian Mounted Police*. Toronto: Ryerson Press.

———. 1956. *The Marching Call*. London: Thomas Nelson.

Steele, John C. 1974. "Reminiscences of a Pioneer" (originally published in the *Orillia Packet* 1893–1894), *Simcoe County Pioneer and Historical Society: Pioneer Papers* No. 4. Canadiana Reprint.

Steele, S.B. 1915. *Forty Years in Canada: Reminiscences of the Great North-West with Some Account of His Service in South Africa*. Toronto: Dodd, Mead and Company.

Stewart, Robert. 1979. *Sam Steele: Lion of the Frontier*. Toronto: Doubleday Canada.

Stewart, William. 2013. "Frustrated Belligerence: The Unhappy History of the 5th Canadian Division in the First World War," *Canadian Military History* (Spring).

Stonechild, Blair, and Bill Waiser. 1997. *Loyal Till Death: Indians and the North-West Rebellion*. Calgary: Fifth House.

Strachan, Hew. 2001. *The First World War*. Vol. 1, *To Arms*. Oxford: Oxford University Press.

Strange, Thomas Bland. 1988. *Gunner Jingo's Jubilee*. Edmonton: University of Alberta Press. First published 1893 by Remington and Co. (London).

Thompson, Leonard. 1960. *The Unification of South Africa 1902–1910*. London: Oxford University Press.

Titley, Brian. 1986. *A Narrow Vision: Duncan Campbell Scott and the Administration of Indian Affairs in Canada*. Vancouver: University of British Columbia Press.

———. 1993. "Hayter Reed and Indian Administration in the West." In *Swords and Plowshares: War and Agriculture in Western Canada*, edited by R.C. Macleod. Edmonton: University of Alberta Press.

———. 2009. *The Indian Commissioners: Agents of the State and Indian Policy in Canada's Prairie West, 1873–1932*. Edmonton: University of Alberta Press.

Torrance, David E. 1996. *The Strange Death of the Liberal Empire: Lord Selborne in South Africa*. Montreal and Kingston: McGill-Queen's University Press.

Turner, John Peter. 1950. *The North-West Mounted Police 1873–1893*. 2 vols. Ottawa: King's Printer.

Utley, Robert M. 2003. *The Indian Frontier, 1846–1890*. Rev. ed. Albuquerque: University of New Mexico Press.

Vanderhaeghe, Guy. 1996. *The Englishman's Boy*. Toronto: McClelland and Stewart.

Vronsky, Peter. 2011. *Ridgeway: The American Fenian Invasion and the 1866 Battle of Ridgeway that Made Canada*. Toronto: Allen Lane.

Waiser, Bill. 2006. "Too Many Scared People: Alberta and the 1885 Rebellion." In *Alberta Formed—Alberta Transformed*, vol. 1, edited by Michael Payne, Donald Wetherell, and Catherine Cavanaugh. Edmonton and Calgary: University of Alberta Press and University of Calgary Press.

Wallace, Jim. 2003. *No Colours, No Drums: Canadians in the South African Constabulary*. N.p.: Bunker to Bunker Books.

Warwick, Peter. 1983. *Black People and the South African War 1899–1902*. Cambridge: Cambridge University Press.

Whitehead, Margaret (ed.). 1988. *They Call Me Father: Memoirs of Father Nicolas Coccola*. Vancouver: University of British Columbia Press.

Williams, Jeffery. 1983. *Byng of Vimy: General and Governor General*. London: Leo Cooper.

# Index

*Page numbers in italics refer to maps and photographs. SS refers to Sam Steele.*

Abbott, John J.C., 141, 143, 344n13
Aboriginal peoples. *See* First Nations; Indigenous peoples; Métis
Adamson, Agar, 213–14, 217, 218
Aitken, Max, 297, 300, 311
Alaska. *See* Klondike Gold Rush (1898–1899); Skagway
Alberta
    military district, 258–59
    *See also* Calgary; Canadian Pacific Railway (CPR); Edmonton; First Nations; Fort Macleod; Fort Macleod and SS (1886–1898); Military District No. 13 (Alberta and western Saskatchewan) and SS (1907–1908)

Alberta Field Force
    about, 76–77, 81
    Alberta Mounted Rifles, 75, 77, 81, 85, 337n19
    map and routes, *70*, *78*
    militia units, 75–76
    Perry's forces, 75, 77, 87, 229
    Quebec militia units, 76
    SS's command of mounted troops, 77, 81
    Steele's Scouts as NWMP detachment, 76–77
    Strange's command, 75–79, 81–85, 336n11
    uniforms, 77
    weapons, 77, 78, 82, 85
    Winnipeg Light Infantry, 76, 78
    *See also* Rebellion (1885); Steele's Scouts (1885)
Alberta Mounted Rifles, 75, 77, 81, 85, 337n19
alcohol. *See* liquor

Alderson, E.A.H., 286, 288, 290, 295, 300
Allan, John Beresford, 95–96, 98
Almighty Voice, 149–50, 156, 160
Antrobus, W.D., 95–99
Archibald, Adams G., 17–18
Assiniboine, 25, 29–30
Atlin Lake, 164, 176–77
autobiography, SS's. See *Forty Years in Canada* (SS's memoir)

Baden-Powell, Lord
  Boy Scouts, 269
  inspector general of British cavalry, 246
  SAC leadership, 232–35, 241, 246–47, 247, 355n10
  South African War, 232
  SS's friendship, 246–47, 254, 355n10
  WWI training, 283
Badfontein, 192, 219
Bagnalls, Mr. and Mrs. (SS's servants), 260
Baker, James, 101, 106
Barker, J.S., 224
Barton, Geoffrey, 221–22
Batoche, 70, 71, 72, 75, 81
Battleford
  Antrobus matter, 97
  Big Bear, 75–76
  map, 28, 70
  MD No. 10 training camp (1913), 274
  NWMP farm instructors on reserves, 92
  NWMP post, 91–96, 99–100, 146
  oats incident, 94–96
  Rebellion (1885), 75, 85
  SS's command of divisions, 91–96, 99–100
  SS's social life, 92–94
Beahen, William, 99, 145
Bear's Head, 62–65, 334n55
Beaver River, 65–67, 67, 84
Belcher, Robert, 169, 200, 204, 215, 353n57
Belfast, 192, 217
Bennett-Goldney, Francis, 297
Bennett Lake
  First Nations relations, 172
  gold miners, 172–73, 176, 348n18
  map, 164
  NWMP customs post, 167, 172, 173
  Walsh's residence, 170–71
  Yukon route, 167–68
Bethulie, 192, 223
Big Bear, Chief, 71, 75–76, 78, 81–87
Big Bend, 151
bison, 39, 46, 51, 54, 59, 73–74
Black Diamond Mining, 158–59, 347n55
Blackfoot
  Crowfoot and Riel, 64
  map, 70
  starvation, 54
  tensions with Sitting Bull, 48–49, 54–55
  Treaty 7 negotiations, 48–49
  whiskey trade, 25, 35
  *See also* First Nations; Kainai (Blood); Peigan (Piikani); Siksika; treaties
Bliss, D.C.F., 264–65

Blood. *See* Kainai (Blood)
Blue Quill, 79
Bobtail, 78–79
Boer War. *See* South African War (1899–1902)
Borden, Frederick
　election defeat (1911), 271–72
　reorganization of army (1907), 258, 261–62, 264
　South African War, 197, 199, 201–2
　SS's friendship, 250, 253, 257
Borden, Robert
　conscription, 312, 316
　election extension, 299
　Hughes's dismissal, 299–302
　Imperial War Conference, 308
　military command structure, 290, 299–302
　military vote, 312–13
　Shorncliffe troops review, 292
　SS's friendship, 281, 317
　Unionist Party, 312–13
Botha, Louis, 212, 215, 217–18, 220, 246, 350n6
Boulton's Scouts, 81
Boy Scouts, 269
Bramshott camp, 297–98, 305
Brandon
　Camp Sewell, 275, 275–76
　CPR route, 57
　Fort Ellice (near Brandon), 35, 37–38, 42
Britain. *See* United Kingdom
British Columbia
　CPR construction and routes, 57, 70, 88
　CPR last spike ceremony, 88–89

　First Nations relations, 100–101
　jurisdiction, federal *vs.* provincial, 65, 88, 102, 344n23
　Kutenai relations, 100–107, 110–11
　land claims, 101, 107
　liquor sales, 65, 88
　map, 70, 164
　MD No. 11, 279
　mines, 157–58
　Oblate Fathers, 105–6
　royalties on gold, 183–84
　treaties, 100–101
　*See also* Canadian Pacific Railway (CPR); Fort Steele; Klondike Gold Rush (1898–1899); Kutenai
Brothers, John, 219
Brown, Charles, 160
Brown, John George "Kootenay," 110–11
buffalo, 39, 46, 51, 54, 59, 73–74
Buffalo Lake, 28, 39–40
Bull, William Perkins, 315, 315–18
"Bull Dog Kelly" murder case, 87–88
Buller, Redvers, 210–20, 253, 352nn52–53
Bummer's Flats, 109
Burrows, J.G., 99
Burstall, Henry, 279
Butler, William F., 24, 330n29
Byng, Julian, 218, 300, 305–6, 310–11, 362n35

Calder, Alexander, 317
Calf Robe, 124
Calgary
　about, 61–62, 260

Agricultural Fair, 258
Alberta Field Force, 78
CPR route, 57, 61
fear of 1885 Rebellion, 76–77
maps, 28, 70
MD No. 13 headquarters, 254, 260, 262, 263–64, 266
MD No. 13 training camps, 254, 257–58, 262
NWMP post (1875), 42, 146
SS's family life, 260, 263–65
SS's first murder case, 61–62
Steele's Scouts in, 77, 85–86
Cameron, George, 218
Camp Sewell, 275, 275–76
Canadian Arctic Expedition, 324
Canadian Mounted Rifles (CMR)
Fort William strike, 267–68
name change to Lord Strathcona's Horse (1909), 269–70
soldiers from NWMP, 351n15
South African War, xii–xiii, 198–200, 229
Canadian Pacific Railway (CPR)
about, 57–59
construction, 57–59, 88, 106
Dunmore Line, 102
economic growth along routes, 58, 99–100
First Nations relations, 62
last spike ceremony, 88–89
map of routes, 28, 70
military "aid to the civil power," 267–68
NWMP's detachments, 58–59, 63, 65–66, 67, 88–89

prohibition of liquor on routes, 65
religion in camps, 106
riots, 68–69, 335n63
routes, 38, 40, 57, 62, 70, 72, 88, 157
strikes, 60, 68–69, 267–68, 333n48
*The Canadian Pictorial and Illustrated War News*, 86
*The Canadians in France* (H. Steele), 318
Cape Colony, 192, 195, 220, 223, 232
Cape Town
Green Point Camp, 206, 208
map, 192
SS's Strathconas in, 203–8, 213, 224
SS's visits for SAC, 237
Card, Charles Ora and Zina, 138
Cardston (Lee's Creek), 138, 151, 152, 153
Carlton, Fort. *See* Fort Carlton
Carlton Trail, 36–37, 57
Carson, John
Hughes's representative in WWI, 287, 289, 293–95, 301, 305–6
Shorncliffe troop review, 292
Cartwright, Francis and Richard, 171, 199
Case, Joe, 20
Casement, Roger, 209–11
Catholics
anti-Catholic sentiment, 118, 125–26, 141, 342n28
Jesuit Estates controversy, 125–26
Oblate Fathers, 105–6, 118

SS and Marie's mixed marriage,
118–19, 131–32
Charcoal, 150–56, 160, 346n40,
346n43, 347n47
Chilkoot Pass
map, 164
NWMP customs post, 167, 172
telephone line, 177
Yukon route, 165–66, 168–69, 172
Christie, William, 44–45
Clark, Charles, 109, 111
Clive (steamship), 104
CMR. See Canadian Mounted Rifles
(CMR)
coal mines, 100
Coccola, Nicolas, 105–7, 111
Cochrane, Robert, 203, 211–12
Cochrane Ranch, 128, 258
Coldwater Narrows, 4
Colebrook, Colin, 149
Constantine, Charles, 160–61, 170
Cook, Tim, 361n8, 362n35
Coryell, J.A., 77
courts. See justice system in Canada;
justice system in South Africa
Cowdry, John, 158
CPR. See Canadian Pacific Railway
(CPR)
Craig, Thomas, 129–30
Craigellachie (Eagle Pass), 88–89
Cranbrook, 101
Cree
Almighty Voice incident, 149–50,
156, 160
Big Bear, 71, 75–76, 78, 81–87
divisions between Plains and
Woods Cree, 81, 82–83, 84

Loon Lake skirmishes, 70, 83–86
Plains Cree, 45, 81, 84
starvation, 73
Treaty 6, 44–45
Wandering Spirit, 52
Woods Cree, 45, 81–85
See also First Nations; Rebellion
(1885); treaties
Crowfoot, Chief, 49, 63–64
Crowsnest Pass, 28, 110–11, 157
Crozier, L.N.F., 49, 54, 74–75, 98
Cruickshank, Charles, 219
Currie, Arthur, 295, 310, 311, 312
Custer, George Armstrong, 45
Cut Arm, 83
Cypress Hills Massacre, 25, 28, 29–30,
42, 330n2

Davin, Nicholas Flood, 59, 129,
140–43
Dawson and SS (1898–1899)
career ambitions, 187–89
family separations, 176, 179
Harper incident, 186–87
judicial duties, 179, 185–86, 189
living conditions, 178–79, 185
map, 164
NWMP barracks, 164, 178–79
NWMP command, 175–76, 180,
188–89
postal system, 183
social life, 179, 181–83
supply route to, 168–69
workload and routine, 178–79,
181–82, 189
Yukoner (steamship), 185–86
Yukon Field Force, 178

See also Klondike Gold Rush (1898–1899); North-West Territories; Yukon and SS (1898–1899)
Deane, R. Burton, 148, 327n4
Dempsey, Hugh, 151, 346n40
Dewdney, Edgar, 64, 73, 102, 145
De Wet, Christiaan, 220–24
Dickens, Jeffrey Francis, 87
Dowling, Thomas, 61, 333n48
Drayner, William and Louise Harwood, 115
*Duchess* (steamship), 103–4
Duck Lake, 70, 71, 74–75, 149
Dudley, Stewart, 308, 323
Dufferin, 35–36
Dufferin, Lord, 87
Dumont, Gabriel, 74
Dundonald, Lord, 211–13, 215, 218–19, 227, 351n26
Dunmore Line, 102
Durban, 192, 210–11
Durieu, Paul, 105
Dyea, 164, 165, 167–68

Eagle Pass (Craigellachie), 88–89
Edmonton
　Alberta Field Force in, 78–79
　Carlton Trail, 36–37, 57
　fear of 1885 Rebellion, 76–77, 78
　HBC western hub, 38–39
　maps, 28, 70
　NWMP arrival and post (1874), 36–41, 332n19
　postal system, 38, 41
　Rebellion (1885), 78
　social life, 38–40
　Steele's Scouts in, 79, 85
Edward VII, King, 226–27
Elliot, Frank, 204
Elliott, William J.S., 339n24
Empire mine, 157, 159, 160
England. *See* United Kingdom
*The Englishman's Boy* (Vanderhaeghe), 330n2
Ermineskin, 70, 78–79
Esquimalt naval base, 259
Evans, John, 30
Evans, Thomas, 263, 265

Fall, Percy, 234, 237, 355n16
Family Compact, 4–5
Farwell, BC, 67
Fawcett, Thomas, 178
Fenian raids, 9, 21
Fernie fire, 262–63
First Nations
　about, 30–31, 147–48
　BC treaties and reserves, 100–101, 106–7
　Bear's Head incident, 62–65, 334n55
　Chippewa in Ontario, 2, 3–4
　Cypress Hills Massacre, 25, 29–30, 42
　DIA relations, 62, 72–74, 147–48
　government neglect, 72–74
　Indian agents, 46, 147
　land claims, 107
　NWMP relations, 31, 46–47, 55, 62, 147–49
　pass system, 62, 148, 334n50, 345n33
　prohibition on liquor, 58, 123

racism, 74, 79
reserves, 100–101, 106–7, 147–48, 177
residential schools, 147–48
settler relationships, 55
smallpox vaccinations, 55
SS's relations, 34
starvation, 54, 73, 147–48
transition to farming, 72–74, 92, 147
treaty payments, 45, 55
*See also* Blackfoot; Cree; Kainai (Blood); Kutenai; Peigan (Piikani); Siksika; treaties
First World War, military before. *See* military and SS (1906–1914)
First World War
about, 288–89
1st Division, 269–70, 277–78, 288, 290, 295, 305, 310
2nd Division, 279, 281, 283, 285–87, 289, 290–91, 292, 294, 305
3rd and 4th Divisions, 294, 297–98, 300, 305, 310
Bramshott camp, 297–98, 305
command structure, 289–90, 293, 295, 297–99
conscription, 311–12, 316
gas warfare, 288, 290
historical background, 275–77, 311–12
home front, 280
Hughes's chaotic leadership, 277–81, 289
nurses, 293–94
officers, 295, 305–7

political influences, 278–81, 286, 298–300, 306, 308–11
rejection of Canadian division commanders by British, 281, 285–86
training, 305–6, 305–7, 310
trench warfare, 288, 289
Valcartier camp, 278–79
Vimy Ridge, 310, 311–12
vote, military, 312–13
Ypres, 290
*See also* Hughes, Samuel
First World War and SS
about, 282, 313–15, 319
20th Battalion difficulties, 294
Bull's friendship, 315, 315–18
career ambitions, 285–86, 300, 308–9
commander of 2nd Division, 283, 285–86, 289–91, 292
family in Folkestone (1915–1916), 287, 293–94, 303, 304, 307–8, 308, 317
health, 278, 281, 285, 287, 307, 309
inspector general for western Canada, 280–83, 282
Kitchener meetings, 287–88, 292, 293
pay dispute, 302–3
political influences, 279–81, 286, 295–96, 298–300, 306, 308–11
promotions and ranks, xiii, xv, 280–81, 282
rejection for command due to age, 281, 287–88
reputation, 281
retirement and death, 313–18

381

Index

Ross rifle defects, 289, 299–300
Shorncliffe base, 287, 289–93, 292, 297, 301–5
social life, 297, 315–17
soldiers' relations with locals, 296–97
Spittal court martial, 295–96
training, 294–95, 305–7, 310
Valcartier camp, 278–79
visits to the front, 288, 310–11
*See also* Hughes, Samuel; Shorncliffe training base and SS
Folkestone
SS's family life, 287, 293–94, 303, 304, 307–8, *308*, 317
Fort Alexander, *xviii*, 16–17
Fort Benton, Montana, 30, 46
*See also* Montana Territory
Fort Calgary. *See* Calgary
Fort Carlton
Big Bear's surrender, 84
Duck Lake, 74–75
map, 28
NWMP police post surrender by Crozier, 74
Rebellion (1885), 74–75
Treaty 6 negotiations, 44–45
Fort Edmonton. *See* Edmonton
Fort Ellice, 35, 36, 37, 42
Fortescue, Laurence, 134
Fort Garry
horses, 32–33
map, *xviii*
NWMP quarters, 32–36
Red River Expedition, 17–18
Fort Henry, Kingston, 22–23

Fort Macleod
about, 46, 51, 99–100, 121
CPR route's impact, 123, 143
dignitaries' visits, 122, 127–28
fear of 1885 Rebellion, 76–77
First Nations relations, 148–49
maps, 28, *70*
move from original fort, 46
NWMP post, 44, 61, 121–22, 146
NWT administration, 46, 51
social life, 117, 138–39
tensions with Lakota and Sitting Bull, 45, 47–51, 54–55
Fort Macleod and SS (1886–1898)
career ambitions, 126, 137, 142, 145–46, 160
Charcoal's case, 150–56, 160, 346n40, 346n43, 347n47
courtship and marriage, 114–22, *115*, 125–26, 131–35, *133*
Craig payroll error case, 129–30
dignitaries' visits, 127–28
family life (1890–1898), 137–38
First Nations relations, 148–49, 156
Herchmer misconduct allegations, 129–31, 140–43
home, 122, 128–29, 135, 137–38
investments, 157–60
judicial duties, 122–24
NWMP commander of post, 121–22, 137, *144*, 148–49, *149*
officers, 144
social standing, 138
transfer from Battleford to (1886), 95

transfer from Fort Steele to
(1888), 111–12
*See also* Steele, Marie Harwood,
marriage to SS
Fort Pitt
Dickens's command, 87
map, 28
Rebellion (1885), 71, 78, 80–82,
84–85, 87
Treaty 6 negotiations, 45
Fort Qu'Appelle
about, 55
Alberta Field Force, 75
cadet camp (1914), 276
CPR route, 57–58, 75
dignitaries' visits, 57
First Nations relations, 55
maps, 28, 70
NWMP post, 54–57, 146
Rebellion (1885), 75
SS as commanding officer, 55–57
Fort Saskatchewan
NWMP arrival (1874), 36–41,
332n19
Fort Steele
desertions, 109
Kutenai and NWMP relations,
102–7, 110–11
map, 70
mines, 157
NWMP detachment (1887–1888),
104–11
St. Eugene's Mission, 105–6
typhoid fever, 107–8
Fort Steele Heritage Town, 108
Fort Victoria, 79–80

Fort Walsh
about, 54
criminal justice, 52
Cypress Hills Massacre, 25, 28,
29–30, 42, 330n2
first NWMP killed on the job, 54
map, 28
NWMP post, 42, 46, 51–52, 59
Sitting Bull negotiations, 49–50
supply route, 54
typhoid, 54
Fort William, 267–68, 271
*Forty Years in Canada* (SS's memoir)
about, xiii
composition, 266, 268, 276
dedication to Lord Strathcona,
268
diaries, xv, 331n14, 335n64
early life, 1–2, 7
motives for writing, 270
omissions in, xiii–xiv, 23, 49,
99–100, 335n64
publication (1914), xiii, 266, 283,
364n97
SS's views on, 327n4
title, 266
Fouquet, Leon, 105–6
Frederikstad, 192, 221–22
Freemasons, 54
French, George Arthur, 22, 26, 32–36,
40, 43–44
French-English hostilities, 130–31,
140–44
Frenchman Butte, 70, 81–83, 337n25
Frog Lake Massacre, 28, 70, 71, 76,
79–82, 87

Fury, William, 62, 67, 69, 83, 86, 337n27

Gagnon, Sévère, 36
Galbraith, Robert, 104, 109, 111
Galbraith's Ferry (later Fort Steele). See Fort Steele
Galvin, Pat, 185–86
Garner, Albert, 219
Garry, Fort. See Fort Garry
Gatling gun, 77, 78, 82, 85
George V, King, 292, 293, 296–97
Glengarry Ranch, 138
Godsal, Frederick, 138, 157–58, 160
Golden, 65, 70, 87–88, 107–8
Goldring, Philip, 330n2
Goulet, Elzear, 19
Gouraud, Henri, 311
Graburn, Marmaduke, 54
Great Britain. See United Kingdom
*The Great Lone Land* (Butler), 24, 330n29
Grey, Earl, 257, 358n2
Griesbach, Arthur, 88
Gros Ventres, 123–24
Gwatkin, Willoughby, 287, 293, 299, 306

Hamilton, Ian, 220, 275
Hammond, Henry (Marie's uncle), 132
Hardisty, Richard, 332n19
Hardwick, Thomas, 30
Harper, Frank, 186–87
Harris, Robert, 210
Hartigan, M.M., 238
Harvey, Eric, 321

Harvey, Horace, 155
Harwood, Antoine (Marie's brother), 244
Harwood, Frank (Marie's brother), 244
Harwood, Henry (Marie's uncle), 174
Harwood, Marie. See mother of Harwood, Gertrude, and Flora); Steele, Marie Harwood (SS's wife)
Harwood, Mary Charlotte McGillis (Marie's mother), 114–15, 244
Harwood, Robert William (Marie's father)
  political influences, xii, 174
  as Quebec elite, 114–15, 341n4
  as SS's father-in-law, 119–20, 131
  SS's statements on Yukon maladministration, 187
Hatfield, James, 154
Hatton, George, 77, 99, 336n10
Haultain, F.W., 130
HBC (Hudson's Bay Company)
  Fort Edmonton as western hub, 38–39
  Fort Ellice post, 35, 36, 37
  postal system, 38, 41
  treaty negotiations, 44–45
Heidelberg, 192, 212, 214
Henderson, George, 216
Henderson, G.F.R., 251–52, 357n70
Herchmer, Lawrence W.
  about, 339n24
  Antrobus matter, 97–99
  Bear's Head incident, 62–65, 334n55

boundary commission (Canada–
US), 339n24
British Army service, 339n24
Davin's public criticism of, 129,
140–43
misconduct charges, 129–31,
134–35, 140–45
NWMP commissioner (1886–
1900), xii, 63–64, 97–98, 117,
129–31, 134–35, 229–31
personal qualities, 99
political influences, xii, 97–98
South African War, xii, 198–99,
207, 229
SS's relations, 64, 98–99, 130, 137
Wetmore inquiry and report,
141–45
Herchmer, William M.
anti-French-Canadian tirade,
129–31, 140–44
Davin's public criticism of, 129,
140–43
death (1892), 142
Kutenai land claims, 101–4, 111
misconduct charges, 129–31,
134–35, 140–45
NWMP asst. commissioner,
98–99, 101–4, 111, 131
personal qualities, 130–31
SS's relations, 102–3
Herron, John, 138
Hicks, H.T., 221
Historical Society of Manitoba,
265–66
Hobson, Jonathan, 213
Horrall, Stan, 99, 145
Howard, Donald, 213

Hubert, Richard, 131
Hudson's Bay Company. *See* HBC
(Hudson's Bay Company)
Hughes, Samuel
about, 272
chaotic command structure
(1914–1916), 277–81, 283,
289–90, 293–302, 310
dismissal by Borden (Nov 1916),
299–302
minister of militia (1911–1916),
277–81, 283, 285–86, 298–99
personal qualities, 286–87, 293,
297, 301–2
political influences, 274–75, 299
Shorncliffe troop review, 301–2
South African War, 207–9, 272
SS's dislike for, 208–9, 272,
274–75, 278–80, 286, 288, 297
Valcartier camp, 278
*See also* First World War
Huot, Albert, 104, 132, 144, 145,
343n47
Hutton, E.T.H., 197, 198, 199–200,
204, 206

Ibex Mining Co., 158–59, 347n55
I.G. Baker Company, 46
Indian Affairs, Dept. of
government failures, 72–74, 147,
336n5
transfer of NWMP management
to, 62
*See also* First Nations; treaties
Indigenous peoples
about, 30–31
buffalo, 39, 46, 51, 54

Cypress Hills Massacre, 25, 29–30, 42
dispossession of land, 30
Sitting Bull and Lakota, 47–51, 54–55
voyageurs, 15–16
See also First Nations; Métis; treaties
Inihan Kinyen, Chief, 30
Irvine, Acheson Gosford
  firing of, 64, 87, 339n24
  First Nations relations, 62
  NWMP commissioner, 58, 63, 87
  Rebellion (1885), 75, 85–87, 339n24
  SS's friendship, 64
Isadore, Chief, 101–7, 110–11
Ives, W.B., 145

Jarvis, A.M., 18, 152, 215, 235
Jarvis, W.D., 36–40, 169
Jenkins, Angus, 213
Jesuit Estates controversy, 125–26
Johannesburg, 192, 195, 237
Johnston, George Hope, 66–69, 134
Johnston, Walter, 134
Joseph, Chief, 50
Joseph's Prairie, 101, 106–7
justice system in Canada
  acquittals, 334n55
  Almighty Voice, 149–50, 156, 160
  Charcoal, 150–56, 160, 346n40, 346n43, 347n47
  court costs as judicial pay, 185
  Craig payroll error case, 129–30
  delays, 56
  First Nations relations, 149–50
  first NWMP killed on the job, 54
  hangings, 156
  jurisdiction, federal *vs.* provincial, 65, 88, 344n23
  murder cases, 61–62, 66, 87–88
  NWMP officers as justices of the peace, 59, 68–69, 122–24, 147, 334n55, 335n60
  rule of law, 56, 60, 62
  SS's role, 20, 55, 61–62, 66
  *Yukoner* (steamship) case, 185–86
justice system in South Africa, 246–48

Kainai (Blood)
  Charcoal, 150–56, 160, 346n40, 346n43, 347n47
  cross-border horse raids, 123–24
  dignitaries' visits, 127–28
  Indian agents, 148–49
  map, 70
  NWMP relations, 148–49
  Red Crow, 124, 127, 148, 151, 342n26
  starvation, 148
  Sun Dance, 124
  Treaty 7 negotiations, 49
  See also Blackfoot; First Nations
Kapula murder case, 102, 105, 107
Kelly, "Bull Dog," 86–87
Kemp, Edward, 314
Kennedy, George, 54
Kerr, Jack, 246
Kerr, John, 20–21, 329n26
Ketchen, H.D.B., 265, 281, 303, 310–11, 320
Kicking Horse Pass, 65

King's Royal Rifle Corps, 11–12, 18
Kingston, 22, 24, 26, 258
Kipling, Rudyard, 241
Kitchener, Lord
  death, 302
  SAC commander, 237, 239, 357n49
  Shorncliffe troop review, 292, 293
  South African War, 211, 222, 224, 226, 231–33, 357n49
  SS's relations, 287–88, 290–91, 302
  WWI Canadian division commanders rejected by, 281, 285–88
Klondike Gold Rush (1898–1899)
  early history, 160–61
  map, 164
  population of miners, 178
  royalties on gold, 161, 183–84
  Stikine railway scheme, 166, 168
  See also Dawson and SS (1898–1899); Yukon and SS (1898–1899)
Knox, Charles, 223–24
Kootenay Valley, 103–4, 108–9
Kruger, Paul, 196, 211, 217–18, 239, 239, 356n34
Kutenai
  Herchmer's investigation, 101–4
  Isadore's leadership, 101–7, 110–11
  Joseph's Prairie land claim, 101, 106–7
  Kapula murder case, 102, 105, 107
  NWMP relations, 100–107, 110–11
  SS's relations, 110–11

Labelle, Capt., 132
labour relations
  about, 60
  CPR strikes, 60, 68–69, 267–68, 333n48, 335n64
  Fort William strikes, 267–68
  military "aid to the civil power," 267–68
  mutiny of steamship workers, 185–86
  riots, 68–69, 335n63
Lac des Iles, 84, 85
Lacombe, Albert, 78–79, 118, 126, 131–32, 139
Ladysmith, 192, 210, 212
Laggan (Lake Louise), 65, 70
Lake, Percy, 254, 257, 264
Lake, Tom, 103
Lake Louise (Laggan), 65, 70
Lake Simcoe–Lake Huron Purchase, 3–4
Lake Superior Regiment, 266–67
Lakota and Sitting Bull, 45, 47–51, 54–55
Laurier, Wilfrid
  distrust of NWMP, 145–47, 155, 157, 160, 169–70
  election (1896), 157, 160, 169
  Jesuit Estates controversy, 125–26
  NWMP appointments, xii
  South African War, 197, 207–8
  Yukon-Alaska boundary dispute, 165–66
Law, Andrew Bonar, 291, 297, 306
Leckie, John, 219
Lee's Creek (Cardston), 138, 151, 152, 153

Lessard, François-Louis, 265, 299, 360n82
Lethbridge (Whoop-Up), 28, 100, 143, 148, 156
Lindeman, Lake, 164, 173
Lipsett, Louis, 265, 271
liquor
   about, 58–59, 123
   CPR construction sites, 58–59, 65–66
   federal *vs.* provincial jurisdiction, 88, 344n23
   lack of prohibition in BC, 67–68, 88
   prohibition for First Nations, 25, 58, 123
   prohibition in NWT, 58–59, 123
   smugglers, 25, 58–59, 123
   SS's drinking, xv, 92–93, 100, 274, 279, 311, 325, 338n5, 339n29
   SS's drunkenness, letter clearing him of, 274, 279
   whiskey trade, 25, 29–30, 39–40, 58–59, 123
Little Bighorn, 45
Little Hunter, 79
Logan, Archibald, 219
London, England
   SS's family life (1906–1907), 251–55, 254
   Strathconas' visit (1901), 226–28, 274
Longstreth, T. Morris, 92–93, 100, 338n5
Loon Lake (Makwa Lake), 70, 83–86

Lord Strathcona's Horse and SS (1899–1901)
   about, 199–201, 202, 205, 226–28
   Adamson's relations, 213–14
   awards and honours, 226–28
   "Breaker" Morant event, rumours of similar, 216–17, 353n68
   in Cape Town, 203–9, *208*
   casualties and POWs, 212–13, 215–16, 219
   discipline of soldiers, 204, 206–7, 212, 221, 226
   guerilla warfare, 220–24, 231–32
   horses, 200, 203–6, 207, 220–21
   in London (1901), 226–28, 274
   in Ottawa, 201–5, *202*
   as permanent unit (1909–1912), 231, 259, 269–70
   in Pretoria, 221
   public support, 202–3
   railway operations, 209–11, 221
   scorched earth operations, 222, 231–32, 240
   size, 200
   soldiers, 186, 200–202, *202*, 204–6, 213, 351n15
   South African War operations, 211–22
   SS's career ambitions, xv, 193, 198–200, 229
   SS's family separations, 198, 205, 221, 230–31
   SS's rank (1909–1912), 231, 269–70
   SS's War Diary, 202, 204, 206, 210, 217, 222, 224, 350n12
   travel to Cape Town, 203–6, *205*
   typhoid, 222

uniforms, *202*, 203, *205*, 270
weapons, 201, 207, *208*, 215, 217
*See also* South African War
    (1899-1902)
Lorne, Marquess of, 57
Lotbinière, Henri-Gustave Joly de
    (Marie's cousin), 174, 187
Lougheed, James, 62
Lourenço Marques (Maputo), *192*,
    196, 209
Lydenburg, *192*, 218, 220
Lyttleton, Neville, 220

Macdonald, Allen Bean, 138
Macdonald, D.A., 261, 264
Macdonald, Hugh John, 13, 314,
    363n80
Macdonald, John A.
    Antrobus matter, 97
    Catholic-Protestant hostilities,
        118, 125-26
    CPR project, 57
    death (1891), 137, 141, 145
    First Nations neglect, 72-74
    Herchmer allegations, 129-31,
        134-35, 140
    Jesuit Estates controversy, 125-26
    NWMP support by, 31, 145
    Pacific Scandal (1873), 33, 38, 43
    Rebellion (1885), 73-74
    Sitting Bull and Walsh, 48, 55
    SS's meeting with, 134-35
Macdonell, A.C. (not related to Alex),
    265, 266, 269-70, 279, 281,
    359n43
Macdonell, Alex R.
    death, 260

Fort Macleod post, 121, 128, *144*,
    146, 345n27
investments, 127
NWMP divisions, 121
ranch life, 146, 260, 345n28
Sitting Bull and Lakota, 47-48
SS as division commander, 91-94
SS's friendship, 92, 112, 128, 135,
    146
Wood Mountain post, 47-48
Macdonell, Minnie (Alex's wife;
    Marie's aunt)
    life with SS's family, 260, 266, 272
    Marie's friend and aunt, 114,
        115-16, 135, 146
    remarriage (1913), 272
    widowhood, 260
Macdougall, J.C., 287, 289, 293-96,
    298, 300-301, 305-6
Machadodorp, *192*, 217
Mackenzie, Alexander, 33, 38
Mackie, Ernest, 262
Macleod, Fort. *See* Fort Macleod
Macleod, James F.
    about, 34, 44
    lawyer and judge, 34, 44, 58, 62,
        88
    Native relations, 49-50
    NWMP officer, 34-35, 44, 48
    Red River Expedition, 13
    Treaty 7 negotiations, 48-49
Macleod Company, 158
Macpherson, D.H., 130
Makwa Lake (Loon Lake), *70*, 83-86
Maniputosis, Chief, 30
Manitoba
    Camp Sewell, *275*, 275-76

first election, 20
Manitoba Act (1870), 10
map, *xviii*
military district, 258-59
Ontario boundary dispute, 60-61
See also Military District
    No. 10 (Manitoba and
    Saskatchewan) and SS
    (1908-1914); Red River; Red
    River Expedition and SS
    (1870); Winnipeg
Manitoba Mounted Police, 24
Maple Creek, 28, 60, 146
Maputo (Lourenço Marques), 192, 196
*The Marching Call* (H. Steele), 326
Marsh Lake, 164, 173
Massiah, Kate, 247-48
Matheson, Samuel, 320-21
McCarthy, D'Alton, 98, 118, 125-26
McCormick, Edward, 351n18
McEachran, Duncan, 200, 203
McIlree, John Henry, 61, 142, 161-62, 229
McInnes, Hector, 313-14
McKay, George, 80, 83
McKay, James, 44-45
McLean, C.W.W., 234
McLean, William, 84
McMillan, Daniel H., 12-13, 17, 265, 329n18
McMullen, James, 145-46
MD (Military District), *See entries beginning with* Military District
memoir, SS's. *See Forty Years in Canada* (SS's memoir)
Métis
    Batoche battle, 70, 81
    Battleford, 92, 95
    census by NWMP (1879), 52
    Cypress Hills, 29-30
    Riel's government, 71, 75, 81
    SS's relations, 13, 92, 95
    survey demands by, 72-74
    voyageurs, 15-16
    *See also* Rebellion (1885); Red
        River Resistance (1869-1870);
        Riel, Louis
Middleton, Frederick
    map, 70
    Rebellion (1885), 75-76, 81, 83-85, 87
military and SS (before 1906)
    about, 23-24, 259
    British officers and instructors, 11, 21, 22
    early years, 9-10, 21-24
    historical background, 21, 258-59
    Middleton's forces in Rebellion (1885), 75-76, 81, 83-85, 87
    NWMP relationship, 86
    permanent forces, 258-59
    Red River Expedition forces, 11-12
    SS as young volunteer, 9-10
    training, 21-22
    volunteer militia, 9, 21-22
    Yukon Field Force, 161, 167, 172, 176, 178, 181-82, 188
    *See also* Alberta Field Force; Lord
        Strathcona's Horse and SS
        (1899-1901); Rebellion (1885);
        Red River Expedition and SS
        (1870); Steele's Scouts (1885)
military and SS (1906-1914)
    about, 251-52

British officers on secondment, 271
cadet movement, 274, 276
historical background, 258–59
homesteader exemptions, 276
insufficiencies, 270, 275–76
military "aid to the civil power," 267–68
permanent forces, 258–59
plan for overseas conflicts, 277–78
political influences, 261–62, 271–72
reorganization (1907), 258, 271
Royal Canadian Regiment (RCR), 197, 278, 294
size of force, 258
SS's command of MD No. 10 (1908–1914), 263–69
SS's role as trainer (1906), 251
training of volunteers, 251, 258–59, 271
*See also* Military District No. 10 (Manitoba and Saskatchewan) and SS (1908–1914); Military District No. 13 (Alberta and western Saskatchewan) and SS (1907–1908)
Military District No. 10 (Manitoba and Saskatchewan) and SS (1908–1914)
about, 263–64, 275
"aid to the civil power," 267–68
Camp Sewell, 275, 275–76
career ambitions, 264, 269
equipment shortages, 275
historical background, 258–59
Lord Strathcona's Horse (was CMR), 269–70
officers, 265
permanent forces, 258–59, 267–68
political influences, 274–75
SS's command, 263–69, 272
SS's composition of memoirs, 266, 268
SS's family life, 268–69, 272
SS's rank of colonel, 272
summer training camps, 266, 274–75, 275
training standards, 271
volunteer militia, 267
*See also* military and SS (1906–1914)
Military District No. 11 (British Columbia), 279
Military District No. 13 (Alberta and western Saskatchewan) and SS (1907–1908)
about, 258–62
budget constraints, 261
Calgary headquarters, 254, 260, 262, 263–64, 266
career ambitions, 264
family separations, 260
Fernie fire, 262–63
historical background, 258–59
jurisdiction, 253–54
location of headquarters, 259–60
officers, 261–62
permanent forces, 258–59
political influences, 261–62
reorganization, 258–59
SS in command, 253–54, 259–63, 266

summer training camps, 254, 257–58, 262
*See also* military and SS (1906–1914)
Militia Act, 267–68
Miller, Carman, 197, 352n53, 353n69
Mills, David, 55
Milner, Alfred
　British governor in South Africa, 242, 244–45, 249
　First World War, 281
　SAC planning, 232, 235
　South African War, 209
Minto, Lord, 234, 248, 339n24
Modderfontein, 237
　*See also* Johannesburg
Montana Territory
　cross-border horse raids, 123–24
　Cypress Hills Massacre perpetrators, 42
　Fort Benton, 30, 46
　Riel in, 72
　SS's visits, 52
　supply route, 46, 52, 54
　wolfers and whiskey traders, 25, 29–30, 35
Montreal. *See* Quebec
Moodie, Susanna, 3, 328n2
Moose Hill Creek, 80
Morant, Harry "Breaker," 216–17, 353n68
Morris, Alexander, 44–45
Morton, Desmond, 293
*Mounted Police Life in Canada* (Deane), 327n4
Mount Royal Rifles, 76, 132

Mozambique (Portuguese East Africa), 192, 196
Mulrooney, Belinda, 179, 181
Mulvey, Stewart, 16, 329n18

Nash, Harry, 93
Natal, 192, 195, 210–11, 220, 232
National Historic Sites publications, 330n2
Neale, Percy, 95–96, 122, 144
New York City
　SS's honeymoon, 132, 134
Nez Perce, 50
Nicholson, J.S., 237, 247
9th Voltigeurs, 76
*The Ninth Circle* (H. Steele), 324
North Axe, 124
North-West Mounted Police. *See* NWMP (North-West Mounted Police) (1873–1920)
North-West Rebellion (1885). *See* Rebellion (1885)
North-West Territories
　dignitaries' visits, 57
　Fort Macleod as administration hub, 46
　growth after CPR completion, 123
　Indian commissioners, 74
　international issues, 47
　map, 164
　NWMP officers as justices of the peace, 59, 68–69, 122–24, 147, 334n55, 335n60
　prohibition on liquor, 58–59, 123–24
　Sitting Bull, 45, 47–51, 54–55
　Territorial Council, 44

Territorial Supreme Court, 58, 124
*See also* Dawson and SS (1898–1899); Klondike Gold Rush (1898–1899)
NWMP (North-West Mounted Police) (1873–1920)
  about, 30–31, 46, 146
  archives, 326
  BC as outside jurisdiction of, 65
  British models for, 25
  budgets, 32–33, 42, 145–46
  change to RCMP, 321
  command structure, 32, 61
  CPR detachments, 58–59, 63, 65–66, 67, 88–89
  desertions, 51–52, 109
  detachments, 75, 156
  First Nations relations, 146–48
  formation and goals (1873), 23–26, 30–32
  French as first commissioner, 26, 32–36, 40–41, 43–44
  historical background, 30–31
  horsemanship, 24, 33–37, 43
  Liberals' plan to eliminate, 145, 147, 155, 160, 169, 193
  maps, 28, 70, 164
  married men, 146
  Métis census, 52
  military character, 24–25
  military conversion, proposal for, 43
  militia's relationship, 86
  pay levels, 32, 51–52, 127, 146, 176
  peacekeeping among First Nations, 47
  political influences, 33
  postal system, 41, 43, 46, 173–74
  recruitment, 25–26, 33–34
  size of force (300), 26, 33–34, 36
  size of force (500 and 1,000), 58, 74, 93–94
  size reduction (1890s), 145–46, 156
  tensions with Sitting Bull and Lakota, 45, 47–51, 54–55
  uniforms, 32, 42, 53, 67, 149
  weapons, 24, 36
NWMP and SS (1873–1885)
  about, 53, 67
  boundary dispute (Manitoba and Ontario), 60–61
  British training request by SS (1875), 40, 47, 332n25
  career ambitions, xi–xii, 23–24, 37, 47, 229
  CPR detachments, 58–59, 63, 65–66, 67, 88–89
  Edmonton detachment (1874), 36–41
  enlistment (1873), 23–26
  First Nations relations, 63–64
  horse expert, 33–34, 35–37, 40, 47, 52
  justice of the peace, 59, 63–64, 122–23, 147, 334n55, 335n60
  last spike ceremony, 88–89
  maps, 28, 70
  political influences, 34–35
  promotions and ranks, 26, 41, 52, 53, 55, 61, 91
  recruitment of men, 58, 59, 61
  SS's regimental number, 32

Swan River post (1875), 40–44, 332n21
travel to Manitoba (1873), 29, 31–32
treaty negotiations, 44
US military encounter, 51
visit to Ontario (1882), 58
NWMP and SS (1885). *See* Rebellion (1885); Steele's Scouts (1885)
NWMP and SS (1885–1888)
  about, 91–92
  Antrobus matter, 95–99
  Battleford post (1885–1886), 91–94
  career frustrations, 91–92, 98–100
  Fort Macleod post (1886), 95–96
  Fort Steele post (1887–1888), 102–11
  Kutenai and NWMP relations, 102–7, 110–11
  political influences, 96–97
  Swift Current patrols, 102–3
NWMP and SS (1888–1898). *See* Fort Macleod and SS (1886–1898)
NWMP and SS (1898–1899). *See* Dawson and SS (1898–1899); Klondike Gold Rush (1898–1899); Yukon and SS (1898–1899)

Ogilvie, William, 170, 177–78, 179, 182–84
Ogilvy, J.H.C., 240–41
Oliver, Frank, 79, 259
Ontario and Manitoba boundary dispute, 60–61
Ontario Rifles, 12, 18–20, 23, 329n26

Orange Free State, 192, 195, 220, 232, 249
Orange Order, 125–26, 342n28
Orillia, Ontario
  map, *xviii*
  SS's early life, 1–4, 7–9
  SS's visits (1882, 1899), xi–xii, 58, 113–14, 193–94
  Steele family in, 3–7
Oswald, J.K., 77, 80–81
Otter, William, 70, 84–85, 266
Overseas Estates Ltd., 316

Pakenham, Thomas, 218
Parker, E.C., 201
Patullo, T.D. "Duff," 188
Peigan (Piikani)
  Charcoal incident, 153–54
  maps, 28, 70
  NWMP relations, 148–49
  Treaty 7 negotiations, 49
  *See also* Blackfoot; First Nations
Perley, George H.
  minister of overseas forces, 299, 301–2, 306–7, 311, 313–14
  Shorncliffe troop review, 292
Perry, Aylesworth Bowen
  about, 161–62, 229–30
  career ambitions, 87, 162, 175, 188, 229–30, 355n5
  lawyer, 148, 162, 230
  NWMP commissioner, xii, 229–31
  pass system on reserves, 148
  political influences, 162
  Prince Albert post, 91
  RCMP commissioner, 355n5
  Rebellion (1885), 75, 77, 87, 229

SS's relationship, xii, 231, 355n5
Yukon post, 161-62, 167-68, 175, 229
Pétain, Philippe, 310-11
Phillips, Michael, 111
Piikani. See Peigan (Piikani)
Pitt, Fort. See Fort Pitt
Pocklington, William, 148-49
police in Canada
   historical background, 31
   provincial jurisdiction under BNA Act, 65, 88, 344n23
   See also NWMP (North-West Mounted Police) (1873-1920); and entries beginning with NWMP and SS
police in South Africa. See South African Constabulary and SS (1901-1906)
Policing the Arctic (H. Steele), 324
Portuguese East Africa (Mozambique), 192, 196
postal system, 38, 41, 43, 46, 173-75, 183
Potts, Jerry, 52
Poundmaker, Chief, 45, 81
Powell, F. Hamilton, 104, 107-8
Powell, Israel, 108
Pretoria
   map, 192
   SAC headquarters and posts, 239-41, 249
   SS's family life in, 239, 239, 242-44, 243, 249, 252, 356n34
Prince Albert
   CPR route change, 72
   map, 28

MD No. 10 training camp (1913), 274-75
Métis relations, 92
   NWMP post, 86-87, 91, 146
   Rebellion (1885), 74-75, 86-87
   survey of Métis lots, 72-73
Protestants
   Catholic-Protestant hostilities, 118, 125-26
   Orange Order, 125-26, 342n28
   SS and Marie's mixed marriage, 118-19, 131-32
   SS's church attendance, 92
Public Works Peace Preservation Act, 65

Qu'Appelle. See Fort Qu'Appelle
Quebec
   Alberta Field Force militia units, 76
   anti-conscription riots, 312
   Catholic-Protestant hostilities, 118
   Jesuit Estates controversy, 125-26
   See also Vandreuil, Quebec

Radley, Kenneth, 310
railways. See Canadian Pacific Railway (CPR)
Rand mines, 195, 232-33, 248-49, 250-51
Rawling, Bill, 310
RCMP (Royal Canadian Mounted Police), 321
RCR. See Royal Canadian Regiment (RCR)
Ream, Peter T., 332n19

Rebellion (1885)
  about, 71–85
  Alberta Field Force, 75–82, 85, 87
  Big Bear, 71, 75–76, 78, 81–87
  Cree divisions (Plains *vs.* Woods), 81
  Cree resentment of neglect by government, 72–74
  Fort Pitt, 71
  Frenchman Butte, 70, 81–83, 337n25
  Frog Lake Massacre, 71, 76, 79–82, 87
  lack of Cree support for Riel, 78
  Loon Lake (Makwa Lake), 83–86
  map, 70
  Middleton's forces, 75–76, 81, 83–85, 87
  Perry's forces, 75, 77, 87, 229
  political influences, 73–74
  Riel's provisional government, 18, 71, 74
  SS's scouts, 75–76, 91
  survey and ration demands, 72–74
  terminology (resistance *vs.* rebellion), 334n51
  *War News*, 86
  *See also* Steele's Scouts (1885)
Rebellions of 1837, 4–5
*Red Coats on the Prairies* (Beahen and Horrall), 99, 145
Red Crow, Chief, 124, 127, 148, 151, 342n26
Red Deer, 77, 78–79
Red Deer Investments, 316
Red River
  social life, 34
  travel to, 12–17, 31–32
  *See also* Fort Garry
Red River Expedition and SS (1870)
  about, 10–20
  diaries, xv
  historical background, 10–14, 20–21
  map, *xviii*
  military forces, 10–13, 18
  Ontario Rifles, 11–12, 18–20, 23
  SS's eagerness to learn, 12
  travel to Red River, 12–17, 32
  voyageurs, 15–16
  Wolseley's command, 11, 15, 16–18, 21, 329n16
Red River Resistance (1869–1870)
  historical background, 10–11
  terminology (resistance *vs.* rebellion), 334n51
  *See also* Red River Expedition and SS (1870); Riel, Louis
Reed, Hayter, 74, 148, 336n6
Regina
  about, 59
  Davin's journalism, 59, 129, 140–43
  maps, 28, 70
  NWMP post, 59–61, 75, 137, 146, 161
religion
  SS's relations with clergy, 106
  *See also* Catholics; Protestants
Resistance (1869–1870)
  terminology (resistance *vs.* rebellion), 334n51
  *See also* Red River Resistance (1869–1870)

Rhodes, Cecil, 196
Richardson, Arthur, 213–14
Riel, Louis
   about, 10, 71–73
   Bear's Head incident, 62–65, 334n55
   death of Thomas Scott, 10, 13, 17, 18, 19, 72
   lack of Cree support for, 78
   messianic vision, 73, 336n4
   provisional government, 10, 17–18, 71, 72, 74
   Red River Expedition arrival, 17
   Red River Resistance, 10
   return from US, 72–73
   surrender, 84
   terminology (rebellion vs. resistance), 334n51
   *See also* Métis; Red River Resistance (1869–1870)
*Riot Act*, 69, 267–68, 335n63
Roberts, Lord
   autobiography, 266
   SAC planning, 232–33
   South African War commander, 206, 211, 214, 217, 220
Robertson, J.E., 99
Robertson-Ross, Patrick, 24–25
Rogers, A.B., 60
Rogers, Robert, 276, 279–80, 286, 306, 308–11
Rogers Pass, 65, 88
Rolph, J.W., 92
Rooke, Robert Percy, 216, 217, 353n69
Ross, James, 68
Rosser, Thomas L., 60
Rossland, 157, 347n48

Ross rifles, 289, 299–300
Rouxville, 192, 223–24
Royal Artillery, 11
Royal Canadian Dragoons, 198, 250
Royal Canadian Regiment (RCR), 197, 278, 294
Royal Engineers, 11
Royal Military College, Kingston, 22, 24, 26, 258
Royal North-West Mounted Police, 320

SAC. *See* South African Constabulary and SS (1901–1906)
Saddle Lake Reserve, 79–80
SALH (South African Light Horse), 212, 213, 216, 218, 300
Sandow, Eugen, 238, 272, 303, 318
Saskatchewan
   military district, 258–59
   *See also* Battleford; Fort Qu'Appelle; Fort Walsh; Military District No. 10 (Manitoba and Saskatchewan) and SS (1908–1914); Prince Albert; Regina; Swift Current
Scott, David Lynch, 155
Scott, Duncan Campbell, 336n5
Scott, Thomas, 10, 13, 17, 18, 19, 72
Selborne, Earl of, 249, 250, 358n2
Selby-Smyth, Edward, 42–43
Settle, Herbert, 208
Seymour, Lord, 203
Shaughnessy, Lord, 306
Shaw, Flora, 175, 177, 349n29
Shoal Lake, 28, 56

Shorncliffe training base and SS
　about, 287, 292, 305
　2nd Division, 291, 292
　command structure, 295, 297-98
　Hughes's troop review, 301-2
　SS as commander, 289-93, 302-3
　training, 305-7, 310
　*See also* First World War and SS
Sifton, Clifford
　Alaska boundary dispute, 165-66
　Catholic issues, 118
　political patronage, 169, 170, 174-75
　Walsh's corruption inquiry, 184-85
　Yukon NWMP positions, 169, 174-75
Siksika
　Bear's Head, 62-65, 334n55
　CPR route without consultation, 62
　horse thefts, 76
　map, 70
　NWMP relations, 62-64, 76
　Treaty 7 negotiations, 49
　*See also* Blackfoot; First Nations
*The Silent Force* (Longstreth), 92-93, 100, 338n5
Simcoe County, Ontario
　historical background, 1, 3-6
　militias, 9-12, 20
Simpson, James, 84
Sitting Bull, Chief, 45, 47-51, 54-55
Skagway
　map, 164
　postal system, 174
　railway, 189

SS's base of operations (1898), 167-69, 172
　Yukon route, 165-66, 167-68, 171
Smith, Donald. *See* Strathcona, Lord (Donald Smith)
Smith, W. Osborne, 32
Smuts, Jan Christiaan, 220, 232, 246, 350n6
South Africa
　Black people, 194, 222, 242, 245-46, 248, 350n2, 357n49
　cost of living, 238
　governance, 249
　historical background, 193-98, 350n1
　justice system, 246
　languages, 194, 242, 350n1
　map, 192
　militia, 194
　mines, 195-96, 232-33, 248-49
　racial views, 245-46
　SAC formation, 232-35
　slavery, 194-95
　SS's views on, xiv-xv
　Treaty of Vereeniging (1902), 242, 244
　typhoid, 236
　voting rights, 242
　*See also* Lord Strathcona's Horse and SS (1899-1901); South African Constabulary and SS (1901-1906); South African War (1899-1902); Transvaal (South African Republic)
South African Constabulary and SS (1901-1906)
　about, xiii, 232-33, 239, 247

Afrikaner forces, 244–45
Baden-Powell's leadership,
    232–35, 241, 246–47, 247
Canadian forces, 221, 234–35,
    238–40, 247–48
Canadians as future settlers, 235,
    238
casualties, 239
Chinese miners, 248–49, 250–51
complaints about, 247–48
concentration camps, 240
funding, 247
justice system, 246–48
model of semi-military police
    force, 232, 241–42, 244–45,
    247
non-white policies, 245–46
officers, 237, 247
police posts, 239–41, 244, 246,
    250–51
political influences, 246
Pretoria headquarters, 239–42
reconciliation after war, 241,
    245–46
Royal Commission on SAC (1905),
    249
size of force, 232–33, 237, 238,
    244, 247
SS as senior officer, xiii, 233–35,
    246–49, 247
SS's career ambitions, 229, 233
SS's departure for London (1906),
    250
SS's family life in Pretoria, 239,
    239, 242–44, 243, 249, 251, 252,
    356n34
SS's family separations, 236

SS's racial views, 245–46
SS's rank and pay, 233, 235, 238
training, 241–42
Transvaal duties, 233, 249
Treaty of Vereeniging (1902), 242,
    244
*See also* Transvaal (South African
    Republic)
South African Light Horse (SALH),
    212, 213, 216, 218, 300
South African War (1899–1902)
about, 193–98, 242
"Black Week" (1899), xii, 197
Boer forces and strategy, 210–11,
    212, 215, 217–24, 354n99
Boer operations after treaty,
    220–22, 231–32
Boer weapons, 197, 207, 211
Botha's leadership, 212, 215,
    217–18, 220, 246, 350n6
British command, 210, 220
British forces and strategy,
    210–11, 215, 217–18, 354n99
British weapons, 201, 207, 208,
    208, 211, 215, 217
Buller's leadership, 210–20,
    352nn52–53
Canadian response, 188, 197–203,
    207–8
CMR role, xiii, 198–200
concentration camps, 222, 231–32,
    240
guerilla warfare, 196–97, 211, 212,
    218, 222–24, 231–32
historical background, xii,
    193–98, 227

international response to, 227, 232
map, 192
railway bridge operations, 209–11, 212
scholarship on, 350n6, 352n52
scorched earth policy, 222, 231–32, 240
Treaty of Vereeniging (1902), 242, 244
trench warfare, 212, 217
*See also* Lord Strathcona's Horse and SS (1899–1901); South Africa

South African War, military police after (1901–1907). *See* South African Constabulary and SS (1901–1906)

Spanish flu, 325
Spittal, C.D., 295–96
Spitzkop, 192, 220
Springfontein, 192, 223
SS. *See* Steele, Sir Samuel Benfield (SS)
Stagg, Ronald J., 328n1
Standerton, 192, 212
Stanley, George F.G., 19, 329n17
Stanley, Lord, 127
Starnes, Cortlandt, 130–32, 144, 182, 320, 343n47
Steele, Ann MacIan Macdonald (SS's mother, Elmes Yelverton's second wife), 7–8
Steele, Elizabeth Coucher (Elmes Yelverton's first wife), 3, 6–7

Steele, Elmes (SS's nephew; son of Henry Edward Steele), 204, 351n31, 352n33
Steele, Elmes Yelverton (SS's father), 2–7, 328n1
Steele, Flora (SS and Marie's daughter)
  archival material on SS, 7, 328n1
  birth and death (1891–1948), 139, 323
  early life in Fort Macleod, 139–40, 174, 175, 176
  interest in SS's life and career, 140
  in London, 252–53
  in Montreal, 236, 260, 265
  photos of, 225, 304, 308
  protection of SS's reputation, 325
  publications, 343n1
  in South Africa, 238
  in Winnipeg, 266, 268–69
  in WWI as nurse, 293–94, 303, 304, 307, 308, 312–13
Steele, Fort. *See* Fort Steele
Steele, Fred (no relation), 157–60, 347n55
Steele, Gertrude (SS and Marie's daughter)
  birth (1895), 140
  in Calgary, 260
  early life in Fort Macleod, 140, 156–57, 176, 344n10
  in Folkestone in WWI, 293–94, 304
  in London, 252–53
  marriage to S. Dudley, 140, 308, 323

personal qualities, 303
photos of, 225, 304
SS's relations, 140
in Winnipeg, 266, 269
Steele, Godfrey (SS's brother), 337n19
Steele, Harwood Elmes Robert (SS and Marie's son)
  archival material on SS, xv, 7, 325–26, 328n1, 338n5
  author, historian, and lecturer, 318, 321, 324–25
  birth and death (1897–1978), 140, 326
  Boy Scouts, 269
  CPR public relations, 324
  early life in Fort Macleod, 140, 174, 175, 176
  interest in SS's life and career, 140
  in London, 252–53
  Longstreth's portrayal of SS's drinking, 92–93, 100, 338n5
  military cadet, 276, 283
  military career in WWI, 286–87, 293, 303, 304, 307, 312–13, 317, 323–24
  military career in WWII, 324
  photos of, 225, 304
  protection of SS's reputation, xiii, xv, 93, 100, 325
  SS's relationship with, 273, 283, 286–87, 325
  in Toronto for school, 279
  unfinished biography of SS, xv
  in Winnipeg, 266, 269, 276
Steele, Henry Edward (SS's half-brother), 351n31

Steele, James (SS's brother), 337n19
Steele, John (SS's half-brother), xi, 3, 4, 8, 135, 244
Steele, Marie Harwood (SS's wife; mother of Harwood, Gertrude, and Flora)
  about, 114–16
  death (1951), 323
  early life in Quebec, 114–15
  health, 139, 252, 323
  love of music, 118, 122, 139, 251
  marriage proposals, 114–15
  personal qualities, 114–15, 138, 341n3
  photos of, 133, 225, 243
  widowhood, 323
Steele, Marie Harwood, marriage to SS
  Catholic-Protestant mixed marriage, 118–19, 131–32
  courtship, 114–22, 125
  family separations, 135, 173–76, 198, 205, 230–31, 236
  letter writing, 119–20, 121, 125, 135
  life in Calgary (1907), 260, 263–66
  life in Folkestone (1915–1916), 287, 293–94, 304, 317
  life in Fort Macleod (1890–1898), 137–39
  life in London (1906–1907), 251–55
  life in Montreal (1898–1899), 176
  life in Pretoria (1903–1906), 239, 239, 242–44, 243, 249, 251, 252, 356n34
  wedding and honeymoon (1890), 120–21, 132–34, 133

Steele, Richard (SS's brother), 22, 36, 333n29, 337n19
Steele, Sir Samuel Benfield (SS)
    about, xi–xiii, *11*, *319*, 320–21
    ancestors, 2–7, 237, 253, 328n1
    awards and honours, 83, 227, 281, 291, 297, 313
    birth and death (1848–1919), 1, 318–21
    Canadian pride, xiv–xv, 228, 231, 249–50, 320–21
    career ambitions, xi–xiii, xv, 22–23, 47, 199–200, 229, 250
    diaries, xv, 145, 331n14, 335n64
    falsehoods about his life, 325
    fatherhood, 139–40, 156–57, 225, 269, 273, 304
    funerals (1919), 318–21
    lecturer, xi, 266
    love for the military, 9, 12, 21, 320
    marriage and family life, xiii–xiv, 113–14
    overview of his life, xi–xiii
    political influences, xii, 174
    protection of his reputation by family, xiii, xv, 93, 100, 325
    religious beliefs, 106
Steele, Samuel, early life (1848–1873)
    about, 1–2
    absence of sources on, xv–xvi
    birth (1848), 1, 7
    death of his mother, 7
    drive to excel, 8, 12
    education, 34
    historical background, 2–7, 9–10
    lack of interest in farming, 8–9, 20
    life with John (half-brother), 7–8
    Ontario Rifles, 12, 18–20, 23
    in Orillia, 1, 7–8
    Simcoe infantry battalions, 9–10
    *See also* Red River Expedition and SS (1870)
Steele, Samuel, marriage to Marie
    Catholic–Protestant mixed marriage, 118–19, 131–32
    impact on career decisions, xiv
    life before marriage, 113–14, 341n1
    SS's life before Marie, 113–14
    wedding and honeymoon (1890), 120–21, 132–34, *133*
    *See also* Steele, Marie Harwood, marriage to SS
Steele, Samuel, children
    fatherhood, 139–40, 156–57, 225, 269, 273, 304
    *See also* Steele, Flora (SS and Marie's daughter); Steele, Gertrude (SS and Marie's daughter); Steele, Harwood Elmes Robert (SS and Marie's son)
Steele, Samuel, career in NWMP. *See entries beginning with* NWMP
Steele, Samuel, career in South Africa. *See* Lord Strathcona's Horse and SS (1899–1901); South African Constabulary and SS (1901–1906); South African War (1899–1902)
Steele, Samuel, career in military. *See* military and SS (before 1906); military and SS (1906–1914)

Steele, Samuel, career in First World
    War. *See* First World War and
    SS
Steele, Samuel, finances and
    investments
  about, 157–60, 262
  BC mines, xii, 67, 157–58, 185, 261,
    316
  Bull's enterprises, 316–17
  coal oil and mines, 100, 127
  deceptions and losses, 261–62
  with Johnston, 67–68
  Macdonell ranch, 146, 345n28
  Marie's management, 174–75
  Marie's widowhood, 323
  pensions, 235, 261, 316, 317, 323
  F. Steele's role, 157–60, 347n55
  Strathcona's loans, 273
  Yukon mines, xii, 184–85, 244
Steele, Samuel, health
  bronchitis, 171, 228, 233, 235, 237
  cause of death, 325
  cigar smoking, 92
  depression, 145, 160
  diabetes, 273, 287, 309, 317, 325
  drinking, xv, 92–93, 100, 274, 311,
    325, 338n5, 339n29
  eczema, 317–18
  heart palpitations, 273
  horseback riding injuries, 285,
    286, 287
  physical strength, 16, 38
  typhoid, 54
  unknown serious illness (1893),
    143
  weight, 109, 238, 272–73, 309,
    317–18

Steele, Samuel, memoir. See *Forty
    Years in Canada* (SS's memoir)
Steele, Samuel, personal qualities
  belief in order and discipline,
    18–20
  belief in rule of law, 56, 60, 62
  church attendance, 92
  competitive, 264
  curious, 12, 13, 34–35
  drive to excel, 8, 12
  enjoyment of card games, 52, 54,
    66, 92, 93, 109, 116
  helpful, 250
  love for the military, 9, 12, 21, 320
  love of photography, 111, 236
  love of reading, 24, 109, 251–52,
    253, 266, 271
  racial views, 13, 245–46
  social ambitions, 22–23, 181
Steele Narrows, 83
Steele's Scouts (1885)
  about, 77–86, 336n11
  Alberta Mounted Rifles, 81
  Boulton's Scouts, 81
  career ambitions, 86–87
  casualties, 83–85
  celebrity status, 85–86
  Frenchman Butte, 70, 81–83,
    337n25
  Loon Lake (Makwa Lake), 83–86
  map, 70
  size of force, 77, 83
  SS's rank, 86
  Steele's brothers in, 337n19
  Surveyors Intelligence Corps, 81
  *War News*, 86
  weapons, 336n11

*See also* Rebellion (1885)
Stefansson, Vilhjalmur, 324
St. Eugene's Mission, 105-6
Stikine River railway scheme, 166, 168
St. Laurent, 72
Strange, Thomas Bland
    Alberta Field Force, 75-79, 81-85, 336n11
    early training, 22
    in Edmonton, 78-79
    Rebellion (1885), 75-76
    relations with Cree and Siksika, 79
    SS's friendship, 254
Strathcona, Lord (Donald Smith)
    death, 273-74
    HBC official in Red River, 18
    last spike ceremony, 88-89
    letter clearing SS of charge of drunkenness, 274, 279
    Lord Strathcona's Horse, xiii, 199-201, 227
    SS's relationship, 237, 273-74, 279
    Strathcona Trust, 274, 276
Strathconas. *See* Lord Strathcona's Horse and SS (1899-1901)
Strickland, D'Arcy, 169, 171
Surveyors Intelligence Corps, 81
Swan River, 40-44, 332n21
Swift Current
    Antrobus matter, 96-98
    CPR route, 57, 75
    maps, 28, 70
    NWMP patrols, 102-3
    Rebellion (1885), 75

Tagish Lake, 164, 171, 173, 174, 175, 177
Terry, Alfred, 50-51
Thompson, John, 118, 141, 145-46, 342n26
Thunder Bay, 266-67
Titley, Brian, 336n5
Tobacco Plains, 111
Tobin, Seymour, 213
Toronto
    SS as militia trainer, 22
Traill, Catharine Parr, 3, 328n2
Transvaal (South African Republic)
    Black miners, 248
    Chinese miners, 248-49, 250-51
    historical background, 195-96, 232, 242, 249
    Kruger's presidency, 196, 211, 217-18, 239, 239, 356n34
    labour shortage, 248
    map, 192
    mines, 195-96, 232, 248, 250-51
    railways, 196, 209
    SALH soldiers, 212
    SS's command of SAC division, 233, 239-40, 250-51
    Strathconas' operations, 211, 215
    Uitlanders (foreigners), 196, 212
treaties
    about, 44-45
    in BC, 100-101
    Cree dissatisfactions, 72-73
    famine clause, 45, 72-74
    government failures, 72-74, 336n5
    international issues, 47
    map, 28
    medicine chest clause, 45
    negotiations, 44-45, 48-49

NWMP's roles, 31, 44-45, 92
pass system on reserves, 62, 148, 334n50, 345n33
scholarship on, 332n27
settler violations of, 31
in Simcoe County area, 3-4
transition to farming, 72-74, 92, 147
treaty payments, 45, 55
US Indian wars, 25
Treaty 6, 44-45, 48, 72-73
Treaty 7, 48-49, 101
Treaty 16, 3-4
Treaty of Vereeniging (1902), 242, 244
Tretheway, William, 159
Tupper, Charles Hibbert, 188, 202
Turner, John Peter, 331n14, 332n21
Turner, Richard, 290-91, 293, 303, 306, 311
typhoid fever, 54, 68, 107-8, 222, 236

United Kingdom
abolition of slavery, 195
Aldershot training centre, 251
Imperial War Conference, 308
JCPC appeals, 60-61
military withdrawal from Canada, 21-22
police forces, 31
Shorncliffe training base, 287, 289-93, 292, 301-5
SS in London with family (1906-1907), 251-55, 254
SS in Scotland (1907), 253
SS in Wales, 237, 254, 290
SS's request for cavalry training in (1874), 40

Strathconas in London (1901), 226-28, 274
*See also* South African War (1899-1902)
United States
CPR workers, 66
cross-border horse raids, 123-24
Cypress Hills Massacre perpetrators, 42
Fenian raids, 9, 21
49th parallel, 25, 35
Indigenous peoples, 25, 30-31, 55, 330n4, 331n6
military, 30-31, 51, 55
police forces, 31
postal system, 46
silver monetary policy, 158-59
Sitting Bull and Lakota, 45, 47-51, 54-55
SS's views on Americans, 51, 134
supply route to NWT, 46
Yukon-Alaska boundary dispute, 165-66
*See also* Klondike Gold Rush (1898-1899); Montana Territory; Skagway
University of Alberta
SS's archives, xv-xvi, 328n1

Vancouver
SS's visits, 89, 166
support for Yukon operations, 162, 166-67
Vanderhaeghe, Guy, 330n2
Vandreuil, Quebec
Marie's home, 114, 131-32, 139-40

SS and Marie's wedding (1890),
    132–35, 133
Van Horne, William Cornelius, 89

Wade, Frederick Coates, 178
Wales
    SS's visits, 237, 254, 290
Walker, James, 258
Walsh, Fort. *See* Fort Walsh
Walsh, James Morrow
    corruption inquiry, 184–85
    NWMP officer, 25–26, 34, 47–48,
        57, 169–72
    personal qualities, 57, 171, 178
    resignation (1883), 48, 55, 57, 169
    Siksika wife and child, 55, 113
    Sitting Bull relations, 48, 54–55
    SS's relations with, 57, 169–72
    Yukon post, 169–70, 174, 178
Wandering Spirit, Chief, 52, 81, 82
Wascana, 59
Watson, David, 300, 310
Wetmore, E.L., 141–45
White, Fred
    about, 98, 342n31
    Herchmer investigation, 140–43
    NWMP comptroller, 98
    political influence, 98, 135
    SS's friendship, 126, 134–35, 201,
        257, 342n31
    SS's statements on Yukon
        maladministration, 187–88
    Yukon post for SS, 175–76
White, Thomas, 302, 306
White-Fraser, M.H., 235
Whitehorse, 164, 173, 178

White Pass
    map, 164
    NWMP customs post, 167, 172
    railway route, 164, 189
    Yukon route, 165–66, 171, 172
Wilde, William Brock, 154, 155
Williams, Jeffery, 362n35
Williams, Jesse, 61–62
Williams, Victor, 278–79
Wills, H.T., 181
Wilson, James, 149, 155, 156
Winnipeg
    Boy Scouts, 269
    SS as NWMP recruiter, 58, 59–61
    SS's family home, 266–67
    *See also* Fort Garry; Military
        District No. 10 (Manitoba and
        Saskatchewan) and SS (1908–
        1914); Red River Expedition
        and SS (1870)
Winnipeg Light Infantry, 76, 78
Witwatersrand (Rand) mines, 195,
    232–33, 248–49
wolfers, 25, 29–30
Wolseley, Garnet, 11, 15, 16–18, 21,
    329n16
    *See also* Red River Expedition and
        SS (1870)
Wood, C.E.D., 129
Wood, Zachary Taylor
    about, 104
    First Nations relations, 124
    Fort Macleod post, 121, 144
    Herchmer controversy, 141,
        344n15
    NWMP officer, 121
    SS's friendship, 104, 109, 175–76

Yukon post, 168, 169
Wood Mountain, 48, 50
World War One. *See* First World War
Wright, Alonzo, 98
Wroughton, T.A., 144
WWI. *See* First World War

Yukon and SS (1898–1899)
    boat and business regulations, 172–73, 178
    career ambitions, xi–xiii, 175, 187–89
    customs duties, 167, 172
    family separations, 162, 173–76
    First Nations relations, 172, 177
    gold discoveries, 161
    map, 164
    miners' required supplies, 172–73, 176, 348n18
    NWMP commanding officer, 161–63, 175–76, 180, 188–89

Perry as replacement for SS, 229
political influences, 169, 175, 187–88
postal system, 173–74, 175, 183
royalties on gold, 161, 183–84
social life, 179, 181
SS on Territorial Council, 176, 179, 185
SS's relations with Walsh, 169–71
SS's statements on Yukon maladministration, 187–88
Yukon early history, 160–61
Yukon Field Force, 161, 167, 172, 176, 178, 188
*See also* Bennett Lake; Dawson and SS (1898–1899); Klondike Gold Rush (1898–1899)
Yukon and White Pass railway, 189
*Yukoner* (steamship), 185–86

Zululand, 192, 211

OTHER TITLES FROM UNIVERSITY OF ALBERTA PRESS

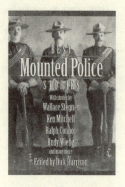

### Best Mounted Police Stories
DICK HARRISON

The Mountie is a uniquely Canadian figure in the great stories of the West. Dick Harrison has collected 22 classic adventure stories by Wallace Stegner, Rudy Wiebe, Ken Mitchell, Ralph Connor, and 18 others.

### Red Serge and Polar Bear Pants
*The Biography of Harry Stallworthy,* RCMP
WILLIAM BARR

From policing and prospecting in the Yukon to coordinating patrols against rum-runners in the Gaspé, Stallworthy's life was an eventful one.

### Outrider of Empire
*The Life and Adventures of Roger Pocock*
GEOFFREY A. POCOCK

A dreamer of dreams, an adventurer, and a man of many ideas, Roger Pocock was an author and world-ranging traveller.

More information at www.uap.ualberta.ca